Lives Lived, Lives Imagined

Lives Lived, Lives Imagined

Biography in the Buddhist Traditions

edited by LINDA COVILL
ULRIKE ROESLER
SARAH SHAW

Wisdom Publications • Boston
in collaboration with
The Oxford Centre for Buddhist Studies

Wisdom Publications
199 Elm Street
Somerville MA 02144 USA
www.wisdompubs.org

Library of Congress Cataloging-in-Publication Data
Lives lived, lives imagined : biography in the Buddhist traditions / edited by Linda Covill, Ulrike Roesler, Sarah Shaw.
p. cm.
ISBN 0-86171-578-0 (pbk. : alk. paper)
1. Buddhist literature—History and criticism. 2. Religious biography—History and criticism. 3. Buddhists—Biography. I. Covill, Linda, 1962– II. Roesler, Ulrike. III. Shaw, Sarah, Dr.
BQ1020.L58 2010
294.3092—dc22

2010024526

14 13 12 11 10
5 4 3 2 1

Cover design by Allison Nealon. Interior design by LC. Set in Diacritical Garamond Pro 11/14.9.

Wisdom Publications' books are printed on acid-free paper and meet the guidelines for permanence and durability of the Production Guidelines for Book Longevity of the Council on Library Resources.

Printed in the United States of America.

This book was produced with environmental mindfulness. We have elected to print this title on 30% PCW recycled paper. As a result, we have saved the following resources: 18 trees, 6 million BTUs of energy, 1,726 lbs. of greenhouse gases, 8,313 gallons of water, and 505 lbs. of solid waste. For more information, please visit our website, www.wisdompubs.org. This paper is also FSC certified. For more information, please visit www.fscus.org.

Publisher's Acknowledgment

THE PUBLISHER gratefully acknowledges the generous help of the Hershey Family Foundation in sponsoring the publication of this book.

Contents

Preface

THE PRESENT VOLUME contains papers presented at a two-day conference on Buddhist biographies held at Balliol College, Oxford, on 28–29 April 2007. Participants from the UK, the United States, and Germany presented their research on biographies and biographical writing in the Buddhist context based on a wide range of sources, including anthropological fieldwork, as well as text-based studies of works in Sanskrit, Pali, Burmese, Chinese, and Tibetan. An article by Jim Rheingans is a welcome addition to the conference papers.

The conference would not have been possible without support from several institutions. I am grateful to the Faculty of Oriental Studies/Subfaculty of South and Inner Asian Studies and to the Faculty of Theology (Oxford) for their generous financial support. Balliol College was a wonderful host, and we wish to thank the College for providing a pleasant and stimulating conference venue that participants were reluctant to leave when the conference was over, and for providing the essentials that are so important for the success of any conference, such as coffee, tea, and computer projectors.

Finally, thanks are due to Richard Gombrich for kindly agreeing to publish this volume in the OCBS Monograph Series.

Ulrike Roesler
May 2010

Introduction

Ulrike Roesler

THE FIRST PART of the autobiography of the German poet, scientist, and politician Johann Wolfgang von Goethe (1749–1832) bears a title that could be considered to epitomize the ambiguities of the genre. Entitled "Dichtung und Wahrheit," it can and in fact has been rendered either as "Truth and Poetry" or as "Truth and Fiction."[1] At first sight this title suggests there *is* a discernible truth to human life, and that it can be told matter-of-factly, or in a poetic and partly fictitious way, or both. This understanding would imply a tension between the truth as such and how it is presented. Such an understanding would be very positivist indeed, and Goethe himself clearly did not intend such a contrast, since in the author's preface to his autobiography he explains the title as referring to "the main object of biography,—to exhibit the man in relation to the features of his time, and to show to what extent they have opposed or favoured his progress; what view of mankind and the world he has formed from them, and how far he himself, if an artist, poet, or author, may externally reflect them" (trans. J. Oxfenford). In a letter to his friend Eckermann he remarks that he called the book "Poetry and Truth" because, "through higher tendencies, it rises from the realm of the base reality."[2] Thus it seems that the autobiography is intended

1. English translations of the autobiography bear the titles "Truth and fiction relating to my life" (trans. J. Oxenford), "Truth and poetry: from my own life" (trans. P. Godwin), "Poetry and truth from my life" (trans. R.O. Moon).

2. Quoted from Frenzel 1979 I: 289. In this context, a statement of Goethe's friend Jacobi is quoted, describing the autobiography as "truer than truth itself." (Translations are mine.)

not to render facts about a life, but a different and somehow more essential type of truth about a person.

Although these deliberations concern a German autobiography from the classical period, the issues addressed above also apply to the topic of the present volume: biography in the Buddhist traditions. The title of this book seems to be equally suggestive of an opposition of a "real life," the "life lived" as opposed to the "life imagined." This, however, is not what is intended; rather, it alludes to the fact that a life is always and necessarily imagined, whether somebody is thinking and writing about the life of another person or about his or her own life. Previous books on the topic of biography have emphasized that biographies are always life stories, with the emphasis on *stories*.[3] The biographies introduced in this volume are also stories or narratives about lives. Most articles deal with the historical and/or the literary aspects of such narratives; some articles create a biographical narrative themselves, or do both of these at the same time, by writing a life story and comparing it with the autobiography of the person. This proves that what we do as scholars is not fundamentally different from what biographers of Buddhist life stories have done in previous times: we are not bystanders who merely observe the "biographical process"[4] from the outside; we actively participate in this process ourselves when we write about the life story of Buddha Śākyamuni or about the sources for the lives of Buddhist monks, siddhas, and scholars.

Biographies and hagiographies contain different types of truth, not just historical ones, and in order to understand these different truths we must consider when and why biographies are written.[5] Life stories are only told if there is a reason to tell them. In a religious context, it is usually an exceptional person, a saint or "spiritual hero" whose story is considered worthy of being rendered, serving to instruct and edify the audience. A religious biography might also describe the exceptional life of a villain, perhaps as an example of the devastating effects of immoral behavior, or it could be a story of conversion where, through various trials and tribulations, the villain becomes in the end as outstandingly virtuous as he had been outstandingly evil in the

3. On "life stories" and "life histories" see Arnold and Blackburn 2004: 9ff.

4. This expression is taken from Reynolds 1976.

5. See the introductory essay by Juliane Schober in Schober 2002: 1–15. See also the examples in books like Granoff and Shinohara 1988 and 1994, and Ray 1993.

beginning. In any case, a biography speaks about an exceptional life, and it is told because it teaches a lesson. Willis has suggested distinguishing between "historical," "inspirational," and "instructional" functions of Tibetan biographies.[6] As previous studies have shown, biographies can express beliefs or illustrate theories,[7] they can function as a commentary on doctrinal issues or authenticate the teaching, and they can be didactic tools, depicting models to be emulated or inspiring faith.[8] Biographies can have collective functions in a given community, like circumscribing and affirming the identity of a group[9] or legitimizing behavior and norms, e.g., when they explain the origin of certain places of pilgrimage, or of rites, customs, and beliefs of the community, or dynastic lineages.[10] One of the special charms of these edifying life stories seems to lie in the pleasant tension between the imperative of the story and the possibility of the listener finding himself at a safe distance from it. On the one hand the Buddha, and hence his life story, is the object of recollection and meditation, and through this recollection, his person and his acts become a significant element in people's religious life (see the remarks on *buddhānussati* in Shaw's article). In this sense, Buddhist biographies in general and the life of the Buddha in particular are guidelines for the path to enlightenment. On the other hand, the life of a saint is a very lofty example that is difficult to fully emulate, for who would really claim to be like the Buddha or an accomplished Buddhist master like Milarepa? Or, if we look

6. Willis 1995: 5f. Although I would agree that Tibetan biographies do have these functions, I am not convinced that these correspond to the categories of "outer," "inner," and "secret" biographies respectively, as Willis seems to suggest.

7. Seen this way, Buddhist biographical literature is at the same time a doctrinal statement. A recent study has interestingly emphasized the opposite aspect, namely, that doctrinal works can (and should) also be read as literature; see Flores 2008.

8. Silk 2003 nicely shows how the apparent contradiction between the Buddha as "the all-knowing infant and the ignorant adolescent" makes very good sense when it is understood as illustrating two different aspects of the Buddhist path: the quest of the ignorant young man shows the situation of someone who sets out on the Buddhist path, while the all-knowing infant illustrates the goal that can finally be achieved through untiring efforts during many lifetimes.

9. Miller 2004 shows how the legends in the "Book of the Kadam Tradition" serve to define the identity of the Kadampa school by creating a complex narrative framework around the figure of its founder.

10. See, e.g., Frank E. Reynolds, "The Many Lives of the Buddha" in Reynolds 1976: 37–66 and "Rebirth Traditions and the Lineages of Gotama" in Shober 2002: 19–39.

at the examples in Ramble's article, who would *want* to be like Ra Lotsāwa, a tantric master who earned his reputation by "liberating" numerous adversaries through murder?

Hagiographies and *jātaka*s may be making only a mild enjoinder to emulate the models found therein. The listener or reader can participate in the hero's adventures without much risk, and safely enjoy the thrill of listening to the hero's trials and tribulations without being directly involved. In addition, the situation in which *jātaka*s and hagiographies are traditionally told can make their effect rather more entertaining and edifying than directly challenging: they are often recounted on festive occasions, where the collective character of the situation grants a secure environment for the individual while also potentially providing space for the exceptional or "liminal" state that the listeners may experience on these occasions.

Thus life stories have various purposes and contain various types of truth. This, however, does not mean that the question of historicity is altogether out of place. It does make a difference whether a life story deals with a historical person like a Burmese or Tibetan teacher who has been involved in the politics of his or her time, or with legends like the one about the Buddha's brother Nanda visiting the nymphs in heaven, a scene that we would obviously not try to verify or falsify as a historical event. Questions about historicity may be inappropriate if they are considered to be the sole purpose of studying biographies,[11] but this should not lead to a general verdict on asking them. It is possible and legitimate to ask whether certain details in a biography are corroborated by other sources. Moreover, through textual comparison we can observe how, for instance, the life stories of the Buddha or a Buddhist master like Milarepa have evolved and changed in the process of retelling and redacting them. Such a comparison may lead to observations about the development of biographical traditions, and reveal possible reasons and motives why biographies have changed over the centuries.

In the Buddhist context, the topic of biography implies a delicate tension. While in Western biographical and autobiographical writing, the development of an individual within his or her specific social and cultural environment

11. Scholars have tried to extract the historical details from the biography of Buddha Śākyamuni by filtering them out from the Buddha legend; on the merits and the problems of such an attempt see, e.g., the remarks in Shober 2002: 3 and Deeg in the present volume.

is the primary focus, such a concern with the individual ego seems contrary to the spirit of Buddhism. Since the self, or ego, accounts for various emotional and intellectual obstacles to enlightenment, it is therefore something to be overcome on the Buddhist path. To inflate it by paying it too much attention would be contrary to Buddhist doctrine. Indeed many Buddhist countries do not have a tradition of autobiographies, since writing about oneself is seen as a form of self-promotion. Traditionally, a disciple writes the biography of his teacher, not the teacher himself. There are a few interesting exceptions to this rule. Tibet has an extensive autobiographical tradition.[12] Moreover, in certain Zen lineages there is the tradition of providing an account of one's own experience with spiritual progress and enlightenment.[13] Similarly, first-person accounts of a personal struggle for enlightenment and of final success are found in some of the *Theragāthā* and *Therīgāthā*, the early songs of the monks and nuns in the Pali Canon.[14] As these examples show, while writing about one's own spiritual progress may not be widespread, it is by no means absent from the Buddhist traditions; it appears at an early stage, and is even a required part of the spiritual path in some later traditions.

The literary genres considered here—autobiography, biography, history, hagiography, and legend—do not correspond precisely to clearly distinguishable genres in Asian literatures. Among the Buddhist types of biographical literature we find, for example, genre designations like Sanskrit/Pali *carita* (deeds or acts, as in *Buddhacarita*), *vaṃśa* (genealogy, as in *Buddhavaṃsa*), or the simple designation as *kathā* (story, as in *Nidānakathā*). Biographical details and legends are part of the Buddhist commentaries (*aṭṭhakathās*), and fragments of the life story of Buddha Śākyamuni are embedded in the Sūtra and the Vinaya sections of the Buddhist canonical scriptures. Stories about previous lives, the *jatakas* and *avadānas* with their respective translations into the different languages of Asia, are an important part of Buddhist life stories, too. The Tibetan tradition uses the designation *rnam thar*, "liberation (story)," for religious biographies, but biographical accounts are also

12. A highly instructive presentation of the Tibetan genre of autobiography (*rang rnam*) and its sub-categories is given in Gyatso 2001: 101–23.

13. A general overview together with two examples is given in King 1995.

14. Some of the songs are very precise about when and how liberation was obtained, and they even "date" this event in retrospect, like Thī 37–38, 39–41, 42–44 and the more elaborate description in Thī 169–74.

found in other genres such as *chos 'byung*, "history of the doctrine," or in doctrinal works, or in eulogies of Buddhist teachers. These examples may suffice to show that the genres and designations are specific to their time and geographical origin, and they do not correspond precisely to our literary category of "biography." Houtman has remarked about Burmese biographies:

> ...I find that what Burmese might refer to as "biography" I would often prefer to call "lineage history." Conversely, what Burmese call "history" could readily be interpreted as a form of biography. (Houtman in Schober 2002: 334)

This observation refers to the genres of "biography" and "history." Both genres share the same complex status with regard to the "truth" contained therein, because just as life stories are narrations with multiple purposes and various kinds of truth, so is history, even if authors of both genres claim to render the events as they have happened. History and biography are equally situated in between the factual and the fictional; they are ways of explaining what has happened, and why, and may contain a truth or a moral without exactly mapping the events that have occurred. With regard to literary genre, we should moreover keep in mind that Asian literatures do not necessarily observe a distinction between works on science or history that are written in a sober prose, as opposed to works of fiction that may be written in a poetical style. The content does not automatically determine the literary form. In South Asian literature what we would call "legend" may be told in a simple factual prose, while a highly abstract theoretical work or a historical record may well be composed in the form of a poetical masterpiece.[15] When considering the biographies discussed in the present volume we should therefore be aware that different modes of expression may have undertones and implications that do not correspond exactly to Western codes of expression and habits of understanding.

The first part of the present collection contains articles devoted to the

15. Slaje 2008 has shown how Kalhaṇa's *Rājataraṅginī*, a historiographical poem from Kashmir, combines the aim of rendering historical events "as they happened" with the form of a highly refined poem that is meant to evoke *śāntarasa*, the emotion of inner peace in the face of the vicissitudes of history. As Slaje sums up, "reliable historiography may even come guised in poetry, inspired by soteriological purposes" (Slaje 2008: 239).

life story of Buddha Śākyamuni. Sarah Shaw's paper can be read as a general introduction to the topic of biography in Buddhist countries as compared to Western autobiographical and biographical literature. She examines the narrative voice in those parts of the canon in which the Buddha speaks about his own life. Records of his present life shift between first-person and third-person accounts and sometimes exhibit rather sophisticated patterns, such as an account by the Buddha (in the first person) about what others said about himself (in the third person). This "skilled layering of personal voice" can be seen as an "embodiment of the middle way," neither overemphasizing the Buddha's presence as an individual agent and storyteller, nor negating his presence altogether. The *jātaka*s, stories about the previous lives of the Buddha, link his present life to the many past lives that prepared him for buddhahood. These stories present him in a much more personalized way, describing the sometimes bold and adventurous actions of the Buddha-to-be, behavior that would be out of the question for Buddha Śākyamuni in his life as the Awakened One.

Max Deeg examines the development of the biography of the Buddha during the early centuries C.E. By comparing different versions of the legend about the birth of the Buddha's son Rāhula, he shows that the Chinese translations of this period contain variations of the story, some even combining contradictory elements. We can observe in these sources that the biography of the Buddha was still in the process of formation, and Deeg suggests that there may have been certain reasons why one or the other version was more appealing to certain readers and traditions.

The two following articles deal with the two great poems of Aśvaghoṣa (second century C.E.): the *Buddhacarita* ("Life of the Buddha") and the *Saundarananda* ("Handsome Nanda"). Roland Steiner has chosen the episode of Siddhārtha's birth to demonstrate the inherent logic of the plot and the poetical aspects involved in its composition, namely, the opposition between the forest and the city. The forest is the typical haunt of hermits and renouncers, and so its location for the Buddha's place of birth foreshadows the future career of the child, a biographical detail that thereby contains a truth beyond mere historical fact.

Linda Covill introduces the story of the Buddha's handsome brother Nanda and his slightly forced conversion to Buddhism, highlighting the poetical methods of the composer. Aśvaghoṣa carefully prepares the reader or listener for the dramatic events to come and creates an intricate pattern of plots that become interwoven as the poem evolves. Metaphors and images serve as links between the scenes and contribute to the work's coherence as well as the development of the characters. Moreover, metaphors serve as tools of understanding, as the author has shown elsewhere in a careful analysis (Covill 2009).

Part 2 not only deals with written biographies, but with the lives of two outstanding Theravāda teachers of recent times. The Venerable Khammai Dhammasami introduces the life and the biographies of Ashin Janakābhivaṃsa (1900–77), a Burmese monk, teacher, and reformer, who tried to make the government and the monastic community work together for the aims of education and rural development. The limited success of this enterprise prompted Janakābhivaṃsa to the unconventional step of writing his own biography in order to explain his ideas and preserve them for future generations, but since writing an autobiography would have been conceived as an act of immodesty and self-promotion, he composed it as a fictitious interview with an imaginary monk, Dhammagutta, who requested his life story, thereby creating a literary form that made the biography acceptable to its readership.

Sarah LeVine adds to biographical writing by sketching a life story herself: that of Ganesh Kumari Shakya (*1934), a Newari girl from the Kathmandu Valley who studied Theravāda Buddhism in Burma for thirteen years and eventually took full ordination in the Chinese tradition in a monastery in California. The life story of this exceptional and uncompromising Buddhist nun reveals a lot about the situation of women in different Asian countries, the social situation of monks' and nuns' communities, the movement for women's ordination, and last not least, the difference that a single courageous individual can make in a community.

Part 3 deals with Tibetan biographies, a field that is peculiar insofar as both biographies and autobiographies form a large and important part of Tibetan religious writing. The articles are arranged according to the chronological order of their protagonists. Peter Alan Roberts focuses on the historical development of a "classic" of Tibetan biographies: the life stories of Milarepa and his disciple Rechungpa. The reader will be surprised to find that such well-known events like the black magic Milarepa used as a young man are absent in the early versions of his biography and were obviously added for edifying purposes later, demonstrating that even a person with extremely bad karma can obtain enlightenment within one lifetime through the practices of the Kagyü tradition. Rechungpa's status is downgraded in the biographical process, thereby enabling the biographer Tsangnyön Heruka to let his own lineage, going back to Milarepa's disciple Gampopa, appear in a more favorable light than the one going back to Rechungpa.

Volker Caumanns analyzes the biographies of Shākya Chogden (1428–1507), a scholar of the Sakya tradition whose works came to be forgotten in Tibet because of their controversial philosopical position and perhaps also because of the political alliances of their author. The two main biographers, Künga Drölchog (sixteenth century) and Shākya Rinchen (eighteenth century), both had close personal links with the figure of Shākya Chogden, the latter even being considered his re-embodiment. The paper introduces the biographies and shows that the later biography tends to expand the hagiographical elements and omit controversial points. The paper mentions in passing interesting details about the pragmatic context of biographies, like the ritual installment of a newly written biography (by giving the *lung*, the reading transmission to the monastic community), and the economical aspects of collecting sources for the "collected writings" of a Buddhist master.

Jim Rheingans presents a vast range of biographical and historical material on the early years of the eighth Karmapa Mikyö Dorje (1507–54), whose recognition and enthronement were overshadowed by attempts to install a rival candidate as the new Karmapa. Rheingans makes clear how the method of establishing spiritual lineages through identifying reincarnations was (and is) embedded into the politics of the day. Biographies and autobiographies reflect this religio-political dimension, and some of the stock elements of such narratives, like the self-recognition of an incarnate young lama or the establishment of the prototypical patron-priest relationship in later years, serve to legitimize the position of the Karmapa and establish the political alliances that were necessary for maintaining a religious legacy.

So far the articles in this volume have been dealing with the exemplary lives of Buddhist saints. Charles Ramble's paper concludes the volume by having a look at the darker side of life stories. He presents a wide range of samples describing the much less exemplary behavior of Buddhist teachers and siddhas, such as eloquent denigrations of well-known Buddhist figures, stories about rather sinister heroes, like the tantric mass murderer Ra Lotsāwa, and accounts that do not deal with heroes at all: records about lives that are neither outstandingly saintly nor outstandingly evil, but simply shabby, mediocre, and "ugly." Since biographies are written for the purpose of edifying an audience, we must turn to other kinds of sources when looking for the more ordinary aspects of life stories. In this case, family archives from Mustang reveal behavior that would never find its way into a biography proper.

The workshop in Oxford was guided not by a fixed agenda or preconceived ideas about what we would discover but by a genuine curiosity in life stories, what they tell and how they are told, and—though this may sound unscholarly—by the simple pleasure in the narratives themselves. The workshop was fulfilling in all these respects. It did not lead to a new overarching theory on biographical narrative, but it inspired many insights into the diverse aspects of life stories and biographical writing. If both the insights and the pleasure in biographical narrative have found their way into this volume, then the book fulfills its purpose.

Bibliography

Arnold, David, and Stuart Blackburn, eds. 2004. *Telling Lives in India: Biography, Autobiography, and Life History*. Bloomington and Indianapolis: Indiana University Press.

Covill, Linda 2009. *A Metaphorical Study of Saundarananda*. Delhi: Motilal Banarsidass.

Flores, Ralph 2008. *Buddhist Scriptures as Literature: Sacred Rhetoric and the Uses of Theory*. Albany: State University of New York Press.

Frenzel, H. A. and E. 1979. *Daten deutscher Dichtung. Chronologischer Abriß der deutschen Literaturgeschichte*. 15th ed., 2 vols. München: Deutscher Taschenbuch Verlag. (First ed. 1962.)

Granoff, Phyllis, and Koichi Shinohara, eds. 1988. *Monks and Magicians: Religious Biographies in Asia*. Oakville, New York, and London: Mosaic Press.

——— 1994. *Autobiography and Biography in Cross-Cultural Perspective*. Buffalo, NY: Mosaic Press.

Gyatso, Janet 1998. *Apparitions of the Self: The Secret Autobiographies of a Tibetan Visionary*. Princeton, New Jersey: Princeton University Press. (Reprint: New Delhi: Motilal Banarsidass, 2001.)

King, Sallie 1995. "Awakening Stories of Zen Buddhist Women." In *Buddhism in Practice*, ed. by Donald S. Lopez, pp. 513–24. Princeton Readings in Religions. Princeton, NJ: Princeton University Press.

Miller, Amy Sims 2004. "Jewelled Dialogues: The Role of The Book in the Formation of the Kadam Tradition Within Tibet." PhD diss., University of Virginia. Available as UMI Number 3131384.

Ray, Reginald 1993. *Buddhist Saints in India*. New York: Oxford University Press.

Reynolds, Frank, ed. 1976. *The Biographical Process: Studies in the History and Psychology of Religion*. The Hague: Mouton.

Schober, Juliane, ed. 2002. *Sacred Biography in the Buddhist Traditions of South and Southeast Asia*. First Indian ed., Delhi: Motilal Banarsidass. (First ed. Honolulu: University of Hawaii Press, 1997.)

Silk, Jonathan 2003. "The Fruits of Paradox: On the Religious Architecture of the Buddha's Life Story." *Journal of the American Academy of Religion* 71.4: 863–81.

Slaje, Walter 2008. "'In the Guise of Poetry'—Kalhaṇa Reconsidered." In *Śāstrārambha: Inquiries into the Preamble in Sanskrit*, ed. by Walter Slaje, pp. 207–44. Abhandlungen für die Kunde des Morgenlandes LXII. Wiesbaden: Harrassowitz Verlag.

Willis, Janice 1995. *Enlightened Beings: Life Stories from the Ganden Oral Tradition*. Boston: Wisdom Publications.

I.

The Buddha: A Life Lived, Imagined, and Living Still

And That Was I

How the Buddha Himself Creates a Path between Biography and Autobiography

Sarah Shaw

THE *Mahāpadāna-Sutta* (DN II 1–54) starts with the low-key and atmospheric introduction often found in the extended discourses of the *Dīgha Nikāya*.[1] A group of monks sit discussing past lives. The Buddha, listening to their conversation with the divine ear, joins them and tells them of his various past lives: of six earlier buddhas who preceded him. These six, he tells them, had many distinctive features, such as great assemblies of varied size, vast lifespans of varied length, chief attendants, and distinct trees under which they gained enlightenment. Bodhisattas who take rebirth in order to become buddhas, he says, share features such as miraculous births, and the fact that they are born to pure mothers. Focusing on Vipassī, the earliest, he delineates the thirty-two marks and relates his life up to the decision to teach, prompted by Lord Brahma, through to the exposition of dependent origination and the recital of the *Pāṭimokkha*: information he never gives in the first person in the canon for himself. Only after this does Gotama move to an autobiographical recollection. He recalls sitting under a sāl tree and deciding to visit the heaven of the pure abodes, where he listens to his own short biography related to him in the third person by several non-returners who have seen many buddhas before him. Descending through the heavens, he hears the autobiographies of the devas (gods) of many realms, who have

1. The openings of the first two *suttas* of the *Dīgha Nikāya* are noteworthy in this regard.

also seen many buddhas, before returning to the human realm. Tathāgatas, he says, have such knowledge of earlier buddhas through the discerning of truth (DN II 53). The Buddha, these witnesses demonstrate, is distinctive, but one of many.

This is the nearest thing to a sequential account of the Buddha's own life, on the part of the Buddha, within the Pali Canon, delivered as a meditation within a conversation, within a teaching text. It is hidden and enclosed in layers of biography and autobiographical discourse. It is heard by the Buddha, within an autobiographical experience, presumably of deep meditation, under a tree, as a third-person validation of his status by elders of an ancient human lineage in the one realm, in which, as bodhisatta, he has never taken rebirth.[2] It is recounted only after the biographies are given of earlier buddhas to a select group of his own followers, who would all, by the nature of their discussion about previous lives, have themselves attained the fourth *jhāna* (meditative state).[3] And this discourse is itself recounted within a third-person biographical account, the sutta remembered by the redactors of the canon. As most suttas are, it is also, of course, opened by the resonant first-person statement, presumably made first by Ānanda and then accurately by each person who repeats it, so that it is one which those in the present hear, and becomes an autobiographical tag to the recitation of any sutta: *evam me sutam*, "Thus have I heard." The skilled layering of personal voice in this sutta, the flexible movement from the intimate to the public, the visionary to the straightforward, the fact that the biography is never recited in the first person but the way that person is used to enclose key moments in the sutta seem like a skilled embodiment of the middle way. It indicates not only the presence of a very alert teacher, attentive to the circumstances in which a biography should be given, but also of a composer or composers of texts who are themselves exercising considerable care in presenting their material for oral recitation. In the canon, biographies hide inside such autobiographical recollections, while autobiographical accounts nest within biographical

2. The word *bodhisatta* is used in this article, as it is in Pali texts and by those in the Southern Buddhist traditions. The "being attached to awakening" or "bound for awakening" is perceived a little differently in that tradition from the way its counterpart, the *bodhisattva*, is understood in Sanskrit texts.

3. The recollection of past lives is recommended in the canon after the practice of the fourth *jhāna* (DN I 79). See also Bhikkhu Ñāṇamoli 1976: 1, XXXIII 13–71.

record. The Pali Canon is a masterpiece in the use of different voices, for which the term *buddhavacana* should perhaps always be qualified by the term *saṅghavacana*, the early accounts of the earliest followers of the Buddha Gotama, who describe where he was, what he did, how he behaved, and the effects on those around him. These followers asked him questions, gained enlightenment themselves, delivered discourses, composed poems that sometimes recounted their own autobiographies, gave advice leading to enlightenment, and described the Buddha as a person, seen from the outside. Their role in recording biographical and incidental information, set with such literary skill in the Nikāyas, is nearly as important, as an embodiment of the dhamma, as the actual words Gotama himself used at the time.

The *Mahāpadāna-Sutta* demonstrates the great difficulty in identifying all genres of biography and autobiography in an Indological context. Rhys Davids does not seem to have liked the *Mahāpadāna-Sutta*, seeing in it the "weed" of Mahāyāna.[4] This sense of a lineage of teachers, however, is not peculiarly Buddhist, but colors our understanding of all ancient Indian texts about specific individuals. The individual exists and is defined by others with whom he is associated. Jain teachers are from the earliest days depicted in multiples, and there is no separate biography of Mahāvīra that excludes earlier tīrthaṅkaras until the ninth century C.E.[5] The Buddha, too, clearly wanted to place himself in a large family and, elsewhere, rebuts Sariputta's claim that he must be the greatest man that ever lived, saying that there have been other buddhas in the past and there will be in the future.[6] To this day, one of the most popular chants in Southeast Asia is that to the twenty-eight buddhas, and in Sri Lankan temples in particular we see the present Buddha sitting, in many forms, at the feet of twenty-four earlier buddhas (*sūvisi vivaraṇa*).[7] We do not have a word for the genre of literature known then as *vaṃsa*, but such

4. Rhys Davids thought that the introduction of the idea of the bodhisatta and many "wonder-workers" in the system "gradually covered up much that was of value in the earlier teaching, and finally led to the downfall, in its home in India, of the ancient faith." Rhys Davids 1977, 2: xvii. This view is not, of course, shared by modern scholars.

5. See Dundas 1992: 29 and Singh 2001: 15, 4041–76.

6. Reference to future buddhas is made only once in the canon, in the *Parinibbāna-Sutta*, to Sāriputta (DN II 82–83).

7. See Gombrich 1980: 62–72. On the visual liturgy of the twenty-four buddhas in Sri Lankan temples see Holt 1996: 58, 66–69, plate 10, 128n23. See also Ap 20–23 and MN II 45–54.

works were and are of as much interest to Southeast Asians as biography and autobiography are to us now.[8] Gotama is one of a specialized familial line: the buddhas themselves.

This brings us to some of the other problems in considering biography and autobiography in Buddhist texts: so many features not found in Western examples of the genres come into play. Western classifications may be helpful in making a differentiation between personal and public accounts, but they do not encompass either the deep sense of *vaṃsa* or the revolutionary idea of many lives. The "I" that may well have a different identity in earlier rebirths, as well as the peculiarly Buddhist doctrine of "no self," whereby the very nature of that "I" is questioned, place these two terms in a context of time, place, and interwoven relationships where many loci of consciousness are protagonists in the narratives and discourses. The Buddha, his own past life, and his own past lives as the character of the bodhisatta—the being described in the jātakas as bound to enlightenment—are all examined. All of these are also linked to those of his followers and their past lives and relationships. The Buddha is also shown in relationship to preceding buddhas, who also have relationships with gods such as those in the pure abodes, beings who still remember their teaching within a single lifetime. The final exemplary life of a buddha is linked by many connections to others. As in the sutta cited here, this netted relatedness is always painstakingly acknowledged and explored within the canon. It is a necessary part of the path that leads him away from further "I" making, a process that has to be described, contextualized, explained, and related to many others, a sangha whose interpretation of these events must be faithful for the requirements of complete buddhahood to be fulfilled.

Biography and Autobiography as Genres

Despite this, the terms autobiography and biography can be applied and, if used carefully, tell us a surprising amount about the early Buddhist texts. Although we use these terms frequently, often with little formal thought

8. In the canon this is evinced by the first-person recollections of the Buddha of earlier renewals of his vow before the twenty-four buddhas in the *Buddhavaṃsa*. Post-canonical works include Kassapa's *Anāgatavaṃsa*, the *Dīpavaṃsa*, the *Mahāvaṃsa*, and the *Cūlavaṃsa*.

given to what they mean, I have found no extended historical comparison between the two genres and, aside from some useful entries in general reference works, surprisingly little attempt at broad differentiation.[9] Most academics working on these genres very sensibly stick to areas in which they have specific knowledge, and rarely venture out of the period and locality in which their texts were composed. So I will say a little about biographies and autobiographies in a general sense, with their many different genres within genres. Autobiographies and biographies at all historical periods are like plants that adapt and grow in specific soils, dependent on readership or audience, intention, the type of text involved, social, personal, and religious expectations, and even economic considerations. As a way of exploring the diversity among these kinds of texts, I will take as a thread one principal theme, that of narrative voice. Who is narrating? Examining this one simple feature tells us a great deal about texts, ancient and modern, and reveals a considerable amount about the author's intent and skill. I will then return and, in brief, explore the Pali use of the two genres.

Biography

A biography is the story of the life of someone else. It is a narrative, not usually constructed by the subject of the text, which can, from an external perspective, look at one lifetime as a continuum. Although sometimes written before its subject's demise, the biography can, and historically usually has been, a finished product with an account of the person's birth and death as well as his or her life. Modern sophisticated biographers sometimes avoid a strict progression in "linear" time, and begin with a funeral or a key moment of fame, but the genre implies a naturally formed narrative with a beginning, a middle, and an end. While biography allows the subject's speech to be recorded, its natural mode is the "scientific" third person: he or she did this, said this, and behaved in such and such a way. Indeed this voice can be sustained without a break throughout the entire narrative. The great excellence of a biography arises precisely from this external and even public viewpoint. Biographies are usually intended for a large audience and for posterity.

9. Particularly helpful has been "E.G." 1926 in a now old but not superseded article, La Fleur 1987, and Gunn 1987.

Because of the distance of the narrator from his subject, the genre also lends itself to great diversity. Any amount of authors, at any time, can assemble details from a variety of sources, interviews, papers, manuscripts, chronicles, and even the imagination, and attach them to their chosen subject. A nineteenth-century biography may list the heroic deeds and adventures of its subject. A twentieth-century one brings to light unconscious motives that might surprise the subject and act to further contextualize the actions and experiences. A twenty-first-century understanding of a life may even supply a spouse for a religious leader, such as Christ.[10] So with enough information, perhaps from many first-hand sources, all sorts of varied biographies by different people can be and are written about any one person. For great world figures, new biographies can be rewritten, adapted, and changed by each new generation in the light of new evidence, reappraisal, or, it has to be said, the wish to suppress or override earlier information and interpretations.

History of Biography

As a genre, biography has an ancient, well-documented ancestry. Although the term does not come into existence until the fifth century, with Damascius's *Life of Isadorus*, biographical composition in the West emerges as a separate form in classical times.[11] Early examples such as Plutarch's *Parallel Lives* (75 C.E.) and Suetonius's account of the twelve Caesars (roughly 119 C.E.), life stories and character sketches that give a public, external account of great men, give some sort of historical and even historicist context. In the West such biographies have always been written about public figures, saints, and

10. The development of biographical writing over the last two centuries has been complex, with trends moving from the Carlylean model of idealized heroes and hero worship, to the inevitable reaction in Lytton Strachey's *psychographia* in *Eminent Victorians* (1918), which prepared the ground for post-Freudian investigation of nineteenth-century heroes, up to the modern "factualization" experimentations of Simon Schama's *Rembrandt's Eyes* (1999). Dan Brown's novel *The Da Vinci Code* (2003) could hardly be called biographical in any sense, but its suggestion of a familial line descending from Christ reawakened animated debate about the effects of biographical research on theological discourse and prompted some smart public rebuttals from the Catholic church. See unattributed, "A Response to *The Da Vinci Code* by the Prelature of Opus Dei in the United States" (2006).

11. *The Encyclopedia Britannica* identifies Damascius (ca. 480–550) as the earliest employer of the term. See "E.G." 1926: 952–54. For the original see Damaskios 1967: 2.

heroes.[12] Oddly enough, we would have to include Caesar's *De Bello Gallico* (concerning events 58–47 B.C.E.) and Xenophon's *Anabasis* (fifth century B.C.E.) under biography or at least biographical history. Although the authors are protagonists in the action, all personal content is utterly subsumed in an exemplary third-person military persona whereby only that which is of interest for the public domain is described—"Caesar did this and that"—not personal deliberation such as "Caesar had a difficult morning and could not decide whether to take a walk before breakfast." By the nineteenth century the term *sacred biography* was coined to describe third-person narratives about a religious figure which could include factual information, such as date, time, and circumstances of birth, but could also include hagiography, in the case of saints and holy men, as well as mythological, symbolic, and even supernatural elements.[13] The historical figure may assume the quality of a "type." This spectrum is represented in many compositions and the nature of its range is often the subject of intense debate—as in the events of Christ's life story, for instance. In this regard, we find another kind of text, the epic. Jasper Griffin has noted usefully in his work on Virgil that epic narrative could include many interpenetrating layers—the "factual" historic, the heroic, the mythological, the symbolic, and the psychological, all of which contribute to the success of the final product: one layer does not exclude another.[14] A composition about a single person's life can be such a narrative, where a multitude of layers may be found: the "objective" historical, the character sketch, the historicist, the heroic, the mythic, the poetic, and the typological. In the case of the Buddha for instance, the figure is certainly a historical figure, exhibiting certain features peculiar to one individual, such as different chief followers, clan, place of birth, and so on. He is also a "type," however—that of a buddha—possessing, as the *Mahāpadāna-Sutta* indicates, heroic and mythic features such as the thirty-two marks and a miraculous birth.

Biographical narratives, with a third-person subject, are of essence external:

12. The fourteenth-century *Gesta Romanorum* provided fables, myths, and allegorical stories concerning holy figures, primarily as exempla and types, within a Christian context: see Herrtage 1879. Many works discussed in this article, such as this, may be inaccessible in some university libraries, so reputable online versions of texts are cited after the bibliography wherever possible.

13. See La Fleur 1987.

14. See, for instance, Griffin 2001: 58–106.

they provide us with public information. A good biography often reveals the inner struggle, torment, or even conversion, but its detail and incident are factual or include events observable in the outside world: accounts of interactions with others, the demonstration of public virtues, epitaphs, documents, archaeological evidence, and even bills and receipts can all contribute to the reconstruction of a single life.[15] Biographies can take many forms: they can be sung in ballads and hymns or painted in murals.[16] Where a figure is of great cultural importance, life stories can be knitted into the rhythms and rituals of the seasons and year, as in Christian celebrations of Palm Sunday, Good Friday, and Easter Sunday, where there is a festive, calendric biography of great events in a religious leader's life, comparable to the way the birth, death, and enlightenment are celebrated on one day in Buddhist countries. Biographies can also be mapped out in geographical locations, as in pilgrimage sites, where the stages of a great man's life can be plotted out in stages for visitors to experience themselves, such as the eight places of pilgrimage for early Buddhists or within temples, in the biographical arrangement of stages of the Buddha's life.[17] Biographies place "he" or "she" in a larger and public context, so that we see, from the outside, and sometimes even in physical form, the cultural imprint of a single life, just as we see the imprint of the Buddha on Adam's Peak, a physical sign of the Buddha's supposed visit to Sri Lanka: probably, of course, an accretion to his life story that occurred after his death.[18]

Autobiography

The essence of an autobiographical composition, however, lies in an internal, single voice. It can only be written from living experience: the narrator

15. Claire Tomalin has, for instance, reconstructed the last days of Dickens's life using records of bills and money changed at his local inn, plausibly concluding that he spent his last day with his mistress rather than at Gad's Hill. See Tomalin 1990: 271–83.

16. Temple murals of the stages of the Buddha's life are widespread throughout Southeast Asian temples. Étienne Lamotte (1958) has identified thirty-four episodes from the Buddha's life at Sanchi, India, in bas-relief depictions that predate literary evidence. Forty poses for each stage of the life were codified by Abbot Prince Paramanuchit Chinorot (1735-1814), supreme patriarch and abbot of Wat Pho in Bangkok: see Matics 1998: 2.

17. On the eight places of pilgrimage, see Strong 2001: 5–13.

18. The Buddha's supposed visits to Sri Lanka are chronicled in the *Mahāvaṃsa*: Geiger 1912.

must also be the subject. Like its kinsmen, the diary, the memoir, the personal letter, the confession, and the apologia, it voices the worries, fears, achievements, and happiness of a unique, particularized continuum. The natural narrator of the autobiography is the first-person singular pronoun. Normally speaking, a first-person narrator cannot speak of the beginning of "I," and so, except from other people's accounts, give a firsthand account of the subject's birth. At some stage the authority of the narrator must be broken by the inclusion of another: "I was born in..." requires hearsay, and in effect means, "I am told I was born in..." or movement to the third person: "My mother was Indian." The same applies to its own death. Recently a large number of works of fiction, cinema, and television have employed the "dead narrator" device, a practice which in fact has an ancient ancestry, dating back to the accounts given by the dead in classical epic or Dante's *Inferno*.[19] Such works of fiction are, however, striking for their oddity. So while there is the potential for a satisfying completeness in biographical composition, the Western autobiographical mode depends upon and is shaped by its lack of completion. There is a mysterious confusion inherent to "I"-ness, for "I" does not know where it began or where and how it will end. Indeed first-person narration has, in modern times, become the articulation of the problems of having an identity, a human body, and a single destiny and arouses our sympathy as an outpouring from and about this both happy and unsatisfactory condition. Many autobiographies share a preoccupation with this search for origins and the source of what it is to be "I," evident also in works of fiction such as early British novels where the hero or heroine narrates through the first person—from very early works such as Defoe's *Robinson Crusoe* (1719), *Moll Flanders* (1722), Sterne's *The Life and Opinions of Tristram Shandy, Gentleman* (1759), the epistolary novels such as Richardson's *Clarissa* (1747–48), up to Charlotte Brontë's *Jane Eyre* (1847).[20] This personal search renders

19. The "me" generation seems to like a dead "I." Recent examples of a deceased narrator have occurred in the novels Alice Sebold, *The Lovely Bones* (2002), and Orhan Pamuk, *My Name Is Red* (2001), the film *American Beauty* (directed by Sam Mendes and produced by Bruce Cohen and Dan Jinks, Dreamworks 1999), and the television program *Desperate Housewives* (produced by Marc Cherry, ABC 2002–7). In all of these a murder victim acts as the main narrative voice. The parallels with encounters with the shades in classical epic and Dante's *Inferno* are striking: see, for instance, the accounts of murder victims Francesca and her lover in Kirkpatrick 2006: Canto 5, ll. 73–142.

20. See Spacks 1976.

"real" autobiography an often private genre, a fact sometimes reflected in its intended readership. Much autobiographical composition may not even be intended for anyone else at all, if a diary or a solitary confession, or may be addressed to a very limited audience, such as a friend, a spiritual confessor, a potentially hostile critic, the recipient of a letter, or even a deity. Any number of contributions can be made to a biographical narrative and offer third-person accounts of a subject's life and actions: only one person, alive, can write autobiography.

History of Autobiography

Perhaps because of their often emotional and internal nature, narratives describing a life through the first person have, as might be expected, a very different and even private history, a feature that has meant that autobiography has only recently become the subject of academic study: it has been termed by Shapiro the "dark continent" of narrative.[21] Indeed recent criticism has focused on the genre as the natural articulation of, for instance, women or Afro-Caribbean minorities whose "public" history may have been overlooked.[22] Even now, the *New Encyclopaedia Britannica* does not give a separate entry under "Autobiography." *The Oxford English Dictionary* gives the earliest use of the term, "the story of one's life written by himself," in 1809.[23] In practice, however, autobiographical composition also has an ancient ancestry. In a monumental study of classical autobiography, George Misch pointed out that first-person pseudo-autobiographies purporting to describe the author's fantastic adventures and first-person inscriptional autobiographies in the Middle East date back to the ninth century B.C.E. Ancient Egyptian funeral epitaphs record the confession of the being as his soul is about to be weighed.[24] Inscriptions, of course, occupy a special position. The edicts of the

21. See Shapiro 1967.

22. For some survey of this and the argument that the emergence of both autobiographical and biographical writing since the eighteenth century involve changing concepts of "self," see Marcus 1994.

23. OED 144. Southey refers to "this very amusing and unique specimen of autobiography" in the *Quarterly Review*, I, 283.

24. See Misch 1998: 20ff. Some care is needed in assessing this material in this context: Elizabeth W. Bruss notes that we can "read older texts, or texts of other cultures, and find in them

Indian king Aśoka are usually delivered with the conventional regal impersonality of the third person, but we assume the content is autobiographical and that he is the author. It is uncertain whether there is any reason for some edicts being recorded in the first person, always a more frequent and immediate occurrence in an Indian context where there is no intermediate mode of indirect speech, and others straightforwardly in the third, but the use of both "I" and "he" renders their mixture of public injunction and confessional autobiography vividly poignant for the modern reader.[25]

The kind of autobiography that we would recognize is generally considered to come into its own with the spiritual autobiography. The historical emergence of the genre is too large a subject to be discussed here, but the earliest, often taken as a paradigm, is the *Confessions of St. Augustine* (398), written in a form that pre-existed and survived his own more famous account of his spiritual journey. In the Middle Ages and early modern period, doctrinal and personal dilemmas are enacted through the genre of spiritual autobiography, which often defends, argues, confesses, or rebels against an established stance. It has been argued that autobiography tends to emerge at times when there is a particular need to assert a single identity. Historically, an "I" narrator often defends an unusual position and a change from the norm.[26] British seventeenth-century spiritual autobiography, for instance, has been identified as the product of revolutionary social change, religious stances which needed defending, and the necessity of asserting a radical entity unbound by conservative viewpoints. "I" autobiographies tend to come at times when the "I" feels that it differs a little from other "I's" that happen to be around.[27]

Readership, audience, and the mode of production are also important elements. Biographies are usually and openly public in appeal and produced for widespread dissemination. Confessional first-person narratives, however, are

---

autobiographical intentions, but it is often our own conventions which inform this reading and give the text this force" (Bruss 1976: 6).

25. See Rastogi 1990. Pillar edicts II and V, for instance, are in the first person; rock edict XIII is in the third. It would be interesting to investigate the use of voice in the edicts in association with geographical area, dialect, and subject matter and see whether any useful conclusions could be drawn.

26. See Obermeier 1999: 256ff.

27. Webber 1979: 6 and Delaney 1969. Other, more general works include Sturrock 1993 and Fleishman 1983.

often intended in the first instance for a very limited audience. Within such texts, the second person starts to assume a prominent and, in much spiritual autobiography, even a numinous presence. Some non-Buddhist examples have striking affinities with accounts of conversions in early Buddhist literature. St. Augustine's *Confessions* take the form of a kind of dialogue with God, in which he describes his own difficulties, explains his position, and attempts to resolve his own spiritual struggle in what often appears a personal communication. Interestingly, spiritual autobiographies written by men through to the medieval period tend to be more direct, and usually address God as the "you" or the "thou" who hears their account. Others are epistolary, written in response to an implied request from a friend or in response to some form of attack, in which case the second person, "you," becomes confidant, father confessor, and even adversary. Abelard's *Calamitatum* (1132–36), for instance, provides a first-person account of his own life in response to a description of a friend's far more straightforward vicissitudes.[28] Nuns writing accounts of their spiritual journey often use a male scribe, and address their narratives to a smaller readership, such as a confessor or a friend, addressing God directly sometimes, but usually invoking the deity rather as a witness to support their spiritual position.[29] This personal element, often expressed in early Buddhist texts through the evocation of the informal, conversational setting described in, for instance, the *Mahāpadāna-Sutta* or the *Meghiya-Sutta* (Ud 34–37), where meditative experience is discussed with a single person or a small group, can be understood today by bearing in one's mind the way that in a Buddhist context meditative experience is usually reported in confidence to a teacher or a "good friend."[30] It is not publicly described, a practice possibly associated with a reluctance to commit the *pārājika* offense of false claims to meditative states.[31] In a talk to a Western Buddhist society, monks might give extensive advice as regards the practice of meditation, but they would not inform the audience of the states they themselves had attained. This ancient convention, followed by the laity too, is felt to protect both meditators and their teachers from the deleterious effects of boasting or

28. See Bellows 1922.

29. See Obermeier 1999: 256.

30. See Shaw 2006b: 10–12.

31. See "The rule about a superhuman state," Norman and Pruitt 1999: 10–11.

proselytizing by those anxious for material support. Such a comparison gives us a sympathetic glimpse into the careful disclosures of Christian spiritual autobiographical writing, which often anticipate the novel and the close psychological analysis of modern autobiography in their exhaustive description of mental states and their transformation.[32] This affinity is strengthened by the possibility that the experiences themselves may be comparable to those of the Buddhist tradition. L. S. Cousins has demonstrated the proximity of, for instance, St. Teresa's autobiographical accounts of the stages of union with God to the stages of Buddhist *jhāna*.[33]

The Life of St. Teresa by Herself (1563–65) was written without a scribe, while its composer knelt on the floor by a window ledge. This perspective informs her writing: her *Life* is addressed to "you," her confessor, whom, she requests in her final chapter, should show it to three other people, who may then in turn speak defending her spiritual experiences against charges such as quietism and heretical practice to the Spanish Inquisition. This adds yet another dimension to the natural reticence a practitioner may feel in making public spiritual experience. Her situation is not unlike that in present-day Tibet or Burma, where extreme caution is necessary in the overt teaching of certain *samatha* meditations, supposed to produce clairvoyance or other psychic powers.[34] St. Teresa enjoys her skilled and even dangerous play with the use of personal pronouns. The description of her interior life constitutes a profound intellectual analysis of closely described meditative experience. In so doing she flatters, cajoles, persuades, and sometimes harangues her small readership into a position, where, she hopes, they will be obliged to accept her experiences as valid within the doctrines of the Roman Catholic Church.[35] Her final chapter is an almost symphonic interplay between different voices, which for its fluidity of expression is, I think, of general interest to those studying Buddhist autobiographies and biographies. God is addressed as Thou, or described in the third person as Him. Her "you" is sometimes her

32. Despite George Eliot's newly atheist stance while writing *Middlemarch*, her heroine Dorothea's agonized reconciliation to her life with Casaubon has been placed within a Christian and humanist context of spiritual awakening and self-development. See Hardy 1970: 55–65.

33. Cousins 1989: 103–20.

34. I have been informed of this by many practitioners from these countries, but for obvious reasons am unable to cite them.

35. For discussion of this, see Sturrock 1993: 86–93.

confessor, sometimes, it seems, those to whom he may show the document, but also, perhaps with some tactful and ironic instructions to her four stated readers, objectified as "Anyone who may benefit from her spiritual experiences." Like other female spiritual autobiographers of the time, she enlists God's support, as both "you" and "Him," to defend her position against potential "yous" and "hims" who might condemn her writings. To conclude her discussion, as protected as the veils and cloisters of her chosen life, she seems to transcend a conventional sense of self, and to find a spaciousness within her own personal dialogue with God, her confessors, and a potential reading public through an objectivity conferred finally by the third person, for both herself and her deity. In the book's final words, Teresa significantly reverts to this person, to describe both herself and God:

> May it please the Lord, since He is powerful and can do what He will, that I may succeed in doing His will in all things, and may He not allow this soul to be lost which so often, by so many methods and devices, His Majesty has rescued from hell and drawn to Himself. Amen.[36]

Through this skilled movement between voices she seems to be deconstructing and dissolving the usual boundaries of selfhood; in her caution we feel not only the voluntary confines of her contemplative cell and the external oppressiveness of sixteenth-century Spain, conditions peculiar to her own time and place, but also the freedom and universality of experience her cloistered life confers upon her internal devotional exploration.

This demonstrates a crucial element in autobiographical and biographical writing, ancient and modern. Some compositions are transformational in intent, using the experiences of first-person or third-person narration, not only to describe spiritual conversion or change but, as Spengemann points out, also to bring it about in others.[37] There are many literary forms in the West of this type, often excluded by critics who confine themselves to discussion of the mainstream of autobiographical discourse. In the *Prelude*, for instance, Wordsworth's memory of the acute alertness of getting lost as

36. See Peers 1991: chapter 39.

37. See Spengemann 1980: 113.

a child is one of a number of profound, transformatory experiences recollected in the poem:

> There are in our existence spots of time, which with distinct pre-eminence retain
> A renovating Virtue, whence,
> ...our minds
> Are nourished and invisibly repaired...
> Such moments
> Are scattered everywhere, taking their date
> From our first childhood.[38]

Autobiographical hymns, such as the six short verses of John Newton's "Amazing Grace" (1772) and John Wesley's "And Can It Be That I Should Gain" (1739), distill an account of religious conversion in a way that reminds us, say, of the *Therīgāthā* and *Theragāthā*, themselves composed as poems, and perhaps even songs. These latter examples are at any rate often pseudo-autobiographical, even if the actual authorship must remain in doubt.[39]

Early Buddhist Autobiography and Biography

So how do early Buddhist texts marry the objectivity of the third person with the personal and the autobiographical? Is narrative voice a useful way of exploring the Pali Canon? The first thing that needs to be said is that much of the Pali Canon, in the form of the Nikāyas, could be termed biographical and is taken that way by, for instance, Ven. Ñāṇamoli and Thomas in their delineation of sources for the Buddha's life story: it is what has been chosen to describe the Buddha by the sangha, whose presence, as I have noted, is indicated by the simple first-person formula that opens most early Buddhist texts.[40] The texts are also intended to be transformational and, when chanted, are intended not only to record the dhamma, but to recreate the Buddha, his teaching, and his followers as living presences for those that recite and hear

38. *The Prelude* XII, ll. 208–25 in Wordsworth 1959.

39. I have taken the term "pseudo-autobiography" from De Looze 1997.

40. See Ñāṇamoli 1978 and Thomas 1927.

them recited. Their intention is to effect some change of mental state and understanding in those listening; the various genres reflect different means of doing this. Simple examination of the use of narrative voice reveals that issues concerning the "personal" interior life of a great figure are addressed in the canon with considerable care, as are the larger questions of many lives and the idea of a "not-self" that participates in them. It becomes clear, for instance, that the early redactors and indeed the Buddha himself seemed to want him to be presented in the suttas as a "type," albeit an inspiring one, a representative of buddhahood. For this, the third person is most frequently employed. They also, however, wanted from time to time to suggest the directness of personal experience, idiosyncrasies peculiar to Gotama Buddha, and, more generally, some sense that he is not removed from others by his attainment of this extraordinary human state. Here the very occasional use of the first person to describe earlier events is significant. One type of literature, the jātakas, also offers the opportunity for more extensive exploration of character than could be attempted in accounts of a final, exemplary life. In this genre the first and third person complement one another to describe the Buddha and his earlier counterpart, the bodhisatta.

The Buddha: Biography

Consideration of the use of narrative voice highlights the great skill and deliberation with which material from the present life of the Buddha is presented. As might be expected, a biographical third person is more prominent. From this narrative it is possible to find historical detail of various kinds, and reconstruct, as Bareau and others have done, a linear "biography" of key events in the Buddha's life in public, historical time.[41] Richard Gombrich has also ascertained a timeline for the Buddha's actual dates.[42] If we look at how such detail is presented, however, we find there is often some personal touch, or first-person recollection, or even a third-person description with a "human" note that leavens the account of a great figure's life. This figure is not being described as a military hero, such as Caesar or Xenophon. Although

41. In, for instance, André Bareau 1963.

42. Gombrich 1992: 237–59. He puts the date of death as 404 B.C.E. I am grateful for some thought-provoking questions he has asked about the topic of this paper.

no sequential biography of the Buddha was composed during his lifetime, or even exists among the earliest canonical material, the *Jātaka-Nidāna*, a work whose verses are considered canonical, does provide this, placed firmly in the context of the Buddha's past lives and the character of the "bodhisatta," the being aiming for enlightenment. Even this early biographical work contains some autobiographical content, however, if the canonical first-person verses of the bodhisatta in an earlier life can be taken as such (e.g. Ja I 11–13, vv. 45–63). Collins has demonstrated that the use of the first-person pronoun in these passages, found also in the *Buddhavaṃsa*, represents a subtle interchange between temporal frameworks, and what he terms "repetitive" and "non-repetitive" time. These elements occur, however, only in the vicinity of an earlier Buddha, with which the narrative opens: in this work "I" is used where the bodhisatta is being validated as part of a *vaṃsa*. The first person is also used to describe the accumulation of the ten perfections. The rest of the narrative, prose and verse, is in the third person.

Autobiography

Autobiography as a genre does not feature in early Indian literature, although there are some autobiographical elements in the Vedas, or at any rate the use of the first person to describe religious experience.[43] Indeed canonical verses of the elders appear to set a precedent in this regard in India. As indicated above, Collins has also comprehensively delineated, with a detail that cannot be emulated here, the skilled shift in the use of narrative voice in the *Buddhavaṃsa* (Collins 1998: 257–67). The Buddha does not give any sequential autobiography in the first person. In the canon the nearest we get to an account of life events of the Buddha is the passage cited in the beginning of this paper, in which Gotama's biography is "told" to him, within what appears to be a first-person recollection of a meditative experience. It is significant, however, that he does not give us first-person accounts of such key events as his own encounter with the deva messengers, the renunciation, or the days after his own enlightenment and the decision to teach others, even though he is willing to relate these "typological" incidents about Vipassī, in the third person. Even the account of the events after the Buddha's enlightenment,

43. See Jamison 2007: 1ff.

which we assume were at one stage told to others, and which largely follow the pattern which the Buddha describes for Vipassī, are recounted in the *Vinaya* entirely through a distanced third person.[44] As the Buddha says, he gives us a handful of leaves, not all the ones in the forest. The early sangha supported him in this, and describe the Buddha as a public figure, with little admitted "past" himself.

The Buddha's Autobiography of His Final Life

We do, however, find some autobiographical incidents, but only in suttas where they directly illustrate teachings. Each recollection seems to occur to answer a particular need. For the Buddha's own life we have his first-person account of the austerities culminating in the delightful account of the first *jhāna* (MN I 246–47). This early memory, somewhat kin to Wordsworth's childhood reminiscences in its transformational intent, is given, we should remember, in the context of an attack on his teaching that culminates with a personal gibe, a criticism of his habit of having an afternoon nap. The "relaxed and friendly atmosphere" of this passage that Bronkhorst notes seems intended to humanize and render more accessible the Buddha's account of his own remembered past and, by implication, the middle way (Bronkhorst 1993: 23). This account also gives, incidentally, a rare account of the Buddha's appearance in dealings with others: his face, apparently, clears and brightens under attack (MN I 250–51). There are other, though few, accounts of the austerities in the first person elsewhere in the canon, as if the Buddha only wishes to draw directly from his own experience to give a direct warning of the pitfalls of these practices.[45] Ānanda relates in the Buddha's presence the account of his miraculous birth, typical of all buddhas: the point is reiterated

44. The encounter with the man who says *hupeyya* and walks on is a nice and, for its unusual choice of dialect wording, probably genuine description of the Buddha's "actual" experience, that gives us a deviation from the usual "type" of events for a new Buddha (Vin I 8). Of course this incident, where the Buddha was on his own with an unknown person, along with other particularized events pertaining to Gotama Buddha, such as the reunion with the five ascetics, must have been related by Gotama to another party to be recorded in this way. The simplicity of the "historical" and public third-person voice is, however, retained, a distance reinforced by the fact that the *Vinaya* lacks the preliminary formula of *evam me sutaṃ* found in the Nikāyas.

45. See, for example, MN I 77–82, MN I 160–75, and Sn vv. 425–49.

throughout the sutta, however, that all tathāgatas experience such wonderful births. The Buddha's only comment is that all tathāgatas also know the arising and falling away of feeling: an attempt, perhaps, to downplay though not deny the wondrous nature of his own arising, which he does not relate here in the first person (MN III 118–24).

From the point of view of the outsider he certainly appears, on occasion, miraculous and out of the ordinary. As the possessor of the thirty-two marks he is observed as a great charismatic teacher, has the voice of Brahma, and shines like Sakka, the lord of the devas (DN II 142–78). He also performs specific, typological, miracles associated with buddhahood (Paṭis I 125–26, Ja IV 263–67). On one or two occasions, however, he seems to drop this persona completely: there are some details in the canon that suggest that he could pass quite comfortably as a "normal" person. He needs to be pointed out to King Ajātasattu in the *Sāmaññaphala-Sutta*, as "the one sitting by a pillar" (DN I 50), presumably an indication that his appearance can, on occasions, be unobtrusive. Another event, recorded in the *Dhātuvibhaṅga-Sutta*, shares with the Ajātasattu incident an odd plausibility. Here he is mistaken by an unsuspecting monk for an ordinary bhikkhu who happens to be sharing a potter's lodging, until the authority of his argument makes his status obvious (MN III 238–47). This incident rings true: perhaps it was possible for Gotama to downplay his shining skin and voice, even if we take the thirty-two marks as literal rather than metaphoric or mythical attributes. He suffers also from normal human ailments. He lives according to the same rules as other monks of his order. He gets backaches now and then and dies of a very non-typological stomach complaint. Unlike other buddhas, he does not have an extended lifespan, due to the fact that Ānanda did not request him to live longer (DN II 118). The diversity of this portrayal, from the divine and supernatural to the mundane, the mythological to the everyday, has prompted many to see contradiction within the Pali texts. It suggests rather something more precise than this: that the teacher could be charismatic, and display miracles, but could also, according to the sangha, drop all personal magnetism and seem like anyone else when the situation demanded it.

From a biographical point of view most of the canonical accounts of the Buddha's final life may be primarily aimed at presenting an exemplary figure. These third-person observations, interspersed with "human" autobiographical touches in the first person, ensure that he does not seem a remote one.

The Buddha's Past Lives as the Bodhisatta

But what about past lives? There is some direct first-person recollection on the part of the Buddha to describe his own past lives. In the *Cariyāpiṭaka*, the *Apadāna*, and in the canonical verses of the *Jātaka-Nidāna* the Buddha uses the same "I" to describe events in earlier lives that he employs to describe the experiences of his own last life. There is not space to consider these works at length, but it is noteworthy that "I" is employed for renewals of vows, the recounting of catalogs of virtues, and by and large for hagiographic description. In the *Cariyāpiṭaka*, for instance, he lists various actions as the bodhisatta with this voice, giving specific life stories, that the bodhisatta took rebirth as a *nāga* (snake spirit), for instance (Cp II.3), or a quail (Cp III.9). The perspective, however, is on those deeds that contribute directly and obviously to the development of a particular perfection. It is as if these events, common to all buddhas, permit Gotama the use of the first person in a way that would not be used for more idiosyncratic, non-exemplary behavior, or, simply, more extensively descriptive narrative.[46]

When E. M. Forster spoke of the successful novel in 1927, he made a famous distinction between "flat" characters that one might find in didactic literature and truly "round" characters: those that seem to develop, to grow, to experience doubts and passions and behave in what could be called a particularized and "human" way.[47] The distinction seems pertinent, if in need of adaptation, to the Buddha's recollections of his past lives. In the "exemplary" texts, the *Cariyāpiṭaka* and the *Jātaka-Nidāna*, the recollections of the first person are concerned with typological events. I am hesitant to use the word "flat" because the descriptions are not: they are rich, beautiful, and heroic. Perhaps more apt would be the term "type" for this kind of depiction: a kind of character rather than a specific one. They describe a wholly inspiring personage, one whose actions are proper to key, exemplary moments in the path to buddhahood. They do not, however, satisfy our perhaps perennial demand for an individualized character, with human foibles and doubts, nor do they

46. For closer analysis of the depiction of the bodhisatta and associated hagiographic elements in the *Apadāna*, see Cutler 1994: 1–42.

47. Forster 1927: 93–112.

indulge in psychological exploration, adventurous narrative, or various other kinds of personal interaction.

The jātaka collection includes some of the kind of material we associate with autobiography: a novelistic exploration of motive and private inner states, dramatic debate in the epic and tragic manner, and the straightforward adventure story. Jātakas cover violent personal conflict, turbulent conflicting emotions, acts of dazzling heroism, unrequited love, and heroic conflict. Phyllis Granoff has demonstrated that Jain stories of often violent and shocking past lives are told in a context where people enter a kind of liminal state, receptive to the intricacies of plot and character delineated in these lengthy tales.[48] The intent, Granoff argues, of these accounts of murder and incestuous relations from earlier lives is to jolt the listener into a desire for the ascetic life. Describing a less starkly shocking form, perhaps more akin to the social, leisurely jātaka style, C. L. Barber, in *Shakespeare's Festive Comedy*, showed the peculiar relationship between local festive conventions, with their tradition of misrule and assumed identities, and the Shakespearean comic pattern: "To relate this drama to holiday has proved to be the most effective way to describe its character. The comedies are plays designed for specific events."[49] This description seems to be closer in spirit to the jātakas, which, for all their sometimes startling violence, are, nonetheless, often buoyant and moving vindications of positive alliances, virtues, and the perfections. To this day in Buddhist countries, when practitioners go to a temple, they hear the stories in a particular context of great festivity, in an apparently chaotic atmosphere that belies the underlying organization and preparation involved.[50] The laity will have taken extra precepts, be wearing white, and will have offered food as

48. In Granoff 1994: 16–34.

49. C. L. Barber demonstrated the way that the spirit of misrule and the controlled folly of the medieval festivals and customs was incorporated into Shakespeare's plays: see Barber 1972. A comparable approach is followed in Liebler (see Liebler 1995). From the point of view of jātaka study it is a shame that this sort of formal criticism is very unfashionable nowadays. Jātakas have not had the benefit of continued critical reappraisal that English literary works have received, and an assessment of their role as, possibly, a festive art form in the context of "holy" day conventions would be welcome.

50. I am grateful to Ven. Dr Paññavaṃsa for accounts of the *Vessantara Jātaka* festivals, described in detail in his unpublished doctoral thesis for Peradaniya University, Sri Lanka, 2008. The subject is also covered by Gombrich in his introduction to Cone's translation of *Vessantara* (Cone and Gombrich 1977: xv–xlv).

well as flowers, incense, and butter lamps. Chants of the *Mettā-Sutta*, wishing happiness to all beings, the *Maṅgala-Sutta*, and the *Ratana-Sutta* may well be going on even at the same time as the traditional recital of the jātaka itself. This restful, cheerful "liminality" is a suitable setting to suspend disbelief—and for the Buddha's "character" to be extended through the adventurous and sometimes reckless persona of the bodhisatta. The often-repeated injunction, largely peculiar to the jātakas, "Be generous, guard the precepts, and keep the *uposatha* day," can be allowed to percolate through all levels of the mind.[51] It is what people who are listening to the jātaka are actually doing. It will be a necessary part of the process of listening, as familiar as the conventional "frame" of the tales. Indeed many, if not most, jātakas involve some exploration of the first two perfections, of generosity and *sīla* ("restraint"), which the tales so frequently enjoin. Perhaps much as an Elizabethan audience would feel within the comic or tragic festivities of a Shakespearean theater, listeners consider themselves protected. There is a familiar form whose outcome is safe within the terms of Buddhist understanding. The "liminal" state of the listeners is also safeguarded by the ritual purity of the precepts taken for the day and the generosity aroused by its festivities. These virtues are constantly rewarded and extolled in the tales.

There is a standard jātaka pattern. A tale from the present describes the exemplary Buddha in the third person; this is followed by the tale from the past and a story about a third-person character, the bodhisatta, an earlier "self," related by the Buddha. Only at the end does the story finish with "*aham eva*," "thus was I," the Buddha's acknowledgement of his relationship with his earlier state.[52] The threads of the Buddha, described in the third person, the "he" of the bodhisatta, and the "I" of the end of each tale are woven in and out of each other like a plait, evoking a succession of lives. These three elements suggest neither the "eternalist" view, an abiding self, nor the "annihilationist" view that the self ceases at death. Patterns repeat; specificity of detail may not. A moving point, like a kind of "middle way," arises from the process itself, in the constant movement between the first person acknowledgment of the Buddha

51. On this see Shaw 2006a: xxxii–xxxvii. The injunction is found at, for instance, Ja I 93, Ja III 52.

52. The same sort of pattern is found in the suttas where jātaka type tales are found: see *Mahāsudassana-Sutta* (DN II 168–98), *Mahāgovinda-Sutta* (DN II 220–52), and *Makhādeva-Sutta* (MN II 74–83).

and his third-person character, the bodhisatta. This shift in personal pronouns permits the Buddha to describe behavior, actions, and arguments he cannot in his final life. In the tales "from the past," the bodhisatta finds out what it is like to be physically unattractive (Ja V 278–312), and to perform sometimes less than exemplary deeds, such as falling in love with a married woman (Ja III 496–501), or killing another being (Ja I 420–21). He could not, as a buddha, use the directness of the first person for these events. The enactment of the bodhisatta vow, of course, allows for many admirable kinds of behavior, too, and these form the major part of jātakas: the bodhisatta lays down his own life for another (Ja III 39–43, Ja III 51–56) and cares for his parents into old age (Ja VI 68–95); he struggles at sea for days on his own (Ja VI 34–38), allows himself to be rescued from death by his wife (Ja IV 282–88), and lives for multiples of 84,000 years as a munificent monarch, constantly making donations to others (Ja I 137–39, Ja I 391–93). These positive features are also things he cannot do in his final, monastic life.[53] A multiplicity of life events, which include large acts of personal heroism and generosity, but also morally equivocal behavior, extensive personal deliberation and debate, and, of course, rebirth as animal, king, outcast, sailor, and priest, are possible. Such a variety of "selves" or "I's" could not be contained within one life story. In the jātaka tales, through the constantly changing and dissolving identities of the bodhisatta and the enactment of karmic patterns over lifetimes, the fully awakened mind, in the search for the perfections, demonstrates its links with many successions of "I's" and types of behavior: the process of rebirth is carefully suggested by the threefold pattern of third-person bodhisatta, third-person Buddha, and the Buddha's "I" that winds through the tales.

The Buddha often has to teach people in very varied circumstances. In the "exemplary" texts, where he does indeed use the first person to describe an earlier life, the material reported is of a typological nature. In the jātakas, in tales acknowledged as the Buddha's own past, a method of mixed narration and participation offers a framework for the full exploration of a real variety of ethical dilemmas, wide-ranging professional experience, personal spiritual conflict, as well as much nobility, wisdom, and kindness. The jātakas, perhaps always told at *uposatha* or "holy" days, allow the disclosure of the

53. I have found discussion with Dr. Naomi Appleton, at the time of my writing this article a doctoral student studying jātaka as biography at Oxford University, helpful on this subject.

laws of karma as it operates over eons. The doctrine of no-self can be enacted through varied autobiographical experience, made possible by a third-person "bodhisatta" who enjoys exciting and daring adventures in "the past" that the Buddha could never have described for the august identity assumed for his final bodily form. The Buddha could not throw himself into a fire, like the generous hare, in his final life, or leap across a chasm to protect others. Such events allow the Buddha to demonstrate his real rapport and compassion for other beings, while always returning to the authority of the "I" of the Buddha in "the present," whose "I"-making and further rebirth has, paradoxically, stopped. In this regard they also claim to be transformational texts. At the conclusion of the tales, recounted in a standard formula, the stories describe many listeners attaining stages of path or enlightenment. In Buddhist terms, by listening to the story of the arising and ceasing of another "I," these important participants in the unfolding of each jātaka are made ready for the teaching that makes them free of "I"-making too.

This leads to consideration of a final feature of the life story of the Buddha, which transcends most modern notions about the function of biographical detail. This is the specific application of the qualities of the Buddha, often exemplified through story events of his final life, within a specifically meditative context. Among the meditative practices recommended in the canon is what is known as *buddhānussati*, the recollection of the attributes of the Buddha, employed to arouse calm, cheerfulness, and composure in daily life. It is particularly enjoined for the lay life, and for those who have attained one of the stages of path (AN V 332–34). In its chanted form it constitutes the traditional opening procedure for most sitting meditations, as recommended by Buddhaghosa, the fifth-century commentator. His work on meditation, *The Path of Purification* (*Visuddhimagga*), is consulted to this day as a practical manual in all Southern Buddhist countries (Vism VII 198–213);[54] he explains the practice in some detail. Analyzing the canonical formula which should be recited to undertake this practice, he makes a number of references to events in the Buddha's life as supporting the recollection of his attributes and in the end of that section in the *Visuddhimagga* says that the mind of the person who practices this recollection "inclines towards the plane of the

54. For the English translation of what has been historically the most frequently consulted manual for meditation in Southern Buddhism, see Ñāṇamoli 1976.

buddhas"; when he sees an opportunity to make a fault in daily life, he feels shame "as if he were face to face with the teacher" (Vism VII 213).[55] The practices of the Southern Buddhist tradition as represented by Buddhaghosa and the Mahāvihāra temple in Sri Lanka do not go so far as to say the Buddha is still actually present, a feature incorporated into some early Indian Buddhism schools which contributed to the development of what we know now as the Mahāyāna.[56] It does nonetheless suggest that the life story of the Buddha is something that can be brought to mind by the practitioner to arouse aspects of the path as a possibility in the present, rather than just an occurrence associated with historical events. The practice of the recollection of the Buddha constitutes part of the core ritual procedures of most Southern Buddhists to this day: the chant recollecting these qualities, the first aspect of the triple gem, is performed daily in both a private and, in temples and festivals, a public context. The manifold aspects of the bodhisatta entertain, move, and suggest ways of action: the Buddha, however, is perceived as a still center, with his life story evoking the fully awakened mind that can provide protection and guidance for the practitioner in the present.

This brings us lastly to another aspect of the triple gem practice that completes the daily practice of most modern Southeast Asian Buddhist practitioners: that of the recollection of the qualities of the sangha, those who have attained any of the four stages of the path. I have focused on the Buddha in this paper, but the early followers of the Buddha are also worthy of consideration. Those who lived at the time of the Buddha not only created the texts that recorded his behavior and speech, but they also give freely of their own first-person voices. First-person poems or songs (*gāthā*) in the *Therīgāthā* and *Theragāthā* are some of the earliest autobiographical compositions in the world. Some of these may not be "genuine": the poems include some duplications of verses found elsewhere, suggesting many could well be

55. Glossing the attribute that the Buddha is a "leader of men to be tamed," for instance, a number of examples from his life are taken in which he actually does this (see Vism VII 207–8 /Ñāṇamoli [1976]: 222). For more discussion of the *Iti pi so* chant remembering the triple gem and recollection of the Buddha as a meditation, see Shaw 2006b: 109–18, Shaw 2009: 96–101, and for the English translation of Buddhaghosa's recommendations for the practice, Ñāṇamoli 1976: 204–30.

56. On this large subject, and the continued "presence" of the Buddha and bodhisattas as revealers of texts and guides for the practitioner, see, for instance, Harrison 1978.

"pseudo-autobiography" (Th 13 and 1063, 15 and 633).[57] Some seem to be more akin to transformational and universalized songs, rather in the manner of the hymns of conversion of Wesley and Newton (Th 171–72, Th 181–82, Th 673–88). The autobiographical content of some lies simply in the aptness of the choice of imagery to describe the process of awakening, as in the verses of Udāyī, who describes the teaching in terms of training an elephant after apparently seeing one himself (Th 689–704).[58] Some, however, are very specific, outlining "factual" details, such as the account of the sad circumstances of Isidāsī's recent past and earlier lives (Thī 400–47). The arahats revealed in these verses, and indeed in incidents throughout the canon, are not just types. In these *gāthās* and in canonical descriptions they seem what we would now call "round" characters, even after the attainment of arahatship: Sāriputta, for instance, loves to describe meditational states in detail, is kindly and humble (Th-a II 116), but has a passion for meal cakes (Ja I 310). Moggallāna likes the grand gesture, such as wiggling his big toe to make a houseful of lazy bhikkhus quake (SN V 269ff). Even the Buddha's beautiful spouse, Rāhulamātā, suffers a bit from flatulence, a difficulty that has a ring of non-typological plausibility (Ja II 392)! With the verses of Aṅgulimāla we find what is, I think, a form of autobiography that has no counterpart in any culture. His personal life story, distilled into one verse, admittedly composed in the first instance by the Buddha, is used as a "statement of truth" and is described as recited in the canon to bring about the safe delivery to a woman suffering in childbirth.[59] The mass murderer's statement, that since he has been a monk he has harmed no living being, is still chanted to this day to

57. On this subject, see Norman 1997: ix.

58. See AN III 344 and Th-a ii 7f.

59. Despite a colorful life as a serial murderer, Aṅgulimāla was converted by the Buddha and soon attained arahatship, though, after taking the robe, was often reviled by the laity. By this stage, he had of course completely rejected his earlier life and lived blamelessly, without defilements. His famous "autobiographical" statement was suggested to him by the Buddha (MN II 98–105). It is what is known in ancient India as a statement of truth (*saccakiriyā*), an announcement that frequently proclaims that a particular virtue has been sustained by the speaker for a long period of time. Such a recollection was thought to possess great magical potency (see also, for instance, Ja I 331–32). Aṅgulimāla's assertion apparently saved both mother and baby, and to this day is used as a blessing chant (*paritta*) to bring good luck in childbirth: "Sister, since I have been born with a noble birth, I do not remember that I have ever intentionally deprived a living being of life. By this truth, may you and your baby be well!" (MN II 103).

laboring women in Southeast Asian countries. Such verses, anecdotes, songs, stories, descriptions, interactions, discourses, and dialogues of the followers of the Buddha are an essential part of the fabric of the canon. The Buddha's first disciples composed with great craft the third-person discourses handed down to us today; their voices are central not only to the content but also to the very production and means of transmitting the Buddha's teaching of the triple gem: the Buddha, the dhamma, and the sangha. Indeed, the recollection of the qualities of these followers, who brought such a great diversity of temperament, disposition, and skill to the process of awakening is itself also a canonical meditative practice, the third element of the triple gem recollection chant. This is also said to arouse happiness, freedom from fear, confidence, and a sense that the practitioner is in the presence of this community (Vism VII 100). The excellences of these historical figures can be brought to mind so that they also act as guides for the Buddhist in the present. A post-canonical chant popular in Southeast Asia is dedicated to the recollection and invocation of the qualities of eight of the principal arahats, who guard each direction in a kind of *maṇḍala* protecting and inspiring the one who chants to them. They are described in the third person, in the present tense: "they sit...all well-established here."[60]

We began by investigating the use of narrative voice as a way of exploring the genres of biography and autobiography, coming to find that such analysis is also useful for examining the way the Buddha, his earlier "selves," and his followers are presented in the canon. Early Buddhist texts encompass many different genres of writing that cannot be examined fully here. These include personal recollection, inspirational "conversion" songs, verses deploying imagery derived from recent observation, detailed autobiography and past-life reminiscences, as well as the "public," exemplary, but sometimes humanized biographical detail of the suttas. A full study in terms of modern understanding of the genres of autobiography and biography has not been attempted. I hope that with regard to the one feature of narrative voice it has become clear that the texts indicate the use of great deliberation. A careful

60. On the chant and life stories of the eight arahats see Shaw 2009: 133–38. On modern versions of the chant see Skilling 2000. The life stories of the various arahats are described in detail in Nyanaponika and Hecker 1997. The practice of the recollection of the sangha is given in Vism VII 218–21 / Ñāṇamoli 1976: 236–40.

interplay of the first with the third person communicates the Buddha's skill as teacher, confidant, and friend, grounding and lending vitality to his portrayal as the figure of factual, historical, devotional, geographic, and calendric biography. His followers, many of whom are arahats, are also particularized and seem "true." Indeed we can see the lives of all of these figures as a still-active influence on the emotional and spiritual worlds of Southern Buddhists to this day: all are regarded as presences that can in some way be invoked and remembered, through daily ritual and meditative practice, as guides, friends, and teachers on the spiritual path. Early Pali texts thus achieve something rather difficult. Through a number of narrative voices they depict the Buddha, and many other exemplary beings, at various stages of awakening. Their journey and expression of that state is, nonetheless, made to seem memorable and diverse: both "lived" and "living" now.

Abbreviations

Pali texts cited are those produced by the Pali Text Society. See http://www.palitext.com/. Abbreviations of Pali texts are according to recent conventions of the Pali Text Society:

AN	Aṅguttara Nikāya
Ap	Apadāna
Cp	Cariyāpiṭaka
DN	Dīgha Nikāya
Ja	Jātaka
MN	Majjhima Nikāya
Paṭis	Paṭisambhidāmagga
Sn	Suttanipāta
SN	Saṃyutta Nikāya
Th	Theragāthā
Th-a	Theragāthā-aṭṭhakathā
Thī	Therīgāthā
Ud	Udāna
Vin	Vinaya
Vism	Visuddhimagga

Bibliography

Bareau, A. 1963. *Recherches sur la biographie du Buddha dans les sūtrapiṭaka et les vinayapiṭaka anciens: de la quête de l'éveil à la conversion de Śāriputra et de Maudgalyāyana*. Paris: École Française d'Extrême-Orient.

Barber, C. L. 1972. *Shakespeare's Festive Comedy: A Study of Dramatic Form and Its Relation to Social Custom*. Princeton: Princeton University Press.

Bronkhorst, J. 1976. *The Two Traditions of Meditation in Ancient India*. Delhi: Motilal Banarsidass.

Brown, D. 2003. *The Da Vinci Code*. New York: Doubleday.

Bruss, E. W. 1993. *Autobiographical Acts: The Changing Situation of a Literary Genre*. Baltimore and London: Johns Hopkins University Press.

Collins, S. 1998. *Nirvana and Other Buddhist Felicities: Utopias of the Pali Imaginaire*. Cambridge: Cambridge University Press.

Cone, M., and R. F. Gombrich 1977. *The Perfect Generosity of Prince Vessantara*. Oxford: Oxford University Press.

Cousins, L. S. 1989. "The Stages of Christian Mysticism and the Path of Purification: *Interior Castle* of St. Teresa of Avila and the *Path of Purification* of Buddhaghosa." In *The Yogi and the Mystic: Studies in Indian and Comparative Mysticism*, ed. by K. Werner, pp. 103–20. London: Routledge, and JSTOR, http://links.jstor.org/sici.

Cutler, S. M. 1994. "The Pāli Apadāna Collection." *Journal of the Pali Text Society* XX: 1–42.

Damaskios 1967. "The Life of Isadorus: Fragmentia Photius Bibliotheca." In *Damascii Vitae Isidori Reliquiae edidit adnotationibusque instruxit Clemens Zintzen*. Hildesheim: Olms.

Delaney, P. 1969. *British Autobiography in the Seventeenth Century*. London and New York: Columbia University Press.

De Looze, L. 1997. *Pseudo-autobiography in the Fourteenth Century: Juan Riz, Guillaume de Machant, Jean Froissart and Geoffrey Chaucer*. Gainesville: University of Florida Press.

Dundas, P. 1992. *The Jains*. London and New York: Routledge.

"E.G." 1926. "Biography." In *Encyclopaedia Britannica*. 13th ed. in 3 vols. pp. 952–54. London: Encyclopaedia Britannica Co.

Fleishman, A. 1983. *Figures of Autobiography: The Language of Self-Writing in Victorian and Modern England*. Berkeley: University of California Press.

Forster, E. M. 1927. *Aspects of the Novel; The Clark lectures, delivered under the auspices of Trinity College, Cambridge, in the Spring of 1927*. London: Edward Arnold.

Geiger, W., trans. 1912. *The Mahāvaṃsa or the Great Chronicle of Ceylon*. London: PTS.

Geiger, W., and B. Ghosh, trans. 1978. *Pāli Literature and Language*. Third reprint. New Delhi: Oriental Books.

Gombrich, R. F. 1980. "The Significance of Former Buddhas in the Theravādin Tradition." In *Buddhist Studies in Honour of Walpola Rahula*, ed. by Somaratna et al., pp. 62–72. London: Gordon Fraser.

——— 1992. "Dating the Buddha: A Red Herring Revealed." In *The Dating of the Historical Buddha*, ed. by H. Bechert, part 2, pp. 237–59. Gottingen: Vandenhoeck & Ruprecht.

Granoff, P. 1994. "Life as Ritual Process: Remembrance of Past Births in Jain Religious Narratives." In *Autobiography and Biography in Cross-Cultural Perspective*, ed. by P. Granoff and K. Shinohara, pp. 16–34. Oakville, Canada / Buffalo, NY: Mosaic Press.

Griffin, J. 2001. *Virgil*. Bristol: Bristol Classical Press.

Gunn, J. V. 1987. "Autobiography." In *Encyclopedia of Religion*, ed. by M. Eliade, vol. 2, pp. 6–11. New York and London: Macmillan.

Hardy, B. 1970. "The Moment of Disenchantment in George Eliot's Novels." In *George Eliot: A Collection of Critical Essays*, ed. by G. R. Creeger, pp. 55–65. Englewood Cliffs, NJ: Prentice-Hall.

Harrison, P. 1978. "*Buddhānusmṛti* in the *Pratyutpanna–Buddha saṃmukhāvasthitasamādhisūtra*." *Journal of Indian Philosophy* 6: 35–57.

Herrtage, S. J. H., ed. 1879. *The Early English Versions of the Gesta Romanorum / formerly edited by Sir Frederic Madden for the Roxburghe Club, and now re-edited from the mss. in British Museum (Harl. 7333 & Addit. 9066) and University Library, Cambridge (Kk. 1–6), with introduction, notes, glossary.* London: Early English Text Society, N. Trübner & Co.

Holt, J. C. 1996. *The Religious World of Kīrti Śrī: Buddhism, Art, and Politics in Late Medieval Sri Lanka.* New York: Oxford University Press.

Jamison, S. W. 2007. *The Rig Veda between Two Worlds.* Paris: College de France.

Kirkpatrick R., ed. 2006. *The Divine Comedy 1 (The Inferno).* Harmondsworth, Middlesex.: Penguin.

La Fleur, W. R. 1987. "Biography." In *Encyclopedia of Religion*, ed. by M. Eliade, vol. 2, pp. 220–24. New York and London: Macmillan.

Lamotte, E. 1958. *Histoire du Bouddhisme Indien.* Louvain: Publications Universitaires, Bibliothèque du Muséon. Translated by S. Boin-Webb as *History of Indian Buddhism.* Louvain and Paris: Peeters Press, 1988.

Liebler, N. C. 1995. *Shakespeare's Festive Tragedy: The Ritual Foundations of Genre.* New York: Routledge.

Marcus, L. 1994. *Auto/Biographical Discourses: Theory, Criticism and Practice.* Manchester and New York: Manchester University Press.

Matics, K. I. 1998. *Gestures of the Buddha.* Bangkok: Chulalongkorn University Press.

Misch, G. 1998. *A History of Autobiography in Antiquity.* 2 vols., trans. of Leipzig 1907 version by E. W. Dickes. London: Routledge.

Ñāṇamoli Bhikkhu, trans. 1976. *The Path of Purification (Visuddhimagga) of Bhadantacāriya Buddhaghosa.* 2 vols. Berkeley and London: Shambhala.

——— 1978. *The Life of the Buddha as it appears in the Pali Canon, the oldest authentic record.* Kandy, Sri Lanka: Buddhist Publication Society.

Norman, K. R. 1997. *Poems of Early Buddhist Monks (Theragāthā).* Oxford: Pali Text Society.

Norman, K. R., and W. Pruitt, ed. 1999. *The Bhikkhupāṭimokkha.* Oxford: Pali Text Society.

Nyanaponika Thera, and H. Hecker, 1997. *Great Disciples of the Buddha: Their Lives, Their Works, Their Legacy.* With intro. by Bhikkhu Bodhi. Boston: Wisdom.

Obermeier, A. 1999. *The History and Anatomy of Auctorial Self-Criticism in the European Middle Ages.* Amsterdam, Atlanta, GA: Rodipi Bv.

Pamuk, O. 2001. *My Name Is Red.* London: Faber.

Peers, E. A. 1991. *The Life of Teresa of Jesus: The Autobiography of Teresa of Ávila.* New York: Doubleday.

Rastogi, N. P. 1990. *The Inscriptions of Aśoka.* With foreword by K. Deva. Varanasi: Chowkhamba Sanskrit Series Office.

Rhys Davids, T. W., trans. and ed. 1977. *Dialogues of the Buddha.* 3 vols. 4th ed.; reprinted London, Henley, and Boston: Routledge/PTS.

Schama, S. 1999. *Rembrandt's Eyes.* London: Penguin.

Sebold, A. 2002. *The Lovely Bones.* Boston: Little, Brown, and Company.

Shapiro, S. A. 1967. "The Dark Continent of Literature: Autobiography." *Comparative Literature Studies* 5: 421–58.

Shaw, S. 2006a. *The Jātakas: The Birth Stories of the Bodhisatta.* New Delhi: Penguin.

——— 2006b. *Buddhist Meditation: An Anthology of Texts.* Oxford Centre for Buddhist Studies. London: Routledge.

——— 2009. *An Introduction to Buddhist Meditation.* London and New York: Routledge.

Singh, N. Kr., ed. 2001. *Encyclopedia of Jainism.* Indo-European Jain Research Foundation. 27 vols. Delhi: Anmol Publications.

Skilling, P. 2000. "The Arahats of the Eight Directions." *Fragile Palm Leaves for the Preservation of Buddhist Literature* 6: 12, 22.

Spacks, P. M. 1976. *Imagining a Self: Autobiography and Novel in Eighteenth Century England.* Cambridge, MA: Harvard University Press.

Spengemann, W. C. 1980. *The Forms of Autobiography; Episodes in the History of a Literary Genre.* New Haven: Yale University Press.

Strong, J. S. 2001. *The Buddha: A Short Biography.* Oxford: Oneworld.

Sturrock, J. 1993. *The Language of Autobiography: Studies in the First Person Singular.* Cambridge: Cambridge University Press.

Thomas, E. J. 1927. *The Life of the Buddha as Legend and History.* London: Routledge and Kegan Paul.

Tomalin, C. 1991. *The Invisible Woman: The Story of Nelly Ternan and Charles Dickens.* Harmondsworth, Middlesex: Penguin.

Geiger W., trans. 1912. *The Mahāvaṃsa or the Great Chronicle of Ceylon.* London: Pali Text Society.

Webber, J. 1979. *The Eloquent "I": Style and Self in Seventeenth-Century Prose.* Madison: University of Wisconsin Press.

Wordsworth, W. 1959. *The Prelude, or, Growth of a Poet's Mind.* Ed. by E. de Selincourt and revised by H. Darbishire. Oxford: Clarendon Press.

Online Texts

Bellows H. A. trans. 1922. *Peter Abelard: Historia Calamitatum: The Story of My Misfortunes.* www.fordham.edu/halsall/basis/abelard-histcal.html.

Caesar, *De Bello Gallico.* Electronic Text Center, University of Virginia Library. http://etext.lib.virginia.edu/toc/modeng/public/CaeComm.html.

Project Gutenberg. http://www.gutenberg.org/etext/1170.

Caesar, Julius 1913. *De Vita XII Caesarum.* Loeb Classical Library ed. in Latin and English. http://penelope.uchicago.edu/Thayer/E/Roman/Texts/Suetonius/12Caesars/Julius*.html.

Herrtage, S. J. H., trans. *Gesta Romanorum.* www.slu.edu/colleges/AS/languages/classical/latin/tchmat/readers/gr/gr1.html.

Peers, E. A., trans. *The Life of Teresa of Jesus*. http://www.catholicfirst.com/thefaith/catholicclassics/stteresa/life/teresaofavila01.html.

Works by Plutarch, John Dryden trans. 1994–2000. http://classics.mit.edu/Browse/index-Plutarch.html.

Wordsworth, W. *The Prelude.* Ed. by Ernest de Selincourt. 2nd ed. http://www.bartleby.com/145/ww298.html.

The Prelature of Opus Dei in the United States, 2006. "The *Da Vinci Code*, the Catholic Church, and Opus Dei." www.opusdei.org/art.php?w=32&p=7017.

Chips from a Biographical Workshop— Early Chinese Biographies of the Buddha

The Late Birth of Rāhula and Yaśodharā's Extended Pregnancy[1]

Max Deeg

ONE OF THE most interesting aspects of Buddhism for Westerners after the so-called discovery of the religion in the early nineteenth century was the figure and the life of its historical founder, Gautama Siddhārtha. In the age of Positivism, only what could be proven historically was deemed worthy of scholarly attention. This attitude led to a long history of investigation into the biography of the Buddha,[2] the peak of which are certainly the volumes on the date of the historical Buddha edited by Heinz Bechert[3] and the constant flow of publications materializing from the research of the

1. It is my pleasant duty to thank my colleague, James Hegarty, for correcting the rough English of the draft version of this paper.

2. This is not the place to give a complete overview of Western scholarly writing on the life of the Buddha, but it may be allowed to outline, in a chronological order (of first publication), some of the major scholarly publications which are not mentioned otherwise in this article: Pischel 1917; Thomas 1949; Foucher 1987; Waldschmidt 1982; Klimkeit 1990; Nakamura 2000 and 2005.

3. Bechert 1991/1992. For a different approach, and one which takes into account the different forms of sources (textual, art-historical, geographical, and archaeological) as sources in their own right without any intention to "search for the origins," and which relates to the birthplace (Lumbinī) and the hometown (Kapilavāstu) of the Buddha, see Deeg 2003. For yet another approach, which reads the biographies in terms of a "bio-blueprint" (Strong) and of "religious architecture" (Silk) see Strong 2001: 10ff. and Silk 2003.

French scholar André Bareau in his *Recherches sur la biographie du Buddha*.[4] The basic sources for this long thread of research activity are, of course, the Buddhist texts from India dealing with the life of the Buddha.

In speaking of Indian texts on the Buddha's life, those that represent a full-fledged biography, we soon become aware that we have quite a restricted corpus of sources at our fingertips.[5] There is nothing that clearly goes back to the pre-common era. The usually quoted texts from outside the Pali tradition, the *Lalitavistara* and the *Mahāvastu* of the Lokottaravādin school, are already elaborated texts, a fact which is also true for the first masterpieces of the poetic genre, Aśvaghoṣa's *Buddhacarita* and *Saundarananda*. Besides these texts there is the more or less connected biography of the Buddha in the Vinaya of the Mūlasarvāstivādins that, though a complex compilation, is relatively young and presents us with clear regional extensions. Here the Buddha has already visited regions—Mathurā and the Indian northwest—to which he could not have traveled in purely historical terms.

For basic episodes and elements of the life of the Buddha in India we have, however, much older evidence than the supposed earliest Indian biographical texts whose time of compilation is hardly datable. This earlier evidence is found in the earliest Buddhist art in places like Sāñcī, Bhārhut, and Ajaṇṭā. Although these sources are aniconic,[6] their motifs are mostly clearly identifiable. There has been a lot of speculation about the literary sources of this earliest form of Buddhist art. Regularly, the *Lalitavistara* or the *Mahāvastu* were taken as the textual blueprints for this art,[7] often due to the fact that they are extant Sanskrit biographies rather than clearly identifiable original and authentic sources.[8]

But there is a problem in this method of simply reading these two strands of sources together in this way, not only because of the late material evidence for the texts, but also because Buddhist art does not provide us with a

4. Bareau 1963, 1970/71, 1995.

5. For an overview of the biography of the Buddha see Strong 2001.

6. See, e.g., Karlsson 2000.

7. See Krom 1926 for the "classical" example of N. J. Krom's work on the great stūpa of Borobudur, Java, and the *Lalitavistara*.

8. In recent times Western scholars like D. Schlingloff (see note 10) in his work on Buddhist art and Karetzky (see note 12) have adequately used Chinese material—as Japanese art historians have long done.

continuous biographical account of the Buddha's life, but only with selected episodes. As Dieter Schlingloff puts it in one of his works on Ajaṇṭā:

> At the time when the oldest Buddhist paintings[9] were made, there was still no Buddha biography in the sense of a continuous account of the life of the legendary founder of the order.[10]

This is, then, in full accord with the episodes and motifs found in the oldest Ajaṇṭā paintings, dated to the second century B.C.E.[11] They were restricted to a fixed set of events in the life of the Buddha centered around birth, great departure, enlightenment, first sermon, and physical death, or *parinirvāṇa*. This accords with what one of the canonical biographical texts, the *Mahāparinirvāṇasūtra*, recommends as the (in this case four) great events that are to be commemorated as places of pilgrimages and worship. It is not before the full-fledged narrative art of Gandhāra is developed that we grasp, sometimes in combined freezes and panels, a well-developed and datable biography of the Buddha on South Asian soil.[12]

The investigation into the growth and development of the Buddha-*vita* is a complex and difficult matter. Already Étienne Lamotte and Erich Frauwallner have argued that the first biographical textual tradition about the life of the Buddha was not extant at a very early period but was patched together during the course of time. As Frauwallner pointed out, some of the Vinayas still represent this process.[13] Lamotte discerns the following periods:

1. biographical fragments incorporated into the early Sūtras;
2. complete or fragmentary biographies included in the Vinayas;

9. And, one could add, sculptures.

10. Schlingloff 2000: 39.

11. Schlingloff 2000: 41–71.

12. The basic reference work on Gandhāran narrative art is still Foucher's monumental work, see Foucher 1905/1918/1951. In Japanese, Kurita's 2008 book must be mentioned which, though often quoted for its illustrations, is noteworthy also for its textual references, within which the author frequently refers to Chinese biographical sources. A comparison of the early Chinese sources and Gandhāran art has been made by Karetzky 1992.

13. Frauwallner 1956: 42ff. For a re-assessment of Frauwallner's Vinaya studies see Clarke 2004.

3. autonomous but incomplete "Lives," elaborated by various Buddhist schools at the beginning of the Christian era;
4. a complete biography in the Mūlasarvāstivādin Vinaya and related texts, dating from approximately the fourth century;
5. Nidānakathā and an outline of annals compiled in the fifth century by Sinhalese commentators.[14]

Lamotte's first, fourth, and fifth stage of development are accessible to the specialist of Indic languages. For the second and third part this is only partly true because here we only have the Vinaya of the Theravādins and texts such as the *Buddhacarita* and the *Lalitavistara*. It is exactly in these two groups where the early Chinese independent biographies of the Buddha become important as sources for the historical development of the Buddha's biography.

If we leave aside for a moment the Chinese translations of the Vinayas of the different schools (*nikāya*) containing biographical material *in extenso*, it is striking that the above-mentioned texts cover only the first half of the Venerable One's life, up to either the enlightenment or the first conversions. The second half of the Buddha's life, the main teaching period until the Buddha's *parinirvāṇa*, is not covered by some of the older texts, although the "canonical" *Mahāparinirvāṇasūtra* obviously represents an early stage of formulation of narrative episodic texts in the history of Buddhist literature.[15] This text extends the actual events around the physical death and cremation of the Buddha backward to his last journey from Magadha to the north in the last weeks or months of his life.

This textual situation seems to indicate that between the second and fourth centuries of the Common Era, to which the earliest Chinese biographical texts have to be dated, the story of the life of the Buddha was still in the process of formation. This contention finds further support from the fact that the Indian textual tradition itself has brought to light a lot of "incomplete" biographies of the Buddha, which find their "extension" in, and corre-

14. Lamotte 1988: 649ff. (For the sake of convenience I quote from the English translation of the French original, published Louvain 1958.) Lamotte first presented this developmental scheme in his article 1947–48.

15. Cp. Waldschmidt 1944/48 and Waldschmidt 1950/51. For a German translation of the text see Weber 1999.

lation with, the oldest Chinese material.[16] In many cases, without a detailed investigation of these Chinese sources, it seems impossible to reconstruct the connection and interrelation of the different strings of the different Buddha-*vitae*. The Chinese biographical material represents a biography of the Buddha in the making much more than does the Indian material. These partial biographies are chips from a biographical workshop.

Before I discuss one particular episode from the biography of the Buddha, let me briefly introduce some of the aforementioned early Chinese biographies. I take into account here only those biographical texts that follow the career of the bodhisattva continuously over a substantial period of his life—texts which are comparable with the Sanskrit *Catuṣpariṣatsūtra*[17] (which covers the events between the enlightenment and the first conversions after it)—and thus leave aside the sūtras which concentrate on a specific event or a shorter period in the Buddha's life. These texts are:

- the *Xiuxing-benqi-jing* 修行本起經, "*Avadāna* of the practice (of the bodhisattva)" (T.184),[18] translated in the year 184 by Zhu Dali 竺大力 (active 197) and Kang Mengxiang 康孟詳 (active 194–99 and 207); this work ends with the defeat of Māra.
- the *Zhong-benqi-jing* 中本起經, "*Avadāna* of the middle (period of the life of the Buddha)" (T.196), translated by Tanguo 曇果 (possibly Dharmaphala) (active 207) and Kang Mengxiang; from

16. See Lamotte 1988: 654f. This does not, of course, solve the problem of the first appearance of a "blueprint" of a biography structure as represented in the *Mahāvadānasūtra* (Pali: *Mahāpadānasuttanta*) with its stereotypical description of the lives of the buddhas of the past. The archaeological and art-historical evidence, at least, seem to indicate a rather early date. We have, therefore, for the development of the life of the Buddha, the situation of an early skeleton structure versus incomplete episodic biographies. It is also beyond question that the writing of biographies in the Buddhist traditions went on after the shaping of complete life-circles: see Reynolds 1976.

17. For a translation of the *Catuṣpariṣatsūtra* see Kloppenburg 1973 (English), and Weber 1999 (German); for text editions Waldschmidt 1952/1957/1962.

18. This text and the following one have been translated into Dutch by Zürcher 1978. In my translation of the title of some of the following texts I omit *-jing* 經, *-sūtra*, in cases where the title already contains *-benqi* 本起, *-avadāna*.

the achievement of enlightenment until after the conversion of Mahākāśyapa.[19]

- the *Taizi-ruiying-benqi-jing* 太子瑞應本起經, "*Avadāna* of the auspicious (deeds) of the prince (Siddhārtha)" (T.185), translated between 222 and 229 by Zhi Qian 支謙 (active 220–52); this work ends with the conversion of the three Kāśyapas.
- the *Puyao-jing* 普曜經, "Sūtra of the display (of the deeds of the Buddha)" (T.186), a kind of proto-*Lalitavistara*, translated by Zhu Fahu 竺法護 / Dharmarakṣa (active 265–313).
- the *Fangguang-dazhuangyan-jing* 方廣莊嚴經, "Extended garland (of the deeds of the Buddha)" (T.187), another version of the *Lalitavistara*, translated by Dipoheluo 地婆訶羅 / Divākara (613–88, arrived in China 680); this work ends with the first sermon in the Mṛgadāva near Benares (Sarnath).
- Aśvaghoṣa's *Buddhacarita*, *Fo-suo-xing-zan* 佛所行讚, "Praise of the Deeds of the Buddha" (T.192), translated by Tanwuchen 曇無讖 / Dharmakṣema (385–433, active 414–21).
- *Zabao-zangjing* 雜寶藏經, "The basket of miscellaneous jewelry (of *avadāna*s)" (T.203), translated by Jijiaye 吉迦夜 / Kiṃkārya (active 472) and Tanyao 曇曜 (active ca. 462).
- *Fo-benxing-ji-jing* 佛本行集經, "Sūtra of the collection of authentic deeds of the Buddha," a text "translated" by Jñānagupta / Zhe'najueduo 闍那崛多 (532–600, arrived at Chang'an 560) and rendered into English by Samuel Beal. This text is rather more of a compilation than a real translation, but it has some references to concurrent versions of legends in the Vinayas of the Mahāsāṅghikas[20] and the Mahīśāsakas.[21]

The Chinese were clearly aware that there were different, incomplete, lives of the Buddha in Indian languages at a relatively late period. It is specifically from Sui, Tang, and later Song dynasty encyclopedias that the compil-

19. This text, in terms of content, shows the closest connection with the *Catuṣpariṣatsūtra*.

20. T.190.663a.21; 685b.26; 733b.29; 804a.19; 873c.16; 875c.11f.; 826b.23; 882b.19; 895b.25; 908c.3; 923a.17 (see below).

21. T.190.663b.5; 671b.5 and 7; 884c.24; 816c.19; 923a.21 (see below).

ers draw upon those biographies in the introductory portions of their works in which the life of the Buddha was narrated.[22]

There was also an awareness of life cycles of the different *śrāvaka*-denominations, the *nikāyas*. At the end of the *Fo-benxing-ji-jing* 佛本行集經 we read:

> At that time there were people like the three, the *sthavira* Puṇyavasu[23] (in the language of the Sui this means "well-dweller"), the *sthavira* Gumbhira[24] (in the language of the Sui this means "snake") and the *sthavira* Nandika[25] who only knew about how he (the Buddha) had left the householder's life, but sadly enough did not know the matter of the cause of his birth, and also did not know where he existed in former times and what he did (otherwise). So they asked: "How should we call this sūtra?" And (they) were answered: "The teachers of the Mahāsāṅghika call it 'The Great Events' (*Mahāvastu* / *Dashi* 大事), the teachers of the Sarvāstivāda call this sūtra 'The great garland' (**Mahāvyūha* (?) / *Da-zhuangyan* 大莊嚴), the teachers of the Kāśyapīya call it 'The (karmic) cause of the Buddha's birth' (**Buddhajātinidāna* / *Fosheng-yinyuan* 佛生因緣), the teachers of the Dharmaguptaka call it 'The original deeds of the Buddha Śākyamuni' (**Śākyamunibuddhāvadāna* / *Shijiamouni-fo-benxing* 釋迦牟尼佛本行), and the teachers of the Mahīśāsaka call it 'The root of the Vinayapiṭaka' (**Vinayapiṭakamūlika* / *Pini-zang-genben* 毘尼藏根本)."[26]

22. On the early compilation process of these biographical collections see Durt 2006.

23. *Fennaposu* 分那婆素 / EMC **pun-na'-ba-sə^h*; reconstructions of Early Middle Chinese (EMC) are given according to Pulleyblank 1991.

24. *Gongpiluo* 宮毘羅 / EMC **kuwŋ-bji-la*.

25. *Nantijia* 難提迦 / EMC **nan-dɛj-kɨa*.

26. T.190.932a13ff. 爾時，復有長老分那婆素(隋言：‘井宿’)，長老宮毘羅(隋言：‘蛟龍’)，長老難提迦等，如是三人，唯得知其出家由緒，不知所生因緣之事；亦不知彼於往昔時，作何業也。或問曰：“當何名此經？”答曰：“摩訶僧祇師名為《大事》，薩婆多師名此經為《大莊嚴》，迦葉維師名為《佛生因緣》，曇無德師名為《釋迦牟尼佛本行》， 尼沙塞師名為《毘尼藏根本》。 On this passage see already Beal (1875), v.f.

It is interesting that the *Mahāvastu* is mentioned in this passage although this text has never been translated into Chinese. It is, however, even more interesting that the text states that there was a *Mahāvastu*-like Buddha biography extant within the most important *nikāyas*. I would argue that the relatively old text of the extant *Mahāvastu*, with its repetition and only partial Sanskritization, represents a stage of transition toward a fully developed biography of the Buddha. I would furthermore suggest that a version of it was known to the compiler of the *Fo-benqi-ji-jing*, Jñānagupta, and thus was known in China more generally.

One particular story that provides an excellent resource for our study here is that of Yaśodharā's extended pregnancy with Rāhula over a period of six years. In contrast to most of the other better-known versions of the life as found in the *Nidānakathā* (being originally a commentary on the Pali jātaka stories),[27]

27. *Jātaka* I, 60 (ed. Fausbøll): *Tasmiṃ samaye "Rāhulamātā puttaṃ vijātā" ti sutvā Suddhodanamahārājā "puttassa me tuṭṭhiṃ nivedethā" 'ti sāsanaṃ pahiṇi. Bodhisatto taṃ sutvā "Rāhulo jāto, bandhanaṃ jātan" ti āha.* ("When then the great king Suddhodana heard [the news]: 'The mother of Rāhula has given birth to a son,' he sent out the message: 'Tell my son about this happy [event].' When the bodhisattva heard this he said: 'Rāhula has been born, a fetter has been born.'"); 62: *Bodhisatto pi kho Channaṃ pesetvā va "puttaṃ tāva passissāmîti" cintetvā nisinnapallaṃkato vuṭṭhāya Rāhulamātāya vasanaṭṭhānaṃ gantvā gabbhadvāraṃ vivari. Tasmiṃ khaṇe antogabbhe gandhatelappadīpo jhāyati. Rāhulamātā sumanamallikādīnaṃ pupphānaṃ ammaṇamattena abhippakiṇṇasayane puttassa matthake hatthaṃ ṭhapetvā niddāyati. Bodhisatto ummāre pādaṃ ṭhāpetvā ṭhitako va oloketvā "sac' āhaṃ deviyā hatthaṃ apanetvā mama puttaṃ gaṇhissāmi devī pabujjhissatîti, evaṃ me gamanantarāyo bhavissatîti, Buddho hutvā va āgantvā passissāmîti" pāsādatalato otari.* ("After the bodhisattva had sent out Channa [to get Kaṇṭhaka] he thought: 'Let us now look at [our] son.' He rose from the divan where he had sat and went to the residence of the mother of Rāhula and opened the door of the bedchamber. At that time a lamp with fragrant oil burnt inside the bedchamber. The mother of Rāhula slept on a bed covered over the width of an *ammaṇa* with jasmine, Arabic jasmine and other flowers, her hand resting on the head of the son. The bodhisattva, standing on the threshold, looked [at them and thought:] 'If I remove the hand of the queen and take my son, the queen will wake up and thus it will be a hindrance to my going away. I will come and look [at him] after I have become a Buddha.' And he descended from the roof of the palace.") See also the English translation of the two passages in Jayawickrama 1990: 81 and 83. The *Buddhavaṃsa* (36.15) just gives the names of the Buddha's wife (Bhaddakaccā) and son (Rāhula) without specification of the time of birth.

the *Buddhacarita*,[28] and others,[29] this text places the birth of the Buddha's son in a dramatic biographical parallelism during the night of the enlightenment instead of shortly before the great departure (*abhiniṣkramaṇa*).[30] This, of course, strips the biography of one of the most touching scenes, that of the

28. Obviously placed a considerable time before the great departure: *Buddhacarita* 2.46.: *kāle tataś cārupayodharāyāṃ yaśodharāyāṃ svayaśodharāyām, śauddhodane rāhusapatnavaktro jajñe suto rāhula eva nāmnā.* ("Then in the course of time the fair-bosomed Yaśodharā, bearing her own fame, bore to the son of Śuddhodana a son, Rāhula by name, with the face of Rāhu's adversary.") (text and translation of Johnston 1936: I, 18 and II, 29). Aśvaghoṣa does not allude to the bodhisattva's moving farewell to his wife and his child which follows, as his point is obviously that the sight of the women in the harem prompted the prince's final decision. The *Lalitavistara*, in the fourteenth chapter, relates the dreams of the bodhisattva's wife's—here called Gopā—and the bodhisattva's explanation, but has not even an allusion to a child or making love to each other; see Foucaux 1884: 172ff.

29. See Lamotte 1949: 1001n1. It is striking in terms of the history of the reception of the Buddha biography that this tradition is found in texts which have been used by Western scholars for reconstructing a "mainstream blueprint" for the Buddha's *vita* although quantitatively more texts preserve the alternative version discussed here. The reason for this is certainly that the Sanskrit and Pali tradition were held in higher esteem as "historical" sources and that the Chinese (and Tibetan) tradition was used as confirmative material for the Indian and discarded as minor in case it differed from it. For a discussion of a much later Sanskrit *avadāna* tradition of the six-year pregnancy, see Tatelman 1998.

30. Lamotte (1949: 1002n1) points out a parallel version which is referred to in the *Fo-benxing-ji-jing*, that according to the Kāśyapīyas Rāhula was already two years old when his father left home. Lamotte, in my opinion mistakenly, obviously combined two different text passages to draw his conclusion, while the evidence of these passages shows only that there were different versions of Rāhula's story in different nikāyas: T.190.908c.3f. 其迦葉維復有別說。 ("The Kāśyapīya now have a different version [of Rāhula's meeting with his father]."); 909c.24f. 或有異說作如是言：其羅睺羅生二年後，菩薩爾時方始出家，苦行六年。 ("There is another version which says that it was not before two years after Rāhula had been born that the bodhisattva left his household and underwent austerities for six years.") The *Kāśyapīya-Vinaya*, according to the earliest existing catalogue, Sengyou's 僧祐 (445–518) *Chu-sanzang-jiji* 出三藏集記, had not been transferred to China: T.2145.20a.16f. and 21b.5ff. In the *Lidai-sanbao-ji* 歷代三寶記 (finished 598) of Fei Zhangfang 非張房, a partial translation of this Vinaya from the Wei dynasty 魏 is mentioned T.2034.87a.3 解脫戒本一卷(興和二年出，僧昉筆受，出迦葉毘律) ("Jietuo-jieben in one fascicle: translated in the second year of [the era] Xinghe; Sengfang was the scribe; [this is] an extract from the *Kāśyapīya-Vinaya*."), to which the Sui and Tang catalogues add Qutan Banruoliuzhi 瞿曇般若流支 / Gautama Prajñāruci as translator (see, e.g., the Sui-catalogue *Zhongjing-mulu* 眾經目錄, T.2146.140a.18; the work is preserved as T.1460 with an introduction by Sengfang). As this Vinaya, or rather a part of it, is the only Kāśyapīya work documented in the Chinese canon, it is quite likely that Jñānagupta refers to this text or to the parts of it available to him.

bodhisattva's farewell to his sleeping wife and son which has been—as John Strong has noted[31]—anthologized by Western Buddhologists.[32]

Indian art historical evidence does not document this version, as far as I am aware,[33] but does have some examples of the other version.[34] The most prominent scene concerning the Buddha's son and wife here occurs when Rāhula donates the food to his father that his mother has prepared.[35] Textual sources take this as a means for Yaśodharā to prove that Rāhula is indeed the Buddha's son and not an illegitimate child, since Rāhula is able to recognize his father without having seen him before.

My chosen episode has already been to a certain extent analyzed by Lamotte,[36] and was discussed in another article by John Strong, but I think there is still space for detailed analysis in the light of the Chinese sources. Lamotte, for instance, used this narrative complex in order to explain what he calls "justification of details": "When a given source is in contradiction with a universally accepted tradition over a point of detail, the old biographers,

31. Strong 1997: 113.

32. And, due to the translations they used, by early Western propagators of the Buddha's biography such as Carus; see Carus 1915: 22, and the art nouveau illustration of the episode by Olga Kopetzky on page 23. Carus' sources here have been Beal's translation of Zhu Fahu's Chinese rendering of the *Buddhacarita* (see "Table of Reference," p. 260) and—not explicitly mentioned—the Pali texts. In Arnold's poem "Light of Asia" the episode is obviously taken from Beal's "Romantic Legend"—Arnold 1998: 87ff.—although Arnold, probably to avoid the embarrassment of his Victorian audience and because of Beal's ambiguous rendering (see below), skips the sex scene and has Yaśodharā bear the baby Rāhula already on the night of the departure (p. 87: "Alas, my Prince! I sank to sleep most happy, for the babe I bear of thee Quickened this eve..."). The two different versions of the episode were known at least since Hardy's "Manual," as he remarks in a footnote (referring to Hodgson), Hardy 1995: 156: "The Karmikas of Nepaul assert that Râhula remained six years in the womb of his mother. The pain and anxiety of mother and son were caused by the karma of their former birth."

33. Evidence in Gandhāran art is given in Kurita 1988: plates on pages 70ff., discussed 286f. Kurita points out one fragment in which, he suspects, a blur between the conception scene of the Buddha and the conception of Rāhula on the night of the great departure may have occurred.

34. One piece was found in Lumbinī, the birth place of the Buddha. On the pieces presented by Kurita there is no trace of a baby Rāhula.

35. See Schlingloff 2000: I, 402ff.; II, 79. For Gandhāran depictions of the Buddha's return to Kapilavāstu see Kurita 1988: plates on 164ff., and the discussion 298f.

36. Lamotte 1947–48: 60f.; Lamotte 1988: 662ff.

never at a loss, invented a new story to explain the contradiction."[37] As true as this may be, Lamotte's statement seems to reflect a very positivistic view of the development and growth of the life story of the Buddha. It presumes a kind of master text that included the main events, while other sources, and especially the Chinese ones, just indicated that there were different versions of certain episodes existent at the same time and that later compilers used these as a kind of lego-box to build their narratives without having to invent something new.

Yaśodharā's extended pregnancy is alluded to in the *Mahāvastu* (III 172) in the frame story (Pali *paccuppannavatthu*, "matter of arising," and the final *samodhāna*, "connection") of a jātaka of Rāhula (*Rāhulapūrvayoga*):

> The monks asked the Exalted One, "Lord, as a maturing of what karma was Prince Rāhula's stay in the womb as long as six years?" The Exalted One replied, "This long stay, too, was the maturing of an old karma."[38]

The jātaka then relates the story of the two princes Sūrya and Candra. The older of the brothers, Sūrya, decides to become a *ṛṣi*, so Candra must become the king. But upon drinking from the jar of another *ṛṣi*, Sūrya feels great remorse because he believes he has committed theft. It is only after his royal brother announces a general amnesty and hosts him in an Aśoka grove for six days that he accepts that he is purified from the assumed crime.[39] As I will argue below some of the features of this jātaka reappear as blind motives in one of the Chinese collections, and thus reflect some knowledge of a *Mahāvastu*-like text at least by the translator of this life of the Buddha.

> The Exalted One said, "It may be, monks, that you will think at that time and on that occasion King Candra was somebody else. Prince Rāhula here was then him. I was him who was then Sūrya

37. Lamotte 1988: 662.

38. Translated by Jones 1956: 167. For the original text see Senart 1897: 172: *Bhikṣū bhagavantam āhansuḥ: kasya bhagavan karmasya vipākena rāhulasya kumārasya ṣaḍvarṣāṇi garbhāvāso abhūṣi? Etasya vaiṣa bhikṣavo rāhulasya kumārasya paurāṇaṃ karmavibhākaṃ.*

39. A similar version is found in the *Mūlasarvāstivāda-Vinaya* and in the *Mahāprajñāpāramitopadeśaśāstra*, T.152 (CCC 53); on the latter see below.

> the seer. Because Sūrya the seer was confined in the Aśoka grove for six nights, as a maturing of that karma Prince Rāhula's stay in the womb was six years long."[40]

What is clear here is that the *Mahāvastu* was aware of a story of Rāhula having spent six years in his mother's womb, and that this is the only Indian text which brings forth this fact in an explicit way. The other Indian text that refers to Yaśodharā's becoming pregnant on the night of the bodhisattva's departure is the *Vinaya* of the Mūlasarvāstivādins in the *Saṅghabhedavastu* section,[41] and Bareau has seen a direct line of development from the *Mahāvastu* to the *Vinaya*.[42] The narrative complex has been studied by John Strong,[43] who shows that the complex compositional structure of the narrative reflects a strong parallelism between the bodhisattva's striving for enlightenment and the events around the pregnant Yaśodharā in Kapilavāstu. This is enough reason to again emphasize the relatively late final composition of this monastic corpus. Strong emphasizes that in the fully developed life of the Buddha

40. Jones 1956: 170; Senart 1897: 175: *Bhagavān āha: Syāt khalu bhikṣāvaḥ yuṣmākam evam asyādanyaḥ sa tena kālena tena samayena candro rājā. Eṣa tadā rāhulabhadrakumāro abhūṣi. Yaḥ sūryo ṛṣis tadā aham evābhūvaṃ. Yat sūryo ṛṣi aśokavanikāyā ṣaḍrātraṃ uparuddhaḥ tasya karmasya vipākena rāhulo kumāro ṣaṭvarṣāṇi garbhāvāsasthito abhūṣi. Rāhulabhadrasya pūrvayogaṃ.* This goes together with a relevant passage in the Chinese translation of the *Vinaya* of the Mahāsāṅghika (see below).

41. For the versions in the different translations of the *Mūlasarvāstivāda-Vinaya* see (Tibetan) Rockhill 1885: 24 and 32, (Sanskrit) Strong 2002: 10 and 17f. Rockhill's paraphrase of the last night interestingly conceals the conception: "...and now it was that he knew Yaçôdhâra [sic] his wife." The Sanskrit text is quite frank about the conception when the bodhisattva, having been reproached with being unmanly (*apumān*, Chinese: *wo bu shi zhangfu* 我不是丈夫), decides to make love to Yaśodharā (ed. Gnoli: 81): '*...yannv ahaṃ yaśodharayā sārdhaṃ paricārayeyam' iti; tena yaśodharayā sārdhaṃ paricāritam; yaśodharā āpannasattvā saṃvṛttā.* ("'...I now should amuse myself with Yaśodharā!' And he amused himself with Yaśodharā (and) Yaśodharā conceived."); see also the Chinese translation by Yijing 義淨: T.1450.115a.28f. 爾時菩薩，在於宮內嬉戲之處，私自念言："我今有三夫人及六萬婇女。若不與其為俗樂者，恐諸外人云：我不是丈夫。我今當與耶輸陀羅共為娛樂。"其耶輸陀羅因即有娠。("At that time the bodhisattva, as he amused himself in the palace, got to think: 'I now have three wives and sixty thousand concubines. If I do not give them worldy pleasure I am afraid that ordinary people will say that I am not a real man. I should now amuse myself with Yaśodharā.' Therefore Yaśodharā became pregnant.") A paraphrase of the Chinese version of the Buddha's return (T.1450.158c.16ff.) is given by Lamotte 1949: 1003f., note 1.

42. Bareau 1982.

43. Strong 1997.

there is not only an extension into the past (by means of the various jātakas), but also an interpersonal dimension which interlinks—in the case of the episode discussed—Yaśodharā and Rāhula with the career of the bodhisattva/Buddha; it represents what Schober has called: "...longitudinal and lateral extensions that transcend individual life spans."[44]

The *Mūlasarvāstivāda-Vinaya* clearly shows a patchwork structure in promoting two karmic explanatory narratives for Rāhula's long stay in the womb and one "naturalistic" one. Because Yaśodharā undergoes severe austerities, like the bodhisattva on his path toward enlightenment, the growth of the embryo in her womb is retarded.[45] One of the karmic stories relates why Yaśodharā had to bear the child for six years: in a former existence she had, instead of doing it herself, let her mother carry a vessel of milk over a distance of six miles (*krośa*).[46] Another story provides different reasons for the lengthy pregnancy: two brothers, the ascetics Śaṅkha and Likhita, live in a forest hermitage. The younger, Likhita, once drinks from the water-pot of his brother, and feeling guilty for having taken what was not offered, goes to Benares to ask King Brahmadatta to punish him. Brahmadatta tells him that he has committed no crime and asks him to wait for him because he has other business. The king, who was Rāhula in one of his former existences, completely forgot about his visitor and had him wait for six days. This is the reason for his six-year stay in the womb.[47] So here two biographies and karmic "destinies" meet in one event, which is, as it were, an inversion of the normal jātaka or avadāna formula where the karmic "destinies" of the same persons overlap in the narrated past and in the auctorial present.[48]

Although the early Chinese biographies do not usually relate the return of the Buddha to Kapilavāstu after enlightenment because they terminate

44. Schober 1997: 111.

45. See Strong 1997: 117f.; Panglung 1981: 96–99. For an attempt of Māra to inflict damage on Yaśodharā's and the unborn Rāhula's life and health see Strong 1997: 118 and Strong 2002: 17f.

46. Strong 1997: 116.

47. In the later Indian sources but in the Chinese context these two karmic narratives are only found in the *Fo-benxingji-jing*—see Beal 1875: 360ff.—and in the *Mahāprajñāpāramitopadeśa*.

48. See the normal final formula in the jātakas where the Buddha explains that the respective protagonists in the jātaka are now the Buddha himself, Ānanda, Śāriputra, etc.

before these events, they include, of course, the episode of the great departure, and here we can usually decide if a text has the "standard" version, with Rāhula's birth before the departure, or not. In the light of the *Mahāvastu* reference, let us now turn to the Chinese versions of this episode. It is found, as far as I am aware, in five versions that clearly reflect a historical sequence.

The nominally earliest version is the *Taizi-ruiying-benqi-jing* 太子瑞應本起經 (T.185), translated by, or rather attributed to, Zhi Qian 支謙. Even if this attribution (and thereby the dating) deduced from the Chinese sūtra catalogs may not be correct, the text seems to have been produced in an early period, probably in the fourth or early fifth century. The very short text reads as follows:

> When the prince had reached the age of seventeen, the king, in order to find a royal consort for him, inspected the kingdom and innumerable thousands of women well known (for their beauty and status). The last one was called Gopī, beautiful and delicately pure, the best of the world, surpassing all people in terms of virtue and talent, well mannered and well equipped. Because of her (karmic) destiny she was a girl who sold flowers. Although she was married (to him), (the bodhisattva) for a long time did not accept her (as a consort). But (with) the passion of a wife she wanted to be close (to him). The prince said: "Get beautiful flowers and put them between us. Let us look at them together. Are they not beautiful?" Gopī arranged the flowers and again wanted to be close (to him). The prince said: "But these flowers have liquid and pollute our bed." Some time later he said again: "Get some nice white weed and put it between us. (If we) two watch them—are they not nice?" The wife arranged them and again wanted to be close (to him). The prince said: "But you are not clean; you will pollute this weed." (His) wife did not dare to come close (to him). The female servants all had the suspicion that he was impotent. The prince pointed with his hand to the belly of the consort and said: "In six years time she will give birth to a boy." As a consequence

she became pregnant, and the prince started his journey and left through the eastern gate.[49]

A similar narrative complex is found in the *Mahāprajñāpāramitopadeśa*, the *Da-zhidu-lun* 大智度論, attributed to Nāgārjuna, and "translated" into Chinese by Kumārajīva. It most likely belongs to the same period as the former text because it is almost certainly a contribution by Kumārajīva, narratively commenting on the doctrinal issue that touching (*sprașțavya*) pleasant things is to be rejected by telling the story of Yaśodharā.[50] Kumārajīva refers to a text *Luohouluo-mu-bensheng-jing* 羅睺羅母本生經, "Avadāna of Rāhula's mother,"[51] which is unfortunately not extant in the available editions of the canon. There the Buddha is said to have had two wives, Gopiyā and Yaśodharā. When Yaśodharā becomes pregnant on the night of the great departure, she carries the child for six years. The Śākyas blame her for having been unfaithful, but Gopiyā protects her, claiming that she had been together with Yaśodharā all the time. Yaśodharā then gives birth to Rāhula on the night of the Buddha's enlightenment. The text also provides a jātaka similar to the one found in the *Mahāvastu* and in the *Mūlasarvāstivāda-Vinaya* in order to explain why Rāhula had to stay in his mother's womb for six years. Thus, the *Mahāprajñāpāramitopadeśa* represents the earliest stage of the full-fledged legend-complex as it is found in the *Mūlasarvāstivāda-Vinaya* with the story of Yaśodharā and Rāhula itself and the two explanatory jātakas.

References to the six-year pregnancy of Yaśodharā are also found in the *Mahāsāṅghika-Vinaya / Mohesengzhi-lü* 摩訶僧祇律 (T.1425), translated by Fotuobatuoluo 佛陀跋陀羅 (359–429, arr. Chang'an between 406 and 408) and Faxian 法顯 (approx. 370–430):

49. T.185, j.1, 475a.10ff. 太子至年十七，王為納妃，簡閱國中名女數千，無可意者。最後一女，名曰：'瞿夷'，端正，好潔，天下第一，賢才過人，禮義備舉。是則宿命賣華女也。女子雖納，久而不接。婦人之情欲，有附近之意，太子曰："常得好華，置我中間，共視之。寧好乎？"瞿夷即具好華，又欲近之。太子曰："却此華有汁，污瘀床席。"久後復曰："得好白褻，置我中間。兩人觀之，不亦好乎？"婦即具褻，又有近意。太子曰："却汝有污垢，必污此褻。"婦不敢近。傍側侍女咸有疑意，謂不能男。太子以手指妃腹曰："却後六年，爾當生男。"遂以有身。於是太子復啟遊觀，出北城門。

50. For a full translation of the relevant passage see below.

51. Lamotte 1949: 1002, reconstructs *Rāhulamātṛjātaka.

> And then, when the Buddha was (still) a bodhisattva, cherished in his father's home, and (the father) was concerned whether (the son) would become a cakravartin king or not, (the bodhisattva) grieved and cried because he did not receive permission to leave his house. And because (Yaśodharā) was pregnant with Rāhula he refrained still more from leaving his house....All the bhikṣus said to the Buddha: "O World-honored One! For what reason did Rāhula stay for six years in the womb (of his mother)?" The Buddha told the bhikṣus: "In the past there was a seer called Libodu[52] who went to a king who had asked to see him. The king (wanted) to recompense him (and said): 'Wait here in this Aśoka grove. I will soon come to meet you.' After this request he went away and did not return for six days. The king at that time was Rāhula. Therefore he stayed in (his mother's) womb for a period of six years." As it is told in the jātakas, the Buddha related it to the bhikṣus.[53]

Here we have quite a strange combination of material. It is stated that Yaśodharā's pregnancy prevented the bodhisattva from becoming a *śramaṇa*, but it is then also suggested that Rāhula stayed in the womb for six years. These two pieces of information do not complement each other well, as in another passage inserted between them it is emphasized that the bodhisattva practiced austerities for six years before he reached enlightenment.[54] It should however be noted that the quoted Vinaya does not specify the night

52. This transliteration does not correspond to the other versions where the name is clearly Likhita, Chin. Liqiduo 利棄多 / EMC **li*^{h}-*k*^{h}*ji*^{h}-*ta* (*Mūlasarvāstivāda-Vinaya*, T.1448. j.16, 77c.); Lamotte 1949: 1006n1, strangely gives the form *Li po* without any further suggestion, but I think that the underlying name—correct or blurred—is Revata: see Fan-fanyu 翻梵語, T.2130.1022b.1. 梨波都(應云：'離波多'譯者曰：'星名'也。) ("*Libodu* (*EMC *li-pa-tə*), should be: *Liboduo* (*EMC *liə-pa-ta*); the name of a star").

53. T.1425, j.17, 365b.12ff. 復次佛為菩薩時，在家父王愛惜，恐轉輪王種滅，愁憂泣涙，不聽出家。以懷妊羅睺羅故，便捨出家。 ... (365.11ff.) 諸比丘白佛言："世尊！有何因緣羅睺羅六年在胎。"佛告諸比丘："往昔有仙人，名梨波都，詣王求相見。王報仙人：'汝且住無憂園中。須臾當與相見。'作是教已，乃至六日，不與相見。爾時王者，羅睺羅是。以是因緣故，六年在胎。如生經中廣說，佛告諸比丘。

54. T.1425.365b.16ff. 諸比丘白佛言："世尊！何故乃六年苦行如是。"佛言："非但今日，如鳥本生經中廣說。" ("All the bhikṣus said to the Buddha: 'World-honored One! Why now have you practiced austerities for six years?' The Buddha answered: 'This is not only now [but also in former times] as explained in the *Śakuna-Jātaka*.'")

of the great departure as the night of Rāhula's conception, as do other texts such as the *Mūlasarvāstivāda-Vinaya* and, on the Chinese side, the *Fo-benxing-ji-jing* 佛本行集經.

The *Mahāvastu*, as has been shown above, knows about the conception on the night of the great departure but seems reluctant to state the fact of the matter—the bodhisattva had sex with his wife on the night of his departure. The conclusion, however, is clear:

> Rāhula, passing away from Tuṣita, entered his mother's womb at the hour of midnight.[55]

This accords with the *Fo-benxing-ji-jing* 佛本行集經, the full-fledged life of the Buddha from the late sixth century. Here we find two allusions to Rāhula's conception on the night of the departure, the first one of which states:

> On this very night the consort of the prince, Yaśodharā, realized that she was pregnant.[56]

It is interesting to see how this text is presented by Samuel Beal in his *Romantic Legend of Śākya Buddha*. Beal renders the passage—and it may be worthwhile again to mention that his work is rather more of a paraphrase than a true translation—as follows: "On this night the Queen Yaśodharā found herself about to be delivered," and in an extensive note he comments:

> This is an ambiguous sentence. According to the subsequent narrative Yasôdharâ was not delivered till six years after. Doubtless the passage in the text is an attempt to reconcile the accounts found in the different schools. We may observe, however, that the agreement of the passage cited from the...[Lalitavistara], with the

55. Jones 1952: II, 154; *Rāhulo tuṣitabhavanāc cyavitvā mātuḥ kukṣim okrame ardharātre samaye*. The text goes on to describe the bodhisattva waking up and seeing the damsels of his harem, a sight which finally prompts him to leave the house.

56. T.190.727a.24f. 其太子妃耶輸陀羅，即於是夜便覺有娠。

> events narrated in the subsequent pages, proves that the work we are now translating is known in Thibet.[57]

Beal here obviously wants to dispel us of the fact that the Buddha had sex with Yaśodharā and to harmonize the text with the mainstream narrative. He should have known better because a little bit later, after the dreadful dreams of Siddhārtha and Yaśodharā, which the bodhisattva discards as meaningless, he, in order to console her, expressly makes love to her:

> After hearing the words of the prince, Yaśodharā, who had just experienced pain which her pleasant body had not experienced before, went back to her bed and fell asleep. The prince wanted to soothe and console Yaśodharā, and with the pleasures of the five (senses) they entertained each other and then slept together.[58]

Whatever the practical implications of this description may be, Beal renders this slightly differently: "Then Yasôdharâ, having heard the words of the prince, returned to her couch and slept, whilst the prince reposed by her side." and—quite correctly!—remarks: "The original is more explicit."[59]

The *Fo-benxing-ji-jing* has used various sources, but a strong influence has obviously come from the Mahāsāṅghika-Lokottaravādin narrative tradition. Of course this needs further detailed study, but it can be seen in the many parallels of the episode discussed with the *Mahāvastu*, a text belonging to the Vinaya of this *nikāya*, and with the *Mahāsāṅghika-Vinaya* itself. It may also be detected in minor details: for instance, the jātaka which is offered in the *Mahāvastu* as a reason for Rāhula's extended stay in his mother's womb speaks of an Aśoka grove in which the *ṛṣi* was forgotten by the king; in the *Fo-benxing-ji-jing*—and only there—it is in an Aśoka grove that the Śākyas discuss how to punish Yaśodharā for her embarrassing pregnancy. It looks as if both versions wish to reflect a karmic connection between the cause of

57. Beal 1875: 126n1.

58. T.190.728a.24ff. 耶輸陀羅，以受樂身未曾經苦，既聞太子如是語已，還臥而眠。太子為欲安恤慰喻耶輸陀故，以五欲樂共相娛樂，更同睡眠。

59. Beal 1875: 128n1.

the extended pregnancy and its consequences in the biographical present by placing the respective events in a similar place.

We find in the Buddhist narrative tradition two concurrent versions of Rāhula's conception and birth. What gives the version of Rāhula's conception on the night of the great departure and the extended pregnancy at least the same right of consideration as that in which Rāhula is born earlier and still seen by his father before he left the palace is the dramatic tension created not only for the great departure but also for future events when the Buddha revisits his home town. There was certainly embarrassment over the miraculously extended pregnancy and the sexual intercourse on the night of the great decision, and the romantic notion of the bodhisattva taking farewell from his family in the alternative version prompted Western scholars to opt for the latter.[60]

Now what can we say in the light of these different versions of a deviant episode reflected mainly in the Chinese biographical literature? The narrative of the life of the Buddha has been elaborated and extended over the first centuries of the Common Era, and it is especially through the Chinese sources that we can understand the differences and developments reflected in our scarce and chronologically uncertain Indic biographical material—not least because the Chinese texts are usually datable.

I thus agree with Étienne Lamotte's statement that "[t]he life of Śākyamuni is a skein of interwoven legends, and cunning indeed is he who could unravel it."[61] But for doing so, we must follow the example of the great Belgian master and take into account the Chinese sources.

60. One Chinese version, the *Shijia-rulai-yinghua-lu* 釋迦如來應化錄 by Baocheng 寶成 from the Ming dynasty 明 (1368–1644), keeps the reproach of Yaśodharā's extramarital intercourse in the narrative of the Buddha's return to Kapilavāstu but does not refer to the conception in the events of the great departure; see Wieger 1951: 107.

61. Lamotte 1958: 665.

Appendices

The full story of Yaśodharā's six-year pregnancy in the *Fo-benxing-ji-jing* is related after a jātaka of a deer king and his faithful hind, and is given here in translation:

> The Buddha said to Upāli: "Now, you should know: this deer king—how could he be another man?—is no other than me. The hind is no other than Yaśodharā. At that time Yaśodharā followed me and underwent great pain. She is all the more able to follow me today and to undergo even greater austerities, because (there are) people in all periods who cannot undergo and (some who) are able to undergo (such austerities). This Rāhula now stays in (Yaśodharā's) womb for six years, forced (by the power) of the stains of (her) past karma. (Because) Yaśodharā harbored a bitter grief for the bodhisattva, she did not adorn herself. Thus King Śuddhodana, when the Tathāgata had attained the *anuttarasamyaksaṃbodhi* after six years, sent envoys with a message. Because these envoys saw that the venerable Buddha had (already) risen from his seat, they went (back) to King Śuddhodana. After they came to the king they told him: 'The king should know that the prince, after having undergone strict austerity, is now called a full-enlightened (*manxinyi*) and has risen from his seat.' When King Śuddhodana heard these words he ordered two different men (to come) and told them: 'You will now go to the prince, and when you have arrived there you should tell the prince what I tell you: "You have now undergone severe austerity, and you should now come back quickly to take care of affairs of state and become a cakravartin, endowed with the seven precious items."' When the two men told (him) the king's message as the king had ordered them, they bowed their head and kept it in mind as custom prescribes; they went to the holy prince in order to bring him this message. They greeted (the Buddha's) feet with their forehead, stood to the side, and told the holy prince: 'Lo, holy prince! King Śuddhodana ordered us two to approach the holy prince and to tell him: "You have now undergone severe

austerity and now you should come back quickly to take over my position and become a cakravartin, endowed with the seven precious items."' At that time the World-honored One, after he had heard what the two men had said, spoke the following verses:

> When men are fully tamed, the world is under control.
> The realms of the buddhas are unlimited, without traces and without coming and going.
> If men do enter the net (i.e., the right teaching) from the absence of passion there is no birth.
> The realms of the buddhas are unlimited, without traces and without coming and going.

"When Yaśodharā in her palace heard that the prince had undergone severe austerity she still hoped that he would soon return and take over the throne, rule the country and the people, and become a cakravartin king. (Therefore) she thought: 'If the prince becomes a holy cakravartin king I will be his first royal consort.' After having thought this, her whole body trembled with joy and she could not control herself. She perfumed herself with all kinds of fragrant substances and adorned herself with different invaluable bejeweled cloths and necklaces, she ate delicate food, slept in her bedroom, (took) soft and fine bedding. After having done so she happily awaited the prince. At that time Rāhula, over a period of six years, had consumed his former karmic substance. Yaśodharā had provided for herself all kind of provisions such as food and drink, and therefore Rāhula finally was born. After he had been born the other consorts consulted King Śuddhodana and said: 'This is indeed very strange, O great king, that Yaśodharā has now given birth to a son!' When King Śuddhodana heard this he became angry and said: 'My son has now abandoned his home, has left the household, and now after six years Yaśodharā gives birth to this son. How can this be?' Then the Śākya scion Devadatta said: 'This is my son.' Thereupon King Śuddhodana became even angrier, summoned all the Śākyas for a meeting, and told them: 'You should know that Yaśodharā has not been faithful to the prince, and (therefore) has also not been truthful to me and has not been truthful to the Śākyas. She does not value (our) good name. She indulges freely and insults our clan. What should we do now to punish her?' Thereupon the Śākyas, in full accord, said the following: 'Yaśodharā insulted her family. We must punish her according to the regulations concerning the insulting of one's own family.' There was a high official in this assembly who said: 'She should be shaven and beaten with a stick, and after having been beaten she should receive a stigma.' Another official said: 'One should cut off her ears and her nose.' Another official said: 'One should poke her eyes.' Another official said: 'One should impale her on a tree.' Another official said: 'One should throw her into an empty pit.' Another official said: 'One should encompass her with a heated and blazing pillar.' Another official said: 'One should tie her hands and feet and let a huge crowd of cattle trample over her in order to kill her.' Another official said: 'One should have her lie down on the ground and send white elephants over her.' Another official said: 'One should saw her apart from head to foot.' Another official said: 'Step by step one should dismember her into eight pieces.' Thereupon King Śuddhodana said to these officials: 'I now order Yaśodharā and the son born to her to be put to death.' At that time the Buddha, who had attained the *anuttarasamyaksaṃbodhi*, saw the calamity of Yaśodharā and the son born to her, and because they were suffering, he compassionately looked all around. At that time the god Vaiśravaṇa was not far away from the Buddha, and this heavenly king knew what the Buddha thought. Taking a brush and a *tāla* leaf he went to the Buddha. The World-honored One with his own hand wrote to the king: 'The child born recently is my own son. May you not be in doubt about this.' Thereupon the god Vaiśravaṇa took the letter and went from the Buddha to the middle of the assembly around King Śuddhodana, and gave this letter (to the king, but) the king was still suspicious (about the authenticity of the letter). But, at that time, there was a proven and (authenticated) seal on this letter. King Śuddhodana, after seeing this seal, pondered: 'This is really a letter written by the hand of my son, the prince Siddhārtha.'

Because of (this letter) King Śuddhodana and the assembly were full of joy about Yaśodharā. Yaśodharā, when she had heard that the great king of the human realm had ordered herself and her son to be killed, she went quickly, in order to protect herself and her son, to Mahāprajāpatī Gautamī and said: 'Well, O venerable royal consort, I have not committed any offense. This child born (to me) is the offspring of the prince. I have heard that the prince will soon come here, and once he is here he will know this. Now they want to kill us and this is (both) without any justice and just absurd.' When Mahāprajāpatī heard what Yaśodharā said her heart was full of joy, and she sent a messenger to King Śuddhodana in the Aśoka forest. When the messenger arrived in the forest he said to the king: 'The king should know that Yaśodharā, the girl of the Śākya clan, has come to me and has said: "I have not committed any offense. This child born (to me) is the offspring of the prince. As soon as the prince comes here in person, he will understand that (all this) is an empty (accusation)." May the great king therefore not do (what he ordered) but wait until the prince has arrived—he will recognize the truth and tell how it (really) is.'

"This Rāhula was not born until six years after the Tathāgata had left his home. On the day when the Tathāgata returned to his father's house, this Rāhula was already six years old.[62] Now the Tathāgata arrived in Kapilavāstu and the mother of Rāhula thought: 'Previously I have been slandered by my relatives because of this Rāhula. Now today I have to purify myself from this accusation and clear my own karmic (account). I have to invite the Buddha and the sangha for a meal and also invite all our relatives so that they clearly understand (the situation).' With these thoughts, that evening Yaśodharā prepared all kinds of delicate

62. This shows that at least this passage is not based on an Indian original as it is not Indian custom—in contrast to the Chinese—to count the time in the mother's womb as belonging to the age of a person. On the other hand—as becomes clear through what follows—Rāhula definitely was considered to have the real age of six when he recognized his father. It seems that here we can discern the compositional fissure where the story of Yaśodharā's pregnancy of six years and the mainstream story of the Buddha's visit were put together. An indication for this is also the change between the name Yaśodharā and the epithet "mother of Rāhula."

food and drinks. And after she had prepared them, she sent a messenger during the night who said: 'The meal is prepared. May the World-honored One indicate the proper time.' She also told all her relatives that they should all come as invited.

"At that time, in the morning when the sun stood in the east, the Buddha, the World-honored One, put on his (upper) garment, took his alms bowl, and surrounded by a crowd of monks and leading a great assembly of 1,250 monks, went to the royal palace and sat down on the arranged seats.

"Thereupon the mother of Rāhula made a big 'happy-ball.'[63] She called Rāhula, put the happy-ball into his hands and said to him: 'You, Rāhula, go—in this assembly of monks is your father. Give the happy-ball to him.' And the mother of Rāhula also said to all her relatives: 'Today this Rāhula will look for his father.' Then Rāhula took the happy-ball, and after he had examined the assembly of monks, he went directly to the Buddha and said to him: 'The coolness of this *śramaṇa* is pleasant indeed! The coolness of this *śramaṇa* is pleasant indeed!'

"Thereupon King Śuddhodana addressed the Buddha: 'O World-honored One! What now: did this Yaśodharā commit all these offences?' The World-Honored one told King Śuddhodana the following: 'The great king should now not doubt (that) Yaśodharā has not committed an offense (and) that Rāhula is really my son, but for reason of former karmic ties he stayed in (his mother's) womb for six years.' When King Śuddhodana and all the family members heard these words of the Buddha, they were full of joy and they could not prevent their whole bodies trembling (with joy). Each of them took all kinds of sacrificial food[64] and donated it to the Buddha and to the sangha so that they were completely satisfied. After having eaten, the Buddha and the sangha washed their alms bowls. (The Śākyas) gave them small cushions

63. In the *Saṅghabhedavastu* of the Mūlasarvāstivādin (Skt.) this is called *vaśīkaraṇamodaka*, "empowering ball of sweetmeat." It is taken to be an aphrodisiac—Strong 1997: 120, calls it "aphrodisiac sweetmeat"—which the Chinese obviously did not want to admit as such.

64. This term again shows a tendency towards a "Sinification" of the text.

and sat down to the Buddha's left and right side. At that time King Śuddhodana, out of respect for the Buddha, could not ask in detail about the earlier karmic bonds, (and so) he talked to the crowd of monks: 'Would you, O teachers, please ask the World-honored One (to explain) about the former karmic bonds of the actions of Rāhula here and of Yaśodharā?' Thereupon these monks said to the Buddha: 'By which kind of retribution of former action did Rāhula here stay in his mother's womb for six years? And by which kind of retribution of former action has Yaśodharā been pregnant for a period of six years?' Then King Śuddhodana said to the Buddha: 'O World-honored One! How is it now: is what happened to Yaśodharā a sin?' Thereupon the World-honored One said the following to King Śuddhodana: 'May the great king now have no doubt! Yaśodharā has not committed a sin: this Rāhula is really my son. But because of the force of these former karmic binds he stayed in the womb for six years.'"[65]

65. T.190, j.51, 888a.21ff. 佛告優陀夷："汝今當知，彼鹿王者 - 豈異人乎？ - 即我身是。時牝鹿者，耶輸陀羅即其是也。耶輸陀羅於彼之時，尚隨順我，受大苦厄。況於今日能隨順我，行大苦行。於諸世人莫能行事而能行也。其羅睺羅今以過業所逼惱故在胎六年。耶輸陀羅為是菩薩懷愁毒故，不自嚴飾。然其如來過六年後證阿耨多羅三藐三菩提，於時輸頭檀王所遣使人候消息者。彼等使人見佛世尊從坐起故，即詣輸頭檀王之所。到王所已而白王言："大王當知，太子今者苦行已徹，稱滿心意，已從坐起。"爾時輸頭檀王聞此語已，別勅二人而告之曰："汝等今當詣太子所。至彼處已，當宣我言告彼太子：'汝於今者苦行已徹，當可速來統領國事，為轉輪王，具足七寶。'"時彼二人奉王勅已，依王教命，如法頂受，承是勅意，詣太子所，頭面禮足，却住一面，白太子言："善哉聖子！輸頭檀王勅我二人到聖子所，告聖子言：'汝於今者苦行已徹，今可速來，承受我位，為轉輪王，七寶之具令悉備足。'"爾時世尊聞彼二人作是語已，而說偈言：

"若人已調伏，　　世無不伏者。
諸佛境無邊，　　無跡，無來去。
若人不入網，　　愛無所從生。
諸佛境無邊，　　無跡，無來去。"

爾時耶輸陀羅於其宮內聞是太子苦行已徹，猶望不久必應還來，當受王位，政國治民，作轉輪王，便生是念："太子若作轉輪聖王，我即當作第一妃后。"如是念已，歡喜踊躍，遍滿其體，不能自勝。持種種香塗其身體，即著種種無價寶衣，及諸瓔珞而自莊飾；食諸妙饌，眠寢寶床，柔軟臥具。作如是事，豫待太子。時羅睺羅過六年已，盡其往業。耶輸陀羅即以種種資物食飲而自供養。以是因緣，其羅睺羅便即出生。既出生已，時諸內人尋共諮白輸頭檀王作如是言："異哉，大王！耶輸陀羅今乃生子。"輸頭檀王聞此事已，心大瞋怒，即作是言："今我太子捨家出家已經六歲。耶輸陀羅今生此子。何從而得？"是時釋子提婆達多作如是言："此是我子。"輸頭檀王倍增瞋恚，召諸釋種悉令聚集，即告之曰："卿等當知，耶輸陀羅不護太子，亦不護我，不護諸釋。不惜名聞。縱恣其意，辱我宗族。我等今者應作何事而苦治也？"爾時釋種皆共同聲作如是言："耶輸陀羅污辱家

T.203, j.10, 496b26ff, *Zabaozang-jing* 雜寶藏經, translated by Jijiaye 吉迦夜 / Kiṃkārya (around 472) and Tanyao 曇曜 (second half of the fifth century):[66]

117: *Rāhulāvadāna.* Once I heard that Rāhula entered his mother's womb only on the evening that the Buddha left his home. The

---

者。我等應當如辱家法而苦治之。"時彼眾內有一大臣作如是言："當髡其髮，以杖打之。打已印記。"復有一臣作如是言："當截其耳，劓去其鼻。"復有一臣而作是言："當挑兩目。"復有一臣作如是言："槍貫木上。"復有一臣作如是言："擲著空井。"復有一臣作如是言："擲著火內。"復有一臣作如是言："令抱熾然大熱鐵柱。"復有一臣作如是言："繫縛手足遣大群牛蹈而殺之。"復有一臣作如是言："令臥地上白象蹈之。"復有一臣作如是言："從頭至足以鋸解之。"復有一臣作如是言："節節支解分為八段。"爾時輸頭檀王告諸臣言："我今勅令耶輸陀羅及所生子俱當就死。"是時如來已成阿耨多羅三藐三菩提，便自觀見耶輸陀羅及所生子在厄難處，以慈悲心，所逼惱故，處處顧視。於時而有毘沙門天去佛不遠。時彼天王知如來意，即持筆墨及陀羅葉往詣佛所。爾時世尊手自作書而白王言："其所生兒是我之息。願莫有疑。"爾時毘沙門天王從世尊所受是書已，尋即往至輸頭檀王大眾之內，即出其書王懷裏。爾時彼書有證有驗。輸頭檀王見是驗已，思尋："此書真是我息悉達太子手自書處。"爾時輸頭檀王及諸大眾為此因緣於耶輸陀羅生歡喜心。耶輸陀羅傳聞人道大王有勅欲殺其身及所生子，護身命故，速疾往至摩訶波闍波提憍曇彌所，作如是言："善哉，尊后！我無是過。此所生子太子體胤。聽聞不久太子來到。若其到已，自應當知。今欲殺我，是虛枉耳。"爾時摩訶波闍波提聞耶輸陀羅作是語已，心復歡喜，即遣使請輸頭檀王至阿輸迦樹林之內。到林處已，而白王言："唯願大王當知，今者耶輸陀羅釋種之女至於我邊而作是言：'我無此過。我所生子太子體胤。若彼太子身來到已，自知虛實。'是故大王莫作是事，應須待彼太子來到，即知此事定實云何。"

其羅睺羅，如來出家六年已後，始出母胎。如來還其父家之日，其羅睺羅年始六歲。爾時如來至迦毘羅婆蘇都城，羅睺羅母作如是念："我昔因此羅睺羅故，為諸眷屬之所誹謗；今日時至，我於彼事，應自清淨以明其身。以是因緣必須請佛及比丘僧布施飲食，及請一切諸眷屬等以自明白。"耶輸陀羅作是念已，於其彼夜。辦具種種微妙飲食。既備辦已，過於彼夜，即遣使人往白佛言："所設飲食辦具已訖。世尊知時。"兼告一切諸眷屬等悉令聚集來赴所請。爾時世尊，於晨朝時，日在東方，著衣持鉢，與諸比丘左右圍遶；佛為導首與大比丘一千二百五十人俱詣向王宮，如所鋪座次第而坐。爾時羅睺羅母別作一枚大歡喜丸，喚羅睺羅，內著手裏，作如是言："汝羅睺羅，往至比丘僧眾之內，是汝父者施歡喜丸。"羅睺羅母復告一切諸眷屬言："是羅睺羅今當覓父。"時羅睺羅持歡喜丸，遍觀一切諸比丘已，直往佛邊而白佛言："如是沙門蔭涼快哉！如是沙門蔭涼快哉！"爾時輸頭檀王白佛言："世尊！此事云何？耶輸陀羅頗有如此過患已不？"爾時世尊告輸頭檀王作如是言："大王今日莫作是疑耶輸陀羅無此過患。其羅睺羅真我之子。但是往昔業緣所逼，在胎六年。"爾時輸頭檀王及諸眷屬聞佛此語，皆悉歡喜，踊躍遍身，不能自勝。各各以手持諸種種飲食餚饍，供佛及僧，令得充足。自恣飽已，佛及大眾洗鉢澡手。各將小座，遶佛左右，坐一面。爾時輸頭檀王以敬佛故，不能廣問如上因緣，而白眾中諸比丘言："願諸師等！請問世尊其羅睺羅及耶輸陀羅往昔造業因緣之事。"爾時諸比丘即白佛言："是羅睺羅往昔造作何業因緣，以何業報處胎六歲？耶輸陀羅復作何業懷孕六年？"爾時輸頭檀王白佛言："世尊！此事云何？耶輸陀羅頗有如此過患已不？"爾時世尊告輸頭檀王作如是言："大王今日莫作是疑耶輸陀羅無此過患。其羅睺羅真我之子。但是往昔業緣所逼，在胎六年。"

66. Paraphrase in Chavannes 1962: 136f.

bodhisattva Siddhārtha underwent austerities under the bodhi tree for a period of six years, subdued the four *māras*, eradicated all hindrances (*nīvaraṇa*), developed great insight and achieved the highest enlightenment, became endowed with the ten (supernatural) powers and the four fearlessnesses, realized the eighteen unmixed dharmas and the four eloquences, and resting in all *pāramitā*s he reached the other shore to expound the dharma of all the buddhas, surpassing all śrāvakas and pratyekabuddhas. It was only on the evening when (the Buddha) attained enlightenment that Rāhula was born, and thereby all the palace women were annoyed and said: "How strange that this evil Yaśodharā did not think about her offense, is reckless about what she has done, does not act more carefully for herself, and causes pollution for all of us here in the palace. The bodhisattva Siddhārtha has long left his house and yet she finally gives birth to a son. This is a great humiliation (for us)." Then there was a Śākya maiden called Vidyutī (Dianguang) who was Yaśodharā's maternal aunt's daughter; she beat her chest and clapped at her hips, stared at her angrily, and scolded her: "Yaśodharā, why do you injure the kinfolk you (should) respect? Six years have passed since the prince Siddhārtha left his home to search for enlightenment. You give birth to this child at an inappropriate time. From whom did you receive it? Are you not ashamed to insult our clan? Considering it as (your own) clan, do you not protect it from (acquiring) a bad reputation? The bodhisattva Siddhārtha has great merits and his fame is widespread. Why don't you now show him mercy, rather than disgracing him?" King Śuddhodana, who at this time was dwelling in his lofty pavilion, saw the earth trembling in six different ways and was puzzled by these ominous signs. King Śuddhodana,[67] having seen these signs, considered them to mean that the prince was dead, and the arrow of sorrow penetrated his heart and caused him great pain; and he said: "The incense of the precepts (kept by) my son fills the four distant (regions); he is adorned with

67. Here, instead of the former name form Jingfan 淨飯 ("Pure Rice"), the text suddenly has the alternative name form Baijing 白淨 ("White Rice").

(portentous) marks such as lotus-like hair. He is now dried out by the sun of death; the deep and firm root of the precepts is lacking branches and leaves. The fragrance of fame is of great compassion and (provides) broad shadow—my son (who) was like a tree has now been trampled by the elephant of death, my son, the king of the golden mountains. Big as a golden mountain he was, adorned by all kinds of gems. His body was embellished by the marks (of a great being). He is now smashed to pieces by the diamond-bolt of impermanence. He was like a vast ocean, full of jewels; like an ocean teeming with *makara* fishes—my son, the great ocean, is like this: he is now swallowed by the *makara* fish of death. Or like the full moon around which the stars revolve, my son has such great merit, is adorned with (portentous) marks; now he is swallowed by Rāhula[68] of impermanence. Our clan stems from great men, (and) the great men of (Kapi)lavāstu[69] are of true purity; such kings have succeeded each other until the present. Will the (succession line) of my clan not be interrupted in the future? I explicitly hoped that my son would become a sacred cakravartin king, or would achieve the enlightenment of a Buddha. How now can it possibly be that he has died? If now I have lost my son, I will wither away from grief and my life will be diminished. I had hoped, seeing him leave home, taking the monastic robes and the almsbowl, to behold him expound immortality and this sort of thing, (but now) I will certainly not see these." In remembering his son, he grieved deeply. When he now heard the great lamenting in the prince's palace he became even more afraid that the prince might be dead. He asked a female servant to come forward and said to her: "Why all this lamenting? Is it not because my son is dead?" The girl told the king: "The prince is not dead. Yaśodharā has given birth to a child today and everybody in the palace is embarrassed. That is why they lament." When the king heard this

68. I.e., Rāhu; this clearly alludes to the dreams of Yaśodharā on the night of Rāhula's conception of Rāhu swallowing the moon, which was the reason for the son-to-be-born's name, Rāhula.

69. Luwei 盧越 is the abridged form of Chaopiluyue(-Shijia) 超毘盧越(釋迦) / EMC **trʰiaw-bji-lə-wuat-°*, "(Śākyas of) Kapilavāstu."

he was even more worried and strongly lamented and cried out loud: "This is strange! This is an extreme shame! Six years have passed since my son has left his home. But how now can she bear a son?" Now, according to the regulations of the kingdom, the drum was beaten to assemble all the troops. And all the 99,000 Śākyas came together and called for Yaśodharā. Thereupon Yaśodharā put on white clothes, held the baby at her bosom, and was not scared at all; (herself) experiencing little affliction, she stood in the middle of her kinsmen, holding the baby. The Śākyas, holding their weapons, were very angry and yelled at Yaśodharā in the following way: "Stupid (girl)! How dare you shame (us) in such a manner, and insult our clan?! You (should) feel ashamed to stand in front of us." There was a Śākya called Biniu-tian (*bji-nruw-°; P. Veṇhu-deva), Yaśodharā's maternal uncle, who said: "Yaśodharā is a stupid (girl) and has the naivety of an infant, (but) she has not committed this. (As your) maternal uncle in the Śākya clan (I) should like (to hear) the truth: where did you beget this child?" Yaśodharā, honestly and without shame, said: "It is from that Śākya who left the household called Siddhārtha from whom I begot this child." As King Śuddhodana heard these words he was enraged and said: "(You will) not protect (the child) whom you have borne even if you speak different words, be they true or false! As the Śākyas know, my son Siddhārtha, while he (still) lived in the house, would not even listen when he heard of the five lusts—how now can he have been full of lust and produced a child? If (you) say so (you) are indeed respectless. From whom have you begotten the child? You are insulting us and just (trying to) ingratiate yourself with us. This is not honesty. Before, when my son Siddhārtha was (still) at home, he was not even affected by jewels and food. Now that he is undergoing austerities and eats (only) sesame(-flavored) rice every day, how can he now be slandered by this?" King Śuddhodana,[70] extremely enraged, asked the Śākyas:

70. Here the text uses the semantic rendering Jingfan 淨飯 for the name Śuddhodana instead of the earlier transcriptional Yuetoutan 悅頭檀 / EMC **jwiat-dəw-dan* (*yue* 悅 here probably should be read *shuo* / EMC **ɕwiat* like *shuo* 說).

"Now by which (kind of) torture should we kill her?" There was a Śākya who said: "In my opinion we should make a fiery pit and throw mother and child into the fire (and burn them) until nothing is left of them." All the people said: "This is the best (solution)." They dug out a fiery pit, piled *khadira* wood in it, and set it on fire. As soon as Yaśodharā came near and saw the fiery pit, she was extremely terrified, like a helpless (person) without refuge, surrounded and watched on four sides by wild beasts. Thereupon Yaśodharā became disheartened, (although) she certainly felt no guilt and had accepted (her) misery. She looked at all the Śākyas, and because no one helped her, she heaved a deep sigh, embraced (her) child, thought of the bodhisattva, and said: "You have mercy and compassion for everybody. Gods, nāgas, and spirits all respect you. Now we, mother and child, are short of protection and innocently undergo hardship. Why does the bodhisattva not take care (of us)? Why does he not rescue us (both), mother and child, from today's danger? The gods and the benevolent spirits do not think of us. Formerly, when the bodhisattva (still) dwelt among the Śākya clan, he was like the full moon amid the host of stars. But now (we) do not catch even a glimpse of him." Thereafter she paid respect in the Buddha's direction, honored the Śākyas, too, folded her palms, went toward the fire, and said the true words: "My child is really not from somebody else, but is his [i.e., the bodhisattva's] child. If it is true and not false that he dwelt in my womb for six years, the fire should extinguish itself and not harm us, me and (my) child." After she had said so she went into the fire, but the fiery pit turned into a water pond and she saw herself resting on lotus flowers. She was without fear and her face expressed calmness. She folded her palms toward the Śākyas and said: "Had I lied (to you) I should have been burned to death. As it is now (established) that this child is really the bodhisattva's son and that I have told the truth, I should be exempted from the fire ordeal." There were some Śākyas who said: "Look at (her) appearance: she is not frightened and has no fear. Therefore let us push her (into the fire) and we certainly will know if this is true." Other Śākyas said: "But this fiery pit has turned into a clear pond! We know that she is innocent, because we have seen this with our own eyes." Thereupon the Śākyas took Yaśodharā home to the palace and respected and admired her even more. They found her a nurse to look after the child, and things were the same as they where when [i.e., before] (the boy) had been born. His grandfather Śuddhodana loved (the boy) deeply, and when he (could) not see Rāhula he was not able to eat. Whenever he remembered the bodhisattva he took Rāhula into his arms in order to relieve himself from his worried thoughts. To make a long story short: after six years King Śuddhodana, (who) greatly admired the Buddha, sent messengers with an invitation for the Buddha. The Buddha, feeling compassion, returned to his home kingdom. After he had arrived at the palace of the Śākyas the Buddha converted 1,250 monks, who all, without exception, had bodies like the Buddha with its shining marks. Yaśodharā told Rāhula: "Go to the side of the one who is your father!" Thereupon Rāhula saluted the Buddha, went toward (him), and stood just at the Tathāgata's left foot, and the Buddha, with his hands showing the wheel marks of merit accumulated during innumerable kalpas, touched Rāhula's head. Then all the Śākyas thought: "The Buddha still bears affection for his own (offspring)." The Buddha recognized what the Śākyas thought and uttered the (following) verses:

> I have no partial affection for my inborn son,
> no more (affection) than for my own kinsmen; by touching his head
> I only eradicate forever the bonds of love and hate.
> The delay in my son's birth should cause you no doubts.
> He also will leave the householder's life and become my son in the dharma, too.
> To briefly state his merits: he will leave the householder's life, will study the true path,
> and will become an arhat.[71]

71. （一一七）羅睺羅因緣。我昔曾聞：佛初出家夜，佛子羅睺羅始入于胎。悉達菩薩六年苦行，於菩提樹下降伏四魔，除諸陰蓋，豁然大悟，成無上道，具足十力四無所畏，成就十八不共之法，具四辯才，悉於諸度，得到彼岸，解了一切諸佛之法，過諸聲聞緣覺之上。於初成道夜生羅睺羅，舉宮婇女咸皆慚恥，生大憂惱而作是言："怪哉！大惡耶

輸陀羅不慮是非，輕有所作，不自愛慎，令我舉宮都被染污。悉達菩薩久已出家，而於今者卒生此子。甚為恥辱！"時有釋女，名曰電光，是耶輸陀羅姨母之女；椎胸拍髀，瞋恚呵罵："耶輸陀羅！汝於尊長所親何以自損？悉達太子出家學道，已經六年。生此小兒，甚為非時。從誰而得？爾無慚愧辱我種族？不數種族，不護惡名？悉達菩薩有大功德，名稱遠聞。汝今云何不護惜彼，而方恥辱？"淨飯王當于爾時在樓閣上見此大地六種震動，奇異相現。白淨王見是相已，謂菩薩死，憂箭入心，生大苦惱，而作是言："我子戒香充塞四遠。相好莊嚴如蓮花鬘。今為死日之所乾枯戒深固根慚愧枝葉。名譽之香大悲厚蔭。我子如樹為死象所蹋。大如金山，眾寶莊嚴。我子金山王相好莊嚴身。為無常金剛杵之所碎壞。猶如大海滿中眾寶；如摩竭魚擾亂海水，我子大海亦復如是：為死摩竭魚之所擾惱。猶如滿月眾星圍繞。我子如是無量功德，相好莊嚴。今為無常羅睺羅所吞。我種從大丈夫，丈夫盧越真淨；如是等王相續至此。今日將不斷絕我種耶？特望我子為轉輪聖王，或成佛道。而於今者寧可死耶？設失我子，憂愁憔悴，命必不全。冀其出家法服持鉢，敷演甘露，如此種種諸事；必不得見。"以憶子故，種種愁思思惟是。時聞子宮中舉聲大哭，王倍驚怖謂太子死。問前走使女言："是何哭聲？將非我子死耶？"女白王言："太子不死。耶輸陀羅今產一子，舉宮慚愧。是以哭耳。"王聞是語，倍增憂惱，發聲大哭，揚聲大喚，唱言："怪哉！極為醜辱！我子出家以經六年。云何今日而方生子？"時彼國法擊鼓一下，一切軍集。九萬九千諸釋悉會，即喚耶輸陀羅。時耶輸陀羅著白淨衣，抱兒在懷，都不驚怕，面小有垢，於親黨中抱兒而立。時執杖釋作色瞋忿，罵耶輸陀羅，叱爾："凡鄙！可愧之甚，辱我種族！有何面目，我等前立！"有釋名毘紐天 - 是耶輸陀羅舅 - 語："耶輸陀羅凡鄙嬰愚，無過於爾。舅於種族宜好實語：竟為何處而得此子？"耶輸陀羅都無慚恥，正直而言："從彼出家釋種名曰悉達，我從彼邊而得此子。"悅頭檀王聞是語已，瞋恚而言："不護所生，便作異語，若實，若虛，諸釋所知我子悉達本在家時，聞有五欲耳尚不聽。況當有欲而生於子？如斯之言深為鄙媟。從誰得子？毀辱我等，實是諂曲。非正直法。我子悉達昔在家時，及眾珍寶餚饍，都無染著。況今苦行，日食麻米，以此謗毀？"淨飯王極大瞋恚，問諸釋言："今當云何苦毒殺害？"復有釋言："如我意者，當作火坑，擲置火中，使其母子都無遺餘。"諸人皆言："此事最良。"即掘火坑，以佉陀羅木積於坑中，以火焚之，即將耶輸陀羅至火坑邊。時耶輸陀羅見火坑已，方大驚怖，譬如野鹿獨在圍中四向顧望，無可恃怙。耶輸陀羅便自呵責，既自無罪受斯禍患。遍觀諸釋，無救己者，抱兒，長嘆，念菩薩言："汝有慈悲憐愍一切。天，龍，鬼，神咸敬於汝。今我母子薄於祐助，無過受苦。云何菩薩不見留意？何故不救我之母子今日危厄？諸天善神無憶我者。菩薩昔日處眾釋中，猶如滿月在於眾星。而於今者更不一見。"即時向佛方所，一心敬禮，復拜諸釋，合掌向火而說實語："我此兒者實不從他而有斯子。若實不虛，猶六年在我胎中者，火當消滅，終不燒害我之母子。"作是語已，即入火中。而此火坑變為水池，自見己身處蓮花上。都無恐怖，顏色和悅。合掌向諸釋言："若我虛妄，應即燋死。以今此兒實菩薩子，以我實語，得免火患。"復有釋言："視其形相：不驚不畏。以此推之，必知是實。"復有釋言："而此火坑變為清池。以是驗之，知其無過。"時諸釋等將耶輸陀羅還歸宮中，倍加恭敬讚嘆。為索乳母，供事其子；猶如生時等無有異。祖白淨王愛重深厚。不見羅睺羅，終不能食。若憶菩薩，抱羅睺羅，用解愁念。略而言之：滿六年已，白淨王渴仰於佛，遣往請佛。佛憐愍故，還歸本國，來到釋宮。佛變千二百五十比丘，皆如佛身，光相無異。耶輸陀羅語羅睺羅："誰是汝父，往到其邊。"時羅睺羅禮佛已訖，正在如來左足邊立。如來即以無量劫中所修功德相輪之手摩羅睺羅頂。時諸釋等咸作是念："佛今猶有愛私之心。"佛知諸釋心之所念，即說偈言：

"我於生眷屬　　及以所生子
無有偏愛心。　　但以手摩頂
我盡諸結使　　愛憎永除盡。
汝等勿懷疑　　於子生猶預！
此亦當出家，　　重為我法子。

Da-zhidu-lun, T.1509.182b12ff.:

> Furthermore, as it is said in the "Avadāna of Rāhula's mother": The bodhisattva Śākyamuni had two wives; one was called Gopiyā,[72] the other was called Yaśodharā. Yaśodharā was the mother of Rāhula. Gopiyā was the preferred wife[73] and therefore did not bear a child. On the night when the bodhisattva left the household, Yaśodharā felt that she was pregnant. The bodhisattva underwent austerities for six years, and in the same way Yaśodharā was pregnant for six years without delivering (a child). The Śākyas questioned her: "The bodhisattva has left the household—how can this be?" Yaśodharā said: "I have not committed adultery.[74] The child I am bearing is really the offspring of the bodhisattva." The Śākyas said: "How can it be that after such a long time, you have not delivered (a child)?" She answered: "This is something I don't know." The Śākyas held a meeting and asked the king how he wanted to punish the crime. Gopiyā addressed the king: "Please forgive her. I have been constantly together with Yaśodharā. I bear witness to her innocence. Wait until the child is born, and you will know if it resembles the father. It will not be (too) late to punish her." Thereupon the king generously left (the case). After six years the bodhisattva finished his austerities and realized buddhahood—and that same night (she) gave birth to Rāhula. The king saw that he resembled his father, loved him greatly, and forgot his worries (in his presence). He said to his officials: "Although my son has now gone away, I have this child who is no different from my son." Yaśodharā had avoided expulsion

---

略言其功德： 出家，學真道，
當成阿羅漢。"

72. See Lamotte 1949, 1003. Qupiye 劬毘耶 / EMC **guə-bji-jia*.

73. I have not found the meaning "infertile woman" for *baonü* 寶女 although this seems to be the logical translation in the context—Lamotte translates "sterile (*bandhya*)"—and would rather stick to the literal meaning here: see Hirakawa, 389a., s.v. (*strī-ratna*, *ratna-dārikā*, *vara-bhāryā*). The logic of the text would then be that Gopiyā, because she was the preferred woman, did not have to bear a child.

74. Literally "transgression with somebody else," *tazui* 他罪.

because of her (supposed) crime, yet she had developed a bad reputation throughout the kingdom, and she wanted to get rid of it. After the Buddha had realized buddhahood, he returned to Kapilavāstu to convert the sons of the Śākyas. At that time King Śuddhodana and Yaśodharā frequently invited the Buddha to the palace for a meal. Then Yaśodharā took a bowl of happy-balls with a hundred flavors, gave it to Rāhula, and asked him to offer it to the Buddha. Thereupon the Buddha with his magical power transformed five hundred arhats so that they had bodies like the Buddha, without any difference. The seven-year-old Rāhula took the happy-balls, approached the Buddha, and offered it to the World-honored One. There the Buddha enacted his magical power and changed the monks' bodies back to their former (shape); and they sat down with empty bowls. Only the bowl of the Buddha was filled with happy-balls. Thereupon Yaśodharā said to the king: "This proves that I am innocent." Yaśodharā then asked the Buddha: "Why have I been pregnant for six years?" The Buddha said: "Your son Rāhula, in the past, in former times, had been a king. Once there was a seer (*ṛṣi*) (endowed) with the five magical powers who came to the kingdom and said to the king: 'The king's duty is to punish thieves. Punish my crimes!' The king said: 'What are your crimes?' He answered: 'I came to this kingdom and committed the crime of taking what is not given, namely: I have drunk the king's water and have used the king's poplar twigs.' The king said: 'I will deal with whoever has committed a crime. When I first ascended the throne, I donated the water and the poplar twigs to everybody.' The seer said: 'Although the king donated (these), I am concerned that there (will really) be no (punishment) for my crimes. I wish you would investigate it now, so that later there will be no (punishment) for my crimes.' The king said: 'If you insist on this, then stay a little bit and wait for me (until) I return from (the palace).' The king entered the palace and did not come out for six days. The seer stayed in the royal garden for six days, suffering hunger and thirst. The seer thought: 'This is how the king punishes me.' After six days the king came out and apologized to the seer: 'I may have forgotten (you), but I cannot be blamed.' It is for this reason that he suffered the punishment of evil forms of existence over five hundred generations. Five hundred generations are as long as the six years in his mother's womb. Thereby it is proven that Yaśodharā is without guilt."[75]

75. 復次如《羅睺羅母本生經》中說：釋迦文菩薩有二夫人；一名劬毘耶，二名耶輸陀羅。耶輸陀羅羅睺羅母也。劬毘耶是寶女，故不孕子。耶輸陀羅以菩薩出家夜，自覺妊身。菩薩出家六年苦行，耶輸陀羅亦六年懷妊不產。諸釋詰之："菩薩出家何由有此？"耶輸陀羅言："我無他罪。我所懷子實是太子體胤。"諸釋言："何以久而不產？"答言："非我所知。"諸釋集議，聞王欲如法治罪。劬毘耶白王："願寬恕之。我常與耶輸陀羅共住。我為其證知其無罪。待其子生，知似父不。治之無晚。"王即寬置。佛六年苦行既滿，初成佛時，其夜生羅睺羅。王見其似父，愛樂，忘憂，語群臣言："我兒雖去，今得其子，與兒在無異。"耶輸陀羅雖免罪黜，惡聲滿國；耶輸陀羅欲除惡名。佛成道已，還迦毘羅婆度諸釋子。時淨飯王及耶輸陀羅常請佛入宮食。是時耶輸陀羅持一鉢百味歡喜丸，與羅睺羅令持上佛。是時佛以神力變五百阿羅漢，皆如佛身，無有別異。羅睺羅以七歲身持歡喜丸，徑至佛前，奉進世尊。是時佛攝神力，諸比丘身復如故，皆空鉢而坐。唯佛鉢中盛滿歡喜丸。耶輸陀羅即白王言："以此證驗我無罪也。"耶輸陀羅即問佛言："我有何因緣懷妊六年？"佛言："汝子羅睺羅過去久遠世時，曾作國王。時有一五通仙人來入王國，語王言：'王法治賊，請治我罪！'王言：'汝有何罪？'答言：'我入王國，犯不與取，輒飲王水，用王楊枝。'王言：'我以相與何罪之有。我初登王位，皆以水及楊枝施於一切。'仙人言：'王雖已施，我心疑悔罪不除也。願今見治，無令後罪。'王言：'若必欲爾，小停待我入還。'王入宮中六日不出。此仙人在王園中六日飢渴。仙人思惟：'此王正以此治我。'王過六日而出，辭謝仙人：'我便相忘，莫見咎也。'以是因緣故，受五百世三惡道罪。五百世常六年在母胎中。以是證故，耶輸陀羅無有罪也。" In the following episode it is not Rāhula who gives the happy-ball dumplings to the Buddha but Yaśodharā herself. See Lamotte 1949, 1001ff.

Bibliography

Arnold, Edwin 1998. *The Light of Asia or The Great Renunciation (Mahâbhinishkramana) Being the Life and Teaching of Gautama, Prince of India and Founder of Buddhism (As Told in Verse by an Indian Buddhist)*. Los Angeles: The Theosophy Company. (Originally published 1891.)

Bareau, André 1963. *Recherches sur la biographie du Buddha dans les Sūtrapiṭaka et les Vinayapiṭaka anciens: de la quête de l'éveil à la conversion de Śāriputra et Maudgalyāyana*. Publications de l'École Française de l'Extrême-Orient 53. Paris: École Française de l'Extrême-Orient.

——— 1970/71. *Recherches sur la biographie du Buddha dans les Sūtrapiṭaka et les Vinayapiṭaka anciens: II. Les derniers mois, le Parinirvāṇa et les funérailles*, tôme I + II. Publications de l'École Française de l'Extrême-Orient 77. Paris: École Française de l'Extrême-Orient.

——— 1982. "Un personage bien mystérieux: l'épouse du Buddha." *Indological and Buddhist Studies. Volume in Honour of Professor J.W. de Jong on his Sixtieth Birthday*, pp. 31–59. Canberra: 1982 (reprinted in 1995: 119–47).

——— 1995. *Recherches sur la biographie du Buddha dans les Sūtrapiṭaka et les Vinayapiṭaka anciens: III. Articles complémentaires*. Paris: École Française de l'Extrême-Orient.

Beal, Samuel 1875. *The Romantic Legend of Śākya Buddha: A Translation of the Chinese Versions of the Abhiniṣkramaṇasūtra*. London: Trübner & Co. (Reprint: Delhi: Motilal Barnassidas, 1985.)

Bechert, Heinz 1991/92. *The Dating of the Historical Buddha / Die Datierung des historischen Buddha, Part 1 & 2*. Symposien zur Buddhismusforschung, IV, 1 and 2 = AAWG 189 and 194. Göttingen: Vandenhoeck & Ruprecht.

Carus, Paul 1915. *The Gospel of Buddha: Compiled from Ancient Records*. Chicago and London: The Open Court Publishing Company.

Chavannes, Édouard 1962. *Cinq cents contes et apologues extraits du Tripiṭaka Chinois et traduits en Français. Tôme III*. Paris: Libraire d'Amérique et d'Orient Adrien-Maisonneuve.

Clarke, Shayne 2004. "Vinaya-Mātṛkā: Mother of the Monastic Codes, Or Just Another Set of Lists? A Response to Frauwallner's Handling of the Mahāsāṅghika Vinaya." *Indo-Iranian Journal* 47.2: 77–120.

Deeg, Max 2003. *The Places Where Siddhārtha Trod: Lumbinī and Kapilavastu*. Occasional Papers 3. Lumbinī: Lumbinī International Research Institute.

Durt, Hubert 2006. "The Shijiapu of Sengyou: The First Chinese Attempt to Produce a Critical Biography of the Buddha." *Journal of the International College for Postgraduate Buddhist Studies* X / 国際仏教学大学院大学研究紀要第10号: 51–86 (Japanese pagination: 154–119).

Karetzky, Patricia Eichenbaum 1992. *The Life of the Buddha: Ancient Scriptural and Pictorial Traditions*. Lanham, New York, London: University Press of America.

Fausbøll, V. 1962. *The Jātaka Together with Its Commentary: Being Tales of the Anterior Births of Gotama Buddha*. London: Luzac & Company. (Originally published London: Trübner & Co., 1877.)

Foucaux, P. E. 1884. *Le Lalitavistara. L'histoire traditionelle de la vie du Bouddha Çakyamuni traduit du sanscrit*. Paris: Édition Leroux. (Reprint: Paris: Les Deux Océans, 1988.)

Foucher, Alfred 1905/1918/1951. *L'art Graeco-Bouddhique de Gandhāra*. Étude sur les origines de l'influence classique dans l'art bouddhique de l'Inde et de l'Extrême-Orient, 3 vols. Paris: Imprimérie Nationale, Hanoi.

——— 1987. *La vie du Bouddha d'après les textes et les monuments de l'Inde*. Paris: Adrien Maisonneuve. (Reprint of first ed. Paris: Payot, 1949.)

Frauwallner, Erich 1956. *The Earliest Vinaya and the Beginnings of Buddhist Literature*. Serie Orientale Roma VIII. Roma: Istituto Italiano per il Medeo ed Estremo Oriente.

Fukita Takamichi 2003. *The Mahāvadānasūtra: A New Edition Based on Manuscripts Discovered in Northern Turkestan*. Sanskrit-Wörterbuch der buddhistischen Texte aus den Turfan-Funden 10. Göttingen: Vandenhoeck & Ruprecht.

Gnoli, Raniero, ed. 1977. *The Gilgit Manuscript of the Saṅghabhedavastu: Being the 17th and Last Section of the Vinaya of the Mūlasarvāstivādin. Part I*. Serie Orientale Roma XLIX, 1. Roma: Istituto Italiano per il Medeo ed Estremo Oriente.

Hardy, Spence R. 1995. *A Manual of Buddhism in Its Modern Development: Translated from Singhalese MSS*. Delhi: Munshiram Manoharlal Publishers. (First published 1853.)

Hirakawa Akira 平川彰 1997. *Bukkyō-kanbon-daijiten* 佛教漢梵大辭典 / *Buddhist Chinese-Sanskrit Dictionary*. Tokyo: The Reiyukai.

Jayawickrama, N. A. *The Story of Gotama Buddha: The Nidāna-kathā of the Jātakaṭṭhakathā*. Oxford: The Pali Text Society.

Johnston, E. H. 1936. *The Buddhacarita or Acts of the Buddha*. 2 parts. Lahore: University of the Punjab. (Reprint: Delhi: Motilal Banarsidass, 1972.)

Jones, J. J. 1956. *The Mahāvastu (Translated from the Buddhist Sanskrit)*, vol. III. London: Luzac & Company.

Karlsson, Klemens 2000. *Face to Face with the Absent Buddha: The Formation of Buddhist Aniconic Art*. Acta Universitatis Upsaliensis 15. Uppsala: Uppsala Universitet.

Klimkeit, Hans-Joachim 1990. *Der Buddha: Leben und Lehre*. Stuttgart, Berlin, Köln: Verlag W. Kohlhammer.

Kloppenborg, Ria 1973. *The Sūtra on the Foundation of the Buddhist Order (Catuṣpariṣatsūtra): Relating the Events from the Bodhisattva's Enlightenment up to the Conversion of Upatiṣya (Śāriputra) and Kolita (Maudgalyāyana)*. Leiden: E. J. Brill.

Krom, N. J. 1926. *The Life of the Buddha on the Stūpa of Barabuḍur according to the Lalitavistara-Text*. The Hague: Martinus Nijhoff.

Kurita Isao 栗田功 1988. *Gandāra-bijutsu / Gandhāran Art, 2 vols.: I. Butsuden / The*

Buddha's life story—II: Budda-no-sekai / The world of the Buddha ガンダーラ美術，I. 佛伝 / II. 佛佗の世界. Tokyo: Kodai-bukkyō-bijutsu-sōkan / Ancient Buddhist Art Series 古代佛教美術叢刊.

Lamotte, Étienne 1947–48. "La légende du Buddha." *Revue de l'histoire des religions* 134: 37–71.

——— 1949. *Le Traité de la Grande Vertu de Sagesse de Nāgārjuna (Mahāprajñāpāramitāśāstra), tôme II, châpitres XVI–XXX.* Bibliothèque de Muséon 18. Louvain/Leuven: Institut Orientaliste / Institut voor Oriëntalistiek.

——— 1988. *History of Indian Buddhism: From the Origins to the Śaka Era.* Translated from the French by Sara Webb-Boin under the supervision of Jean Dantinne. Louvain-La-Neuve: Publications de l'Institut Orientaliste de Louvain.

Nakamura, Hajime 2000. *Gotama Buddha: A Biography Based on the Most Reliable Texts, Volume One.* Tokyo: Kosei Publishing Co.

——— 2005. *Gotama Buddha: A Biography Based on the Most Reliable Texts, Volume Two.* Tokyo: Kosei Publishing Co.

Panglung, Jampa Losang 1981. *Die Erzählstoffe des Mūlasarvāstivāda-Vinaya analysiert auf Grund der Tibetischen Übersetzung.* SPB Monograph Series III. Tokyo: The Reiyukai Library.

Pischel, Richard 1917. *Leben und Lehre des Buddha* (Durchgesehen von Heinrich Lüders). Leipzig, Berlin: B. G. Teubner. (Reprint: Wiesbaden: Franz Steiner Verlag, 1982.)

Reynolds, Frank E. 1976. "The Many Lives of the Buddha: A Study of Sacred Biography and Theravada Tradition." In *The Biographical Process: Essays in History and Psychology of Religion*, ed. by Frank E. Reynolds and Donald Capps, pp. 37–61. The Hague: Mouton.

Rockhill, W. W. 1885. *The Life of the Buddha and the Early History of His Order: Derived from Tibetan Works in the Bkah-Hgyur and Bstan-Hgyur (Followed by Notices on the Early History of Tibet and Khoten).* London: Kegan Paul, Trench, Trübner & Co.

Schlingloff, Dieter 2000. *Ajanta: Handbuch der Malereien / Handbook of Painting 1, Erzählende Wandmalereien / Narrative Wall-paintings, Vol. I: Interpretation.* Wiesbaden: Verlag Otto Harrassowitz.

Schober, Juliane, ed. 1997. *Sacred Biography in the Buddhist Traditions of South and Southeast Asia.* Honolulu: University of Hawaii Press.

Senart, Émile 1897. *Le Mahâvastu: Texte sanscrit*, vol. III, Paris: Imprimérie Nationale.

Silk, Jonathan 2003. "The Fruits of Paradox: On the Religious Architecture of the Buddha's Life Story." *Journal of the American Academy of Religion* 71.4: 863–81.

Strong, John 1997. "A Family Quest: The Buddha, Yaśodharā, and Rāhula in the Mūlasarvāstivāda Vinaya." In Schober 1997: 113–28.

——— 2001. *The Buddha: A Short Biography.* Oxford: Oneworld.

——— 2002. *The Experience of Buddhism: Sources and Interpretations.* 2nd ed. Belmont, CA: Wadsworth.

Tatelman, Joel 1998. "A Synopsis of *Bhadrakalpāvadāna* II–IX." *Buddhist Studies Review* 15.1: 3–42.

Thomas, Edward J. 1949. *The Life of Buddha as Legend and History*. London: Routledge, Kegan, Paul.

Waldschmidt, Ernst 1944/48. *Die Überlieferung vom Lebensende des Buddha: Eine vergleichende Analyse des Mahāparinirvāṇasūtra und seiner Textentsprechungen*. Anzeiger der Akademie der Wissenschaften zu Göttingen 29 + 30. Göttingen: Vandenhoeck & Ruprecht.

——— 1950/51. *Das Mahāparinirvāṇasūtra: Text in Sanskrit und Tibetisch, verglichen mit dem Pāli nebst einer Übersetzung der chinesischen Entsprechung im Vinaya der Mūlasarvāstivādins*. 3 parts. Abhandlungen der Deutschen Akademie der Wissenschaften zu Berlin, Klasse für Sprachen, Literatur und Kunst Jahrgang 1949 Nr. 1, Jahrgang 1950 Nr. 2, Jahrgang 1950 Nr. 3. Berlin: Akademie Verlag.

——— 1952/57/62. *Das Catuṣpariṣatsūtra: Eine kanonische Lehrschrift uber die Begründung der buddhistischen Gemeinde. Text in Sanskrit und Tibetisch, verglichen mit dem Pāli nebst einer Übersetzung der chinesischen Entsprechung im Vinaya der Mūlasarvāstivādins*. 3 parts. Abhandlungen der Deutschen Akademie der Wissenschaften zu Berlin, Klasse für Sprachen, Literatur und Kunst Jahrgang 1952 Nr. 2, Jahrgang 1956 Nr. 1, Jahrgang 1960 Nr. 1. Berlin: Akademie Verlag.

——— 1953/56. *Das Mahāvadānasūtra: Ein kanonischer Text über die sieben letzten Buddhas. Sanskrit, verglichen mit dem Pāli nebst einer Analyse der in chinesischer Übersetzung überlieferten Parallelversionen*. 2 parts. Abhandlungen der Deutschen Akademie der Wissenschaften zu Berlin, Klasse für Sprachen, Literatur und Kunst Jahrgang 1952 Nr. 8, Jahrgang 1954 Nr. 3. Berlin: Akademie Verlag.

——— 1982. *Die Legende vom Leben des Buddha: In Auszügen aus den heiligen Texten, aus dem Sanskrit, Pali und Chinesischen übersetzt und eingeführt*. Graz: Verlag für Sammler.

Weber, Claudia 1999. *Buddhistische Sutras: Das Leben des Buddha in Quellentexten*. München: Diederichs.

Wieger, Léon 1951. *Les vies chinoises du Buddha*. Paris: Les Humanités d'Extrême-Orient, Bouddhisme Chinois.

Zürcher, Erich 1978. *Het leven van de Boeddha. Xiuxing Benqi jing & Zhong benqi jing. Vertaald uit de vroegste Chinese overlevering en ingeleid door E. Zürcher*. De Oosterse Bibliotheek 10. Amsterdam: Meulenhoff.

Truth Under the Guise of Poetry

Aśvaghoṣa's "Life of the Buddha"[1]

Roland Steiner

In a plain, somewhat trivial sense, a "biography" belongs to a genre of literature that is based on written or oral accounts of individual lives. We usually associate this genre with non-fictitious subjects, or at least with a non-fictitious person. In other words, a biography is usually a *written* history of a real person's life. As a "history," however, it is not only a mere list of plain facts such as birth, education, works, caste, confession, relationships, and death. It is even more than a chronological record of *significant* events. What we expect from a work of history, over and above that, are explanations, interpretations, analyses, or assessments of the biography itself and the circumstances surrounding it. The biographer should make graphic an individual character or a lively personality and draw a picture of the relevant historical epoch. It is even conceivable that the author of a biography might intend to entertain his readers.

If we review the just-mentioned terms "interpretation," "character," or "entertainment," we notice that a biography has a fictitious or artistic aspect too. The biographer must, in a sense, create his subject; he has to look for a literary shape and a linguistic form. One of the most important German biographies of the twentieth century was written by the historian Golo Mann

1. I am very grateful to Prof. Dr. Walter Slaje for valuable suggestions and corrections and to Dr. Jayandra Soni for checking the English.

on Albrecht von Wallenstein,[2] the famous Bohemian generalissimo of the Thirty Years' War. The well-chosen subtitle of his book runs "His life *narrated* by Golo Mann."[3] Mann's *Wallenstein* combines the qualities of a scholarly biography (including endnotes and references) with those of a historical novel. Actually, it is a narration in the true sense of the word, that is, the work of a creative writer, despite its historical subject—or should we say, *because* of its historical subject?

The title of this collection—*Lives Lived, Lives Imagined*—reflects this twofold nature of biographies. The lived life of a certain person and the "same" life imagined or conceived by an author are the two poles of biographical works. This obviously applies to Western biographies as well as to biographies in the Buddhist traditions. Apte's *English-Sanskrit Dictionary* has under "Biography"—apart from the modern Sanskrit formation *jīvanavṛttāntaḥ*, "report or tale of a life"—the entry *caritaṃ*, which literally means "going, moving," and also "doing, practice, behavior, acts, deeds." One might therefore think that a Sanskrit biography primarily concentrates—or should concentrate—on the various movements or deeds of the described person, but that would give us a somewhat wrong idea of the nature of such works. The most famous example of a biography, or *carita*, from the classical period of Indian literature is Bāṇa's *Harṣacarita* (*Acts* [or *Life*] *of Harṣa*) of the seventh century C.E. In this work the author describes the life of his own sovereign Harṣa, the historically important king of Kanauj, who, especially in Buddhist texts, is later called Śīlāditya, "Sun of Virtue." Bāṇa designates his *Harṣacarita* as an *ākhyāyikā*, that is, a narration formally characterized by its ornate prose. According to Bhāmaha, who competes with Daṇḍin in being the oldest among the Indian critics, an *ākhyāyikā* narrates what actually happened (*vṛttam*; *Kāvyālaṅkāra* 1.26). Bāṇa himself emphasizes, among other things, the use of a not-too-common diction, unlabored double meanings, a language rich in sonorous words, coupled with metrical skills. Evidently, the poet here highlights the formal and stylistic aspects rather than the content of his biography. Nevertheless, the work also contains numerous descriptions of courtly life, contemporary manners and customs, and religious conditions of the time. Finally, we should keep in mind that according

2. Mann 1971.

3. "Sein Leben erzählt von Golo Mann."

to the Indian tradition, the literary genre of the *Harṣacarita* is not "biography" but *ākhyāyikā* ("narration").

Five or six centuries earlier than the *Harṣacarita*, a Buddhist author named Aśvaghoṣa wrote a *mahākāvya* ("great poem") entitled *Buddhacarita*, "Acts (or Life) of the Buddha." The *Buddhacarita* consists of twenty-eight cantos, or *sargas*, "of which only numbers two to thirteen are extant in its entirety in Sanskrit, together with three quarters of the first canto and the first quarter of the fourteenth."[4] Thus only around the first half of the entire poem has survived in the original Sanskrit. "It begins with the conception of the Buddha and, after narrating his life and Parinirvāṇa, closes with an account of the war over the relics, the first council and the reign of Aśoka."[5] Apart from the *Sūtra of the Origin*—a legend dedicated to the present Buddha available in an early Chinese translation (T.184)—the *Buddhacarita* is the oldest coherent narrative of the Buddha's life.[6] Moreover, it is one of the earliest examples of ornate Sanskrit poetry (*kāvya*).

Edward Hamilton Johnston, in his 1936 translation of the *Buddhacarita*, commented that "The textual tradition of the extant portion is bad."[7] Claus Vogel, in his text-critical paper on the first canto of the *Buddhacarita*, remarked: "What remains of the original *Buddhacarita* is preserved in a single palm-leaf manuscript (A) dating from c. 1300 and once consisting of 55 folios (up to xiv, 31), the first, third, seventh, and eighth being no longer extant."[8] This manuscript was called "A" by Johnston, and is what his 1935 edition is based upon. "The Cambridge and Paris manuscripts (C, D, P) [on which Cowell's older edition of 1891 rests] are merely copies of a revised and augmented transcript (β) made in 1830 by Amṛtānanda, the Residency pundit at Kathmandu, directly from [Johnston's manuscript] A."[9] In order to better understand and establish the transmitted Sanskrit text and to study the *Buddhacarita* as a whole, it is necessary to make use of the Tibetan translation which is contained in the five known Tengyur

4. Johnston 1936: xviii.
5. Johnston 1936: xviii.
6. Vetter 2000: 11–19.
7. Johnston 1936: xviii.
8. Vogel 1965–66: 267n5
9. Vogel 1965–66: 267n5.

editions.[10] The translation was made in the thirteenth century by the Nepali Pandit Sa dbang bzang po, who also rendered the grammatical text *Vibhaktikārikā* of *Siṃhabhadra (or Haribhadra), and Blo gros rgyal po.[11] The quality of this Tibetan translation is mediocre, to put it mildly, if not sometimes "disappointingly poor."[12]

In this paper, my focus will be on the first chapter of the *Buddhacarita*. Mention was made above of the non-fictitious and at the same time fictitious nature of biographies: the two poles of the actually lived life of a historical person and the "same" life conceived by the author. With regard to the *Harṣacarita* of the seventh century, we noted that the formal, stylistic, and artistic aspects can become dominant or at least very important. We may assume that the highly literary character of the *Harṣacarita* should also augment the glory and fame of King Harṣa himself, since Bāṇa was a poet at Harṣa's court and adorned his patron with a literary masterpiece. Further, Harṣa himself was a gifted poet and author of three dramas and several hymns. Thus, a literary biography in the form of a historical narration appears especially appropriate for such a poet king.

The subject of the *Buddhacarita* is not a contemporary king, but the Buddha Śākyamuni. Therefore the motives of the author will—at least partly—be different from Bāṇa's. We do not know the literary models of Aśvaghoṣa, but it is fair to assume that he was influenced by the *Rāmāyaṇa*, which can be considered a "Rāmacarita." According to the colophons Aśvaghoṣa belongs to the city of Sāketa (Ayodhyā). From the very start of both the *Buddhacarita* and his other poem, the *Saundarananda*, he emphasizes the descent of the Śākyas from the Ikṣvāku dynasty. There are several indications of Aśvaghoṣa's acquaintance not only with the *Rāmāyaṇa*, but also with the *Mahābhārata*. This has also been discussed by Gawroński, Johnston, and, recently, Hiltebeitel, to name but a few.[13] One further motive seems to have been the illus-

10. The Tibetan translation of the *Buddhacarita* is found in the section *mdo* of the Tengyur editions of Cone (C) *ge*, 1–112b, Derge (D) *ge*, 1–103b2, Ganden ("Golden Manuscript") (G), *spring yig snyan ngag*, *nge*, 1–147a3, Narthang (N) *nge*, 1–119b7, and Peking (Q) *skyes rabs*, *nge*, 1–124b8.

11. Jackson 1997: 41–62.

12. Jackson 1997: 42.

13. Hiltebeitel 2006: 229–86.

tration of the contrast between the Buddhist and the Brahmanical dharma. For details, one would have to refer to the relevant articles of these scholars.

However, what I would like to ask here is whether we can learn from Aśvaghoṣa himself about his general or main motives. We saw already that Bāṇa, in the introductory stanzas of his *Harṣacarita*, tells us what he expects from a historical narration (*ākhyāyikā*). It is not at the beginning, but at the very end of the *Buddhacarita* that Aśvaghoṣa informs the reader (or hearer) about his aims. The very last stanza of his poem, which is available only in Tibetan translation, runs as follows:

> Thus, this [work] has been composed out of respect for that best man among the sages, following the canonical texts (*lung*, Skt. **āgama*) of the Sage, not for [displaying] the qualities of [my] learning nor [my] poetical (*snyan dngags*, Skt. **kāvya*) ability; may [this] be for the benefit and happiness of mankind.[14]

Obviously, neither beauty nor learning nor literary skill were the main aim of this poem. The purpose of the work is to promote the good and happiness of all people in accordance with the Buddhist scriptures, which ultimately means liberation or salvation (*mokṣa*, Tib. *thar pa*)—a word which is not expressly mentioned here. This statement is confirmed and elaborated by the two final stanzas of Aśvaghoṣa's second poem, the *Saundarananda*, "which has for its subject the conversion of the Buddha's half-brother, Nanda, in the course of which the opportunity is taken to set out at length the author's view

14. *Buddhacarita* 28.74 (C 112a3–4; D 103a4–5; G 146b2–3; N 119a7–b1; Q 124b1–2):
de ltar thub pa'i skyes mchog de yi gus pa yis | |
mkhas nyid yon tan las min snyan dngags nus pas min | |
thub pa'i lung gi rjes su 'brangs nas 'di brtsams te | |
skye dgu rnams kyi phan dang bde ba'i phyir gyur cig |
b: *yon tan*] CDNQ : om. G; c: *rjes su*] CDQ : *rjesu* GN.

The second quarter of the Tibetan translation seems to reflect a somewhat elliptical diction of the poet's self-justification for composing his text. The reason—which is not self-evident—for differentiating between the ablative *yon tan las* and the instrumental *nus pas* might go back to the Sanskrit original, where metrical requirements could have been decisive for the choice of these cases.

of the Path to Enlightenment."[15] At the end of this work, he gives an even more detailed explanation of his goals than in the *Buddhacarita*:

> Thus, this work, which has liberation at its theme, has been composed for tranquility, not for pleasure, with the intention of capturing through the use of poetry hearers/pupils whose minds are fixed on other things. For (the fact) that I have dealt with something other than liberation here has been done because of the laws of poetry, having thought about how it could become agreeable, as bitter medicine is mixed with honey to make it drinkable.
>
> Having seen that the world is solely devoted to sensual pleasures and repelled by liberation, I here have told the truth under the guise of poetry, having thought that liberation is supreme. Having understood this, what leads to tranquility should be attentively drawn/understood from it, not what is lovely/agreeable; usable gold is obtained from metallic dust.[16]

Here we come across a justification of poetry. In ancient Buddhist circles it does not seem to have been self-evident that poetry is a good thing in any case. Thus paid poetry, poetry composed in order to earn one's living, is expressly rejected by the Buddha in the Pali *Dīghanikāya* (I 11, 10). The main purpose of the *Saundarananda* is to lead the hearer toward liberation (*mokṣa*) and tell him the truth (*tattva*). The poetical form is a means to capture "hearers" who are devoted to other things. The world indulges in sensual pleasures;

15. Johnston 1936: xviii–xix.

16. *Saundarananda* 18.63–64:
ity eṣā vyupaśāntaye na rataye mokṣārthagarbhā kṛtiḥ
śrotṝṇāṃ grahaṇārtham anyamanasāṃ kāvyopacārāt kṛtā |
yan mokṣāt kṛtam anyad atra hi mayā tat kāvyadharmāt kṛtaṃ
pātuṃ tiktam ivauṣadhaṃ madhuyutaṃ hṛdyaṃ kathaṃ syād iti || 63 ||
(meter: Śārdūlavikrīḍita)
prāyeṇālokya lokaṃ viṣayaratiparaṃ mokṣāt pratihataṃ
kāvyavyājena tattvaṃ kathitam iha mayā mokṣaḥ param iti |
tad buddhvā śāmikaṃ yat tad avahitam ito grāhyaṃ na lalitaṃ
pāṃsubhyo dhātujebhyo niyatam upakaraṃ cāmīkaram iti || 64 ||
(meter: Suvadanā)

therefore the dharma has to be told in an agreeable form. Otherwise worldly people will not be ready to hear the dharma. "Pleasure" or "affection" is the opposite of "tranquility" in both stanzas. Hence, the somewhat paradoxical situation arises that poetry tempts the hearers by means of pleasure in order to lead them to tranquility. Similarly, Āryaśūra, in the third *maṅgala* stanza of his *Jātakamālā*, declares that he wishes to make his inspired (*prātibha*) poem agreeable to the ears (*śrutivallabhatva*) by means of examples of the Buddha's extraordinary deeds in accordance with the holy scriptures (*śruti*), with the Buddha's tradition (*ārṣa*), and with reasonable arguments (*yukti*). The motif of making bitter medicine drinkable by putting something sweet into it reminds one of Bhāmaha's statement in his *Kāvyālaṅkāra* (5.3) which remains a topos in later works of poetics:

> One enjoys even a teaching manual, mixed with the taste of sweet poetry; those who have first licked sweet fluids/honey drink pungent medicine.[17]

The central statement is that the ultimate truth has been told under the guise of poetry—*kāvyavyājena tattvam*—with the assumption that ultimate liberation is the supreme goal. It makes sense that these stanzas appear at the very end of the poem, in contrast to the *maṅgala* stanzas of Āryaśūra's *Jātakamālā* or the introductory verses in Bāṇa's *Harṣacarita*. If it is justifiable to take these stanzas seriously, then it would not have been a good idea, in either a realistic or a literary sense, to "warn" the hearer or reader right at the beginning and thus perhaps to prevent him from reading on.

If these declarations are sincere, it will be possible to detect Aśvaghoṣa's intentions as well as the precise meaning of "truth" also in the first chapter of his *Buddhacarita*, the subject of which is the birth of the Buddha. In 1939, Friedrich Weller[18] wrote a lengthy—and still undisputed—article on

17. *Kāvyālaṅkāra* 5.3: *svādukāvyarasonmiśraṃ śāstram apy upayuñjate | prathamālīḍhamadhavaḥ pibanti kaṭu bheṣajam ||*

18. Weller was the editor and translator of the first seventeen chapters of the Tibetan translation of the *Buddhacarita* 1926; he also edited two fragments of the *Buddhacarita* from Central Asia (1953) and published a study of the textual history and development of the Tibetan text (1980).

the scene ("*Schauplatz*") and action ("*Handlung*") of the *Buddhacarita*,[19] in which he harshly criticizes some factual problems that he finds in the text, especially in the first chapter. According to him, the unity of the scene cannot be preserved, the scene of the action is contradictory, and as a narration of events, the first chapter is simply nonsense.[20] On the other hand, Weller is of the well-founded and well-considered opinion that these problems do not stem from textual corruptions. He concludes that the introductory chapter is based on fragments of two different versions of Buddha's birth, which, during Aśvaghoṣa's time, had not yet formed a compact narration but existed in fragmentary reports only. The question would therefore be why Aśvaghoṣa was either incapable or unwilling to create a logically coherent story of the events around the Buddha's birth. Such a task indeed would not have been too difficult for him, as will be shown later. Weller attempts another interpretation: could it be that Aśvaghoṣa's poem is not based on narrated episodes but on fine arts, sculptures, reliefs, and the like?

At this point we should take a closer look at what is described in the first chapter. For the sake of clarity, attention will be given to events that have, or could possibly have, a connection to a specific locality. Two geographical places play a part in this chapter: Kapilavāstu, the capital of the Buddha's father King Śuddhodana, and a forest region named Lumbinī. In the beginning of the poem, the king and his queen appear to reside in Kapilavāstu. Then the queen longs for Lumbinī. Thus, she asks the king about going and staying there (stanza 6). Both go to the forest (stanza 7). Then we hear that the queen awaits the time of her delivery in this forest (stanza 8). The birth takes place, evidently in the forest (stanza 9). The next event connected to a locality is encountered in stanza 23:

> And in the northeastern part of the palace (*prāguttare cāvasatha-pradeśe*)[21] a well containing white/pure (*sita*) water appeared on

19. Weller 1939.

20. Cf., also, Vogel 1965–66: 285: "[...] the same fixed idea [...] that the poet observes in his narrative a strictly logical sequence of events, which is obviously not the case."

21. Or: "In one part of the palace of the northeastern quarter" (Tib. *shar dang byang gi mtshams kyi khang pa'i gcig na*, Skt. **prāguttaraikāvasathapradeśe*?).

> its own, at which the amazed household carried out its rites as if it were a holy bathing-place (*tīrtha*).[22]

Then, again, a scene in the forest is described (stanza 24); it is important for us to know that the newborn child is obviously still there, since the heavenly beings come to see him. A certain conclusion of these occurrences is given in stanza 27:

> When the teacher (*bla ma*, Skt. **guru*) of the liberation of all living beings was born, the world became exceedingly peaceful, as though, being in a state of disorder, it had obtained a ruler. Only Kāmadeva (the god of sexual desire) did not rejoice.[23]

In the next stanza (28), the king, who was last mentioned in stanza 7, feels joy and sorrow after seeing the birth (*skye ba*) of his son. It is not expressly stated at which place exactly this happens. The same is true of the events of the subsequent stanzas, 29 to 48, but we can assume that here there is no change of place. Stanzas 49 to 81 describe the visit of the sage Asita to the royal palace. We learn that the king's son, and perhaps also the queen, are in the palace (stanza 59). When Asita finally departs "as he had come, through the path of the wind" (stanza 80), he sees his nephew, the son of his younger sister, and charges him to listen to the words of the sage (*muni*) and to follow his teaching (stanza 81). With regard to the events that follow—the king opening the prisons, causing the birth ceremony to be performed, making sacrifices, and giving a hundred thousand cows to the brahmans (stanzas 82–84)—there is no explicit statement of place. In stanza 85, however, the king decides to enter or visit the city (*purapraveśe*), which seems to imply that he is not in the city or, somewhat more cautiously formulated, that he is either outside the city or inside his city residence, his palace. The queen enters a palanquin together with her son (stanza 86), and in the next stanza (87), the king makes her go ahead into the city. Finally, the king enters the residence (stanza 88).

22. *prāguttare cāvasathapradeśe kūpaḥ svayaṃ prādur abhūt sitāmbuḥ* | *antaḥpurāṇy āgatavismayāni yasmin kriyās tīrtha iva pracakruḥ* || Bc 1.23.

23. *rgud par gyur la mgon ni nye bar thob nas bzhin* || *'jig rten dag kyang mchog tu rab zhi thob gyur la* || *'jig rten rnams kyi thar pa'i bla ma rab bltams tshe* || *'dod pa'i lha nyid kho na dga' ba med par gyur* | Bc 1.27; a: *rgud*] CD : *rgyud* GNQ.

These are the objective findings with regard to localities when we confine ourselves to explicit statements. Weller interprets the scene of the first chapter thus: Stanzas 5 to 7 take place in Kapilavāstu. Then the royal couple goes to the forest, where the child is born. Further events continue to occur in the forest. Weller finds it strange that stanza 23 describes the appearance of a well in the palace, which in his eyes is an unmotivated change of the location. In stanza 28 we hear that the king saw the birth of his son, which, according to Weller, implies that the king has been in the forest all the time and that all three—parents and child—are still there. Consequently, the action of the following stanzas should also take place in the forest, which, especially in the case of the talk with the learned brahmans (stanzas 31–48), does not seem very appropriate. Should the immediately following episode with Asita (stanzas 49–80) definitely take place in the palace, this would represent a real break in the plot, for according to Weller's interpretation, we would expect the king and his son to be in the Lumbinī forest and not in the palace in Kapilavāstu. In stanza 85, however, the king decides to return ("*zurückzukehren*") to Kapilavāstu, implying that he is not yet there. On the basis of such an interpretation, Weller could hardly avoid coming to the conclusion that the first chapter is "simply nonsense" when taken as a narrative. But what could have been the reasons for such a failure? Aśvaghoṣa's version of the Buddha's life differs from other known versions on several points, leading us to safely presuppose that different versions or fragmentary versions already existed by Aśvaghoṣa's time. It is at least imaginable that he combined them in the introductory chapter, but in this case we have to ask precisely why he would have done it in such a clumsy way. We would not expect a poet and playwright such as Aśvaghoṣa to have serious difficulties with such a task. Moreover, I do not find it very plausible that Aśvaghoṣa would have taken reliefs or sculpture as his models, at least not as his main models. As a poet, Aśvaghoṣa naturally stood in the general literary tradition of Buddhist and non-Buddhist *kāvya* works, and, especially as a playwright, he would be capable of developing a plot even if he were forced to rely simply on sculptures.

As I see it, we can interpret the first chapter without any significant problems arising. The queen, located in Kapilavāstu, longs for the Lumbinī forest. The king and the queen leave the city (stanza 7), which means only that the king accompanied his wife on the journey to Lumbinī. In contrast to other versions of this story, the queen has a spiritual or religious motive for going there: the forest is "free from defilements" and is suitable for meditation (*dhyāna*). In a later stanza (36) we learn that someone who desires liberation would go to the forest, which is depicted as the ideal place for renunciants. From the very beginning, the poet creates the two separate spheres of the capital, the town of the king, and the forest, the place for renunciants. This corresponds to the worldly and the religious aspect of a cakravartin monarch, which already in this very first chapter presents itself as a theme. In stanza 8 we read that the queen awaits (*yang dag mngon gzigs shing*) the time of the birth (*rab tu bltams pa'i dus*) in this forest (*nags der*). The king does not appear on the scene again until stanza 28, which leads me to assume that the king did not remain in the forest (we are not even informed of his arrival there) but had already returned to the city. This would also correspond to the poetic logic of this chapter because the king, representing the urban world of royal duties, will later be concerned about the religious aspirations of his son. Subsequent events take place in the forest (stanzas 9–27) with the exception of the appearance of the well in the palace (stanza 23), which is not a narrative problem at all. As already stated, stanza 27 has the function, in a way, of concluding the occurrences already described: when the teacher was born, the world became peaceful; only Kāmadeva did not rejoice.

A new section begins with stanza 28. After the birth of the child, many marvelous things happened. Thereafter the queen returns to the palace together with her son, and it is not until this point that the king sees his newborn child. The Tibetan expression "after having seen the birth of his son" does not necessarily mean that he observed the actual, indeed remarkable birth, for the child was born "from the side (*pārśvāt*) of the queen" (stanza 9). Aśvaghoṣa does not inform the reader whether or not the king knows of the supernatural aspect of this birth at all. The rest of this chapter up to stanza 86, including the Asita episode, takes place in the royal palace. The above interpretation obviates several minor difficulties with regard to the narrative that could not be referred to in this paper. There remains only one problem: at the end of the canto the king decides to visit the city, and he makes his wife, accompanied by elderly women and her child, go ahead into the city. According to our interpretation the whole royal family is already in the palace, in the city. So does this truly create a problem? In my opinion, "to visit the city" has here the same referential meaning as "to leave the palace." "When a fortunate, auspicious day had been determined, he gladly decided to go into the city" (stanza

85) in order to show his son, who had never left the palace until then, to the citizens for the first time. Finally, the royal family returns to the palace.

Contrary to Weller's harsh verdict, the scene and the plot of the first chapter seem to be coherent. And this is what we would expect of ornate poetry, otherwise it would not exercise its disguised effects (*vyāja*) for the ultimate truth. But the "truth" is not a reasonable plot. It is decisive, for instance, that the queen sets her mind on the pure and impeccable forest, that she longs for the forest region named Lumbinī, which is suitable for meditation, and that her son is born from the side of the queen "for the welfare of the world," "without her suffering either pain or illness" (stanza 9). All these circumstances are described only in order to show that the newborn baby will be the true Buddha who is to be distinguished from a certain type of "historical" Buddha.

In a modern biography of the same title—"The Historical Buddha"—we read about the birth of Siddhattha Gotama (Pali; Skt. Siddhārtha Gautama):

> The *Nidānakathā* tells us, with the ornament of legend, that Māyā, then already forty years old, had set out, shortly before the birth of her child, to the house of her parents in Devadaha in order to give birth to the child with the help of her mother Yasodharā. The journey in a rumbling horse or ox cart on a hot dusty road led to an untimely birth before the arrival in Devadaha. Near the village of Lumbinī, in the open air, sheltered only by the top of a sāla tree (*shorea robusta*), and without competent help, the little Siddhattha saw the light of the day in May of the year 563 B.C.
>
> [...] In addition, a slab probably going back to the second century A.D. has been found in Lumbinī [...]. It represents the upright Māyā, who is gripping a branch of the sāla tree, bearing the child. Evidently, an upright delivery was the custom of the times. Because of the exertions of the childbirth, Māyā was unable to continue her journey to Devadaha. Being exhausted, she was brought back by her small entourage to Kapilavatthu [...]."[24]

24. Schumann 1982: 20. The German original runs: "Wie die Nidānakathā [...] in legendenhafter Ausschmückung erzählt, hatte sich die damals bereits 40jährige Māyā kurz vor der

This is certainly not the "truth" in the sense intended by Aśvaghoṣa. It is not even the historical truth, but evidently a misunderstanding of the nature of the sources.[25]

Geburt ihres Kindes nach Devadaha zum Haus ihrer Eltern aufgemacht, um das Kind dort mit dem Beistand ihrer Mutter Yasodharā zur Welt zu bringen. Die Reise im rumpelnden Pferde- oder Ochsenkarren auf heiß-staubiger Straße führte dazu, daß die Geburt vor Erreichen Devadahas eintrat. Unweit des Dorfes Lumbinī [...], im Freien, beschirmt nur von der Krone eines Sāla-Baumes (shorea robusta) und ohne fachkundige Hilfe für die Gebärende, erblickte der kleine Siddhattha im Mai des Jahres 563 v. Chr. das Licht der Welt.
[...] Auch eine wohl aus dem 2. Jh. n. Chr. stammende Steinplatte wurde in Lumbinī gefunden [...]. Sie zeigt Māyā, die sich, das Kind gebärend, stehend an einem Ast des Sāla-Baumes festhält. Offenbar war Entbindung im Stehen die Sitte der Zeit. Nach den Strapazen der Geburt war Māyā außerstande, ihre Reise nach Devadaha fortzusetzen. Erschöpft wurde sie von ihrem kleinen Gefolge nach Kapilavatthu zurückgebracht [...]."

25. Cf. Snellgrove's (1973: 399) criticism of the methodology at the bottom of such would-be historical reconstructions: "[...] it can easily be shown that the whole process of deliberately abstracting everything of an apparent unhistorical and mythical character, all too often leads away from any semblance of historical truth. This is because the elements that are deliberately abstracted, usually those relating to religious faith and the cult of the Buddha as a higher being, may be older and thus nearer the origins of the religion, than the supposed historical element." Cf. also Schlingloff 1994, esp. pp. 575–77.

Appendix 1

Aśvaghoṣa's *Buddhacarita*, canto 1 (structural analysis). Passages that refer—or could possibly refer—to geographical places or specific localities have been underlined.
Stanzas 1–8b (Tibetan); 8b–24d (Sanskrit); 24d–40c (Tibetan); 40c–89 (Sanskrit)

No maṅgala stanza (= *Saundarananda*).

1: Śuddhodana, king of the Śākyas.
2: Śuddhodana's wife: *Mahāmāyā[26] (*sgyu ma chen mo*).
3: She received the fruit of the womb.
4: Before she conceived, she saw in her sleep a white lord of elephants entering her body.
5: [Description]; she set her mind on the pure (*gtsang*) and impeccable (*nyon mongs med pa*, "free from defilements") forest (*dgon pa*). [Cf. I.36: Someone who desires salvation will go to the forest.]
6: She longed for the <u>forest region named Lumbinī</u>, which is suitable for meditation/contemplation (*bsam gtan*, **dhyāna*), and asked the king if she could go and stay there.
7: The king recognized her righteous/pious and noble dearest wish and <u>left the fortunate city</u>.
8: The queen awaited the time of her delivery <u>in this forest</u> (*nags der*); she lay down on a bed (*śayyā*) overspread with an awning (*vitānopahita*), being welcomed by thousands of women.
9: Birth of a son "from the side (*pārśvāt*) of the queen," "for the welfare of the world," "without her suffering either pain or illness."
10–13: Description and characterization of this birth.
14: Seven steps of the child.
15: He uttered the speech: "I am born for enlightenment" (*bodhāya jāto 'smi*), etc.

26. The reconstructed form Mahāmāyā is unmetrical in the *upajāti* meter; cf. Hahn 1975: 80.

16: Two streams of water poured forth from the sky and fell down on his head.

17: The yakṣa lords surrounded him who was lying on a bed (*śayana*) with a beautiful canopy (*śrīmadvitāna*).

18: Blessings of the "dwellers in heaven" (gods).

19: Great snakes fanned him, etc.

20: Joy of the Śuddhādhivāsa gods.

21: The earth trembled; from the cloudless sky, rain with sandalwood and lotuses showered down upon the earth.

22: Winds blew; the sun shone more brightly; the fire (*agni*) burned.

23: "And in the northeastern part of the palace" (*prāguttare cāvasathapradeśe*) or "In one part of the palace of the northeastern quarter" (*shar dang byang gi mtshams kyi khang pa'i gcig na*, Skt. **prāguttaraikāvasathapradeśe*?) "a well containing white/pure water appeared by itself, at which the amazed household carried out its rites as if it were a holy bathing-place (*tīrtha*)."

24: The forest was filled with hosts of heavenly beings in order to see him (*taddarśanārtham*) [i.e. the child is still in the forest]; blossoms fell from the trees at the wrong time (*dus ma yin par*).

25: Wild creatures consorted with each other and did not hurt each other; diseases were cured.

26: Birds, deers, rivers (silence, calm); the quarters became clear, the bright/auspicious sky was beautiful; drums of the gods resounded.

27: The world became peaceful; only Kāmadeva did not rejoice.

28: On seeing the birth of his son (*sras kyi skye ba mthong gyur nas*) the king felt joy and sorrow, and because of his affection he shed tears. [Locality open to interpretation.]

29: The queen was filled with fear and joy.

30: Old women, seeing only reasons for alarm, prayed to the gods for the sake of the lovely child.

31: The learned brahmans had heard about these omens and said to the king (32–38):

32–38: "Your son will become either an enlightened seer or a cakravartin monarch. He is the best of men."

39: The king asked the brahmans for the reason why he himself was the only king to see such an excellent son.

40–46: Answer of the brahmans.

47: The king was consoled and made happy by the brahmans.

48: The king gave gifts (*pradadau dhanāni*) to the brahmans and wished that his son might become a cakravartin and that he should not got to the forests (*vanāni*) before reaching old age.

49: After having learned of the birth of the bodhisattva by means of the signs and through the power of his austerities, the great seer (*mahārṣi*) Asita came to the residence of the king (*śākyeśvarasyālayam ājagāma*); cf. I.80: He departed, as he had come, through the path of wind (*pavanapathena yathāgataṃ jagāma*).

50: The spiritual teacher (*guru*) of the king brought Asita into the king's palace (*praveśayām āsa narendrasadma*).

51: Asita entered the precincts of the royal women's inner apartments (*pārthivāntaḥpurasaṃnikarṣaṃ* [...] *viveśa*); he remained steadfast, deeming himself to be, as it were, in a forest (*vanasaṃjñayeva*).

52–53: The king properly honored the sitting (*āsanastha*) Asita and then adressed him: "I am your disciple and you should show confidence in me."

54: Invited in this befitting fashion by the king, Asita answered:

55–58: Asita's answer. The reasons and circumstances of Asita's arrival at the palace.

59: After having heard these words, the king became extremely delighted; "he took the prince who was sitting on his nurse's (or: on his mother's; Tib. *yum gyi*, **mātr°* instead of *dhātry°*) flank and showed him to Asita" (*ādāya dhātryaṅkagataṃ kumāraṃ saṃdarśayām āsa tapodhanāya*). Cf. 1.61: *dhātryaṅkasaṃviṣṭam*, Tib. *ma ma'i pang na {b}zhugs*). In this stanza, the king's son resting on the nurse's flank is compared to Agni's son resting on the flank of Devī (or Devīs, taken as a plural for the divine mothers [i.e., the six Kṛttikās] who nursed Skanda [as son of Agni and Gaṅgā]).

60–61: Asita beheld some of the characteristic marks of a superior person on the body of the prince and was moved to tears.

62–66: The king trembled from affection for his son and asked Asita about the reason for his tears and the future of his son.

67–77: Asita's answer. The king's son will become a *dharmarāja*.

78: Having thus learned the reason for Asita's tears (he will not hear the dharma because of his old age), the king rejoiced.

79: The king becomes anxious that his son might follow the noble path (*āryeṇa mārgeṇa*) and could thus annihilate the lineage of his family.

80: (Beginning with this stanza: *puṣpitāgra* meter): Asita departed, as he had come, through the path of the wind (*pavanapathena yathāgataṃ jagāma*).

81: Asita saw the son of his own younger sister and instructed him to listen to the words of the sage (*muni*) and to follow his teaching.

82: The king opened all the prisons in his realm and caused a birth ceremony (*jātakarma*) to be properly (*yathāvat*) performed for him in the manner that befitted his family (*kulasadṛśam*).

83: And when the ten days were fulfilled, he made sacrifices to the gods with muttered prayers, burnt offerings, and auspicious objects for the paramount welfare (or: for the last birth; *śleṣa*: *paramabhavāya*) of his son.

84: The king gave one hundred thousand cows to the brahmans for the prosperity of his son.

85: After having performed/prescribed (*vidhāya*, Tib. *byas nas*) manifold ceremonies, when a fortunate, auspicious day had been determined (*guṇavati niyate śive muhūrte*), the king decided to go into the city (*matim akaron* [...] *purapraveśe*).

86: After having made obeisance to the gods (*devatā*), the queen, together with her son (*tanayavatī*), entered a costly palanquin (*śivikā*).

87: The king made his wife, attended by elderly women (*sthavira-jana*, Tib. *gnas brtan skye mo*) and accompanied (or: protected;

śleṣa: *apatyanātha*) by her child, go ahead into the city (*puram* [...] *purataḥ praveśya*); then the king went (*jagāma*) [into the city] saluted by hosts of citizens (*paurasaṃgha*).

88: After having entered (*vigāhya*, Tib. *rnam khyab mdzad de*) the palace complex (*bhavana*; Tib. *grong khyer*, usually "large town," but may also be used in the sense of "house"), the king gave orders to prepare all the necessary arrangements.

89: The town (*pura*) named after Kapila (Kapilavāstu) rejoiced together with its surrounding territory (*sajanapada*) at the prosperous birth of the prince.

Appendix 2

Aśvaghoṣa's *Buddhacarita*, canto 1 (text)[27]

bu ram shing par mthu mnyam bu ram shing pa'i rgyud[28]
thub dka' shākya rnams la spyod pa rnam dag pa
'phrog byed zla ba lta bur skye dgu rnams la sdug
rgyal po zas gtsang zhes bya'i ming can byung bar gyur | 1.1

dbang po dang mtshungs de yi bdag po ldan ma yin
nus mthu rjes mtshungs gzi brjid lha mo bde sogs dang
padmo can 'dra phun sum tshogs pa sa bzhin brtan
sgyu ma chen mo zhes bya dpe med sgyu 'dra byung | 1.2

mi skyong rgyal po 'di ni de dang thabs cig tu
dga' ba nyer ldan rnam thos sras kyi dpal bzhin rol
de nas yang dag ting 'dzin ldan pa'i rig ma bzhin
sdig bral ma de mngal ni rnam par bzung[29] *bar gyur* | 1.3

mngal dang nye bar ldan pa nyid kyi sngon rol tu[30]
de ni gnyid song glang po'i dbang po dkar po zhig
rang nyid la ni rab tu zhugs sogs mthong gyur la
de yi mtshan ma nyam thag pa yang[31] *thob ma yin* | 1.4

27. Abbreviations: A: Johnston's Ms. A; C: Cone Tengyur; D: Derge Tengyur; G: Ganden Tengyur; Ha.: Hahn 1975; Jo.: Johnston's edition of the Sanskrit text; Jo.n.: note in Jo.; N: Narthang Tengyur; Q: Peking Tengyur; T: Tibetan translation; Vo.: Vogel 1965–66; We.: Weller's edition of the Tibetan text; We.n: note in We.; Ω: all Tengyur editions. < >: enclose editorial additions; { }: enclose editorial deletions. Trivial and exclusive errors of single Tengyur editions are omitted. A glossary (Sanskrit, German, Tibetan) to the first canto of the *Buddhacarita* is found in Steiner 2008.

28. *rgyud*] Ω : *brgyud* We. (ex coni.).

29. *bzung*] GNQ : *gzung* CD.

30. *tu*] GNQ : *du* CD.

31. *yang*] GNQ : *nas* CD.

lha dang rab tu mtshungs pa de yi lha mo de
mngal gyis[32] *rigs kyi dpal ni rab tu 'dren byed cing*
sgyu ma ngal ba dang ni mya ngan sgyu med par
gtsang la nyon mongs med pa'i dgon par blo gros mdzad | 1.5

de ni lum bi zhes bya'i nags mthar gyur pa'i sa
sna tshogs ljon shing sna tshogs shing rta mngon dga' bar
bsam gtan la bzod dben pa'i nags kyi mtha' bzhed ma
'gro ba'i ched dang gnas phyir mi skyong la zhus so | 1.6

de yi chos dang ldan la 'phags pa'i zhe 'dod dag
rnam par shes nas ya mtshan dga' ba yis gang ste
zhi ba'i grong nas sa yi bdag po gshegs gyur te
de yi dga' ba'i rgyu yin rnam par rgyu phyir min | 1.7

dpal dang ldan pa'i nags der rgyal po'i bdag ldan ma
rab tu bltams[33] *pa'i dus ni yang dag mngon gzigs shing*
bla re nye bar phul ba'i gzims mal rab thob ste
mi mo stong phrag dag gis mngon par dga' bar byed | 1.8

[34]<x — ⏑ — — ⏑ ⏑ — ⏑ — — | x — ⏑ — — ⏑ ⏑ — ⏑ >māṇā |
śayyāṃ vitānopahitāṃ prapede nārīsahasrair abhinandyamānā | | 1.8

tataḥ prasannaś[35] ca babhūva puṣyas tasyāś ca devyā vratasaṃskṛtāyāḥ |
pārśvāt suto lokahitāya jajñe nirvedanaṃ caiva nirāmayaṃ ca | | 1.9

ūror yathaurvasya pṛthoś ca hastān māndhātur indrapratimasya mūrdhnaḥ |
kakṣīvataś caiva bhujāṃsadeśāt[36] tathāvidhaṃ tasya babhūva janma | | 1.10

32. *gyis*] CD : *gyi* GNQ.

33. *bltams*] GNQ : *bltam* CD.

34. *dpal dang ldan pa'i nags der rgyal po'i bdag ldan ma* | | *rab tu bltams* (GNQ : *bltam* CD) *pa'i dus ni yang dag mngon gzigs shing* T (*tasmin vane śrīmati rājapatnī prasūtikālaṃ samavekṣamāṇā Jo.).

35. prasannaś] Jo. : *ldan par gyur pa'i tshe* T (*prapannaś Vo.).

36. bhujāṃsadeśāt] Jo. : *lag pa'i cha shas gsang ba nas* T (*bhujāṃśaguhyāt Jo.n.).

krameṇa[37] garbhād abhiniḥsṛtaḥ san babhau cyutaḥ khād iva yonyajātaḥ |
kalpeṣv anckeṣu ca bhāvitātmā yaḥ samprajānan suṣuve na mūḍhaḥ | | 1.11

dīptyā ca dhairyeṇa ca yo rarāja bālo ravir bhūmim ivāvatīrṇaḥ |
tathātidīpto 'pi nirīkṣyamāṇo jahāra cakṣūṃṣi yathā śaśāṅkaḥ | | 1.12

sa hi svagātraprabhayojjvalantyā dīpaprabhāṃ bhāskaravan mumoṣa |
mahārhajāmbūnadacāruvarṇo vidyotayām āsa diśaś ca sarvāḥ | | 1.13

anākulānyubjasamudgatāni[38] niṣpeṣavadvyāyatavikramāṇi[39] |
tathaiva dhīrāṇi[40] padāni sapta saptarṣitārāsadṛśo jagāma | | 1.14

bodhāya jāto 'smi jagaddhitārtham antyā bhavotpattir iyaṃ mameti |
caturdiśaṃ siṃhagatir vilokya vāṇīṃ ca bhavyārthakarīm uvāca | | 1.15

khāt prasrute candramarīciśubhre dve vāridhāre śiśiroṣṇavīrye |
śarīrasaṃsparśasukhāntarāya nipetatur mūrdhani tasya saumye | | 1.16

śrīmadvitāne kanakojjvalāṅge[41] vaiḍūryapāde śayane śayānam |
yadgauravāt kāñcanapadmahastā yakṣādhipāḥ saṃparivārya tasthuḥ | | 1.17

<x — ⏑ — — ⏑ ⏑ — >kasaḥ[42] khe yasya prabhāvāt praṇataiḥ śirobhiḥ |
ādhārayan pāṇḍaram ātapatraṃ bodhāya jepuḥ paramāśiṣaś ca | | 1.18

37. krameṇa] Jo. : *gzugs mdzes te* T (*rūpeṇa Jo.n.).

38. anākulānyubjasamudgatāni] Jo. : *'khrugs pa ma yin yon po'i skyon dag rab bsal zhing* T (≈ *anākulo nyubjamalojjhitāni Jo.n.).

39. niṣpeṣavadvyāyatavikramāṇi] Jo. : niṣpeṣavanty āyatavikramāṇi A : *shin tu brtan pa dang ldan rnam par yangs pa'i 'gros* T (*rnam par yangs pa* ≈ vyāyata).

40. tathaiva dhīrāṇi] Jo. : *de ltar mi g.yo rab tu brtan pa'i* T (≈ *tathācalāny atidhīrāṇi Jo.n.; unmetrical).

41. °āṅge] Jo. : *mtshan* T (*°āṅke We.n.).

42. *mi mngon gyur pa'i lha rnams kyis kyang* T (≈ *adṛśyabhūtāś ca divaukasaḥ Vo.).

mahoragā dharmaviśeṣatarṣād buddheṣv atīteṣu kṛtādhikārāḥ |
yam avyajan bhaktiviśiṣṭanetrā[43] mandārapuṣpaiḥ samavākiraṃś ca | | 1.19

tathāgatotpādaguṇena tuṣṭāḥ śuddhādhivāsāś ca viśuddhasattvāḥ |
devā nanandur vigate ’pi rāge magnasya duḥkhe jagato hitāya | | 1.20

yasya prasūtau girirājakīlā vātāhatā naur iva bhūś cacāla |
sacandanā cotpalapadmagarbhā papāta vṛṣṭir gaganād anabhrāt | | 1.21

vātā vavuḥ sparśasukhā manojñā divyāni vāsāṃsy avapātayantaḥ |
sūryaḥ sa evābhyadhikaṃ cakāśe jajvāla saumyārcir anīrito[44] ’gniḥ | | 1.22

prāguttare cāvasathapradeśe[45] kūpaḥ svayaṃ prādur abhūt [46]sitāmbuḥ |
antaḥpurāṇy āgatavismayāni yasmin kriyās tīrtha iva pracakruḥ | | 1.23

dharmārthibhir bhūtagaṇaiś ca divyais taddarśanārthaṃ vanam āpupūre |
kautūhalenaiva ca pādape< — | x — ⏑ — — ⏑ ⏑ — ⏑ >[47] | | 1.24

chos dang ldan pa’i lha dang ’byung po’i tshogs rnams kyis
de ni lta[48] ba’i don du nags tshal rab gang ste
rmad byung ngo mtshar gyur pa nyid kyi shing las kyang
me tog rnams ni dus ma yin par nges par brul | 1.24

’tshe bar byed pa’i sems can rnams kyang de yi tshe
phan tshun dag tu phyin te gnod pa mi byed la
’tsho ba’i ’jig rten dag na nad gang ji snyed pa
de dag rnams kyang ’bad pa med par de tshe bcom | 1.25

43. bhaktiviśiṣṭanetrā] Jo. : *gus pa’i mig gzir cing* T (≈ *bhaktivikliṣṭanetrā Vo.; unmetrical).

44. anīrito] Jo. : *’dus ma byas pa’i* T (*asaṃskṛto Vo.?).

45. prāguttare cāvasathapradeśe] Jo. : *shar dang byang gi mtshams kyi khang pa’i phyogs gcig na* T (*prāguttaraikāvasathapradeśe Vo. ?).

46. sitā°] Jo. : *bsil ba’i* T (*śītā° Jo.n.; unmetrical).

47. *shing las kyang* | | *me tog rnams ni dus ma yin par nges par brul* T (*pādapebhyaḥ puṣpāṇy akāle vinipātitāni Vo.).

48. *lta*] CD : *blta* GNQ.

mkha' 'gro'i bya ni mtho min sgra sgrogs ri dags kyang
chu klung dag[49] *ni chu yang zhi bar bab gyur la*
phyogs rnams rab snang dge ba'i nam mkha' rab mdzes shing
lha yi rnga rnams mkha' la rab tu grags par gyur | 1.26

rgud[50] *par gyur la mgon ni nye bar thob nas bzhin*
'jig rten dag kyang mchog tu rab zhi thob gyur la
'jig rten rnams kyi thar pa'i bla ma rab bltams tshe
'dod pa'i lha nyid kho na dga' ba med par gyur | 1.27

shin tu ngo mtshar sras kyi skye ba mthong gyur nas
mi bdag brtan pa yin yang rnam par 'gyur nas song
rab dga' skyes pa nyid dang yid mi bde skyes te
brtse ba las ni mchi ma rnam pa gnyis byung ngo | 1.28

mi ma yin pa'i sras po nyid kyi nus pa dang
ma mi rang bzhin kyang ni stobs chung nyid kyi phyir
grang dang dro ba'i chu dag 'dres pa'i chu klung bzhin
lha mo 'jigs pa dang ni dga' bas gang bar 'gyur[51] | 1.29

lhag ma spangs te 'jigs pa nyid ni shes byas nas
yid 'ong 'dod pa'i ched du rtogs pa ma yin pa'i
bud med rgan mo rnams kyis[52] *bde legs gyur byas shing*
gtsang mar byas te lha rnams dag la phyag 'tshal lo | 1.30

de yi mtshan nyid dag kyang shes shing thos gyur nas
spyod dang thos dang tshig la grags thob bram ze rnams
rnam rgyas zhal ni ya mtshan dga' ba yis[53] *gang ste*
dga' dang 'jigs par gyur pa'i mi yi lha la smras | 1.31

49. *dag*] CD : *dang* GNQ.
50. *rgud*] CD : *rgyud* GNQ.
51. *'gyur*] CD : *gyur* GNQ.
52. *kyis* CD] : *kyi* GNQ.
53. *yis*] CD : *yid* GNQ.

mi dag sa la bu ma gtogs pa'i khyad 'phags pa
gzhan gang cung zad 'dod min zhi ba de yi phyir
khyod kyi sgron ma 'di ni rigs kyi sgron ma ste
khyod nyid dga' bar mdzod cig dga' ston da ltar[54] *bgyi* | 1.32

de phyir brtan pa[55] *rnam dpyod med par dgar mdzod dang*
rigs ni nges pa nyid du mchog tu 'phel bar 'gyur
'di ni khyod kyi bu zhes skyes par gyur pa ste
'jig rten sdug bsngal dag gis mngon par bcom pa'i mgon | 1.33

mchog gyur 'di la mchog gyur gser gyi 'od mnga' zhing
sgron ma'i 'od zer dag gi[56] *mtshan rnams gang gyur pas*
de nyid rtogs par gyur pa'i thub par 'gyur ba 'am
yang na mi bdag sa steng[57] *'khor los sgyur bar 'gyur* | 1.34

sa yi bdag po nyid la gal te dga' 'gyur na
stobs dang chos dag gis ni de'i tshe sa steng du[58]
rgyal po kun gyi thog tu 'di ni gnas 'gyur te
skar ma'i 'od rnams la ni nyi ma'i 'od bzhin no | 1.35

de ni gal te thar bzhed nags su gshegs gyur na
mkhyen dang de nyid kyis ni de tshe sa steng du[59]
lugs kun zil gyis mnan nas 'di ni gnas 'gyur te
mtho ba kun la ri rab ri yi rgyal po bzhin | 1.36

ji ltar lcags rnams la ni gser dag mchog yin la
ri rnams la ni ri rab chu bo rnams la mtsho

54. *ltar*] CD : *lta* GNQ.
55. *pa*] Ha. (ex coni.) : *par* Ω.
56. *gi*] We. (ex coni.) : *gis* Ω.
57. *steng*] We. (ex coni.) : *stengs* Ω.
58. *steng du*] GNQ : *stengs su* CD.
59. *steng du*] GNQ : *stengs su* CD.

gza' rnams la ni zla ba dud[60] *byed rnams la nyi*
de ltar khyod kyi sras ni rkang gnyis rnams kyi mchog | 1.37

gang gi spyan dag mi 'dzum mi[61] *gzir rnam par spangs*[62] *pa ste*
brtan zhing shin tu ring la dkar min rdzi ma dang
gzi brjid ldan pa yin yang 'on kyang zhi ba nyid
'di ni kun nas gzigs pa'i spyan mnga' ci la min | 1.38

de nas[63] *gnyis skyes rnams la mi bdag*[64] *gis smra pa*
bdag nyid chen po mi skyong snga mas ma mthong ba
mthong zhes khyad 'di gang yin 'di la rgyu mtshan ci
de nas bram ze rnams kyis[65] *de nyid la smras pa* | 1.39

blo dang thos pa las dang grags pa rnams la ni
mi skyong sngon dang phyi ma nyid ni tshad ma min[66]
dngos po'i lugs la 'dir ni bya ba rgyu yin la
'dir yang bdag gi[67] *dper brjod dag ni mkhyen par mdzod* | 1.40

<x — ⏑ — — ⏑ ⏑ — ⏑ — — | x — ⏑ — >traiva ca no nibodha[68] | | 1.40

yad rājaśāstraṃ bhṛgur aṅgirā vā na cakratur vaṃśakarāv ṛṣī tau |
tayoḥ sutau saumya sasarjatus tat kālena śukraś ca bṛhaspatiś ca | | 1.41

sārasvataś cāpi jagāda naṣṭaṃ vedaṃ punar yaṃ dadṛśur na pūrve |
vyāsas tathainaṃ bahudhā cakāra na yaṃ vasiṣṭhaḥ kṛtavān aśaktiḥ | | 1.42

60. *dud*] GNQ : *gdung* CD.
61. *'dzum mi*] GNQ : *'dzums mig* CD.
62. *spangs*] Ω : read *yangs* (ex. coni.)? Cf. Eimer (2008): 68–69.
63. *nas*] CD : *na* GNQ
64. *bdag*] CD : *dag* GNQ.
65. *kyis*] CD : *kyi* GNQ.
66. *min*] GNQ : *yin* CD.
67. *gi*] CD : *gis* GNQ.
68. *'dir yang bdag gi dper brjod dag ni mkhyen par mdzod* T (*dṛṣṭāntam atraiva ca no nibodha Vo.).

vālmīkir ādau ca sasarja padyaṃ jagrantha yan na cyavano maharṣiḥ |
cikitsitaṃ yac ca cakāra[69] nātriḥ paścāt tad ātreya ṛṣir jagāda | | 1.43

yac ca dvijatvaṃ kuśiko na lebhe tad gādhinaḥ sūnur avāpa rājan[70] |
velāṃ samudre sagaraś ca dadhre nekṣvākavo yāṃ prathamaṃ babandhuḥ
| | 1.44

ācāryakaṃ yogavidhau dvijānām aprāptam anyair janako jagāma |
khyātāni karmāṇi ca yāni śaureḥ śūrādayas teṣv abalā babhūvuḥ | | 1.45

tasmāt pramāṇaṃ na vayo na vaṃśaḥ[71] kaścit kvacic chraiṣṭhyam upaiti loke |
rājñām ṛṣīṇāṃ ca hi tāni tāni kṛtāni putrair akṛtāni pūrvaiḥ | | 1.46

evaṃ nṛpaḥ pratyayitair[72] dvijais tair āśvāsitaś cāpy abhinanditaś ca |
śaṅkām aniṣṭāṃ vijahau manastaḥ praharṣam evādhikam āruroha | | 1.47

prītaś ca tebhyo dvijasattamebhyaḥ satkārapūrvaṃ pradadau dhanāni |
bhūyād ayaṃ bhūmipatir yathokto yāyāj jarām etya vanāni ceti | | 1.48

atho nimittaiś ca tapobalāc ca taj janma janmāntakarasya buddhvā |
śākyeśvarasyālayam ājagāma saddharmatarṣād[73] asito maharṣiḥ | | 1.49

taṃ brahmavidbrahmavidāṃ[74] jvalantaṃ brāhmyā śriyā caiva tapaḥśriyā ca |
rājño gurur gauravasatkriyābhyāṃ praveśayām āsa narendrasadma | | 1.50

sa pārthivāntaḥpurasaṃnikarṣaṃ kumārajanmāgataharṣavegaḥ |
viveśa dhīro vanasaṃjñayeva tapaḥprakarṣāc ca jarāśrayāc ca | | 1.51

69. cakāra] Jo. : *mthong ba* T (*dadarśa Jo.n.).

70. rājan] Jo. : *rgyal po la* T (*rājñe ? Jo.n.).

71. vaṃśaḥ] Jo. (ex coni., *rigs dag* T) : kālaḥ A.

72. nṛpaḥ pratyayitair] Jo. : *yid ches te | | mi skyong* T (*nṛpaḥ pratyayito Vo.).

73. saddharmatarṣād] Jo. : *dam pa'i chos la gus pa'i* T (≈ *saddharmabhakter Jo.n., Vo.).

74. °vidāṃ] A : °vidaṃ Jo. *tshang<s> rig rnams kyi tshang<s> rig de la* T (*taṃ brahmavid-brahmavidaṃ).

tato nṛpas taṃ munim āsanasthaṃ pādyārghyapūrvaṃ pratipūjya samyak |
nimantrayām āsa yathopacāraṃ purā vasiṣṭhaṃ sa ivāntidevaḥ || 1.52
dhanyo 'smy[75] anugrāhyam idaṃ kulaṃ me yan māṃ didṛkṣur bhagavān upetaḥ |
ājñāpyatāṃ kiṃ karavāṇi saumya śiṣyo 'smi viśrambhitum arhasīti || 1.53

evaṃ nṛpeṇopanimantritaḥ san sarveṇa bhāvena munir yathāvat |
savismayotphullaviśāladṛṣṭir gambhīradhīrāṇi vacāṃsy uvāca || 1.54

mahātmani tvayy upapannam etat priyātithau tyāgini dharmakāme |
sattvānvayajñānavayo'nurūpā snigdhā yad evaṃ mayi te matiḥ syāt || 1.55

etac ca tad yena nṛparṣayas te dharmeṇa sūkṣmeṇa[76] dhanāny avāpya |
nityaṃ tyajanto[77] vidhivad babhūvus tapobhir ādhyā vibhavair daridrāḥ || 1.56

prayojanaṃ yat tu mamopayāne tan me śṛṇu prītim upehi ca tvam |
divyā mayādityapathe śrutā vāg bodhāya jātas tanayas taveti || 1.57

śrutvā vacas tac ca manaś ca yuktvā jñātvā nimittaiś ca tato 'smy upetaḥ |
didṛkṣayā śākyakuladhvajasya śakradhvajasyeva samucchritasya || 1.58

ity etad evaṃ vacanaṃ niśamya praharṣasaṃbhrāntagatir narendraḥ |
ādāya [78]dhātryaṅkagataṃ kumāraṃ saṃdarśayām āsa tapodhanāya || 1.59

cakrāṅkapādaṃ sa tato maharṣir jālāvanaddhāṅgulipāṇipādam |
sorṇabhruvaṃ vāraṇavastikośaṃ savismayaṃ rājasutaṃ dadarśa || 1.60

75. dhanyo 'smy] Jo. : *nor ldan* T (*dhanyaṃ hi Vo.). T 1.53a: *bdag gi rigs ni rjes su bzung phyir nor ldan des*; read *gzung ba* (Vo.) instead of *bzung phyir*?

76. sūkṣmeṇa] Jo. : sūkṣmāṇi A. T 1.56b: *phra mo'i chos kyis* (GNQ : *kyi* CD) *nor rnams rab tu thob byas nas* (*dharmeṇa sūkṣmeṇa dhanāny avāpya).

77. tyajanto] Jo. : *mchod sbyin byas* T (*yajanto We.n, Jo.n).

78. dhātry°] Jo. : *yum gyi* T (*mātr° We.n.).

dhātryaṅkasaṃviṣṭam avekṣya cainaṃ devyaṅkasaṃviṣṭam ivāgnisūnum |
babhūva pakṣmāntavicañcitāśrur[79] niśvasya caiva tridivonmukho 'bhūt | | 1.61

dṛṣṭvāsitaṃ tv aśrupariplutākṣaṃ snehāt tanūjasya nṛpaś cakampe |
sagadgadaṃ bāṣpakaṣāyakaṇṭhaḥ papraccha sa prāñjalir ānatāṅgaḥ | | 1.62

alpāntaraṃ yasya vapuḥ surebhyo bahvadbhutaṃ yasya ca janma dīptam |
yasyottamaṃ bhāvinam āttha cārthaṃ taṃ prekṣya kasmāt tava dhīra
bāṣpaḥ | | 1.63

api sthirāyur bhagavan kumāraḥ kaccin na śokāya mama prasūtaḥ |
labdhā kathaṃcit salilāñjalir me na khalv imaṃ pātum upaiti kālaḥ | | 1.64

apy akṣayaṃ me yaśaso nidhānaṃ kaccid dhruvo me kulahastasāraḥ |
api prayāsyāmi sukhaṃ paratra supto 'pi putro[80] 'nimiṣaikacakṣuḥ | | 1.65

kaccin na me jātam aphullam eva kulapravālaṃ pariśoṣabhāgi |
kṣipraṃ vibho brūhi na me 'sti śāntiḥ snehaṃ sute vetsi hi bāndhavānām | | 1.66

ity āgatāvegam aniṣṭabuddhyā buddhvā narendraṃ sa munir babhāṣe |
mā bhūn matis te nṛpa kācid anyā niḥsaṃśayaṃ tad yad avocam asmi | | 1.67

nāsyānyathātvaṃ prati vikriyā me svāṃ vañcanāṃ tu prati viklavo 'smi |
kālo hi me yātum ayaṃ ca jāto jātikṣayasyāsulabhasya boddhā | | 1.68

vihāya rājyaṃ viṣayeṣv anāsthas tīvraiḥ prayatnair adhigamya tattvam |
jagaty ayaṃ mohatamo nihantuṃ[81] jvaliṣyati jñānamayo hi sūryaḥ | | 1.69

duḥkhārṇavād vyādhivikīrṇaphenāj jarātaraṅgān maraṇogravegāt |
uttārayiṣyaty ayam uhyamānam ārtaṃ jagaj jñānamahāplavena | | 1.70

79. pakṣmāntavicañcitāśrur] Jo. : *rdzi ma'i mtha' ru mchi ma rnam{s}* T (*pakṣmāntavibhāvitāśrur Vo.)

80. putro] A : putre Jo. (ex coni.). T 1.65d: *bu ni phye ba'i mig gcig yod* (putro 'nimiṣaikacakṣuḥ).

81. nihantuṃ] Jo. : *rnam 'joms phyir* T (*vihantuṃ Jo.n.).

prajñāmbuvegāṃ sthiraśīlavaprāṃ samādhiśītāṃ vratacakravākām |
asyottamāṃ dharmanadīṃ pravṛttāṃ tṛṣṇārditaḥ pāsyati jīvalokaḥ || 1.71

duḥkhārditebhyo viṣayāvṛtebhyaḥ saṃsārakāntārapathasthitebhyaḥ[82] |
ākhyāsyati hy eṣa vimokṣamārgaṃ mārgapranaṣṭebhya ivādhvagebhyaḥ || 1.72

vidahyamānāya janāya loke rāgāgnināyaṃ viṣayendhanena |
prahlādam ādhāsyati dharmavṛṣṭyā vṛṣṭyā mahāmegha ivātapānte || 1.73

[83]tṛṣṇārgalaṃ mohatamaḥkapāṭaṃ dvāraṃ prajānām apayānahetoḥ |
vipāṭayiṣyaty[84] ayam uttamena saddharmatāḍena durāsadena || 1.74

svair mohapāśaiḥ[85] pariveṣṭitasya duḥkhābhibhūtasya nirāśrayasya |
lokasya saṃbudhya ca dharmarājaḥ kariṣyate bandhanamoksam eṣaḥ || 1.75

tan mā kṛthāḥ śokam imaṃ prati tvam asmin sa śocyo 'sti manuṣyaloke |
mohena vā kāmasukhair madād vā yo naiṣṭhikaṃ śroṣyati nāsya dharmam
|| 1.76

bhraṣṭasya tasmāc ca guṇād ato[86] me dhyānāni labdhvāpy akṛtārthataiva |
dharmasya tasyāśravaṇād ahaṃ hi manye vipattiṃ tridive 'pi vāsam || 1.77

iti śrutārthaḥ sasuhṛt sadāras tyaktvā viṣādaṃ mumude narendraḥ |
evaṃvidho 'yaṃ tanayo mameti mene sa hi svām api sāramattām[87] || 1.78

82. °patha°] Jo. : *'jigs par* T (*°bhaya° We.n.).

83. tṛṣṇārgalaṃ moha°] Jo. : *sred pa'i sgo gtan ma rig* T (*tṛṣṇārgalāvidyā° Jo.n.; unmetrical).

84. vipāṭayiṣyaty] Jo. : vighāṭayiṣyati add. marg. A. : *rnam par 'byed par 'gyur* T (vipāṭayiṣyaty/vighāṭayiṣyaty).

85. svair mohapāśaiḥ] Jo. : *rang gi las kyi zhags pa rnams kyis* (GNQ : *kyi* CD) T (*svakarmapāśaiḥ Jo.n.).

86. guṇād ato] Jo. : *yon tan rgya mtsho* T (*guṇārṇavād We.n., guṇārṇavān Vo.).

87. sāramattām] A : sāravattām Jo. (ex coni. Böhtlingk).

āryeṇa[88] mārgeṇa tu yāsyatīti cintāvidheyaṃ hṛdayaṃ cakāra |
na khalv asau na priyadharmapakṣaḥ saṃtānanāśāt tu bhayaṃ dadarśa | | 1.79

atha munir asito nivedya tattvaṃ sutaniyataṃ sutaviklavāya rājñe |
sabahumatam udīkṣyamāṇarūpaḥ pavanapathena yathāgataṃ jagāma | | 1.80

kṛtamitir anujāsutaṃ ca dṛṣṭvā munivacanaśravaṇe ca tanmatau ca |
bahuvidham anukampayā sa sādhuḥ priyasutavad viniyojayāṃ cakāra | | 1.81

narapatir api putrajanmatuṣṭo viṣayagatāni vimucya bandhanāni |
kulasadṛśam acīkarad yathāvat priyatanayas tanayasya jātakarma | | 1.82

daśasu pariṇateṣv ahaḥsu caiva prayatamanāḥ parayā mudā parītaḥ |
akuruta japahomamaṅgalādyāḥ paramabhavāya sutasya devatejyāḥ | | 1.83

api ca śatasahasrapūrṇasaṃkhyāḥ sthirabalavattanayāḥ sahemaśṛṅgīḥ |
anupagatajarāḥ payasvinīr gāḥ svayam adadāt sutavṛddhaye dvijebhyaḥ | | 1.84

bahuvidhaviṣayās tato yatātmā svahṛdayatoṣakarīḥ kriyā vidhāya |
guṇavati niyate śive muhūrte matim akaron muditaḥ purapraveśe | | 1.85

dviradaradamayīm atho mahārhāṃ sitasitapuṣpabhṛtāṃ maṇipradīpām |
abhajata śivikāṃ śivāya devī tanayavatī praṇipatya devatābhyaḥ | | 1.86

puram atha purataḥ praveśya patnīṃ sthavirajanānugatām apatyanāthām |
nṛpatir api jagāma paurasaṃghair divam amarair maghavān ivārcyamānaḥ
| | 1.87

bhavanam atha vigāhya śākyarājo bhava iva ṣaṇmukhajanmanā pratītaḥ |
idam idam iti harṣapūrṇavaktro bahuvidhapuṣṭiyaśaskaraṃ vyadhatta | | 1.88

88. āryeṇa] A : ārṣeṇa Jo. (ex coni.). T: *'phags pa'i* (āryeṇa).

iti narapatiputrajanmavṛddhyā sajanapadaṃ kapilāhvayaṃ puraṃ tat |
dhanadapuram ivāpsaro'vakīrṇaṃ muditam abhūn nalakūbaraprasūtau || 1.89

iti buddhacarite mahākāvye bhagavatprasūtir nāma prathamaḥ sargaḥ

Bibliography

Apte, Vaman Shivram 1920. *The Student's English-Sanskrit Dictionary*. 3rd rev. and enlarged ed. Poona. (Reprint: Delhi: Motilal Banarsidass, 1983.)

Covill, Linda 2007. *Handsome Nanda by Aśvaghoṣa*. Clay Sanskrit Library. New York: New York University Press and JJC Foundation.

Eimer, Helmut 2008. "Überlegungen zur Überlieferungsgeschichte des tibetischen *Buddhacarita*." In *Bauddhasāhityastabakāvalī: Essays and Studies on Buddhist Sanskrit Literature*, dedicated to Claus Vogel by Colleagues, Students, and Friends, ed. by Dragomir Dimitrov, Michael Hahn, and Roland Steiner, pp. 65–77. Indica et Tibetica 36. Marburg: Indica et Tibetica.

Hahn, Michael 1975. "Buddhacarita I, 1–7 und 25–40." *Indo-Iranian Journal* 17: 77–96.

Hanisch, Albrecht 2005. *Āryaśūras Jātakamālā. Philologische Untersuchungen zu den Legenden 1 bis 15*. Teil 1. Einleitung, Textausgabe, Anhänge, Register. Indica et Tibetica 43/1. Marburg: Indica et Tibetica.

Hiltebeitel, Alf 2006. "Aśvaghoṣa's *Buddhacarita*: The First Known Close and Critical Reading of the Brahmanical Sanskrit Epics." *Journal of Indian Philosophy* 34: 229–86.

Jackson, David P. 1997. "On the Date of the Tibetan Translation of Aśvaghoṣa's *Buddhacarita*." In *Aspects of Buddhism: Proceedings of the International Seminar on Buddhist Studies. Liw, 25 June 1994*, ed. by Agata Bareja-Starzyńska and Marek Mejor, pp. 41–62. Warszawa: Oriental Institute Warsaw University.

Johnston, E. H. 1935. *The Buddhacarita: Or, Acts of the Buddha*. Pt. I—Sanskrit Text. Punjab University Oriental Publications 31. Calcutta: Baptist Mission Press.

——— 1936: *The Buddhacarita: Or, Acts of the Buddha*. Pt. II: Cantos i to xiv trans. from the original Sanskrit supplemented by the Tibetan version, together with an introduction and notes. Punjab University Oriental Publications 32. Calcutta: Baptist Mission Press.

Mann, Golo 1971. *Wallenstein: Sein Leben erzählt*. Frankfurt am Main: S. Fischer, ^{1}1971, ^{8}2004.

Parab, Kâśinâth Pâṇḍurang 1897. *The Harshacarita of Bâṇabhaṭṭa: With The Commentary (Saṅketa) of Śankara*. 2nd rev. ed. Bombay: Nirṇayasāgara Press.

Śarmā, Batuk Nāth, and Baldeva Upādhyāya 1981. *Kāvyālaṅkāra of Bhāmaha*. 2nd ed. The Kashi Sanskrit Series 61. Varanasi: Chaukhambha Sanskrit Sansthan.

Schlingloff, Dieter 1994. "Die wunderbare Überquerung der Gaṅgā. Zur Text- und Bildtradition einer buddhistischen Legende." In *Festschrift Klaus Bruhn zur Vollendung des 65. Lebensjahres*, ed. by Nalini Balbir and Joachim K. Bautze, pp. 571–84. Reinbeck: Dr. Inge Wezler.

Schumann, Hans Wolfgang 1982. *Der historische Buddha*. Köln: Eugen Diederichs.

Snellgrove, David L. 1973. "Śākyamuni's Final *Nirvāṇa*." *Bulletin of the School of Oriental and African Studies* 36: 399–411.

Steiner, Roland 2008. "Glossar (Sanskrit-Deutsch-Tibetisch) zum ersten Gesang von Aśvaghoṣas *Buddhacarita*." In *Bauddhasāhityastabakāvalī: Essays and Studies on Buddhist Sanskrit Literature*, dedicated to Claus Vogel by Colleagues, Students, and Friends, ed. by Dragomir Dimitrov, Michael Hahn, and Roland Steiner, pp. 291–338. Indica et Tibetica 36. Marburg: Indica et Tibetica.

Vetter, Tilmann 2000. "Die Gestalt des Buddha: In buddhistischer Überlieferung und im Lichte der Geschichtsforschung." In *Der Buddhismus als Anfrage an christliche Theologie und Philosophie. Fünfte Religionstheologische Akademie St. Gabriel. Referate—Anfragen—Diskussionen*, ed. by Andreas Bsteh, pp. 11–19. Studien zur Religionstheologie 5. Mödling: St. Gabriel.

Vogel, Claus 1965–66. "On the First Canto of Aśvaghoṣa's *Buddhacarita*." *Indo-Iranian Journal* 9: 266–90.

Weller, Friedrich 1926. *Das Leben des Buddha von Aśvaghoṣa: Tibetisch und Deutsch*. Veröffentlichungen des Forschungsinstituts fur Vergleichende Religionsgeschichte an der Universität Leipzig II.3. Leipzig: Eduard Pfeiffer.

——— 1939. "Schauplatz und Handlung im Buddhacarita." *Zeitschrift der Deutschen Morgenländischen Gesellschaft* 93: 306–38.

——— 1953. *Zwei zentralasiatische Fragmente des Buddhacarita*. Abhandlungen der sächsischen Akademie der Wissenschaften zu Leipzig. Philologisch-historische Klasse 46.4. Berlin: Akademie Verlag.

——— 1980. *Untersuchung über die textgeschichtliche Entwicklung des tibetischen Buddhacarita*. Abhandlungen der sächsischen Akademie der Wissenschaften zu Leipzig. Philologisch-historische Klasse 69.3. Berlin: Akademie Verlag.

Handsome Is as Handsome Does

Aśvaghoṣa's Story of the Buddha's Younger Brother

Linda Covill

THE *Saundarananda* is a Sanskrit poem written in eighteen cantos by the Buddhist monk and poet Aśvaghoṣa.[1] We are fortunate to have the complete Sanskrit text, discovered in 1908 by H. Shāstrī, and critically edited by E. H. Johnston in 1928. The Sanskrit text was translated by Johnston as *Nanda the Fair* in 1932 and by myself as *Handsome Nanda* in 2007. The protagonist and eponymous hero of the *Saundarananda* is Nanda, the handsome half-brother of the Buddha, while its topic is Nanda's evolution from besotted young husband to enlightened sage. The *Saundarananda* is beautiful in form and engrossing in content; there can be little doubt that it succeeds both as a work of poetry and as a Buddhist spiritual biography.

The purpose of this chapter is to provide an overview of the *Saundarananda* which will give a flavor of the many joys of this poem—Aśvaghoṣa's skilled poetic and narrative technique, the psychological accuracy of his portrayal of Nanda's character, his clever intertwining of Buddhist and poetic (*kāvya*)[2]

1. The poem's colophon identifies the author as Aśvaghoṣa, a teacher, great poet, and eloquent speaker. It also tells us his mother's name and that he lived in Sāketa, now Ayodhya in the modern Indian state of Uttar Pradesh. Informed guesses based on paleography, linguistic style, and apocryphal biographical data linking Aśvaghoṣa to the Kuṣāṇa king Kaniṣka place him in the early second century C.E.

2. *Kāvya*: a refined and rather fastidious type of literary Sanskrit, marked by such features as varied poetic meters, ornate descriptive passages, numerous figurative expressions, euphonic blend of sound, and the purposeful evocation of aesthetic delight.

elements, and his sensitive handling of the central theme of conversion—with the hope that the interested reader will be persuaded to seek closer acquaintance with the Buddha's handsome brother.

The poem's opening canto (*Description of Kapilavāstu*, *kapilavāstu-varṇana*) at first glance appears to have little to do with its later preoccupations. We start far back in the mythological past with a description of the sage Kapila and his ashram. Aśvaghoṣa is at pains to establish an appropriate spiritual ancestry for his heroes, providing a vision of the renunciant, ascetic strain of Brahmanism as a backdrop for the story that he is about to unfold. The mood of religious observance and piety changes when certain Ikṣvāku princes arrive and adopt Kapila as their guru. They possess qualities that indicate their authority—they are great-armed and lion-chested, of great splendor and renown.

Kapila wishes to secure prosperity for the princes, so at one point he flies through the air, sprinkling water on the ground from a pitcher while the princes follow in their chariots. The grooves made by their chariot wheels are to be the boundaries of a new city. After Kapila's death, the princes go astray, indulging in hunting and wild behavior. But in time the princes discover treasure and build an attractive town full of fine buildings, pleasant gardens, and virtuous citizens as per the usual *kāvya* criteria for a city. Since the Buddha's actions in the following story may seem heavy-handed, it is important that from the outset a figure of spiritual authority is seen to have his disciples' welfare as his primary consideration.

It would be a mistake to dismiss this canto as an accretion of irrelevant Buddhist mythology and *kāvya* convention. The account serves a number of purposes. Firstly, it establishes the spiritual credentials of the Buddha's and Nanda's heritage. The zealous asceticism of the brahman Kapila and the warrior ethos of the kṣatriya princes combine in the making of the Śākyan race. Secondly, the guru-disciple relationship between Kapila and the Ikṣvāku princes to some extent foreshadows the story of the Buddha and Nanda. Both the Buddha and Kapila are great sages seeking to guide and tame the behavior of their charges. When Kapila dies and his controlling influence is removed, the princes revert to type, like tiger cubs, and it is emphasized that this is no good thing. When the brothers finally do what Kapila has told them to do, that is, build a city, they grow in wealth and virtue. Furthermore, the catchy anecdote of the sage marking out the city limits concerns boundary setting.

The sage orders the brothers not to overstep (*anatikramya*, 1.29) the boundary. Later, Nanda too will attempt to live by the disciplinary rules without transgressing them, and he too will discover that when he eventually follows his teacher's advice he will make great progress. Canto 1 therefore provides a fitting introduction to the poem's major theme of transformation, or conversion—the princes are transformed into wise rulers, while nature, within the demarcated area at least, is transformed into a teeming city with fine mansions, highways, and public gardens. The remarkably concrete vision of a city springing up in the space laid out by the sage is a vivid demonstration that flourishing best occurs within the prescribed limits set by a wise and authoritative guide.

In a manner that is typical of *kāvya's* introductory scenes, the wide-angle view of the city shifts in canto 2 (*Description of the King*, *rāja-varṇana*) to a narrower focus on the figure of King Śuddhodana, who has succeeded to the throne of Kapilavāstu. Though the king epitomizes kṣatriya attributes, his spiritual leanings are much in evidence, as is fitting for the father of the future Buddha. In addition to orthodox behavior such as offering sacrifices and drinking *soma*, he also offers a foretaste of dharma, a word that is freely used in this canto.

This portrayal of kingship, an essential ingredient of *kāvya*, is replaced by the traditional Buddhist material of the bodhisattva's descent from the heavens, Queen Māyā's dream of a white elephant, and the birth of the bodhisattva (here named Sarvārthasiddha, as in the *Mahāvastu*). Nanda is first mentioned toward the end of canto 2:

> As fire-sticks give rise to fire, so the younger queen too gave birth to a son named Nanda, a bringer of constant joy to his family. (2.57)

Although it is commonplace to liken the baby resulting from sexual activity to the fire resulting from twirling the fire-sticks, it is noteworthy that Nanda is associated with fire in his very first appearance in the poem. Fire is a prominent Buddhist metaphor for desire, and this verse is an early indication that desire will prove to be Nanda's chief hindrance on his spiritual journey. We learn too that he is handsome, like springtime, like the rising of the new moon, like the god of love embodied. Differences in temperament between Nanda and his half-brother become evident as the boys grow up; Sarvārthasiddha remains dispassionate while Nanda idles away his time in pleasures.

The Buddha's attainment of enlightenment is the initial subject of canto 3 (*Description of the Tathāgata, tathāgata-varṇana*), after which he returns to his home city and preaches to the townsfolk. The rest of the canto describes the effects of the Buddha's presence on the city of Kapilavāstu; the king and many others achieve stream-entry, many leave their homes, and those who remain at home follow the precepts; and the entire city is free from disease and calamity. Doubtless the purpose of this section is to contextualize Nanda's conduct in the next canto, for without the foreknowledge that every other citizen of Kapilavāstu has put the Buddha's teaching into practice, we would not find Nanda's absorption in his beautiful wife out of the ordinary. Verse 38 sounds an ironic note, since it declares that no one desires even a happy rebirth, and that everyone understands the danger of continued existence. Everyone, that is, except Nanda, who by canto 10 is planning a rebirth among the apsarases, the exquisite nymphs of heaven.

The first half of canto 4 (*His Wife's Request, bhāryā-yācitaka*) is justly renowned for its charming depiction of the loveplay of Nanda and his wife Sundarī, with the couple's close sexual relationship being evident throughout, for instance by frequent mention of parts of the body—breasts, lips, hands, moustache, cheeks, feet, and so on. Aśvaghoṣa chooses just one small incident to encapsulate the relationship of the pair, but presents it powerfully enough to carry the weight of Nanda's yearning for the next few cantos. The poet has Nanda hold a mirror for Sundarī, while she playfully draws his moustache on her own face. When Nanda blows on the mirror to cloud her reflection, she feigns anger and smears some makeup on his face. Nanda pretends remorse and throws himself at her feet, and she raises him up, laughing. Nanda then continues to hold the mirror while she completes her makeup. The short but effective mirror episode is Aśvaghoṣa's invention, appearing in no other version of the Nanda legend. Though brief, it reveals that Nanda is entirely besotted with his wife. These verses contain a number of features typical of the *kāvya* portrayal of a happy love affair, including the standard comparison of the lady's eyes to bees and the lovers playfully feigning various emotions.

A serious note is struck when the Buddha appears at Nanda's house for alms but goes away again unnoticed. When Nanda finds out about this, he asks Sundarī's permission to go and pay his respects to the Buddha. She reluctantly agrees, but makes him promise to come back before her cosmetics are dry. Sundarī is trading on her sexuality and their recent intimacy in making this request, for she has just applied the cosmetics in his presence. The remainder of canto 4 is a masterful depiction of Nanda's painful hesitation as he is torn between his duty of respect to the Buddha and his longing to stay with his wife. The canto ends when Nanda finally turns from his wife and catches sight of the Buddha being honored by the crowd, a clear indication of his eventual spiritual destination.

At this relatively early stage, Aśvaghoṣa has already begun to prepare for the poem's turning point and key narrative event, the visit to heaven in canto 10. From a Buddhist perspective, any new existence is transient, unsatisfactory, and fraught with danger. Hence a life spent consorting with the apsarases in heaven is not essentially preferable to a life spent with Sundarī in Kapilavāstu. Aśvaghoṣa makes this point several times, in this case by taking care to confer semi-divine status on Nanda and Sundarī. Thus she is like a divinity walking in the garden of delight, while Nanda's house is likened to a celestial palace.

Canto 5 (*The Ordination of Nanda*, *nanda-pravrājana*) is a powerful and potentially controversial depiction of Nanda's ordination. The Buddha is shown separating Nanda from the crowd and leading him down a quiet side-road, rejecting his invitation to take food at his house, giving Nanda his bowl to hold, and blocking Nanda's way when Nanda tries to sneak off. The Buddha leads Nanda to the monastery and tells Ānanda to ordain him. Throughout these events, Nanda makes his disinclination clear, to the point of announcing "I will not go forth" (*na pravrajiṣyāmy aham ity uvāca*, 5.35). Yet he finally agrees to do as the Buddha wishes, weeping as his hair is shaved.

At no point does Aśvaghoṣa soft pedal the Buddha's intervention in the life of a reasonably happy person. Sundarī could have been portrayed as flighty or shrewish, but instead she is charming and lovable. The manner in which Nanda was induced to the monastery could have been glossed over; instead we are exposed to a blow-by-blow account of the event. The point of the story is that Buddhist happiness is better and happier than even the happiest of lay lives. Sundarī's delectableness and Nanda's contentment are intended to strengthen rather than to undermine this position. In fact, those things that Nanda believes are making him happy are preventing his true happiness. Thus the Buddha's actions are justified on the grounds that Nanda's life really can be improved; furthermore, Aśvaghoṣa makes it clear that the Buddha goes out of his way to do a favor for Nanda. His action is described as a favor (*anugraha*, 5.11, 5.48), beneficial (*hita*, 5.46, 5.47, 5.48, 5.50), and an effort (*yatna*, 5.18). However, Nanda does not yet appreciate the Buddha's actions on his behalf, and is pictured at the end of the canto in his faded ochre garment. He has lost his radiance, and is likened to the waning moon at dawn.

Of the *Saundarananda*'s eighteen cantos, canto 6 (*The Wife's Lament*, *bhāryā-vilāpa*) comes closest to a developed *kāvya* style. Its subject is one of *kāvya*'s favorites, separated love (*vipralambha-śṛṅgāra*), since the entire canto is devoted to depicting the calamitous effect of Nanda's departure on his wife. Sundarī's distress is sympathetically and delicately drawn in a series of miniature portraits. First she leans out expectantly from the palace roof, her pearls and earrings dangling down, then she collapses on a couch with her slippers half falling off. After hearing the rumor that Nanda has been ordained, her distress reaches a crescendo; she casts off her ornaments, and tears at her face and clothes. The canto is embellished with a number of lovely similes, and the comparison of Sundarī's pale face to the pale moon at the onset of winter echoes the similar comparison made of Nanda in the previous canto, and is a poignant reminder of the bond between the two.

Sundarī's despair is of course antithetical to the Buddhist tranquility and bliss advocated by Aśvaghoṣa. She sinks down and then leaps up and runs across the palace roof, agitated movements that reveal her distraction along with her restless eyes and her haphazard thinking as she berates the absent Nanda. The images of Sundarī weeping hot tears and assailed by the fire of grief and longing, while recalling the *kāvya* notion of love as a fire, draw more heavily on the Buddhist metaphor of suffering as a fire. Their purpose, and that of the whole canto, is to depict the suffering engendered by desire.

Having heard of Sundarī's reaction to her husband's sudden departure in canto 6, canto 7 (*Nanda's Lament*, *nanda-vilāpa*) gives us Nanda's response. He is found wandering around a pleasant grove, but unlike a monk that he sees meditating beside a waterfall, Nanda fails to apply himself. Instead, the reader is informed straightaway, in a simple phrase embellished with *yamaka* (chime), that Nanda is not happy (*na nananda nandaḥ*, 7.1). In a sequence of lovely verses the beauty of the trees, flowers, and creatures around him serve only to stimulate Nanda's memories of Sundarī. Whatever Nanda sees, however innocent and natural, he subverts to an image of his wife. In the solipsistic manner common to lovers, he interprets his environment as a reflection of his own state of mind. He sees a cuckoo and imagines it as Sundarī's hair. He notices the white *priyaṅgu* blossom and remembers her pale face. A creeper wound round a mango tree reminds him of her embraces. The forest fails to calm him since it irritates his overwrought nerves and oversensitized mind. The appearance of several stock attributes used in *kāvya* to signify an amorous situation—spring, bees buzzing in mango trees, the peacocks calling—indicate that Nanda remains firmly embedded in his relationship with Sundarī, despite his physical separation from her.

Though Nanda's distress is the focal point of canto 7, there is a hint that his situation is not entirely hopeless. His journey of conversion inches along with his realization that the practice of renunciation is very difficult indeed. This first glimmer of insight deepens when he begins to see that he is in bondage, caught in the snare of love. Throughout canto 7 Aśvaghoṣa demonstrates great skill in tracing Nanda's unhappiness and sexual frustration, while simultaneously hinting at tiny gains in his self-knowledge.

Just as Nanda's self-pitying ruminations reach a climax, an unnamed monk approaches him at the beginning of canto 8 (*The Attack on Women*, *strīvighāta*) and asks why he has been weeping. Nanda agrees to confide in him, and they retire to a quiet part of the wood and sit down in a bower of creepers, which is said to embrace them with its tender young shoots—a reflection of Nanda's continuing preoccupation with his wife, as well as a continuation of the eroticization of nature found in canto 7. Nanda bluntly states that he cannot be happy without his lover. The unnamed monk responds with a set of verses likening Nanda to an animal, culminating in the splendidly anti-romantic, anti-*kāvya* vision of Nanda wishing to return to his wife as a greedy dog wanting to eat its own vomit (8.21). The monk then launches into a misogynistic diatribe that identifies the home as bondage and women as dangerous, ignoble, and duplicitous. Women, he says, are like poisonous creepers, like hordes of crocodiles in a river, like cows wandering from field to field. Furthermore, their bodies are just as repulsive as their characters.

Before we take this opinion as representative of Aśvaghoṣa's attitude toward women, we should remember his sympathetic treatment of Sundarī. Furthermore, we can note that this vitriol is put into the mouth of an unidentified *śramaṇa*, and is carefully distanced from the Buddha and any of his named disciples.[3] In fact, the invective of this canto is directed at Nanda's specific fixation with the physical and emotional pleasure to be found in a sexual relationship.

In canto 9 (*The Denunciation of Infatuation, madāpavāda*) the unnamed *śramaṇa* renews his efforts to stiffen Nanda's resolve, this time by stressing the impermanence of Nanda's strength, beauty, and youth. The word *bala* (which indicates general vitality and robustness, and not just sheer muscle power) appears twenty-seven times in this canto, a statistic that indicates how serious is Nanda's assumption of enduring physical well-being. After the denunciation of physical strength, good looks and youth are similarly treated. The relentlessness of the aging process is vividly depicted, with one particularly fine simile envisaging old age as a sugar mill squeezing the juice out of a sugarcane stalk. Canto 9's emphasis on the frailness of the body and the perniciousness of the senses is well placed, occurring just before Nanda reaches the apotheosis of desire in the following canto.

Canto 10 (*A Lesson in Heaven, svarga-nidarśana*) presents the crux of the traditional Nanda legend, one of the few constant narrative elements through the many versions of the story, and the center of gravity of the poem. This is Nanda's visit to heaven and his sighting of the nymphs, an occasion engineered by the Buddha in order to jolt Nanda out of his obsession with Sundarī. The canto opens with the Buddha taking Nanda's hand and flying upward, a physical motion that parallels his desire to give Nanda spiritual uplift. It also reminds us of Kapila flying up into the air in order to benefit the princes in canto 1.

Their first stop is a Himalayan mountain where they notice a female monkey with a damaged eye and its face red with lac—a reminder of Sundarī and her makeup. The Buddha asks Nanda whether he finds Sundarī or the monkey more attractive. Nanda replies that there is no comparison between the two. The Buddha and Nanda now depart for Indra's realm, which, in keeping with the ancient Indian conception of heaven, is a jeweled and artificial paradise. Now the ravishing apsarases appear, pulling the leaves off lotuses and with their pearl necklaces disordered by their breasts like true *kāvya* pinups. They throw Nanda sidelong glances and generally imply their sexual

3. A harder attitude is evident in the Chinese *Abhiniṣkramaṇa Sūtra*, in which the Buddha himself delivers a denunciation of women.

availability. The seductive apsarases have a catastrophic effect on the hapless Nanda, worked out in images of fire and heat. When the Buddha again asks Nanda's preference, Nanda is quick to declare his wife's inferiority. Now the Buddha cuts a deal with Nanda: Nanda can buy the apsarases as his future sexual playmates if he pays in advance by persevering with the monastic discipline. The Buddha himself will act as Nanda's guarantor in this matter. Nanda agrees and the two return to earth.

Canto 11 (*The Condemnation of Heaven, svargāpavāda*) finds Nanda keeping to his promise and forcing himself to submit to a life of renunciation, though without any real enthusiasm. Tellingly, his continuing obsession with the apsarases has made the normally handsome Nanda physically ugly (*vairūpyam*, 11.6). Ānanda approaches him at this point, and with a great deal of delicacy questions Nanda's true motivation. Nanda says nothing, but his expression indicates that he is indeed, as Ānanda has suggested, a hireling for the apsarases. Ānanda is moved to both compassion and mirth, and the rest of the canto is taken up with his efforts to prove to Nanda that a heavenly rebirth is ultimately as unsatisfactory as any other, since it is temporary, and would be followed by a far less pleasant rebirth.

Following Ānanda's denunciation of heaven, Nanda experiences a crisis in canto 12 (*Understanding, pratyavamarśa*) during which he reorients himself to a new goal. The word chosen to indicate his crisis is *saṃvega*, a term that suggests an emotional shock stimulated by a painful experience.[4] This critical moment in Nanda's career is condensed into a powerful simile of a great chariot turning round. Nanda approaches the Buddha to tell him that he no longer desires the apsarases and therefore withdraws from the contract, and he asks the Buddha to teach him. The Buddha responds with a eulogy of faith (*śraddhā*) as a springboard to further development.

In canto 13 (*The Conquest of the Senses through Discipline, śīlendriya-jaya*), after a brief aside in which Aśvaghoṣa once again stresses that even the Buddha's rougher methods are entirely motivated by compassion, the Buddha embarks on a long speech of instruction to Nanda which takes up the rest of this canto and the three following cantos, a total of 266 verses. The Buddha's

4. For example, in the Pali *Aṅguttara Nikāya* a dissolute monk experiences *saṃvega* when the Buddha admonishes him (AN 1.280). Coomaraswamy 1977 explores how *saṃvega* is elicited and how it precipitates spiritual growth.

first topic is moral self-restraint, which he expounds using an underlying metaphor of cleanliness. Nanda is "to clean up his act" by keeping a close guard on his conduct and by controlling the operation of his senses.

The Buddha's guidance to Nanda continues in canto 14 (*The First Steps, ādi-prasthāna*), often in the form of lively similes that counterbalance the canto's tendency to preachiness. However, the generally didactic character of the canto is marked by frequent imperatives, future passive participles, and √*arh* with an infinitive as Nanda is robustly told what to do. The Buddha's subject matter is fourfold—eating, sleeping, mindfulness, and solitude. With regard to eating, moderation is key, and the urge to either over or under eat should be resisted. The Buddha's advice on sleep is more austere; sleep is imagined as an enemy who must be combated. The endorsement of wakefulness shades into an advocacy for mindfulness (*smṛti*). Aśvaghoṣa uses military language to explain that mindfulness, functioning as armor or a guard, should remain protectively focused on the body (14.38–39). As the canto draws to a close its recommendations become progressively more ascetic, with the last verse asserting that the state of bliss available to the renunciant who likes to live alone is superior to the sensual delights of Indra's heaven.

In canto 15 (*Leaving Notions Behind, vitarka-prahāna*) the Buddha introduces Nanda to meditation. The bulk of the canto is devoted to the perils that obstruct the meditator's progress, all of which are thoughts (*vitarka*) of varying degrees of unskillfulness. These hindering thoughts are presented in a graduated list from the most obvious to the subtlest, and are accompanied by exhortations to abandon them. For each unskillful thought the Buddha offers Nanda an alternative, more beneficial thought on which to concentrate.

In the first half of canto 16 (*Explanation of the Noble Truths, ārya-satya-vyākhyāna*) the Buddha instructs Nanda in the four noble truths, giving an initial definition (16:3–6) before discussing each of them individually, and finally offering a summary in the form of the well-known medical metaphor (16.40). The second half of the canto emphasizes the importance of choosing the right time and method of meditation. This topic is illustrated by two metaphors, one based on the medical treatment of the three humors, the other envisaging the meditator as a master goldsmith. As the canto moves to a close, the quality of heroic endeavor (*vīrya*) receives particular mention, which appropriately paves the way for the battle scenes of the next canto.

Spurred on by the Buddha's exhortations, Nanda goes to war in canto 17 (*The Attainment of Deathlessness, amṛtādhigama*) and fights a battle with himself in the battleground of his own mind. This basic allegory is spun out in stanza after stanza of military imagery and aggressive language. Wearing the armor of mindfulness and carrying the bow of true knowledge, he uses his arrows of impurity meditation to destroy his great enemy, passion. In such metaphors we find a fulfillment of the concept of *vīrya* that was named as an essential quality of the liberation-seeker at the end of the canto 16, as well as a full flowering of the kṣatriya mores introduced in canto 1. Then, the princes went hunting with their great quivers bristling with arrows before establishing the city of Kapilavāstu; now Nanda slays malice with arrows of loving-kindness, kept in a quiver of constancy, prior to acquiring the "city" of nirvāṇa. The Buddhist practitioner is revealed as the true kṣatriya. With his newfound resolution, Nanda advances swiftly along the Buddhist path until he wins liberation. Canto 17 presents the final stage in the metamorphosis from Nanda's passive acceptance of the Buddha's interventionist policy to his active control of his own spiritual future.

The last canto (*His Instructions Revealed, ājñā-vyākaraṇa*) consists mainly of a dialogue between Nanda and the Buddha, beginning with Nanda's acknowledgment of his indebtedness to the Buddha. At the end of his speech Nanda throws himself at the Buddha's feet. Nanda's prostration reflects his genuine reverence for the Buddha, in contrast to his mock prostration to Sundarī in canto 4. The Buddha responds by saying what a welcome sight Nanda is to him:

> For even an uncomely man is pleasing to behold when he is well-adorned with his own most excellent virtues, but a man, however handsome, is really ugly when he is encompassed by befouling faults. (18.33)

It is at this point that Nanda can truly be labeled "handsome," since true beauty is not the result of surface appearance or cultivated artifice, but the inner loveliness of the perfected person. Nanda's story ends with a vision of him entering the city of Kapilavāstu for alms and preaching to those in need, a final and vivid demonstration of the shift from libertine to liberated man.

Since the poem presents Nanda's spiritual biography, the emphasis falls on internal events and psychological nuance rather than external action and incidents of plot. Nanda's flow of thought is brilliantly traced: his indecision as he is torn between desire for his wife and respect for the Buddha, his initial passivity and emotional dependence that slowly shade into personal responsibility and self-determination, his daydreaming that is eventually replaced by concentrated meditation, and his maturing insight into his own condition are all conveyed with precision and sensitivity—so much so, indeed, that one intuits that the plight of the *Saundarananda*'s vacillating hero had a personal resonance for Aśvaghoṣa.

Bibliography

Coomaraswamy, A. 1977. "*Saṃvega*: Aesthetic Shock." In *Coomaraswamy I: Selected Papers; Traditional Art and Symbolism*, ed. by R. Lipsey, pp. 179–85. Princeton: Princeton University Press.

Covill, L. 2007. *Handsome Nanda*. New York: New York University Press and the Clay Sanskrit Library.

——— 2009. *A Metaphorical Study of Saundarananda*. New Delhi: Motilal Banarsidass.

Johnston, E. H., ed. 1928. *The Saundarananda of Aśvaghoṣa*. London: Oxford University Press.

Johnston, E. H., trans. 1932. *The Saundarananda or Nanda the Fair*. London: Oxford University Press.

Shāstrī, H. 1909. "The Recovery of a Lost Epic by Aśvaghoṣa." *Journal of the Asiatic Society of Bengal* 5: 165–66.

II.

Theravāda Biographies in the Twentieth Century

Seeing Myself as Another Person

The Autobiography of a Burmese Monastic Thinker in the Twentieth Century

Venerable Khammai Dhammasami

Introduction

Traditionally, in most Southeast Asian cultures Buddhist monks have held back from writing autobiographies, which could be seen as an act of self-promotion and self-regard. Specifically the Buddha's teaching of *anattā*, non-self, teaches Buddhists not to promote themselves, for self-promotion stems from the ego. The fear of being seen as advertising oneself was, and indeed still is, so pervasive that historically even the Southeast Asian authors of Pali works often left out their names in their compositions, an omission that can nowadays make for an extra burden for those interested in the history of literature. But one of the twentieth century's leading monastic leaders of Burma, the late Venerable Ashin Janakābhivaṃsa (1900–1977), was not afraid of any accusatory labels: so, just before he died, he did write an account of the story of his life as a pioneer in the reform of monastic education.

In this paper I will describe in brief the life, work, and aims of Ashin Janakābhivaṃsa. On the basis of this I will explore why Ashin Janakābhivaṃsa did eventually decide to write an autobiography, and why he chose to do so in the particular style that he did.[1]

1. I am forever indebted to Dr. Sarah Shaw for improving my presentation and various suggestions and to Venerable Vicitta for his kind assistance and translation of Ashin Janakābhivaṃsa's syllabus.

Ashin Janakābhivaṃsa: His Life and His Work

Ashin Janakābhivaṃsa was born at the turn of the twentieth century in Thayine village, Wetlet township, Shwebo district, Sagaing Division. When he was five years old he was taken to the local monastery and initiated as a *sāmaṇera* for the first time, as was the local custom. Nine years later he entered the order as a full novice, this time for life. At the age of eighteen he passed first in the government monastic exam at the higher level, even though he was still a novice. Because of this, when he took his full monastic vows two years later, in 1920, he was permitted by his preceptor to choose his Pali name. He selected Janaka, the name of the bodhisatta in one of the jātakas, the stories of Gotama's earlier lives as he prepared himself for buddhahood. This favorite tale of his describes the bodhisatta swimming for seven days, struggling on his own when others were drowned in a shipwreck, and is traditionally associated with the development of the perfection of vigor (*viriya*). In 1928 Janakābhivaṃsa was given the title of *Pariyattisāsanahita Dhammācariya*, after passing the full monastic training exam. Taking further training in Pali, the commentaries, and the exegetical literature, not only in the rigorous system at Mandalay but also in the other great training center, Pakhokku, he was well equipped to embark on a scholastic career. Mandalay and Pakhokku were the two most important centers of Buddhist learning in Burma throughout the twentieth century. Mandalay paid attention to developing skills in the interpretation of the dhamma and therefore used formal written and oral examinations; Pakhokku, on the other hand, emphasized reading the whole of the Tipiṭaka with its commentaries and sub-commentaries thoroughly, page by page. Pakhokku set no formal examinations, on the grounds that they would act as potential corruptions on the minds of student-monks, introducing notions of fame and competition into monastic life. Mandalay, as a result of its system, developed syllabi to master dharma through "a short cut"; Pakhokku, for its part, was famed for mastering the "sleeping canonical texts" or "great texts," which were not part of the Mandalay curriculum. After some years of writing, teaching, and scholarship, Janakābhivaṃsa, skilled in both methods, established himself at what was then a dilapidated monastery at the ancient capital of Amarapura, eight miles from Mandalay. It had few resident monks at that time but, within the space of a few years, was to become one of the most prominent teaching monasteries in Burma. He remained at this temple for the rest of his life.

Mahagandhayon, which Janakābhivaṃsa developed fully as a training monastery during World War II, is today considered a model for all others in both teaching and discipline. Ashin Janakābhivaṃsa was considered not only one of the most learned monks of his time but also one who was very strict in the Vinaya, the monastic way of life. His commitment was imparted through his methods and teaching. As recently as March 2007, when I went there with representatives from Theravāda Buddhist colleges and universities from South and Southeast Asia, I was told that there were 1,500 monks and novices currently studying at Mahagandhayon, and that the monastery is so popular among devotees that meal offerings are booked months in advance.

In many respects the way of life developed by Ashin Janakābhivaṃsa follows a traditional monastic pattern.[2] The monks and novices training there have collective extended chanting sessions and meditations in the evening. The meditation practice is a combination of *Buddhānussati*, the recollection of the Buddha, and *mettābhāvanā*, the meditation on loving-kindness. These are traditional calm (*samatha*) practices, often used to complement insight meditation, or in this case, the demands of the scholastic curriculum. Each morning, there is a short chanting session, followed by a daily dharma talk, given by Janakābhivaṃsa himself when he was alive. These talks are known as "morning spiritual advice" (*nan net khin ovada mya*), and many of them have been published. While Ashin Janakābhivaṃsa had contact with famous insight (*vipassanā*) teachers, such as Ledi Sayadaw and Mahagandhayon Sayadaw of Sagaing, his own meditative training had included a considerable amount of samatha too. Janakābhivaṃsa practiced and gave talks on meditation while all the time pursuing his scholarly interests. For those studying in his monastery, Ashin Janakābhivaṃsa compiled his own syllabi, still employed, which reflect this. According to him, if a novice of

2. In his autobiography, Abhijankābhivaṃsa lists the qualities needed in his monastery: "In this Mahagandhayon Monastery, there are ten principles for all resident monks and novices. They are (1) One has to have good intention. (2) One has to respect the Vinaya rules. (3) One has to be healthy. (4) One has to be clean and tidy. (5) One has to follow decorum and table manners. (6) One has to behave well. (7) One has to speak appropriately and gently. (8) One has to observe the disciplines in walking and travel. (9) One has to follow the rules and regulations of the monastery. (10) One has to be learned." The order indicates their importance. See Abhijankābhivaṃsa 1997c: 358–59.

twelve or thirteen years of age studies Pali for eighteen months, he should be able to read Pali well and also compose some Pali verses. Within four and a half years, a novice will have studied Pali grammar, Anuruddha's famous work on the *Abhidhamma*, the *Abhidhammatthasaṅgaha*, the Pali *Dhammapada* and commentary, the whole of the *Vinaya-piṭaka* and the whole of the *Aṅguttara Nikāya*.[3] He placed particular emphasis on reading and listening to lectures rather than learning by rote and memorization, the more usual concerns of Burmese monastic training. He felt that for monks, spiritual development was as important as the academic, and so did not wish for such a great emphasis on examination, which he felt was a recent, regressive development.[4] To this day, under a system established at his instigation, each student is assigned a moral tutor who supervises his spiritual and monastic life as well as his academic training. The current syllabus used in Mahagandhayon Monastery, Amarapura, Burma, was written by Sayadaw Ashin Janakābhivaṃsa and, with explanatory comment in his own words, gives a flavor of his approach. All the texts in the curriculum, except the Pali canonical and commentarial ones, were compiled by him.

The Mahagandhayon Syllabus for Novices: Various Subjects and Their Benefits[5]

1. Pre-elementary (six-month learning period)

a. *Yatana-gun-ye* (*The Qualities of the Triple Gem*)
b. *Yup-po-shin-kyint-wut* (*Illustrated Training for the Sāmaṇera*)
c. *Pāli-sikkhā* (*Basic Pali Language Exercises*)
d. *Thaddā-kyinn* (*Short Basic Pali Grammar*)

3. The *Abhidhammatthasaṅgaha* is better known in the West under the title of a popular English translation, *A Manual of Abhidhamma*, by Narada Mahā Thera, an edition which includes the Pali text, too (see Narada 1978/2002). The *Dhammapada* has frequently been translated in the West. The commentary to this text is better known through its name in Burlingame's translation in the Harvard Oriental Series, *Buddhist Legends* (Burlingame 1921/1990).

4. He is quoted in Dhammasāmi 2007: 24n3, translating from Janakābhivaṃsa 1994: 23–24.

5. This translation of Ashin Janakābhivaṃsa's advice for teaching Pali to monastic novices, delineated in his autobiography, was made by Ven. Vicitta, Oxford Buddha Vihara, 2008.

a) By learning the *Yatana-gun-ye* (*The Qualities of the Triple Gem*) students will gain knowledge of what the triple gem is, the precepts, the nature of good and bad deeds, karma and its fruit, and so on; such is the foundation in Buddhism.
b) By learning the *Yup-po-shin-kyint-wut* (*Illustrated Training for the Sāmaṇera*) students will gain knowledge of the ordination procedure, novice discipline, the way to use the four requisites (robe, food, shelter, and medicine), basic meditation on parts of the body, and the duties and obligations of a sāmaṇera.
c) Through familiarity with the *Pāli-sikkhā* (*Basic Pali Language Exercises*) students will gain knowledge of basic Pali structures such as the subject, verb, object, *vibhatti* (inflection), first, second, and third person, etc. At this level, students learn how to write in Pali a little and how to translate.
d) By study of the *Thaddā-kyinn* (*Short Basic Pali Grammar*), students gain knowledge about the declension of nouns, verbs, word combination, and division; they also learn about compounds, nominal derivation, and verbal derivation.

2. Elementary A (six-month learning period)

a. The *Dhammapada-aṭṭhakathā* (*Dhammapada Commentary*): *Yamaka vagga* ("The Pairs")
b. The *Akhye-byu thaddā* (*Basic Pali Grammar*), *sandhi* (combinations), *nāma* (nouns), and *ākhyāta* (verb)
c. The *Pāli-kathā-sallāpa sikkhā* (*Basic Pali Dialogue Exercises*)

a) The commentary to the *Dhammapada* is the first text to be introduced to young students learning to read the Tipiṭaka in Pali. Students will gradually learn the meaning of the Pali words in the text by enjoying reading the stories therein. They have a chance to use their knowledge of Pali grammar, and by the end of the course they will be able to interpret some short Pali stanzas.
b) This grammatical training is to reinforce knowledge for young students, who have already learned some basic Pali grammar.

Basic Pali Language Exercises and the *Short Basic Pali Grammar* are made for the students like a tiny boat for them to cross the ocean. They might be able to cross with the help of that tiny boat, but they are not yet strong enough to resist the storm. So, they need a higher level of grammar, like a strong boat that has been well reinforced.

c) This is a class in basic dialogue, which enables students to speak a little Pali. The Pali course at Mahagandhayon Monastery does not just aim for translation from Pali, but for students to be able to write their own sentences in Pali too. Therefore most students from this monastery are able to sit the government exam in Pali.

2. Elementary B (six-month learning period)

a. The *Dhammapada Commentary, Appamāda-vagga* ("Heedfulness")
b. *Akhye-byu thaddā* (*Basic Pali Grammar*): *kitaka* (verbal derivatives), *uṇādi* (suffixes of nominal derivatives), *kāraka* (cases)
c. *Akhye-byu thingyo* (*The Foundation of Abhidhamma*) [Janakābhivaṃsa' own work on the *Abhidhammatthasaṅgaha*]: the first three chapters: chapter I—*citta* (consciousness), chapter II—*cetasika* (mental states), chapter III—*pakiṇṇaka* (miscellaneous)

a) Over the last six months students have completed the first part (*vagga*) of the *Dhammapada Commentary*; now another is taught so that they can enjoy reading stories that they have never heard before.

b) This section is intended to encourage students with exercises in Pali grammar, by using lines of Pali from the *Dhammapada Commentary*, which they have already been reading.

c) This section is the first lesson where students learn the *Abhidhamma*, the profound teaching. This deals with the basics: consciousness, mental factors, and the combination of consciousness and mental factors. For example, in the case of an angry person, they find out the number of types of consciousness in which anger can arise, and so on. By learning the *Abhidhamma* like this, students will become used to applying it in their daily life. Students will have spent one and a half years studying by the end of this level.

3. Level 1 (six-month learning period)

a. *Mahāvagga* Pali (*Vinaya*)
b. *Aṅguttara Nikāya* Pali ("The Ones" to "The Threes")
c. *Dhammapada Commentary* ("The Pairs," "Heedfulness")
d. *Akhye-byu thaddā* (*Basic Pali Grammar*): *samāsa* (compounds) and *taddhita* (nominal derivatives).
e. *Akhye byu thingyo* (*The Foundation of Abhidhamma*): chapter I—*citta* (consciousness), chapter II—*cetasika* (mental states), chapter III—*pakiṇṇaka* (miscellaneous), chapter IV—*vīthi* (analysis of thought processes), chapter V—*vīthimutta* (process freed) and chapter VI—*rūpa* (analysis of matter)

a) As students have been getting used to canonical texts by starting reading the *Dhammapada Commentary* in Pali, now they are able to go to the next step in Pali, with the *Mahāvagga* section of the *Vinaya*. Students are supposed to go through this text little by little, daily, in accordance with the policy of the saying "the mountain should be climbed slowly." So students should get to learn this kind of "topmost" text slowly but regularly.
b) The *Aṅguttara Nikāya* is another text that students are here encountering for the first time. It should be taught as a method of climbing to a higher mountain. In addition, students will be stimulated by reading a canonical text that is quite new for them.
c) At this level students are now quite familiar with the *Dhammapada Commentary* and feel at home with it. While learning this text they are also taught grammar and *Abhidhamma*. By

the end of this course they will have been learning for two years.

4. Level 2 (six-month learning period)

a. *Cūlavagga* and *Parivāra* (*Vinaya*)
b. *Aṅguttara Nikāya* ("The Ones" to "The Sixes")
c. *Dhammapada Commentary* (from the beginning up to *Daṇḍa vagga*)
d. *Akhye-byu thingyo* (*The Foundation of Abhidhamma*), the whole text

a) As the next step, students learn more about monastic discipline through studying the *Cūlavagga* and *Parivāra* sections of the *Vinaya piṭaka*. This is a more advanced study in discipline for them.
b) There is also more advanced study of the *Aṅguttara Nikāya*, for those who have become familiar with this text at the previous level.
c) [No explanation given in the original.]
d) At this level students become used to doing grammar and *Abhidhamma* studies through canonical texts. Through studying the *Abhidhamma* they will be able to apply its principles in their daily life, following good states and avoiding bad states. In Pali grammar they will be able to do *viggaha*, the separation of words, in *samāsa*, *taddhita*, and *kitaka* form. In *Abhidhamma* they will be able to conduct an analysis of the thought process. They can sit the level 2 in the *Sāmaṇera-sakya sikkhā* examination in Mandalay and the junior level in Pathamapyan, the government-held examination.

5. Level 3 (six-month learning period)

a. *Pārājika-kaṇḍa* and *Pācittiya* (offenses outlined in the Vinaya)
b. *Aṅguttara Nikāya* (the whole text)
c. *Dhammapada Commentary* (the whole text)

a) Although the *Pārājika-kaṇḍa* and the *Pācittiya* are the first two books in the *Vinaya*, students will have already read the *Mahāvagga*, the *Cūlavagga*, and the *Parivāra* in Pali when they come to study them. This is because the latter consists of stories, which will arouse students' interest.
b) This course covers more material to be read in *Aṅguttara Nikāya*.
c) In order fully to understand the stories and the Pali forms in the *Dhammapada*, students are made to repeat the whole text of *Dhammapada-aṭṭhakathā*. Now there has been a three-year learning period, and students are eligible to sit level 3 in the *Sāmaṇera-sakya sikkhā* examination in Mandalay and the middle level in Pathamapyan, the government-held examination.

After finishing all five levels according to this syllabus, within three years students have read five Vinaya texts, the whole of the *Aṅguttara Nikāya*, and the whole of the *Dhammapada* with its commentary. That means they are well prepared in discipline as well as in the suttas. If a student starts learning at fifteen he could easily finish it at eighteen; even if for any reason he is physically unwell, he could still finish it by the age of twenty, within his novicehood.

An Overview of His Writings

In addition to his teaching work, Ashin Janakābhivaṃsa was equally renowned as one of the most respected authors in Burma of the last century. He differentiated his own writing from that of his predecessors, as well as that of his contemporaries, in two ways. First, he entitled all his works on textual interpretations *bhāsā-ṭīkā*, meaning (Burmese) "vernacular sub-commentary." He wrote a number of bhāsā-ṭīkās such as the *Kaccāyana-bhāsā-ṭīkā*, *Pātimokkha-bhāsā-ṭīkā*, or *Mahāvagga-bhāsā-ṭīkā*; these works ran as a series of sorts, begun in the late 1930s. By the mid 1970s, when he was seventy-four, he had written a *bhāsā-ṭīkā* on nearly every book of the Pali Tipiṭaka. All four *nikāyas* of suttas received his scrutiny, as did the entire *Vinaya* and the seven books of the *Abhidhamma*: he wrote sixty-three such books in all. He rendered his work distinctive not only in his use of a generic title, but also through his writing style. He studied Sanskrit and English with the intention of developing a suitable style of writing and composition. He came to take very seriously the idea of identifying an audience, and when he was writing a commentary on the *Abhidhammatthasaṅgaha*, he commented that his first draft had no clearly targeted readership. Some parts of it were too burdensome for beginners, while some materials were not necessary for the advanced students. As a result, he revised the draft and divided it into three parts: one for beginners in the monastic schools, *Akhye-byu thingyo*, one for laypeople, *Ne-zin ko dwe Abhidhamma*, and the other for advanced learners, *Thingyo-bhāsā-ṭīkā* (a vernacular commentary on the *Abhidhammatthasaṅgaha*). In fact, it was the book for the advanced learners that won him the honorary *aggamahāpandita* title, the first to be offered after Burma's independence from Britain in 1948. Burmese laypeople, as well as monastics, are noted for their particular interest in *Abhidhamma*, a subject sometimes thought too difficult by those in other Southeast Asian countries. His book for this readership, *Ne-zin ko dwe Abhidhamma*, translated in English as *Abhidhamma in Daily Life*, has earned worldwide respect and is even available on the Internet.

Another distinguishing feature of Janakābhivaṃsa's writing is his ideas for reform. When he first took up this topic, he was the only monk to have written rather than just spoken on this subject. His ideas were mainly about the relationship between Buddhism and politics, and he argued that in a country like Burma, where Buddhism had been long established with a population that was largely Buddhist, it was essential that the government should become involved in maintaining the purity and development of the teaching. He argued that the sangha, for their part, should assist in developing the nation, specifically by providing education, both secular and moral, to people living in the rural areas, who at the time numbered over 80 percent of the population.

Some of His Reformist Ideas

In order for the government to help keep the dispensation of the *Buddhasāsana* pure, members of the government themselves, he argued, should be well informed of the true dharma and the *Vinaya*, as expounded in the Pali Tipiṭaka. It was a cause of great concern to him that the first generations of leaders of independent Burma were all educated in non-Buddhist schools and therefore had not been encouraged to appreciate their Buddhist background and culture. For the sangha to be able to assist in nation building, monastic education had to change. In a country where the clergy are known for their conservative outlook, he began his debate on reform with the *Kālāma-Sutta* (AN I 187–93), promoting freedom of thought and critical thinking among the sangha and influential Buddhists through a text in which the Buddha guides his followers to make their own judicious assessment of the views of others.

One of his most important works, to which he refers repeatedly in his autobiography, is *Anagat-sasana-yay* (*The Future of Buddhism*), first published in 1948 (Janakābhivaṃsa 1995). Published on the eve of the declaration of the independence of Burma, when he had become a senior *thera* (elder) with extensive experience administering a monastery, the work gave voice to his hopes for the new state.[6] The book begins with a general presentation on the Buddha, dhamma, and sangha; the work is simple in style, and so more suitable for a modern and perhaps less well-informed reader. He then touches on the history of some Burmese monarchs, whom he believed to have been great supporters of Buddhism as well as builders of the nation. The book continues with a discussion about the need for freedom of thought and critical thinking, in Buddhist practice as well as in nation building.

As to the sangha, he said that all the monasteries should be put into four categories in order to be truly operational. The first is the village monastery, providing a Buddhist and a general education to the villagers. Janakābhivaṃsa stipulated that there should not be two such monasteries in the same village. The abbot should be well versed to a certain extent both with the Tipiṭaka and with secular subjects so that he could offer children a basic education up to middle-school level, that is, up to fifteen years of age. The abbot should also have contact with and be familiar with the local populace and their mores so that his advice on social matters can be relevant.

The second type of monastery is a city monastery, strongly devoted to teaching the Tipiṭaka, among a few other sources, to a greater number of monks and novices. He proposed a syllabus of ten years for students, beginning at the age of fifteen, so that by the age of twenty-five, students would

6. For an account of this, see U Ko Lay, introduction to *Abhidhamma in Daily Life* (1997): http://www.dharmaweb.org/index.php/Abhidhamma_In_Daily_Life_By_Ashin_Janakabhivamsa (page last modified 2005).

have mastered the Tipiṭaka. He recommended that there should not be many of these in the same city so as not to burden the lay people who are supporting the material needs of these monasteries.

The third kind of monastery is a Pali university, which would be established in the major cities: Rangoon and Mandalay. The purpose of these Pali universities would be to introduce the younger generation of the sangha, after they have mastered the Tipiṭaka in the second type of monastery, to modern languages, the Western method of study, and comparative study. In this his aims were partially successful, although he did not live to see the results of his efforts: although centers in Mandalay, Pakhokku, Rangoon, and Sagaing were well established when he wrote, none of the existing Buddhist universities seems to have emerged as the kind of institution he had envisaged.

The last type of monastery is a meditation center, with simple, small, and eco-friendly meditation huts, instead of the multi-story buildings that we see today. In the 1930s the great interest in vipassanā meditation among the urban middle classes, which has persisted until the present day, promoted building work on big local centers, often in noisy locations. These lack the peace and tranquility of rural, secluded meditation centers, which Ashin Janakābhivaṃsa felt should also be supported.

With a few exceptions, Ashin Janakābhivaṃsa's efforts to influence the government were not especially successful. Although his book earned widespread respect, there is no record of him ever meeting with any important figure from the government, which was under the premiership of U Nu from 1948–58 and 1960–62. For example, when the government of independent Burma passed a parliamentary act to set up Pali universities, it was giving the existing traditional monasteries that could produce ten graduates of the *Dhammācariya* degree within three years a status of Pali university. None of Janakābhivaṃsa's "suggestions for modernization," for example the inclusion of the study of Sanskrit and modern languages and a teachers' training program, were included. Janakābhivaṃsa envisaged a Pali university not just as an academic institution with excellent teachings on meditation but also as a sangha body that would work with the government in developing the nation (Janakābhivaṃsa 1997c: 300–302).

The first category of monastery, that is, his ideal of a village monastery, seems to be the one that was most dear to his heart. It was more than monastic education; indeed it was also about rural development. He said that the abbot of a village monastery should know also about healthcare, nutrition, and social matters important to the people in his village. He admired Christian missionaries for their dedication to education and involvement in social development. Without a good village monastic school, he argued, children from the village would have to be sent far away from their families to urban areas in order to receive their education. This would put an emotional strain on many families, and an economic strain on both families and urban centers. So it is important that village monasteries have competent abbots to grow the seeds of the dharma in the mind of the people and to help the government in developing their villages, particularly in the area of education.

The U Nu Government did encourage the establishment of primary schools in the monasteries under the leadership of the abbot of a village monastery. Those schools accepted boys and girls as well as novices. However, the sangha as a whole was not able to agree on a new syllabus that would provide both a Buddhist and secular education. So these monastic schools simply borrowed the syllabus used in government schools from the city. Moreover, some influential and senior members of the sangha even questioned if it was in accordance with the *Vinaya* for novices to study what they considered to be secular subjects such as math, geography, science, and English.[7]

While the debate was still going on, the military that came to power in 1962 soon closed all monastic primary schools because they had been established by the previous government. But even before the military came to power, the government under U Nu had not wanted to alienate the highly influential sangha by forcing their monasteries to study secular subjects. We may roughly conclude that monastic education in Burma has never really been modernized because the syllabuses and methods of teaching and assessment have undergone little change in three hundred years.

In *Anagat-sasana-yay*, Ashin Janakābhivaṃsa talked a great deal about cultural reform. He argued that Burma should not build more *chaitiyas* (pagodas/stūpas) in areas where there already was one, on the grounds that it was a waste of money. Buddhism should not be associated with extravagant ceremonies and rituals; instead, simplicity should be encouraged in every Buddhist activity. But the government found it difficult to simply halt the construction of monasteries and pagodas, and some even accused him of

7. See Dhammasāmi 2004: 280–92 and Dhammasāmi 2007.

being a "communist" (Janakābhivaṃsa 1997: 180). Monasteries and pagodas were seen as a sign of economic prosperity and religious commitment, and the dedication of wealthy patrons from the community.

As a result of this, some decades later, Ashin Janakābhivaṃsa would blame the lack of good village monastic schools, as he had envisioned them, for the increase of crime and underdevelopment. He blamed politicians for not taking rural development seriously and giving only lip service to its objectives. He repeated this claim continuously from the time of independence in 1948 to his death in 1977. As his "biography" laments:

> Oh, the opportunity is lost again! It is so frustrating. It is not easy to get another opportunity like this. When an opportunity arises—which happens only once or twice in a century—the sangha does not seize it with unity; so, it is gone again. It is so difficult. Many do not consider the whole sāsana, but only themselves. That is obvious if we look at the grounds on which they object.
>
> Some half a century ago, there was such an opportunity. That was during the British rule. The British administrators said that the sangha should modernize its education system; so they held a meeting for the sangha in Mandalay so that members of the sangha could consult with each other. At that time, my teacher, Ashin Aggadhamma of Abayārāma Monastery in Mandalay, proposed two changes: (1) to add an elementary level to the existing system, and (2) to introduce math, geography, and Burmese language into the curriculum. At that time, the majority of senior sayadaws objected to his proposal on the grounds that subjects such as math are considered modern subjects and also as *tiracchānakathā*, ["animal training," and hence not suitable for monks].[8] So, the proposal was not successful.
>
> Another chance was offered in 1965 at a meeting of the whole sangha at Hmawbi, about fifty miles from Rangoon, convened by Gen. Ne Win, who had seized power three years earlier. The meeting could not agree on any reform on education or administration. At this meeting his proposal to make textbooks more

8. For a full discussion of this see Dhammasāmi 2007.

> readable, easier, modern, quicker to learn but more effective in quality, was turned down. The monks who did vote for reforms, and who introduced them elsewhere, had students who went on to become national figures, while students from the other schools who did not support reforms did not fare well.[9]

Why He Wrote an Autobiography

Despite his interest in the national stage, the external facts of Janakābhivaṃsa's life are spare: once he had made a success of his own monastery, he never left it. Four years before his death he was made leader of his own nikāya, the Shwe-kyin. Throughout his monastic career he adhered to the simple routine and daily custom he had established in his own temple. So why did he feel it necessary to write an account of his life? His own stated reason was to put the record straight. He explained that a biography, that is a Burmese biography at any rate, contains usually only "prominent events" in the life of the subject; not how that person has brought about those prominent events through his own intelligence and effort. Inspiring it may be, but such a traditional biography has no direct lessons for the next generation. He therefore decided to write one for two reasons. The first was to leave some record of "the way he applied his knowledge and effort for the many which may benefit future generations." The second was to "set the record straight for both good and bad things that have happened in his life. I do not want a biography which is usually written by others after one dies and in which only praiseworthy things are discussed" (Janakābhivaṃsa 1997c: 7–8).

In his autobiography, which he calls *Tatbhava-thanthaya* (*One Life in Saṃsāra*), he provides both personal elements and life experiences as well as ideas for reform and nation building. One of the repeated messages is that although one should not believe politicians, it is very important to work with them. Perhaps his own inability to convince the politicians was his biggest regret, and he failed in this undertaking partly because he was not trained to negotiate and partly because of the modesty of his own monastic nikāya, the Shwe-kyin, which, although respected for its scholarship and meditative work, was traditionally reticent and did not feature much on the national

9. Cited in "Anon" 2000: 183–85.

stage. One of his contemporaries, Ashin Vicittasārābhivaṃsa—who was from the largest nikāya, the Sudhamma, was the first to have memorized the whole Tipiṭaka, and was also one of the leading figures in the sangha—was able to convince the government to set up the two Pali universities mentioned earlier, in Rangoon and Sagaing, about four years after Janakābhivaṃsa died. Vicittasārābhivaṃsa, also known as Min Goon Tipitakadhara Sayadaw, was skillful and patient in his dealing with the political establishment. A stronger social background, like that of Prince Patriarch Vajirayan, who was a comparable reformer in Thailand, would also have helped him to convince the politicians.

On the whole, it's possible that by the time he decided to write his autobiography, in his early seventies, he had already concluded that his ideas would not be heeded by the government, be it a democratically elected one or a military dictator, despite their honoring him with the *aggamahāpandita* title and recognizing his monastery as a model for the whole country ("Anon" 2000: 311). He wanted to revisit his reformist ideas in the hope that they might still be of benefit to future generations. He stated in his autobiography that he was not a quitter but someone who would persist until he got his way. Perhaps he hoped that if he created some record of the recommendations he felt had largely failed so far, they might be achieved after his own death. He communicated his desire to be reborn again in Burma in order to implement his ideas: saṃsāra consists of many lives, but this is only about one life and it will go on. It seems to me as if he accepted a failure in one life but not a long-term defeat over many: a perspective, of course, not generally found in Western biographies and autobiographies, which assume that this life is the only one available. This conviction is indicated also in his choice of the title: *One Life in Saṃsāra*.

The Style of the Autobiography

The style of his autobiography indicates the care and thought that contributed to its composition. It was one of his last works, and for several months before his death he broke a lifetime habit and started to work at night, for the first time in his career using the electric light as he composed. When in good health, Janakābhivaṃsa had liked to write himself, often standing, but this work he dictated to a group of senior monks: a teacher imparting information to his disciples, in the manner of the Buddha himself. With a sense of some urgency, he struggled, until thirteen days before his death, to complete various projects, which included the autobiographical record and two other pieces of dharma composition. It was a feat that bore the imprint of the monastic title he had chosen for himself years ago, Janaka, the bodhisatta's name in the life when he swims on his own after being shipwrecked, thus perfecting heroic vigor.[10] The first of these two other works was a commentary on five out of the seven books of the *Abbhidhamma*, excluding the *Dhammasaṅgaṇi* and the *Vibhaṅga*. The second was a discourse on the second book of the *Dīgha Nikāya*—which contains, appropriately enough, the *Parinibbāna-Sutta*, an account compiled by the assembled arahats and disciples of the Buddha's teachings before his own death (DN II 72–168). Perhaps it was a reading of this sutta that influenced the way he approached his record of his own life.

By and large, the autobiography follows a fairly straightforward pattern. The 542-page book covers the progression of events in Janakābhivaṃsa's life as a sequence, with a chapter for each decade. There is a square grid-style horoscope near the beginning of the book, giving the planetary configuration at the time of his birth. This would not be an unusual addition to an Asian biography, as an anticipatory explanation of character, predisposition, and likely future. Its purpose in this one, the author states, is in part so that those proficient in astrology can see the trends that contributed to his character. It is also to record the predictions made at Janakābhivaṃsa's birth by such experts: that he would live for a long time and that he would achieve great things.

One feature of the structure of the autobiography, however, is very creative. To avoid the accusation of self-promotion, he writes his account in the guise of an interview. It is a Buddhist custom that the story must be requested from another person before its telling, whether a book or a biography. In his case there was no one specifically requesting him to write an account of his life. He records, however, that he had been consulted repeatedly about some of the issues he addresses in this work. Under such circumstances, he must

10. This story is one of the last ten jātakas, no. 539, which are all considered important in Southeast Asia. It is often depicted with Janaka being rescued from the ocean after his struggles by the goddess Manimekhalā (Ja VI 30–68).

have thought that it would be suitable to write such a document, even in the absence of a formal request. Indeed by creating an extended imaginary conversation, he has an opportunity for a dialogue where such requests are made, by someone who can listen, give responses, argue, and finally be convinced and record, describing him from the outside. The imaginary interviewer is a monk called Dhammagutta, "the one who protects the dhamma," explained by Janakābhivaṃsa as "the one who looks after the right path" (Janakābhivaṃsa 1997c: 8). Perhaps he felt that the character of Dhammagutta also represents some sort of embodiment of the aspirations of the sangha as exponents of the holy life: his questions are those of a "typical" monk, dedicated to the teaching, who wishes to see the implementation of measures that would protect its health in the long term. In fact Dhammagutta comes up with the kinds of inquiries that might be made by any serious person, lay or monastic. At any rate, the author presumably hoped that, through this means, readers will be with him on the issues he had spent all his life working on, and that they would be perceived as weighty matters: he feels such reformist ideas are of the greatest significance for the future of Buddhism. As he says in the prefatory poem to the book:

> No. Were it for my own achievement,
> no such great effort would be called for.
> It is to not to let it decline further,
> this dignified and noble *Buddhasāsana*, long established by our ancestors,
> that I work so hard.
> May the *sāsana* long endure![11]

Events demanded that the viewpoint of another living person would be represented in this work anyway. Thirteen days before his death he was unable to compose any more, and a chronicle of this last period was written by his devoted disciple Bhaddanta Candobhāsa; it was added as an appendix. Until the day before his death, this concluding piece notes, he continued to attend the usual chanting and meditation sessions of his monastery, giving dhamma talks as usual. He described his body as "an old train." When not

11. Cited in "Anon" 2000: 186.

conducting these activities he had recourse to the repetition of two simple chants. One was the final stanza of the *Aṭṭhasālinī*, the commentary to the *Dhammasaṅgaṇī*, a series of wishes that accurately reflect the preoccupations of his own life: that all men may come to understand the dhamma, so attaining nibbāna, that the dhamma may endure, revered by all, that rain may come in due season, and that the king should guard the welfare of the state as his own child (see Asl 428). The other verse, fittingly for a life devoted to practice of the teaching, was the one employed by all monks in his nikāya on the completion of their group meditation:

imāya dhammānudhammapaṭipattiyā buddhaṃ pujemi
imāya dhammānudhammapaṭipattiyā dhammaṃ pujemi
imāya dhammānudhammapaṭipattiyā saṅghaṃ pujemi
addhā imāya dhammānudhammapaṭipattiya jātijarabyādhimaraṇamā paṭimuccissāmi

With this practice, which is itself the dhamma and undertaken in accordance with the law of the dharma,
I honor the Buddha, his teaching, and the practicing community.
And truly, with this practice, which is itself the dhamma and undertaken in accordance with the law of dhamma,
may I be set free from birth, old age, sickness, and death.

He died at 4:30 P.M. on December 27, 1977. It was an appropriate tribute to Janakābhivaṃsa that the monk describing his final days continued with the chosen method for the autobiography: it is also written as a series of interviews with the imaginary Dhammagutta. A full and exhaustive biography of 693 pages, *One Life in the Sāsana* (*Tatbhava Thathana*), was written posthumously and, again as a reflection of Buddhist reticence, was attributed to an anonymous group of disciples. The principal author of the biography was apparently, however, his disciple Ashin Ghosita.[12]

12. The title echoes in part the subject's own work: *Tatbhava thathana* (*One Life in the Sāsana*), "Anon" 2000. *Tatbhava thathana* was written and published first in 1984, some eight years after Ashin Janakābhivaṃsa died. The fact that it has been reprinted in 1994 and 2000 indicates its popularity. The title proved so catchy that the author, Ashin Ghosita, himself a close disciple of Ashin Janakābhivaṃsa and who credits the work to all other disciples, became

Janakābhivaṃsa, who may have expressed frustration at his failures, had considerable achievements, even for "one life in saṃsāra." He established one of the most successful and popular training programs for monks in Burma and brought a relatively obscure monastery to the forefront of Burmese cultural life. His recommendations, although not followed as he suggested by successive governments, were deeply influential in the monastic orders. In his lifetime monks throughout Burma read his books; after his death they were widely disseminated among the laity as well, while his book on *Abhidhamma* for this audience has found an international readership. His daily teachings in meditation and practice continue in the efforts and teachings of monks he trained himself. Despite his frustration at the way successive governments had ignored his advice, his ideas were promulgated widely and, in some cases, implemented by others after his death.

The style of his autobiography is a reflection of his life's work. In a society that eschews such records, the reconstruction of his life through the imaginary interview creates a way that his ideas and achievements can be seen as "objective," if this word can be used for either autobiography or biography. In life as well as in his autobiography, he was careful to build up a dialogue between himself and others in the sangha, the real Dhammagutta, in order to convince the state. This was brought to fulfillment through people trained or inspired by him and his writings, and perhaps may continue to be so. I conclude with his own words, with their reverence for the monastic life:

> Numerous buddhas, *pacceka-buddha*s, and arahats, who have all removed from its root the desire to be famous, have left their own biographies in the *Apadāna*, a canonical text, so that the future generations can follow their good examples. This noble tradition gives me encouragement; for this, I pay my homage to those noble ones. I bow down to them.[13]

---

one of the best-known writers in Burma; the author then wrote another biography on Mogok Sayadaw.

13. Janakābhivaṃsa 1997c: 8. The *Apadāna* is a canonical text in which some of the principal followers of the Buddha describe the karma and events, often related to past lives, which contributed to their final enlightenment.

Abbreviations

Pali texts cited are those produced by the Pali Text Society. Abbreviations of Pali texts are according to recent conventions of Pali Text Society:

Asl	Aṭṭhasālinī
AN	Aṅguttaranikāya
DN	Dīghanikāya
Ja	Jātaka
MN	Majjhimanikāya

Bibliography

"Anon" 2000. *Tatbhava thathana* (*One Life in the Sāsana*) [Biography of Ashin Janakābhivaṃsa co-written by his senior disciples]. 3rd reprint. Amarapura: Mahagandhayon Press.

Burlingame, E. W. 1921; reprint 1990. *Buddhist Legends: Translated from the Original Pāli Text of the Dhammapada Commentary* (*Dhammapada Aṭṭhakathā*). Harvard Oriental Series 28–30. Cambridge, MA: Harvard University Press / Oxford: Pali Text Society.

Dhammasāmi, Khammai 2004. "Between Idealism and Pragmatism: A Study of Monastic Education in Burma and Thailand from the Seventeenth Century to the Present Day." DPhil diss., Oxford University.

——— 2007. "Idealism and Pragmatism: A Dilemma in the Current Monastic Education Systems of Burma and Thailand." In *Buddhism, Power and Political Order*, ed. by Ian Harris, pp. 10–25. London: Routledge.

Janakābhivaṃsa, Ashin 1999. *Abhidhamma in Daily Life*. Trans. by U Ko Lay. Revised by Sayadaw U Sīlananda. Yangon: International Theravāda Buddhist Missionary University. Available online at http://www.triplegem.plus.com/abdmjnka.htm (page last modified 2004). Also found at: http://www.dharmaweb.org/index.php/Abhidhamma_In_Daily_Life_By_Ashin_Janakabhivamsa (page last modified 2005). Author biography at http://www.triplegem.plus.com/biograp1.htm (page last modified 2004).

——— 1995. *Anagat sasana yay* (*The Future of the Sāsana*). (Reprint.) Rangoon: Department of Religious Affairs, Ministry of Religious Affairs.

——— 1992. *Ashin Janakābhivaṃsa e aso amaint mya* (*Ashin Janakābhivaṃsa's Teachings on Buddhist Ethics*), compiled by Chit Kyi Than (trans. into English by U On Pe). Rangoon: Win Pitaka Sarpay.

——— 1979. *Aṭṭhakathā akhye byu* (*Introductory Commentary*). Rangoon: Dept. of Religious Affairs.

——— 1999. *Bhatha-thwe* (*The Essence of the Religion*). (Reprint.) Amarapura: New Burma Offset Pitaka Press.

——— 1997a. *Bhathayay pyatthana mya aphyay hnint sittat tayadaw* (*Answers to Questions on Buddhism and a Dhamma Talk for the Armed Forces*) (Reprint.) Amarapura: Mahagandhayon Press.

——— 1994. "*Nan net khin ovada mya* (Morning Speeches)" [delivered in 1971]. *Dhamma byuha sarsaung* [a monthly Buddhist magazine]. Rangoon.

——— 1997b. *Nan net khin ovada mya* (*Collection of Morning Speeches*), ed. by Ashin Mahosadhapaṇḍita. 4th ed. Amarapura: Mahagandhayon Press.

——— 1997c. *Tatbhava thanthaya* (*One Life in Saṃsāra*) [autobiography]. 3rd reprint. Amarapura: Mahagandhayon Press.

——— 1975. *Yup pon shin kyint wut* (*Illustrated Training for the Sāmaṇera*). Rangoon: Department of Religious Affairs.

Narada, Mahā Thera 1978. *A Manual of Abhidhamma: Edited in the Original Pali Text with English Translation and Explanatory Notes*. http://www.zencomp.com/greatwisdom/ebud/abhisgho/abhis00.htm (page last modified 2002).

Learning, Living, Spreading the Dharma

A Postmodern Journey from Uku Baha, Lalitpur, to Hsi Lai Monastery, Hacienda Heights, California: How Ganesh Kumari Shakya Became Bhikkhunī Dhammawati

Sarah LeVine

Bhikkhunī Dhammawati, born Ganesh Kumari Shakya in 1934 to a Newar Buddhist family in Lalitpur/Patan in the Kathmandu Valley, is the president of the Theravāda Nuns' Order of Nepal. For more than four decades she has been fighting what she calls the "Asian Disease," a belief (she avows) shared by "almost all Nepalese men," that, regardless of their talents and competencies, all women are inferior to all men, simply by virtue of their sex. In this essay, we will see how from early adolescence until vigorous old age, with her intelligence, self-discipline, humor, and unflagging energy, she has raised the status of monastic and lay women. Drawing on interviews with Dhammawati herself and members of the Theravāda Buddhist community over the past ten years, magazine articles, and biographical publications,[1] I shall discuss three important decisions she has made during her long career: (1) to ordain as a Theravāda Buddhist nun (technically, a ten-precept laywoman); (2) to build her own nunnery in Kathmandu and, resisting repeated interventions by the monks, to develop a multi-faceted program

1. For a fuller account of the Theravāda nuns' community of Nepal, see LeVine and Gellner 2005.

of devotional and life-cycle rituals, education, and social services; and (3) to take full ordination according to Chinese bhikṣuṇī Mahāyāna rites.

When Dhammawati returned to Nepal in 1963 after fourteen years' training in Burma, she joined a small group of Newar nuns, the majority of whom were barely literate even in their own Newari language, and whose activities were closely monitored, if not dictated, by monks. Today she heads a community of more than two hundred nuns, many of them university educated, foreign trained, and multilingual, who, apart from receiving the precepts from a monk preceptor, run their own affairs entirely independently of the bhikkhu sangha. As one prominent monk admitted, "The gurumas [as Nepalese nuns are generally called] are more loved and respected by the laity than we bhikkhus are."

Dhammawati's dedication to raising the status of women as well as teaching buddhadharma has made her a role model for generations of girls and young women. Some have responded to her charge, "You must be as brave as I was!" by following her into "homelessness." But the large majority, as daughters, wives, and daughters-in-law, are demanding a voice in the decisions that affect their own lives, those of their children, and their communities. Dhammawati's resolve and audacity took her from her father's house in Lalitpur to the nunnery in Moulmein, Lower Burma, where she received the *Dhammācariya*, the highest qualification in the Burmese monastic education system and the equivalent of a doctorate in Buddhist Studies. Her life story is chronicled in her biography, *Dear Daughter.* Originally published in Burmese in 1963, it was translated into Newari (1967) and Nepali (1990) and has become required reading for Newar Buddhist girls.

Buddhist Modernism

The Buddhist revival movement, which ultimately transformed Newar Buddhism in Nepal, was launched in Sri Lanka in 1880 by the Theosophists Colonel Henry Olcott, an American, and Madame Blavatsky, a Russian noblewoman. The movement adopted many of the same tools that Christian missionaries on the island and elsewhere in South and Southeast Asia had long been using, notably preaching, teaching converts to read so they could read the scriptures themselves, undertaking Buddhist education for children, and publishing books, magazines, and vernacular translations of sacred texts.

In 1891 Olcott and Blavatsky's Singhalese disciple Dharmapāla established the Maha Bodhi Society. Born Don David Hewarwitarana and educated in Catholic mission schools, Dharmapāla's objectives were to restore the Bodh Gaya stūpa, where the Buddha had attained enlightenment, to Buddhist control and to revive Buddhism in India from which, aside from some remote Himalayan valleys, it had vanished in the thirteenth century. In contrast with many earlier Buddhist revival movements that had focused on purifying monasticism and elevating monks above the laity, Dharmapāla and his *dharmadūta* "dharma messengers" undercut the hierarchical nature of traditional Theravada Buddhism by emphasizing that attainment of enlightenment was possible for all Buddhists, lay as well as monastic, women as well as men (Gombrich and Obeyesekere 1988: 215–16). But though these Buddhist "modernists," as Heinz Bechert (1993–96) termed Dharmapāla and his followers, conceded that women had the same spiritual potential as men, they could not imagine granting them equal status in the sangha. If female monastics had a role to play, aside from domestic servitude, it would be, similar to that of the Roman Catholic nuns they encountered in Sri Lankan and Indian missionary posts, as nurses or primary school teachers, not as preachers or ritual specialists (Bartholomeusz 1994: 91–98).

I call Dhammawati's career a postmodern journey because as a young woman she rejected Buddhist modernist assumptions about gender, brought her subjective analysis to Buddhist practices as she encountered them, and worked steadily to change cultural beliefs and to build institutions in which nuns and lay women are equal—and sometimes, given energy and talents, superior—to monks and laymen.

At the beginning of the twentieth century, female Buddhist renouncers, most of whom were impoverished rural widows, could be found in Sri Lanka, Burma, and Thailand; but given that *upasampadā*, the full ordination rite for Theravāda Buddhist nuns, had died out in the eleventh century, the social and religious status of these "eight-precept" and "ten-precept" laywomen, known as *dasa sil mata* in Sri Lanka, *thilashin* in Burma, and *maechi* in Thailand, was very low. Since donations to these women were believed to generate little spiritual merit, most lay people were unwilling to give them alms. Confined to the back of temples, they performed menial housekeeping tasks for the monks, from whom they received leftover food that the monks had collected on the alms-round. Nevertheless, by the late nineteenth century, the spread of Western-style schooling for girls was beginning to encourage the idea that wife and mother were not the only respectable adult roles available for women. Like a man, a woman should be able to lead a spiritual life if she chose. Thus, in addition to impoverished rural widows, the Buddhist modernist movement began to attract women from a broader demographic. Among them was Catharine de Alwis, a Sinhalese woman belonging to an elite Anglican family who, in middle age, went to study Buddhism in Sagaing, Burma. In 1905, after taking the precepts and a new name, Sudharmacārī, she returned to Sri Lanka, where she established an order of female social activist and educator renouncers, and the first of several nunneries, Upasikaramaya, in Kandy, where she died at age ninety in 1939 (Bartholomeusz 1994: 103). A prominent Burmese thilashin was Daw Malayi (1880–1984) who established a nunnery in Sagaing in 1907 where, over subsequent decades, she trained numerous *ngebyu* (virgin) Buddhist scholars, thereby raising the status of "ordained laywomen" in the eyes of both monks and laity (Kawanami 2000). Thai maechi nuns, however, remained despised and marginal for much longer. One of the earliest to come to prominence was Voramai Kabilsingh, the journalist widow of an MP who, in the 1960s, took the precepts and turned her family home into a school and orphanage and, in 1972, took bhikṣuṇī ordination in Taiwan (Batchelor 2000).

Unlike Catharine de Alwis, Daw Malayi, or Voramai Kabilsingh, Dhammawati was not from a privileged family. Furthermore, as a child, she never set foot in a school. During her childhood, Nepal was still being ruled by the Rana family as their private fiefdom, cut off from a rapidly modernizing world across their southern border. Of Nepalese children, less than 1 percent—most of whom were scions of princely families or Hindu courtiers' sons—were attending Western-type schools. The first girls' school in Kathmandu opened in 1942 and the first in Lalitpur in 1948. Almost all the few dozen students in both schools were from a small circle of progressive high-caste Hindu families (LeVine 2006). As late as the mid-nineteenth century the majority of the population of the Kathmandu Valley had been Newar (Mahayana) Buddhist. But after 1846 when the brahmanically orthodox Nepali-speaking Rana family took control of the kingdom, Buddhists found themselves pushed to the margins of the society. In order to improve their prospects, ultimately a majority of Newars identified themselves as Hindus and sought to assimilate to the now-dominant Nepali Parbatya (hill people) culture. The residual Buddhist population pursued traditional caste occupations as farmers, traders, icon-makers, and goldsmiths. Since these required minimal literacy, for decades after Western-model schooling became widespread in Nepal, Buddhists were typically less interested than Hindus in formal education, especially for girls.

The Newar society from which Ganesh Kumari, the future Dhammawati, came, was and largely still is today, a caste society divided into a complex hierarchy of about twenty castes (Gellner 1995: 1–37). Ganesh Kumari, Dhammawati's given name at birth, was a Shakya; that is, she belonged to the Newar Buddhist caste whose male members, unlike Vajracharya household priests, were part-time temple priests. As they had no *jajman* and therefore could not make a living as priests, they pursued traditional craft occupations. Ganesh Kumari's father, Harsha Man Shakya, had taken initiation in Uku Baha, his ancestral temple, and he and his family lived just outside the temple gate where he had a goldsmith's workshop.

Buddhist Modernism Comes to Nepal

In the 1920s a few young Newars from the Kathmandu Valley became dissatisfied with their indigenous Buddhism, which they regarded as ritually baroque and elitist. After taking tantric initiation, members of the Buddhist upper castes had access to Sanskrit texts which most didn't understand, and participated in esoteric rituals whose meaning was opaque; religious activities of the middle and lower castes were restricted to making donations to the temple and sponsoring protective rituals. Meanwhile, aside from the wives of Vajracharya household priests who played a supportive, albeit essential, role in ritual performance, women of all castes were relegated to giving *dāna* and performing domestic rituals for the welfare of their families.

The dissidents began searching for a form of Buddhism that was socially more inclusive and free of many Hindu features that had been incorporated into Buddhist practice over the centuries. After considering and rejecting Tibetan Buddhism, they encountered Maha Bodhi missionaries at Buddhist sacred sites in India. Persuaded by their modernist message, they determined to strip Newar Buddhism of Hindu accretions, especially blood sacrifice, and to reintroduce the monasticism that had disappeared in the middle ages when, adopting the Hindu model, Buddhist monks had metamorphosed into householder priests. They took the precepts from Chandramani, a Maha Bodhi Society monk resident at Kushinagar, the final resting place of the Buddha, and returned to spread the good news in Nepal. By the early 1930s a few women were shaving their head and taking the precepts from Chandramani, who designated them *anagārikā*, "homeless ones." Back home in Kathmandu, the converts faced the opposition of the Rana government, which, fearful of the free-India movement on the other side of the border, viewed any new idea, religious as well as political, as a potential threat to their regime. Harassed, imprisoned, and even exiled, the Theravādins struggled on until, after Indian independence in 1947, Rana control began to slacken and they attained a measure of freedom to preach and teach (Kloppenberg 1977). It was during this period, shortly before the Rana regime was overthrown and the monarchy was restored to its full powers, that Ganesh Kumari had her first exposure to Theravāda Buddhism.

Decision One: To Ordain as a Nun

Ganesh Kumari's mother, Hira Thaku, an early Theravāda convert, began going to Sumangal Vihara, the first temple that Theravādins established in Patan, to study buddhadharma with a monk named Buddhaghosa who had spent World War II in a monastery in Moulmein, Burma. Thinking that her restless thirteen-year-old daughter, Ganesh Kumari, might benefit from the discipline of daily study, she persuaded her husband, Harsha Man, to let the girl attend Buddhaghosa's class. Ganesh Kumari, who had learned to read her mother tongue, Newari, from the tutor whom her father employed to teach her brothers, soon finished reading the few Newari translations of Buddhist texts that were available, and began to learn Pali in order to read the canon in its original language. When, after a year, Buddhaghosa left Nepal for further study in Burma, she was devastated. She recalls, "I thought, I've had just a glimpse of nirvāṇa—and now it's vanished. Will I ever see it again?" A Burmese monk named Dhammabuddha who happened to be visiting during the Shiva Ratri spring festival (the Rana government only permitted foreigners to enter the Valley if they came as pilgrims during religious festivals), was impressed by her intelligence and, seeing how upset she was at Buddhaghosa's departure, suggested she accompany him to Burma where, after ordination as a thilashin nun, she could continue her studies. As he would be leaving shortly, he told her she only had a few days in which to make up her mind.

Because there were still no nuns living in Lalitpur, Ganesh Kumari had never actually laid eyes on one and had no idea what ordination entailed, other than, as her mother told her, she would have to cut off her long braids of which she was inordinately proud. "But I was determined to go to Burma," she said fifty years later. "All I wanted was study." Two other factors, aside from her enchantment with the dharma, were important. First, her father was arranging her marriage. Her older sister, supposedly exhausted by domestic work and childbearing, had recently died, and the prospect of marriage terrified Ganesh Kumari. Second, her mother very much wanted her to ordain. Four years earlier, when Ganesh Kumari was ten, her mother and her oldest brother's wife had given birth within a few days of each other. In Newar culture, a couple's sexual life should finish when their eldest son brings his bride into the house. That clearly had not been the case with Hira Thaku and Harsha Man. Guilt-ridden and publicly humiliated, Hira Thaku, already a devout upāsikā, became more devout than ever; because giving a child to the sangha is viewed as one of the most meritorious donations a Buddhist can make, she gave her wholehearted consent when the Burmese monk extended his offer to her daughter. She even went so far as to propose that her second son, Kiran, ordain as well.

While she distracted her husband, brother and sister set off on foot with Dhammabuddha; but within the hour Harsha Man discovered they'd left and sent police after them. Ganesh Kumari and Dhammabuddha managed to evade them and make their way out of the Valley and over the Mahabharata Mountains into India but Kiran was caught and brought home. Soon after Ganesh Kumari's arrival at Kushinagar, where she cut off her braids herself, her father dispatched a prominent Nepalese monk named Amritananda to bring her back; but Ganesh Kumari refused to return with him. As she didn't have her father's permission, Chandramani, the resident Maha Bodhi Society monk, was unable to give her the precepts. As she had no passport, passage from Calcutta by ship to Rangoon was impossible as well, so Dhammabuddha had to take her overland by train, bus, and on foot through the jungles of Bengal, Assam, and Manipur to the Burmese border, where both she and Dhammabuddha were jailed, Ganesh Kumari because she had no travel documents and Dhammabuddha because the border guards suspected him of intending to sell the girl into prostitution in Burma. Eventually, after many adventures and a six-month wait in Rangoon for her father to give his permission, she was ordained and given a new name and traveled on to Moulmein, where she enrolled in Kemarama nunnery. Headed by its founder, an upper-class ngebyu virgin nun named Daw Pannachari, Kemarama was a well-known center of Buddhist scholarship. Though only nuns were enrolled there, the curriculum followed was identical to the one pursued by young monks, and the instruction was thought to be equally good if not better than instruction in monastic training centers. Dhammawati was the first Nepalese nun to enter a foreign training institution, and for the first nine of the thirteen years she spent at Kemarama, she was the only foreigner. Even so, she claims she never felt homesick because she was doing exactly what she wanted to do, which was to study the dharma.

In 1963, Dhammawati, who was already becoming known as a gifted scholar and preacher, turned down an offer to stay on as an instructor at Kemarama nunnery. Although she'd had many happy years in Burma (and had almost forgotten her own language), she had promised her mother to come home to teach the dharma, and to teach it to women in particular. She left Moulmein for Kathmandu accompanied by her closest friend, a Burmese nun named Daw Gunawati. At that time Dhammawati, Daw Gunawati, and their teacher, Daw Pannachari, abbess of Kemarama nunnery, were the only female holders of the *Dhammācariya* degree. Several Nepalese monks had studied in Burma but none had attained the *Dhammācariya*; in more than four decades since then, only one monk has done so.

Decision Two: To Establish Her Own Nunnery

When Dhammawati returned to Kathmandu at age twenty-eight, she received a rapturous welcome, but after the cheers and banner waving were over, reality hit her. "It was like going from heaven to hell," she recalled. In the sangha, as in the family, Burmese women enjoyed high status. But now she discovered that the accomplishments that had won her respect in Burma were ignored, at least by men. In Nepal, as an overage unmarried woman and a highly trained anagārikā, she was an anomaly.

She decided not to live in Kimdol Vihara, the only nunnery in the city, which at the time was headed by Dhammacārī, a well-known but self-educated nun. She soon found living at home with her parents impossible because her father, whose health was failing, was constantly at her to exchange her nun's dress for a sari and get married before he died. She and Gunawati moved in with an upāsaka and his family and ran a school for Buddhist children in a nearby temple. Dhammawati also began teaching adults, mostly women; one of these invited her, as well as a prominent monk, to preach at her wealthy husband's funeral. On the grounds that a mere anagārikā could not be on the same program as a bhikkhu, Amritananda Mahāthera, the monk whom her father had sent to bring her back from Kushinagar in 1949, and who by now was the most senior monk in Nepal, forbade Dhammawati to preach at the funeral. "I was enraged," she recalled many years later. "I believe the bhikkhus were scared of me because I'd had more dharma training than any of them, and they knew I'd been invited to speak at the funeral because people liked my preaching more than theirs." The monks were determined to silence her and she was just as determined to preach. It was Gunawati who got her to stand down. "My friend told me, 'a confrontation will only make things worse for you. The way to prove your worth isn't by fighting the bhikkhus, it's by doing good work in the community.' So I decided, all right, if the bhikkhus won't let me preach in their viharas, I'll build my own." Unlike Kimdol Vihara, which housed widows and divorcees who kept talking about children and husbands and love and family matters, Dhammawati decided to follow the Burmese ngebyu model: she would only accept never-married nuns who, being freer of family attachments, would be better able to focus on dharma work. Most important, as she explained, "In my own vihara, I would be free to teach and preach and do whatever I wanted and the bhikkhus wouldn't be able to interfere."

After their father's death, two of her brothers contributed a portion of their inheritance to Dhammawati's mission. This, together with the contributions of a handful of female devotees, some of whom contributed gold bangles rather than cash, allowed Dhammawati to purchase a small plot in Nagha Tol, the courtyard of an ancient stūpa in Kathmandu, and build a modest nunnery, which she called Dharmakirti, "glory of the dharma." Inaugurated in 1965, it initially housed five "virgin" nuns who had been trained in Moulmein. Repeated attempts by Amritananda and other senior monks to interfere in their activities and even to close Dharmakirti down were unsuccessful. Under Dhammawati's leadership and with the quiet encouragement of Buddhaghosa, her first teacher who now headed his own monastery, and steadily increasing lay support, particularly from the wives of wealthy men in the business community, the nuns developed a complex program of devotional and life-cycle rituals, dharma education, pastoral counseling, social and medical services, and mission activities in villages in the Kathmandu Valley and beyond.

A number of factors contributed to Dhammawati's early success in fighting the Asian Disease. She herself emphasized the importance, as role models, of her Burmese scholar nun teachers, most especially her abbess, Daw Pannachari, who had convinced her that women were equal in every way to men. Clearly, she managed to convince the general public of this truth also for, as Dhammawati observed, "All sorts of big men, both monks and laymen, would come to Kemarama seeking my guru's advice." Another important factor was the companionship, talents, stoicism, and quiet wisdom of her Burmese friend Daw Gunawati, who spent more than twenty years working in Nepal before returning to Rangoon to establish her own nunnery. Dhammawati's upper-caste background was crucial too. In the early years of the Theravāda movement in Nepal, recruits to both the monks' and the nuns' order were exclusively from Buddhist upper castes: Vajracharyas, Shakyas, and Tuladhars; the few Hindus who ordained were Shresthas, i.e., also upper-caste. By the 1980s, however, upper-caste recruitment to the monks' order had virtually ceased. With the opening up of the country to trade and foreign influence and the rapid spread of Western-style education after the revolution of 1951, young men from upper-caste families no longer saw ordination as a career option. Their places in the sangha were being taken by poor boys from farming and occupational caste backgrounds whose families looked to the order to provide their sons with educational opportunities—usually in Sri Lanka, Burma, and, later, in Thailand—which they themselves couldn't afford to provide. Options for young *women* from well-placed Buddhist families, however, were little changed. Even if they managed to get a university education and afterward a government post, their accomplishments didn't exempt them from what was still regarded as the only legitimate adult role, namely being a wife and mother devoted to the welfare of the family. At least within memory, a few upper-caste Newar women have remained unmarried, usually because they didn't receive a "good enough" marriage proposal. Given that, by living independently, a single woman would be the object of criticism and salacious gossip, even if she were employed, she would feel obliged to live with her family. Too often, as a woman ages and loses her parents, she incurs the resentment of her extended family. Although nuns may give a variety of reasons for joining the order, such as to study the dharma, to please their mothers, to follow the example of an admired teacher, to have more time for meditation, or to travel abroad, an overwhelming number admit that their main reason was to escape marriage and the sorrows of women who live in a patriarchal society. Among these they include going to live among strangers in one's husband's house, domination and mistreatment by mothers- and sisters-in-law, the dangers of pregnancy and childbirth, and the death of children. Furthermore, unlike monks who disrobe and get married after finishing their monastic education, Nepalese nuns, with very few exceptions, have remained in the order. For them, lifelong celibacy spells freedom, not jail.

Dhammawati offers girls and young women a respectable alternative to marriage and motherhood. Though not all recruits to the nuns' order are from upper-caste families, most, including those from farming and occupational castes, are from relatively wealthy backgrounds. Perceived by their families as fields of spiritual merit, they tend to attract donations of money and other resources to Dharmakirti and to the "virgins only" nunneries that Dhammawati's student-disciples have established in the city and surrounding settlements. Thus, by contrast with the monks who have looked increasingly to foreign donors for funds for education, construction, and even day-to-day maintenance, Dhammawati and her lieutenants have been able to raise large sums of money for their projects from the Newar business community. Upper-caste Buddhist merchants, reluctant to give substantial sums to monks who are the sons of farmers, barbers, or butchers, tend to be generous to nuns with whose families they feast and intermarry (LeVine 2001).

Perhaps the most important factor in Dhammawati's success has been her expansion of the role of laywomen in Buddhist affairs. In traditional Newar Buddhism, upper-caste wives take tantric initiations with their husbands and thereafter are enjoined to perform certain rituals every day for the rest of their married lives. The wives of Vajracharya householder priests accompany their husbands to ritual performances in order to prepare the requisites their husbands use and afterward are paid for their services. They do not read the scriptures and receive no training in Buddhist thought and philosophy, however. Meanwhile the religious role of most Newar Buddhist women, who make up the large majority of devotees visiting any temple on any given day, is confined to giving *dāna* and domestic ritual performance.

While, from the outset, Dhammawati has provided Buddhist education for children, her main objective has always been to teach the dharma to women. Her talents as a preacher soon raised the ire of the monks' order; but once she had her own nunnery her devotees continued to grow in number regardless. Within months, hundreds of people, most but not all women, would crowd into Dharmakirti to hear her preach on Saturdays, the day of rest in Nepal. On weekdays she and her colleagues gave literacy classes for which they provided reading materials at every level of difficulty from simple stories about the Buddha's life to *Abhidhamma*. Dhammawati herself published prolifically, including Newari translations from the Pali Canon, commentaries, and, eventually, a multi-level Buddhist studies curriculum.

In contrast with the traditional Newar Buddhist temple, women play a major role in Dharmakirti and the "branch" nunneries which Dhammawati's disciples have founded elsewhere. As members of the nunnery donors' committee, women have helped organize many temple functions, including *bhojana dāna* celebratory feasts, pilgrimages, educational outreach programs, meditation retreats, and of course fundraising. Until recent changes in the inheritance laws, only Nepalese women who had no brothers could inherit parental property; few of Dhammawati's female devotees had substantial resources of their own. Rather, they were financially dependent on fathers, husbands, and brothers. Thus it had to be to these wealthy businessmen relatives that female devotees and Dhammawati herself turned for support. But as more young women have become highly educated, entered professions, or started businesses, thereby achieving financial independence and relative wealth, they too have been recruited to nunnery committees. Many of these younger women are graduates not only of the childrens' program but also of the Buddhist Studies Circle, which Dhammawati and Daw Gunawati started in 1972. Initially a small group of secondary school girls, the Circle soon expanded to over a hundred young people, including some boys, who met once a week to discuss a range of issues and hear speakers on Buddhist topics; after a few years a subcommittee started publishing a magazine as well as books, some of which were written by Circle members. The Circle continues to meet and some of the original members, now middle-aged women in positions of power and influence, still attend. One woman, a US-trained PhD, who works for an international organization and runs the children's program at Dharmakirti, recalled how, long ago, Dhammawati had supported her in her determination to delay marriage as long as possible while she pursued her education.

Decision Three: To Take Full Ordination According to Mahāyāna Rites

Dhammawati believed that full ordination was neither possible nor desirable until 1987 when she attended the First International Conference of Buddhist Nuns at Bodh Gaya and heard the Dalai Lama observe, in his opening address, that in the Buddha's time the sangha included four categories of disciples: bhikṣu, bhikṣuṇīs, upāsakas, and upāsikās. Although all four still existed in China in modern times, said His Holiness, in other parts of the Buddhist world bhikṣuṇīs were lacking. "Speaking personally as a Tibetan Buddhist," he added, "if an authentic bhikṣuṇī lineage [such as the Chinese lineage] could be established within the Tibetan tradition, this would truly be something to be welcomed" (Tsomo 1988: 44). In a private audience, His Holiness told Dhammawati that in his opinion, men and women had equal potential and that therefore full ordination should be available to all nuns, regardless of the tradition they belonged to, just as it was to all monks.

Until this point, Dhammawati had shared the views of the thilashin by whom she had been trained in Burma. Although highly respected by monastics and laity alike for their scholarship, they believed that, since full ordination according to Theravada rites was impossible, they had no alternative to living as "ordained" laywomen. But now Dhammawati began to undergo a sea change. If, as she had learned at the conference, the Chinese bhikṣuṇī ordination lineage had been introduced from Sri Lanka, albeit in the fifth century, why shouldn't it be reintroduced to South Asia from whence it came? She also began to question the eight *garudhamma/gurudharma* or chief laws that the Lord Buddha had imposed on his aunt and stepmother Mahāprajāpatī and her followers when he agreed to receive them into the order. In particular she questioned the validity and authenticity of the first rule: "A nun who has been ordained (even) for a century must greet respectfully, rise up from her seat, salute with joint palms, and make proper homage to a monk ordained only that day." How could the Lord Buddha, who had admitted that a woman was as capable of attaining enlightenment as a man, then reverse himself and subordinate all nuns, regardless of seniority, to even the most junior monk? Could this really be *buddhavacana* (the word of the Buddha)? Or had misogynist monks misinterpreted the Lord Buddha's words?

A few months later, Dhammawati received a visit in Kathmandu from some Taiwanese nuns belonging to the Fo Guang San order. By that time she had undergone a radical reevaluation of much that she had understood to be unassailable truth concerning the status of women within the sangha. After admiring the work that she and her students were doing, the visitors invited her and two other Nepalese nuns to attend the inauguration of Hsi Lai Monastery, a branch of Fo Guang San in Hacienda Heights, California, and to receive *upasampadā* bhikṣuṇī ordination according to Chinese rites. Fully aware that by doing so she would invite the unanimous condemnation of the Nepalese monks' order, she accepted the invitation. In December 1988 she announced that she was going to Fo Guang San headquarters in Taiwan. With two younger colleagues she did in fact fly to Taipei but then she flew on to California. Daw Gunawati accompanied them but only as an observer. As a Burmese nun who was planning an eventual return to the land of her birth, she didn't dare antagonize her preceptors.

After several months, the newly ordained nuns returned to Nepal only to find that news of their ordination had preceded them. As predicted, with only a couple of exceptions, the senior monks were furious. "They told us that we were no longer Theravādins but Mahāyānists. That we should exchange our pink and orange dresses for yellow Chinese dresses, start chanting the name of Amitābha Buddha in Chinese and doing full-length prostrations, and so on. Of course they have continued calling us anagārikā, not bhikṣuṇī. But we don't care what they say. We are still Theravādins and we have brought back bhikṣuṇī ordination from China." Although about thirty more Nepalese nuns have taken full ordination, some from Taiwanese and others from Mainland Chinese monks and nuns, the monks have still not admitted them to the Mahāsaṅgha, the Theravāda monastic order of Nepal. But the older more conservative monks are dying off and the younger monks are considerably more open-minded than their preceptors. So Dhammawati looks forward to the day when, instead of having to send her disciples abroad for *upasampadā*, it will be possible to assemble a quorum of monks to officiate at an ordination ceremony in Nepal.

What practical difference has full ordination made in the nuns' daily lives? True, they have sworn to abide by the 338 rules of the *Bhikṣuṇī Prātimokṣa*, the rules of conduct for nuns, rather than ten anagārikā precepts. But before ordination they were already observing, albeit informally, all those rules of conduct that were possible to keep as a modern monastic (some rules, for example those which prohibit going out of the nunnery alone and riding in a vehicle, had long been discarded as impractical). Although their Chinese preceptors encouraged them to meet every fifteen days to recite the rules, confess violations, and receive absolution, they never instituted this practice because of the geographical distances between nunneries and their increasingly busy schedules. Instead, at night before sleeping each nun confesses to herself and gives herself absolution. Do the laity hold them in greater esteem now that they are bhikṣuṇī than they did when they were anagārikā? Few of their devotees have a real understanding of what full ordination implies. As Daw Gunawati suggested to Dhammawati more than forty years ago, ordinary people value and esteem the nuns for the work they see them doing in the community and not for picking fights with the monks over status.

Conclusion

To sum up, Dhammawati returned to Nepal from Burma with a mission. Her first objective was to teach buddhadharma to women who had minimal or no access to the Buddha's teaching. Her second more ambitious goal was to raise the status of nuns and, by extension, of women in general. Until she attended the conference at Bodh Gaya in 1987, she had never heard of the Women's Movement or the growing demand for gender equality within the Buddhist sangha. A voracious reader in Burmese, Pali, and Sanskrit, she read—and spoke—Hindi and Nepali with difficulty. After fourteen years away, even her native Newari was rusty. She knew no English—increasingly the essential international language—and still does not. When she receives foreign visitors or travels abroad other than to Burma, she must be accompanied by a translator. As a girl, she never set foot inside a Western-type school; her education was exclusively monastic. In this regard, she differs markedly from other leading activist Theravāda nuns such as Kusuma Davendra of Sri Lanka and Chatsumarn Kabilsingh of Thailand, both former university professors.

Dhammawati's models for how to proceed with her mission were provided by the Burmese nuns under whom she had studied and the Nepalese monks with whom she was destined to struggle for decades. From her teachers in Kemarama nunnery she learned self-discipline, scholarship, and how to transfix an audience; from the monks she learned the tools of Buddhist modernism: how to organize and service the lay community. Using their formulae, she has built an impressively effective structure. The big question is: what will happen to the Nepalese nuns' order and its myriad groups of lay supporters when Dhammawati, the quintessential micro-manager, is gone? Perhaps her greatest strength has been her ability to attract talented monastic women. Ten years ago, when I first got to know her, she was keeping tight control of every aspect of the order. But her highly educated English, Hindi, Thai, Singhala, and Chinese-speaking lieutenants (three have PhDs) who head branch nunneries, run outreach programs in the villages, give papers at foreign conferences, lead pilgrimages abroad, and recruit novices and raise funds, have begun to contest her authority. Despite her simple style—no domestic task seems to be beneath her as she often sweeps floors, washes teacups, and makes beds for visitors—she certainly enjoys her celebrity status; each confrontation with a lieutenant has been turbulent, and delegating authority has certainly been painful for her. Nevertheless, unlike the senior monks who, as their mental acuity starts to falter, tend to cling tenaciously to their authority, delegate she does, despite remaining energetic and sharp. Today her younger colleagues make all but the most major decisions on their own, and she appears to be at peace with it.

Bibliography

Bartholemeusz, Tessa 1994. *Women Under the Bo Tree.* Cambridge: Cambridge University Press.

Batchelor, Martine 2000. "Voramai Kabilsingh: The First Thai Bhikkunī and Chatsumarn Kabilsingh: Advocate for a Bhikkhunī Sangha in Thailand." In *Women In Buddhism, Buddhism's Women: Tradition, Revision, Renewal,* ed. by E. B. Findly, pp. 58–61. Boston: Wisdom Publications.

Bechert, Heinz 1993–96. *Buddhismus, Staat und Gesellschaft in den Ländern des Theravāda Buddhismus.* Frankfurt: A. Metzner / Wiesbaden: O. Harrasowitz.

Gellner, David N. 1995. "Introduction." In *Contested Hierarchies: A Collaborative Ethnography of Caste in the Kathmandu Valley, Nepal,* ed. by D. N. Gellner and D. Quigley, pp. 1–37. Oxford: Clarendon Press.

Gombrich, Richard F., and Gananath Obeyesekere 1988. *Buddhism Transformed: Religious Change in Sri Lanka.* Princeton, NJ: Princeton University Press.

Kawanami, Hiroko 2000. "Patterns of Renunciation: The Changing World of Burmese Nuns." In *Women In Buddhism, Buddhism's Women: Tradition, Revision, Renewal,* ed. by E. B. Findly, pp. 159–71. Boston: Wisdom Publications.

Kloppenberg, Ria 1977. "Theravāda Buddhism in Nepal." *Kailash* 5: 301–22.

LeVine, Sarah 2001. "The Finances of a Twentieth-Century Buddhist Mission: Building Support for the Theravada Nuns Order of Nepal." *Journal of the International Association of Buddhist Studies* 24.2: 217–40.

———— 2006. "Getting In, Dropping Out, and Staying On: Determinants of Girls' School Attendance in the Kathmandu Valley of Nepal." *Anthropology and Education Quarterly* 37.1: 21–41.

LeVine, Sarah, and David N. Gellner 2005. *Rebuilding Buddhism: The Theravada Movement in Twentieth-Century Nepal.* Cambridge, MA: Harvard University Press.

Tsomo, Karma Lekshe, ed. 1988. *Sakyadhita, Daughters of the Buddha.* Ithaca, NY: Snow Lion Publications.

III.

Tibet Re-narrated: Biographies of Tibetan Masters

The Evolution of the Biographies of Milarepa and Rechungpa

Peter Alan Roberts

Introduction

The biographies of Milarepa and Rechungpa evolved in quite distinct and opposite ways. The term *rnam thar*, literally "liberation," is an unusual word for biographies that appears to have originated in the Kadam tradition founded by Dromtön (1005–64), the pupil of Atiśa Dīpaṃkaraśrījñāna (982–1054), who came to Tibet in 1042. *Rnam thar* eventually displaced the use of more straightforward terms such as *lo rgyus*, "account, history." The earliest Kadampa biographies, such as those of Atiśa and Rinchen Sangpo, employ this word. Gampopa (1079–1153), who was schooled in the Kadam tradition and provides us with our earliest biographies of Milarepa, Marpa, Naropa, and Tilopa, also apparently used this term for these biographies. *Rnam thar* is the Tibetan translation of the Sanskrit word *vimokṣa*, which means "liberation" but never has the meaning of biography. The source of this usage of rnam thar appears to be from the Tibetan translation of Śāntideva's *Bodhisattvacaryāvatāra*, which was written in the seventh or eighth century. This text was of great importance for the Kadampa, whose followers would also memorize the text in accordance with the Tibetan approach to studies. The *Bodhisattvacaryāvatāra* makes only a few references to earlier texts, one of which is in the fifth chapter, where Śāntideva advises:

> Learn behavior toward the guru
> from *The Liberation of Śrīsambhava.*[1]

This passage is generally conceived in Tibet, and in English translations from Tibetan, as referring to a biography of a Śrīsambhava, as even the surviving Indian commentaries identifying the text make no reference to its contents.[2] It is a standard view and practice in Tibetan scholarship to emphasize the commentaries over the sūtras and tantras, which are with a few exceptions little studied other than as select quotations. "The liberation of Śrīsambhava" is, in fact, one of the untitled chapters of the *Gaṇḍavyūha-sūtra*, which is itself the final section of the *Avataṃsaka-sūtra.* It relates how Sudhana met a series of fifty-three teachers, each of whom gave him a *vimokṣa*, which here means the method they used for attaining liberation. The Śāntideva reference omits to mention that two teachers, using the dual first person throughout, teach in unison this *vimokṣa*, which is comprised of showing respect to the guru. The other teacher was a woman named Śrīmatī, and the chapter contains no biographical information on either teacher.

The use of the word *rnam thar* to mean a method for liberation was still being used by Gampopa's own nephew in his colophon to a collection of Gampopa's public lecture notes.[3]

The first printing of a *rnam thar* of Milarepa was made in 1488, over three hundred years after his death, together with its companion volume of a collection of songs. The songs are known in English translation as *The Hundred Thousand Songs of Milarepa*, an over-literal translation, as every collection of songs or collected works has *'bum* ("hundred thousand") added to it. This version of his life, written by Tsangnyön Heruka (1452–1507), has become the most widely translated biography in Tibetan literature, and has a claim to

1. *Bodhisattvacaryāvatāra* 5:103. Skt.: *śrīsambhavavimokṣāc ca śikṣed yad guruvartanam* | Tib.: *dpal 'byung ba yi rnam thar las* | | *bla ma bsten pa'i tshul ltar bslab* | |.

2. Prajñākaramati, *Bodhicaryāvatāra-pañjikā; Byang chub sems dpa'i spyod pa la 'jug pa'i dka' 'grel.* sDe dge'i bsTan 'gyur, *dbu ma*, vol. *la*, 41b–288a. Vairocanarakṣita, *Bodhicaryāvatāra-pañjikā; Byang chub sems dpa'i spyod pa la 'jug pa'i dka' 'grel.* sDe dge'i bsTan 'gyur, *dbu ma*, vol. *sha*, 95b–158b. Vibhūticandra, *Bodhicaryāvatāra-duravabodhana-nirṇaya-nāma-grantha; Byang chub sems dpa'i spyod pa la 'jug pa'i rtogs par dka' ba'i gnas gtan la dbab pa zhes bya ba'i gzhung.* sDe dge'i bsTan 'gyur, *dbu ma*, vol. *sha*. 192b–285a.

3. sGam po pa, *Khams gsum chos kyi rgyal po dpal mnyam med sgam po pa 'gro mgon bsod nams rin chen mchog gi gsung 'bum yid bzhin nor bu* (Kathmandu 2000): 646–47.

be Tibet's greatest literary work of this genre. It has inspired a French play,[4] a comic book,[5] an Italian movie,[6] and recently a Tibetan movie.[7]

Tsangnyön Heruka brilliantly transformed Milarepa's life story into a first-person narrative. He separated the bulk of Milarepa's life, which describes his career as a teacher and is primarily composed of songs, into its own volume: *The Hundred Thousand Songs*. Tsangnyön's version uses the literary device of Rechungpa requesting Milarepa to relate his life (even though in earlier versions he learned this upon first becoming his pupil). Therefore, it has become popularly conceived of in Tibet as an autobiography by Milarepa as written down by Rechungpa, and Rechungpa was at first credited as its author in the West. However, as will be shown here, it is the result of almost three centuries of narrative developments. It was preceded by a number of biographies in manuscript form, and by evolving oral traditions of narrative and song. Some became extremely rare, existing as only a few manuscripts, while many of these versions are known of only through references or criticisms.

Tsangnyön Heruka's version has a well-written and dramatic narrative, unlike the usual hagiography where there is little individual character but a series of miracles, visions, and activities that seem easily interchangeable between various biographies. Not only was Tsangnyön a very good writer, but his Milarepa biography is also of great importance to Tibetan Buddhism in general because it fulfills two very significant functions. The first function has to do with the fact that in the Vajrayāna's higher tantras, specifically in Tsangnyön's Kagyü tradition, it is emphasized that through these practices one can attain buddhahood in one lifetime. However, the masters in the lineage of the Kagyü, beginning with Tilopa and Nāropa in India and then Milarepa's teacher Marpa in Tibet, continuing with Milarepa's pupil Gampopa, who created the monastic Kagyü, and Gampopa's pupils, such as the first of the series of Karmapas, are all depicted as emanations who were already enlightened and who only manifested these lives in order to benefit beings. Therefore, to say they all achieved enlightenment in one lifetime is not quite satisfying, for it leaves open the question of whether truly ordinary beings

4. Schmitt 1997.

5. van Dam 1991.

6. Cavani 1974.

7. Neten Chokling, *Milarepa* (Shining Moon Productions, 2006).

could achieve enlightenment in one lifetime. Milarepa stands out within this lineage as being not only an ordinary person who achieves buddhahood through these practices, but as being worse than ordinary, for he was a mass murderer, having killed thirty-five people through the power of sorcery. In spite of having accrued enough bad karma to send him to hell, he not only purified the karma but attained complete enlightenment through the Kagyü lineage practices. His attainment is evidenced by his miraculous abilities, such as flying, walking through rocks, and clairvoyance. Also, after his death, there were myriad miraculous manifestations, and he even sat up on his funeral pyre, the flames taking on the shape of a lotus as he sang a final song of advice. Therefore lamas in all the traditions of Tibetan Buddhism—even Bön in spite of its unfavorable depiction in Tsangnyön's works—reference Milarepa as a touchstone for demonstrating the power of the higher tantras. For example, the current head of the Bön school, H.H. Menri Rinpoche, in a public talk for which I was translator, said to the audience that they can achieve buddhahood if they have the diligence of Milarepa.

This leads to the other pedagogical function that this story has, because the practitioner, accepting the power of these practices, might then wonder why every ordinary person who practices them doesn't become enlightened. Why is buddhahood in one lifetime, for those not already enlightened, so rare? The answer is that the practitioner has to be just like Milarepa in order to attain the same result. This is beyond the capacity of an ordinary being, for the biography depicts a life of extreme endurance and suffering, during which, living without food or clothing in mountain caves for years, he becomes skeletal and turns green through eating nothing but nettles. The biography demonstrates that while the practices work, the readers should have realistic expectations in terms of their own results, because they cannot live the life of Milarepa. In fact, I have translated for lamas advising that one shouldn't even *try* to live like Milarepa: that if you give everything you own away and go to live in a mountain cave, you will only end up miserable, unenlightened, and destitute.

The Life of Milarepa

This is how the version of Milarepa's life is popularly known from Tsangnyön's biography: He is born as Töpa Gawa to a merchant and his wife, and he also has a little sister. His father dies when he is young, and his paternal uncle takes everything from the family, treats them like servants, and refuses to give them their inheritance. Milarepa's mother says she will commit suicide if he doesn't go away to learn sorcery and take revenge. Milarepa does so and his sorcery causes the uncle's house to collapse during a marriage party, killing thirty-five guests. His mother then has him attack the village with a hailstorm to intimidate the villagers so they won't dare take their revenge against her. However, Milarepa becomes tormented by all the bad karma he has accumulated and is terrified of rebirth in hell. He goes to a Dzogchen master, but these instructions have no effect because of his karma, and so he is sent to Marpa. Marpa accepts him as a pupil but refuses to teach him until he has accomplished a task: he has Milarepa use his sorcery to kill a band of bandits that had been robbing his pupils; but then he refuses to teach him for doing such a bad thing. Then he has Milarepa build strangely shaped houses, such as triangular or round, in various locations, each time promising to give him the instructions on completion and each time refusing and making him demolish the house and take the rocks back to where he found them, claiming he did not want the building, or even if he had asked for it he was either drunk or insane when he asked Milarepa to build it. Eventually, when Milarepa is ordered to single-handedly build a nine-story tower, Milarepa gets witnesses to this command to make sure he won't have to take it down again. Nevertheless, his back becomes one big sore from carrying so many rocks on it. Marpa's wife Dagmema is, however, very sympathetic to his cause and vainly tries to help him get the instructions. They eventually form an audacious plan. Dagmema makes some extra strong beer for Marpa who becomes so intoxicated that he passes out. They then steal the relics of Nāropa, Marpa's guru, from his shrine, and forge a letter for Marpa's principal pupil Ngogtön (1036–1102) and Milarepa flees to him. Ngogtön, believing that the letter and the gift of relics are genuine, follows the instruction in the letter to give Milarepa the secret teachings. Milarepa goes on retreat but gets no benefit from the practice since he doesn't have his guru's blessing. Then Ngogtön goes on a visit to Marpa, bringing Milarepa with him, and the entire ruse is exposed. Dagmema locks herself in a room to avoid a beating, while Milarepa goes out to commit suicide. At this low point, Marpa declares that he is not angry, everybody was acting with good motivation, and his mistreatment of Milarepa was his method of removing the bad karma. In fact, if Milarepa had stayed, Marpa would have treated him even worse, but he would have attained buddhahood as a result. Now he will have to practice with great hardship for many years in the mountains to get that result. Eventually, Milarepa goes home to see his mother and discovers that she has died and their house is in ruins. He gives away his land and goes to live in the mountains. His sister, who is now a beggar, comes to visit him, establishing one of the first encounters that inspires a song. The songs recounted in a separate volume form the major part of his life story; the biography itself jumps forward to the end of Milarepa's life.

Even such an extremely brief retelling of some of the main parts of the life story has some peculiar narrative inconsistencies. If practicing sorcery was such a terrible thing, accumulating so much bad karma, why did Marpa make Milarepa do it a second time? We can also add that Ngogtön, before giving Milarepa the instruction, orders him to attack a village with a hailstorm, which kills many animals. Ngogtön reassures a distraught Milarepa that nothing bad has happened, as all these creatures will attain enlightenment as a result of their connection with Milarepa by being killed through his sorcery. Therefore, Milarepa would have no bad karma to be purified. Why did Milarepa give away his land and house as if his sister did not exist or why had she not sold it herself?

These narrative problems are the result of the evolution of the story from its original form, the earliest version of which we find in the account by Milarepa's own pupil Gampopa.[8] This is closely followed temporally by the Milarepa biographies composed by Lama Shang (1123–93)[9] and Dönmo Ripa (1203–64/76/88),[10] both of which are based on Gampopa's account and reveal the version of the life of Milarepa widely disseminated among the

8. sGam po pa bSod nams Rin chen, *rJe mar pa dang rje btsun mi la'i rnam thar* in: *Selected Writings of sGam-po-pa bSod-nams Rin-chen (Dwags-po Lha-rje), with the biography written by his descendant bSod-nams Lhun-grub* (Dolanji 1974): 18–30. *The Collected Works (gSung 'bum) of sGam-po-pa bSod-nams Rin-chen,* ed. by Khasdub Gyatsho Shashin (Delhi 1975): vol. 1, 16–26. *The Collected Works (gSung-'bum) of sGam-po-pa bSod-nams Rin-chen,* ed. by sPyan-snga bSod-nams Lhun-grub (Darjeeling 1982): vol. 1, 23–42. Grub thob O rgyan pa Rin chen dpal, *bKa'-brgyud Yid-bzhin Nor-bu yi 'Phreng-ba,* Smanrtsis Shesrig Spendzod 38 (Leh 1972), 718-29.

9. Bla ma Zhang brTson 'grus grags pa, *Bla-ma Zhang brtson-'grus grags-pa'i gsung 'bum*, vol. 3 (Nepal, Kathmandu 2004), 146–58.

10. rDo rje mdzes 'od, *bKa'-brgyud kyi rNam-thar Chen-mo Rin-po-che'i gTer-mdzod dGos-'dod 'Byung-gnas* (Kangra 1985).

Kagyü at that time. Lama Shang was a pupil of Gampopa's nephew, Gomtsül (1116–69), and had founded the Tsalpa Kagyü. Dönmo Ripa was writing in the far west of Tibet within the Drigung Kagyü lineage that was founded by Drigungpa (1143–1217), a pupil of Pagmo Drupa (1110–70), one of Gampopa's principal pupils.

In these early versions, Milarepa had no mother or sister, just a father. Milarepa does master sorcery, but there is no mention of the sorcery accumulating bad karma for him. Dönmo Ripa emphasizes that it is Milarepa's own idea to cause hailstorms to attack Ngogtön's enemies.[11] There is no mention of a need for purification in these accounts and no hint of irony in Marpa addressing Milarepa as *mthus chen*, "great sorcerer." In fact, *The Blue Annals* relates how another of Marpa's main pupils had to kill a relative of Marpa's in order to receive the teachings.[12] A contemporary of Milarepa, such as Ra Lotsāwa, is extolled in his biography for his ability to slay through sorcery. Lama Shang himself and the first Karmapa, a pupil of Gampopa, killed people with sorcery in their earlier years,[13] with no hint that this was in some way deleterious. In fact the Buddhist tantras, such as the *Cakrasaṃvara-tantra*, are redolent with such practices. The practices that Milarepa is said to have employed are even included in the highly venerated collection known as *The Treasury of Termas*.[14] These practices are said to be the method for liberating wicked people by separating their minds from their bodies and leading them to liberation. Numerous higher tantras and teachings go as far as to state it to be the compassionate duty of a Mantrayāna practitioner to save such beings through this method. Milarepa's pupil Rechungpa is even credited, in the biography composed by Götsang Repa, a pupil of Tsangnyön's, with killing everyone in seven hundred non-Buddhist villages in India![15]

Moreover, in Gampopa's version Marpa does not refuse to give Milarepa the teachings even though Milarepa does not have any money and the

11. Ibid., 185.

12. 'Gos lo tsā ba, trans. Roerich: 414–15.

13. Karma Ngedon Dengye, *Chos-rje Karma-pa sku-'phreng rim-byon gyi rnam-thar mdor-bsus dpag-bsam khri-shing* (Bir 1976): 13–14.

14. *Rin chen gter mdzod*, text 286, vol. *tsa*, in Kong sprul Blo gros mTha' yas, *Rin chen gter mdzod chen mo*. Vol. 26 (Paro 1976): 417–621.

15. rGod tshang ras pa sNa tshogs rang grol, *rJe btsun ras chung ba'i rnam thar* (Zi ling 1992): 108.

teachings are normally expensive. For his own upkeep Milarepa has to do domestic work, but only such menial tasks as carrying water and so on.[16] The later Dönmo Ripa mentions house building and Milarepa's great strength, but has Marpa *prohibit* Milarepa from continuing with such work, as he is such a good pupil. After Marpa has given Milarepa all the instructions, it is he who sends him to Ngogtön to study these in more detail. Milarepa later returns home to see his father, only to discover that he has died and the house is in ruins. As he has no other family and is weary of the world, he gives away his house and land and goes off to live in the mountains.

In other words, this is a comparatively mundane biography, devoid of the later version's drama, but its narrative is devoid of the anomalies that have been created by the enhanced version. The portrayal of Milarepa himself, especially in Gampopa's version, is far more human than in later accounts, with Milarepa having limitations and making errors. A well-known passage in *The Hundred Thousand Songs* describes Milarepa being snowed in during a mountain retreat and after many months the local villagers send a search party to see if he has survived. In Gampopa's version, they are shouting, hoping for an answer, but Milarepa thinks he is hearing the cries of wild animals, and as he does not expect any humans to be in the vicinity, he ignores them. However, eventually he begins to suspect that they may be the shouts of humans, and so he makes a smoke signal. The search party sees the smoke and finds him. This episode repeats in different versions in later texts, but if we leap ahead to Tsangnyön's version, we find that the search party sees a snow leopard and think it might have eaten Milarepa's body, so they follow its footprints which turn into human footprints that lead to Milarepa's cave. Milarepa tells them he was the snow leopard that had been watching them. Thus in a narrative inversion, it is the search party that mistakes Milarepa for an animal.

Gampopa also imparts some amusing anecdotes: Milarepa told him that when he did his first retreat on Marpa's teachings, he had a butter lamp above his head. When after some time he opened his eyes and saw the cave illuminated he thought, "I'm having my first meditation experience!" because he'd forgotten that the butter lamp was there. Self-deprecating details such as these soon vanish from the biographical tradition. Also, Milarepa told

16. *Selected Writings of sGam-po-pa: The Gemur Manuscript* (Dolanji 1974): 22.

Gampopa that sometimes people didn't see him or thought he was a stupa, but he himself was baffled as to why they were ignoring him. He explained it as a perception that arises in the minds of pupils through the interdependence of their faith with the *kāya*s of buddhahood.[17] Later versions, however, have Milarepa consciously and actually transforming himself into a stupa and so on. In particular Milarepa is famous in Tibetan culture for his ability to fly, and he is the lama that flies more than any other in all the hagiographical literature. In Gampopa's account we find this hagiographical detail already forming, for Gampopa reports how he heard that Milarepa had flown once during a blizzard, but when he asks Milarepa about it, Milarepa explains that he only ran ahead of the other pupils, practicing breath retention and leaving barely any footprint.[18] Lama Shang already leaves out these passages, even though he is evidently using Gampopa's text, recycling most of the sentences with some omissions, additions, and synonym substitutions. Milarepa thus becomes more perfect, more transcendent as time goes by, a transformation as would be expected in a hagiographical tradition.

The Gampopa text, which is an account of the lives of both Marpa and Milarepa, is the transcript of an oral account he gave and serves as an addendum to his biographies of Tilopa and Nāropa, which are written in Gampopa's distinctive literary style. It is awkward and often obscure, but Lama Shang used it soon afterward as a source, so that we can see how he understood it through his use of synonyms and so on. The only two incidents that Lama Shang added were when his cousin and aunt visit and are shocked to see his genitalia, and when Milarepa demonstrates his lack of desire by having a group of young girls masturbate him, causing his penis to shrink instead of lengthening. These incidents appear to be the only new material available to him.

The earliest surviving version that has the key elements of the mother, injustice against the family, bad karma through practicing sorcery, and the building and demolition of houses, is to be found in a mid-thirteenth-century Drugpa Kagyü text.[19] The author, Gyadangpa Dechen Dorje, twice mentions as a

17. Ibid., 27.

18. Ibid., 29.

19. rGyal thang pa bDe chen rdo, *dKar-brgyud gSer-'phreng: A Thirteenth-Century Collection*

source of certain passages[20] a now lost text by Khyungtsangpa (1115–76), who was a pupil of Rechungpa. He mentions no other source. This suggests the possibility that we owe these legendary details to that source, although the cited passages are not at all legendary in nature. Khyungtsangpa does have a curious history, for he was a monk, and Rechungpa had a reputation of not teaching monks. However, according to Khyungtsangpa, Rechungpa taught him the entire transmission secretly and in conclusion told him to go far away from his community and not tell anyone that he had received the transmission until Rechungpa had died. This resulted in even some of Khyungtsangpa's pupils such as Lingrepa, the source of the Drugpa Kagyü, to doubt the authenticity of his teachings until he subsequently studied under Sumtön, the principal pupil of Rechungpa, and discovered the instructions were identical.

It is a trend for masters to become recognized as emanations, if not in their lifetimes then in later generations. However, Milarepa is a unique example of this process going in reverse. Gampopa, Lama Shang, and Dönmo Ripa claim Milarepa to be an emanation, though they do not specify whose. Gyadangpa Dechen Dorje is, however, quite specific: Milarepa is the rebirth of Nāgārjunagarbha, who was himself an emanation of the Buddha. Tsangnyön's fifteenth-century version relates a conversation between Milarepa and a few of his pupils that is often referred to by present-day lamas. Milarepa asks them who they think he is and they say he must be a buddha. His response is to acknowledge their devotion but warn them that what they say is slanderous toward the Vajrayāna, as it implies that no ordinary being could achieve buddhahood. This passage has its origins in the version given by Gyadangpa Dechen Dorje two centuries earlier, in which the first part of the conversation, between Milarepa, Rechungpa, and Shiwa Ö, is basically the same, except that Milarepa ends with congratulating them on realizing that he is a buddha and identifies himself as having previously been Nāgārjunagarbha. He is, however, more commonly identified as an emanation of Mañjuśrīmitra, a prominent Indian antecedent for the Nyingma lineage. This occurs in the biography by the second Shamarpa Khachö Wangpo

of Verse Hagiographies of the Succession of Eminent Masters of the 'Brug-pa dKar-brgyud-pa Tradition (Tashijong 1973).

20. Ibid., 365 and 380.

(1350–1405) and also within such termas (*gter ma*) as those of Rigdzin Jatsön Nyingpo (1585–1656) and Garwang Dorje (1640–85). This identification has continued into recent times, in spite of the popularity of Tsangnyön's works. It is found, for example, in the writings of Trinle Gyatso, the abbot of Dragkar Taso Monastery, writing in 1828.[21] Jamgön Kongtrül (1813–98), who composed the Milarepa *guruyoga*, declares in his commentary that Milarepa is an emanation of Mañjuśrīmitra.[22] In fact, Trinle Gyatso presents Milarepa as having *always* been enlightened and never an ordinary being: Vajradhara, the ultimate buddha, manifested as Buddha Vairocana who manifested as the bodhisattva Mañjuśrī, who then manifested as Milarepa.

Tsangnyön Heruka is the very first author to present Milarepa as an ordinary being, running counter to the hagiographical trend, but thereby creating the most inspirational biography in Tibetan literature. Another characteristic of the earlier biographies, which may be surprising in terms of the present-day ubiquity of the Milarepa story, was its code of secrecy. *The Life and Songs of Shepai Dorje (dPal bzhad pa'i rdo rje'i rnam thar)*, an anonymous and probably fourteenth-century biography and collection of songs, contained warnings that it should only be read by initiates, and anyone who made them public would incur the wrath of the ḍākinīs. Tsangnyön, however, made it widely available through the novel medium of block-printing (leaving out the dire warnings in his version), making it ironically the most widely read of Tibetan works.

Tsangnyön Heruka and His Biography of Milarepa

Tsangnyön's entire life could be said to be a fearless contradiction of the rules that he should have followed. Although originally a monk, he would later claim that anyone who was a Cakrasaṃvara practitioner and remained a monk was breaking his commitments. This unique person was one of Tibet's most gifted writers and is responsible along with his pupils for almost all the popular biographies of the early Kagyü masters. He received the lineage of Rechungpa from Ngagwang Dragpa (1418–96), a teacher of the Taglung

21. Phrin las rgya mtsho, *Grub pa'i gnas chen brag dkar rta so'i gnas dang gnas rab bla ma brgyud pa'i lo rgyus mdo tsam brjod pa mos ldan dad pa'i gdung sel drang srong dga' ba'i dal gtam*: 10a–11b.

22. 'Jam mgon Kong sprul Blo gros mtha' yas, *rJe btsun ras pa chen po la brten pa'i bla ma'i rnal 'byor gyi zin bris ye shes gsal byed*: 13a, in *Rgya-chen bka'-mdzod*, vol. 1, (Paro 1975–76): 517.

Kagyü, and began having visions from an early age. His fellow pupils considered him to be either mad or a fraud, but his teacher had confidence in him and passed the Rechungpa lineage on to him.[23] He was also unusual in his appearance. During a period of time, early in his career, he coated his body in human ash, smeared himself in human blood and grease, tied human fingers that he had cut from charnel ground corpses into his hair, and wore human intestines as necklaces and earrings.

Looking like this, he would often go into the market, alternately laughing and crying, and with his penis erect would chase women, or with his penis tied and hidden would run after men shouting "Fuck me!" (*nga la rgyo shog*),[24] the only time I admit I have seen that particular phrase used in a Tibetan text. This is how he earned part of his sobriquet Tsangnyön, "the lunatic from Tsang." People on seeing him would even believe that he was literally a demon.

However, he subsequently went to visit his mother, who did not approve of his appearance. He promised her that he would desist from being so extreme, which he did, relatively speaking, though he still wore a human skin robe, human bone adornments, and the like, and ate human brains and human flesh.

As for how he came to write the famous biography and songs of Milarepa, his hagiography informs us that while in his twenties, he had a vision of Milarepa telling him his life story, this vision clearly being one of the primary sources for his writing.[25] He also had a vision of Nāropa, who told him Milarepa's life story and recited a verse of praise to Milarepa. Tsangnyön later incorporated this praise into his version of the life of Marpa. Tsangnyön has Marpa return to India in his old age to meet Nāropa. Nāropa recites this verse to him and bows in the direction of Tibet, the mountains and trees of the region all bowing in that direction also. However, this made no chronological sense, as Nāropa died while Marpa was still young, and annoyed more sober historians and scholars in Tibet, such as Tāranātha.

In his visions Tsangnyön was also told by Nāropa to write the life story

23. rGod tshang ras pa, *The Life of the Saint of gTsang* (New Delhi 1969): 24.

24. Ibid., 48.

25. Lha btsun Rin chen rnam rgyal, *Grub-thob gtsang-pa smyon-pa'i rnam-thar* (Leh 1971): 45.

of Milarepa and to have it printed. All previous biographies of Milarepa had been in manuscript form. Printing was quite rare in Tibet at that time, and was an arduous process. The text had to be meticulously carved into the wooden printing blocks in mirror writing. Nāropa told Tsangnyön of the area where he would find patronage for this task and of five young girls he should have as his consorts to ensure its completion. In fact when the patrons balked at sponsoring the printing of the songs and asked for a postponement, he was able to insist on their continuing because the presence of his five consorts would ensure success. It took two years of work, and then the spread of this influential work began.[26]

Biographies of Rechungpa

The development of Rechungpa's biographies shows a curious opposite development to that of Milarepa. He became known as an emanation only in much later texts, and yet his character is depicted in a progressively worse manner, until in Tsangnyön's version he regularly quarrels with Milarepa and even becomes furious with him. Some of the more popular parts of *The Hundred Thousand Songs* are those that deal with the conflicts between Milarepa and Rechungpa.

There is a passage where Milarepa interprets a dream of Rechungpa's, in which he shouts at the conjunction of three valleys, to mean that his buddhahood will be delayed for three lifetimes because of three cases of disobedience. The passage has no proper narrative setting or background as no acts of disobedience have yet occurred, but it has its origin in previous narratives of dream interpretation, thoroughly transformed in order to cast Rechungpa in a negative light. Highly positive interpretations of Rechungpa's dreams appear in earlier biographies, but in particular in *The Life and Songs of Shepai Dorje*, the probably fourteenth-century precursor to *The Hundred Thousand Songs.* Milarepa asks Gampopa, Rechungpa, and Seben Repa to report their dreams the next day. Rechungpa's dream of herding a donkey laden with bags of salt while blowing a conch meant that his fame would spread around the world, while Seben Repa's dream of a fire at the conjunction of three valleys

26. Ibid., 96–99.

meant that he would attain liberation only for himself.[27] Tsangnyön Heruka retells this incident, but with major changes: the third person is Shiwa Ö instead of Seben Repa, but more importantly Rechungpa's dream, as we can see, is a version of Seben Repa's, and now given the meaning of delayed buddhahood.

Rechungpa's demotion in Tsangnyön's version from primary pupil (as he is listed in some earlier texts) to secondary is made explicit on a number of occasions. One that is a subtle sleight of literary hand has Milarepa escorting Gampopa as he leaves for the last time. When they are alone, Milarepa tells Gampopa that he is the only one he has given all his teachings to (implying that Rechungpa has not received the entire transmission), but that there was one instruction left that was so profound he was hesitant to pass it on even to him. Eventually, and this scene occurs in the biographies of other masters, Milarepa shows Gampopa his bottom, which is calloused from years of sitting in meditation. As the primacy of meditation is the focus of this passage, the unique supremacy of Gampopa as a pupil just piggybacks in on it, and seems quite natural. When we compare this passage with the earlier version *The Life and Songs of Shepai Dorje*, we find the entire passage is almost the same—except for the identity of the pupil: Rechungpa. Considering that a major part of Milarepa's lineage was obtained in India by Rechungpa and taught by him *to* Milarepa, as well as the fact that he was in effect Milarepa's adopted son, if someone were the sole recipient of the entire transmission it would be Rechungpa, particularly as the practice of sexual yoga (to which there is minimal reference in Tsangnyön's version) was an integral part of this lineage. This earlier version, however, is probably from the fourteenth century and is itself a narrative development; for it is extremely unlikely that Rechungpa, who was brought up by Milarepa, had never seen Milarepa's bottom before, particularly as Milarepa had a penchant for not wearing clothes.

Both sorcery and sexual practice were to become less evident in later biographies than in those of the eleventh and twelfth centuries. Sexual yoga was an important part of the Cakrasaṃvara practice, but its marginalization is already evident in the thirteenth century: Shang Lotsāwa, a holder of Rechungpa's lineage, wrote a text in which he says that one must avoid doing these practices

27. *dPal bzhad pa'i rdo rje'i rnam thar mgur chings dang bcas pa.* Newark ms. 219a–b; Oxford ms. 173b.

with a real woman because they are the source of all problems, and instead the woman should be visualized only. However, Shang Lotsāwa also wrote a text in which he says the first text was for more general practitioners, but secretly it was essential to perform the practice with a real woman.

Why was there this alteration in the portrayal of Rechungpa, particularly as Tsangnyön Heruka was himself a practitioner and teacher of the lineage of Rechungpa's teachings? The answer is that Tsangnyön Heruka identified himself as a Dagpo Kagyüpa,[28] the term for all the Kagyü lineages that identify themselves as descending from Gampopa, who fused the tantric lineage of Milarepa with the monastic, scholastic tradition of the Kadampa, creating the monastic Kagyü. Tsangnyön's principal teacher was a Taglung Kagyüpa, and he was also particularly active within a Drugpa Kagyü context. These are the two Dagpo Kagyü lineages in which Rechungpa's teachings play a major role. In these traditions therefore Rechungpa had a position of great prominence, which he did not initially have in other Kagyü traditions. There was therefore the dichotomy of both Rechungpa's prominence and the requirement to make him secondary to Gampopa, for every tradition portrays its founder as the principal pupil of their guru.

This secondary importance of Rechungpa is made explicit by Tsangnyön Heruka in such passages as that which describes the first meeting between Milarepa and Rechungpa. In the earliest surviving versions, Milarepa meets Rechungpa by accident, but in Tsangnyön's version a ḍākinī tells Milarepa to go to the region where Rechungpa lives, because there he will meet the one who will be his moon-like disciple, while Gampopa will be the sun-like disciple.

The change in the depiction of Rechungpa can clearly be seen in the developments of the account of his departure to and return from India. In early versions such as Gyadangpa's thirteenth-century work, where this episode is first portrayed, following Milarepa's encounter with Kadampa monks who challenged Milarepa to logical debate, he sends Rechungpa to India to obtain the "bodiless ḍākinī teachings" of Tilopa that had not yet been brought to Tibet. Some of Milarepa's followers become worried that Milarepa is sending

28. Lha btsun Rin chen rnam rgyal, *Grub-thob gtsang-pa smyon-pa'i rnam-thar*, 125: *ngas* (sic; [*nga'i*]) *rgyud* (sic; [*brgyud*]) *pa dags* (sic; [*dwags*]) *po bka' rgyud* (sic; [*brgyud*]) *du grags pa de yin*.

Rechungpa to India to learn logic, but Milarepa dispels their misapprehension.[29] When Rechungpa returns from India he brings some logic texts with him. Milarepa burns them while Rechungpa is away from their cave. On his return, Rechungpa asks why, and Milarepa says that he wanted Rechungpa to be a meditator who wears out his cushion, not a scholar who walks around teaching wearing out his shoes. Rechungpa immediately understands and accepts Milarepa's action.[30]

However, in later versions such as *The Life and Songs of Shepai Dorje*, it is Rechungpa's idea to go to India and to do so to learn logic. Milarepa tells him that is not a good idea but sends him to India anyway in order to get the "bodiless ḍākinī teachings."[31] However, following his return there appears a famous passage that shows a strong increase in the negative depiction of Rechungpa. He is now proud that he has obtained these instructions, and Milarepa, in order to humble him, creates a hailstorm and shelters himself inside a yak horn while Rechungpa is caught out in the open and unable to enter. Moreover the unwelcome texts are not logic, but sorcery. When he burns the texts, Rechungpa is furious with Milarepa, and loses his faith in him. Although Milarepa starts manifesting amazing miracles such as revealing deities within his body and flying, Rechungpa remains unmoved until Milarepa finally vanishes in the sky. He is then stricken with remorse and considers suicide, but Milarepa returns and they are reconciled, thus returning to the same conclusion as the original narrative.[32]

Tsangnyön Heruka adds the wish to learn sorcery, as well as logic, to form Rechungpa's initial motive for going to India, as he desires to use it against the monks who oppose Milarepa. When he returns to Tibet and Milarepa burns the texts, Rechungpa's disillusionment with Milarepa and his miracles is even stronger. When Milarepa disappears, Rechungpa actually attempts suicide by leaping off a cliff, but is miraculously saved, Milarepa returns, and they reconcile.

Although Rechungpa's character worsens in the narrative evolution, in the

29. rGyal thang pa, *dKar-brgyud gSer-phreng*: 350.

30. Ibid., 359: *ras chung pa'i bsam pa la / 'o na de rnams kyis / nga la gnod pa'am mi phan pa'i rtags yin snam nas blo zhi lhan song ngo //.*

31. *dPal bzhad pa'i rdo rje'i rnam thar*, Newark ms., 65a1; Oxford ms., 50b.

32. Ibid., Newark ms., 81b–85a; Oxford ms., 62a–65a; Stockholm ms., 78b–80a.

biographies written by Lhatsün Rinchen Namgyal and Götsang Repa, who were Tsangnyön Heruka's own pupils, he is declared to be not only an emanation of Vajrapāṇi but someone who has always been a buddha, and never an ordinary being. However, this is unskillfully added to the biography as an introduction, because after a list of all the buddhas he has been and a description of his mother as a ḍākinī and a miraculous birth, he is immediately suffering from bad karma, and his mother is an absolutely awful person who hates him and mistreats him. In Dönmo Ripa's version, Rechungpa is an orphan, but in Gyadangpa Dechen Dorje's version he has the wicked mother who marries his uncle. However, in later versions she is eclipsed as the principal villain by Rechungpa's uncle, similar to Milarepa's story.

Rechungpa's own lineage was non-monastic, so even though he probably had numerous pupils and originated several lineages, being non-monastic they did not flourish in the great numbers that some of the lineages originating with Gampopa did, which eventually incorporated Rechungpa's lineages.

Rechungpa's lineage, which in particular contains Tilopa's *karṇatantra* (*snyan rgyud*) teachings, became central to the Drugpa Kagyü because that lineage derives from Lingrepa, who was a practitioner of the Rechung Kagyü before becoming a pupil of Pagmo Drupa in the Dagpo Kagyü lineage and giving up his consort. Ngendzong Tönpa, another pupil of Milarepa, received this transmission and was the source of a lineage. Gampopa also received from Rechungpa a simplified version of this lineage. Rechungpa also introduced *mahāmudrā* instructions and the Jinasāgara practice (the *yogottara tantra* version of Avalokiteśvara), which is one of the principal deity practices in the Karma Kagyü tradition. With only Tsangnyön Heruka's works as a source, readers would wonder whether Rechungpa even had any pupils, let alone lineages, whereas in reality Rechungpa's influence and transmission is still widespread.

In summation, the representation of Milarepa and Rechungpa within Tsangnyön Heruka's famous work is not a historical biography, but a visionary and inspirational portrayal that served the needs of the Dagpo Kagyü at the end of the fifteenth century and beyond. Counter to the expected trend of hagiographical elevation of Milarepa that characterized preceding biographies, Milarepa is downgraded to ordinary human status, and even depicted as a person who employed an evil practice like tantric sorcery, thus making his ultimate accomplishment all the more impressive and poignant. Rechungpa on the other hand is demoted both in status as a pupil and in character and achievement. His portrayal contains elements usually reserved for the rivals or enemies of the subject of a hagiography, and indicates a trend toward displacing Rechungpa from his role as foremost pupil in favor of Gampopa, the founder of the Dagpo Kagyü.

Bibliography

I. Tibetan Sources

Bla ma Zhang brTson 'grus grags pa. *Bla-ma Zhang brtson-'grus grags pa'i gsung 'bum*, 9 vols. Kathmandu: Gampopa Library, 2004.

Grub thob O rgyan pa Rin chen dpal. *bKa'-brgyud Yid-bzhin Nor-bu yi 'Phreng-ba: A Precious Rosary of Lives of Eminent Masters of the 'Bri-gun-pa* [sic] *Dkar-brgyud-pa Tradition*. Leh: S. W. Tashigangpa, 1972.

'Jam mgon Kong sprul Blo gros mtha' yas. *Rin chen gter mdzod chen mo*. Paro, Bhutan: Ngodrub and Sherab Drimay, 1976.

———. *rJe btsun ras pa chen po la brten pa'i bla ma'i rnal 'byor gyi zin bris ye shes gsal byed*. In *Rgya-chen bka'-mdzod*, vol. 1, pp. 493–527. Paro: Ngodub, 1975–76.

Karma Nges don bstan rgyas. *Chos-rje Karma-pa sku-'phreng rim-byon gyi rnam-thar mdor-bsus dpag-bsam khri-shing*. Bir, H. P., India: D. Tsondu Senghe, 1976.

lHa btsun Rin chen rnam rgyal. *Grub-thob gtsang-pa smyon-pa'i rnam-thar dad-pa'i spu-slong gyo-ba*. In *bDe-mchog mkha'-'gro snyan-rgyud (Ras-chung snyan-rgyud): Two Manuscript Collections of Texts from the Yig-cha of gTsang-smyon He-ru-ka*, vol. 1. Leh: S. W. Tashigangpa, 1971.

———. *Tshe gcig la 'ja' lus brnyes pa rje ras chung pa'i rnam thar rags bsdus mgur rnam rgyas pa*. In *Bka'-brgyud-pa Hagiographies*, vol. 1, pp. 485–834. Himachal Pradesh: Sungrab Nyamso Gyunphel Parkhang, 1972.

rDo rje mdzes 'od. *bKa'-brgyud kyi rNam-thar Chen-mo Rin-po-che'i gTer-mdzod dGos-'dod 'Byung-gnas*. Kangra, H. P.: Tzondu Senghe, 1985.

rGod tshang ras pa sNa tshogs rang grol. *rJe btsun ras chung ba'i rnam thar (rJe btsun ras chung pa'i rnam thar rnam mkhyen thar lam gsal bar ston pa'i me long ye shes kyi snang ba)*. Qinghai: mTsho sngon mi rigs dpe skrun khang, 1992.

———. *The Biography of Ras-chung*. Bhutan: Tango Monastery, 1982.

———. *Biography and Collected mGur of Ras-chung rDo-rje Grags [rNal-'byor gyi dBang-phyug Badzrakirti'i rNam-par Thar-pa Rin-po-che mi-zad-pa rgyan gyi 'phreng-ba las Ngo-mtshar Nor-bu sNying-po: The Biography with interspersed Songs (mGur) of Ras-chung rDo-rje Grags: A version of the redaction made by rGod-tshang Ras-pa sNa-tshogs Rang- grol]*. Delhi: Tashi Dorji, 1979.

———. *rJe btsun ras chung pa'i rnam mgur mthong pa rang sgrol* [sic: *rang grol*]. In *Ras chung ka 'bum* [sic: *bka' 'bum*]. Manuscript, Nepal German Manuscript Preservation Project. Reel no. L 840/2.

———. *The Life of the Saint of gTsang (gTsang smyon he ru ka phyogs thams cad las rnam par rgyal ba'i rnam thar rdo rje theg pa'i gsal byed nyi ma'i snying po)*. Ed. by Lokesh Chandra. New Delhi: Sharada Rani, 1969.

rGyal thang pa [= rGya ldang pa] bDe chen rdo rje. *dKar-brgyud gSer-phreng: A Thirteenth-Century Collection of Verse Hagiographies of the Succession of Eminent Masters of the 'Brug-pa dKar-brgyud-pa Tradition (dPal dwags po bka' brgyud las / don brgyud dpal ldan dbyar rnga pa'i bstan pa rin po cher byon pa'i 'brug ra lung gdan rabs chos rje dbon ras dang / rgod tshangs pa yan gong ma grub thob gser ri'i 'phreng ba'i rnam par thar pa mdor tshang rags bsdus le tshan rnams phyogs bsgrigs bzhugs).* Tashijong, Palampur, H. P.: Sungrab Nyamso Gyunphel Parkhang, 1973.

rJe rnal 'byor gyi dbang phyug mi la bzhad pa'i rdo rje'i 'gur tshogs lo rgyus kyis spras pa | byin brlabs kyi chu rgyun gyis nyon mongs pa'i tsha gdung sel bar byed pa. Published as *rNal 'byor gyi dbang-phyug mi-la bzhad-pa rdo-rje'i gsung-mgur mdzod-nag-ma: The Life and Songs of realisation of Mi-las-ras-pa (Bzhad-pa-rdo-rje).* Ed. by 3rd Black Hat Karma-pa Raṅ-byuṅ-rdo-rje, 2 vols. Dalhousie: Damchoe Sangpo, 1978.

rJe btsun mi la ras pa'i rdo rje mgur drug sogs gsung rgyun thor bu pa 'ga'. (No publisher cited.)

sGam po pa bSod nams rin chen. *Selected Writings of sGam-po-pa bSod-nams Rin-chen (Dwags-po Lha-rje), with the biography written by his descendant bSod-nams Lhun-grub.* Dolanji, H. P., India: Tibetan Bonpo Monastic Centre, 1974.

———. *Selected Writings of sGam-po-pa: The Gemur Manuscript.* Dolanji, H. P., India: Tibetan Bonpo Monastic Centre, 1974.

———. *The Collected Works (gSung-'bum) of sGam-po-pa bSod-nams Rin-chen.* Prepared from a manuscript in bKra-shis rDzong monastery in Lahul. Ed. by Khasdub Gyatsho Shashin. Delhi: 1975.

———. *Khams gsum chos kyi rgyal po dpal mnyam med sgam po pa 'gro mgon bsod nams rin chen mchog gi gsung 'bum yid bzhin nor bu.* Kathmandu: Khenpo Tenzin and Lama Namgyal, 2000.

———. *The Collected Works (gSung-'bum) of sGam-po-pa bSod-nams Rin-chen.* Ed. by sPyan-snga bSod-nams Lhun-grub. Darjeeling: Kargyud Sungrab Nyamso Khang, 1982.

———. *Dwags-po'i bKa'-'bum: Khams gsum chos kyi rgyal po dpal mnyam med sgam po pa 'gro mgon bsod nams rin chen mchog gi gsung 'bum yid bzhin nor bu.* Kathmandu: Khenpo S. Tenzin and Lama T. Namgyal, 2000.

Shākya Rin chen. *dKar brgyud kyi rnam thar gser gyi phreng ba lta bu.* In *The Collected Works (gsuṅ 'bum) of Shākya Rin-chen, the ninth Rje Mkhan-po of Bhutan,* vol, 1, pp. 1–403. Thimphu: Kunzang Topgey, 1976.

The Life and Songs of Shepai Dorje [*dPal bzhad pa'i rdo rje'i rnam thar mgur chings dang bcas pa*]. Available as:

(1) "Life of the Buddhist Saint Mila-repa." Untitled manuscript no. Ms Tibet.a.11(r); Oriental Reading Room, Bodleian Library, Oxford. 193 folios.

(2) *rJe btsun mid la ras pa'i rnam thar zab mo.* Handwritten manuscript, folio no. 36.280 (IIB R–16), Newark Museum Tibetan Collection, Newark. 161 folios.

(3) *rJe btsun mid la ras chen gyi rnam thar bka' 'bum chen mo grub thob ras pa bcu gnyis kyis bsgrigs pa.* Blockprint. Asian Collections, Folkens Museum Etnografiska, Stockholm.

Phrin las rgya mtsho. *Grub pa'i gnas chen brag dkar rta so'i gnas dang gnas rab bla ma brgyud pa'i lo rgyus mdo tsam brjod pa mos ldan dad pa'i gdung sel drang srong dga' ba'i dal gtam.* [Manuscript in the collection of E. Gene Smith.]

gTsang smyon Heruka. *sGra-bsgyur Mar-pa Lo-tsā-ba'i rNam-thar mThong-ba Don-ldan.* Kulu, Manali: A-pho Rin-po-che'i dgon-pa.

———. *rJe-btsun mi-la ras-pa'i rnam-thar rgyas-par phye-ba mgur-'bum.* Antwerp: Tibetaans Boeddhistisch Meditatiecentrum. [Blockprint.]

———. *Mi la ras pa'i rnam thar: Texte Tibétain de la Vie de Milarépa.* Ed. by J. W. de Jong. 's-Gravenhage: Mouton & Co., 1959.

Zhwa dmar mKha' spyod dbang po. *Mi-la ras-pa'i rnam-thar Byin-brlabs kyi sPrin spungs.* In *The Collected Writings of the Second Zhva dmar Mkha' Spyod Dbang Po (mKha'-spyod dBang-po gSung-'bum)*, vol. 1, pp. 188–317. Gangtok: Gonpo Tseten, 1978.

II. Sources in Translation

['Gos lo tsā ba gZhon nu dpal]. *The Blue Annals.* Trans. by George N. Roerich. 2nd ed. New Delhi: International Academy of Indian Culture, 1976.

Gray, David B. *The Cakrasaṃvara Tantra (The Discourse of Śrī Heruka Śrīherukābhidhāna): A Study and Annotated Translation.* New York: The American Institute for Buddhist Studies at Columbia University, 2007.

[gTsang smyon He ru ka]. *The Hundred Thousand Songs of Milarepa.* Trans. by Garma C. C. Chang. 2 vols. New York: University Books, 1962.

———. *I Centomila Canti di Milarepa*, Vol. 1. Ed. by Roberto Donatoni, trans. by Kristin Blancke and Franco Pizzi. Milano: Adelphi, 2002. Volumes 2 and 3 forthcoming.

———. *The Life of Milarepa.* Trans. by Lobsang P. Lhalungpa. London: Paladin, 1979.

———. *Le Poète Tibétain Mi-la Ras-pa, ses crimes, ses épreuves, son Nirvana.* Trans. by Jacques Bacot. Paris: Editions Bossard, 1925.

———. *Tibet's Great Yogi Mi-la Ras-pa: A Biography from the Tibetan.* Trans. by Lama Kazi Dawa Samdup, ed. by W. Y. Evanz-Wentz. Oxford: Oxford University Press, 1928.

[Lha btsun Rin chen rnam rgyal]. *rJe btsun Mi la ras pa'i rdo rje'i mgur drug sogs gsung rgyun thor bu 'ga'*, translated as:

(1) *Drinking the Mountain Stream: New Stories and Songs by Milarepa.* Trans. by Lama Kunga Rinpoche and Brian Cutillo. Novato, CA: Lotsawa, 1978.

(2) *Miraculous Journey: Further Stories and Songs of Milarepa, Yogin, Poet, and Teacher of Tibet.* Trans. by Lama Kunga Rinpoche and Brian Cutillo. Novato, CA: Lotsawa, 1986.

[rDo rje mdzes 'od]. *The Great Kagyu Masters: The Golden Lineage Treasury.* Trans.

by Khenpo Könchok Gyaltsen, ed. by Victoria Huckenpahler. Ithaca, NY: Snow Lion Publications, 1990.

Thrangu Rinpoche. *Rechungpa: A Biography of Milarepa's Disciple.* Colorado: Namo Buddha Publications, 2002.

III. Other Sources

Cavani, Liliana 1974. *Mi-la Ras-pa, Dal soggetto al film.* Bologna: Cappelli.

van Dam, Eva 1991. *The Magic Life of Milarepa Tibet's Great Yogi.* Boston: Shambhala.

Decleer, Hubert 1992. "The Melodious Drum Sound All-Pervading." In *Tibetan Studies: Proceedings of the 5th Seminar of the International Association for Tibetan Studies Narita 1989,* ed. by Shoren Ihara and Zuiho Yamaguchi, vol. 2, pp. 13–28. Narita-shi, Chiba-Ken, Japan: Naritasan Shinshoji, 1992.

Ehrhard, Franz-Karl 2000. *Early Buddhist Block Prints from Mang-yul Gung-thang.* Lumbini, Nepal: Lumbini International Research Institute.

Everding, Karl-Heinz 2000. *Der Gung thang dkar chag.* Monumenta Tibetica Historica, Abteilung 1, Band 5. Bonn: VGH Wissenschaftsverlag GmbH.

Goss, Robert Everet 1993. "The Hermenutics of Madness: A Literary and Hermeneutical Analysis of the Mi-la'i-rnam-thar by Gtsang-smyon Heruka." PhD. diss., Harvard Divinity School.

Gyatso, Janet B. 1992. "Autobiography in Tibetan Religious Literature." In *Tibetan Studies Proceedings of the 5th Seminar of the International Association for Tibetan Studies, Narita 1989.* Vol. 2: *Language, History and Culture,* pp. 465–78. Narita-shi, Chiba-Ken, Japan: Naritasan Shinshoji, 1992.

——— 1998. *Apparitions of the Self: The Secret Autobiographies of a Tibetan Visionary.* Princeton: Princeton University Press.

Martin, Dan 1997. *Tibetan Histories: A Bibliography of Tibetan-Language Historical Works.* London: Serindia Publications.

——— 1982. "The Early Education of Milarepa." *Journal of the Tibet Society* 2: 53–76.

Pagel, Ulrich 1997. "The British Library Tibetica: A Historical Survey." In *Tibetan Studies: Proceedings of the 7th Seminar of the International Association for Tibetan Studies, Graz 1995,* ed. by Helmut Krasser, Michael Torsten Much, Ernst Steinkellner, Helmut Tauscher, pp. 725–32. Vienna: Verlag der Österreichischen Akademie der Wissenschaften.

Reynolds, Valrae, and Amy Heller 1983. *Introduction to the Newark Museum Tibetan Collection.* Newark: The Newark Museum.

Roberts, Peter Alan 2007. *The Biographies of Rechungpa: The Evolution of a Tibetan Hagiography.* London, New York: Routledge.

Schmitt, Eric-Emmanuel 1997. *Mi-la Ras-pa.* Paris: Albin Michel.

Smith, E. Gene 2001. *Among Tibetan Texts.* Boston: Wisdom Publications.

Tiso, Francis Vincent 1996. "The Biographical Tradition of Milarepa: Orality, Literacy and Iconography." *The Tibet Journal* 21.2: 10–21.

——— 1997. "The Death of Milarepa: Towards a Redaktionsgeschichte of the Mila rnam thar Traditions." In *Tibetan Studies: Proceedings of the 7th Seminar of the International Association for Tibetan Studies, Graz 1995*, ed. by Helmut Krasser, Michael Torsten Much, Ernst Steinkellner, Helmut Tauscher, vol. 2, pp. 987–96. Vienna: Verlag der Österreichischen Akademie der Wissenschaften.

——— 1989. *A Study of the Buddhist Saint in Relation to the Biographical Tradition of Milarepa*. New York: Columbia University.

van Tuyl, Charles D. 1971. "An Analysis of Chapter Twenty-Eight of the Hundred Thousand Songs of Mila-Raspa, a Buddhist Poet and Saint of Tibet." PhD diss., Indiana University.

Urubshurow, Victoria Kennick 1984. "Symbolic Process on the Buddhist Path: Spiritual Development in the Biographical Tradition of Milarepa." PhD diss., University of Chicago.

Winged Wolf (Heather Hughes-Calero) 1994. *Shaman of Tibet: Milarepa—From Anger to Enlightenment*. Deer Harbor, WA: Higher Consciousness Books.

Tibetan Sources on the Life of Serdog Paṇchen Shākya Chogden (1428–1507)[1]

Volker Caumanns

Introduction

There can be little doubt that the Tibetan scholar-adept Shākya Chogden was one of the most eminent masters of the Sakya school during the second half of the fifteenth century.[2] We learn from his biographer Künga Drölchog (1507–66) that already as a young man Shākya Chogden was called "great pandita" (*paṇ chen*), a title only bestowed upon outstanding scholars who had mastered all five traditional fields of knowledge (*pañcavidyāsthāna*; *rig pa'i gnas lnga*).[3] Furthermore, his own tradition acknowledged his profound

1. I would like to acknowledge my gratitude to Prof. David Jackson and Prof. Franz-Karl Ehrhard for their corrections and valuable suggestions. I am also indebted to E. Gene Smith and Dr. Michael Sheehy at the Tibetan Buddhist Resource Center for providing me with pdf files of rare versions of Kun dga' grol mchog's hagiography of Shākya mchog ldan, and to Ralf Kramer for improving my English.

2. See van der Kuijp 1983: 10–16 and Komarovski 2007: 80–143 for a description of Shākya mchog ldan's life.

3. Kun dga' grol mchog, *Paṇḍi ta*, 48.7–49.1. It should be noted that the honorary title *paṇ[ḍi ta] chen [po]* was not an official degree (such as *bka' bcu pa*, i.e., "master of ten scriptures," or *bka' rab 'byams pa*, i.e., "expounder of all scriptures") in the system of monastic education of fifteenth-century Tibet. The locus classicus for the above-mentioned concept of the "five fields of knowledge" is chapter 11.60 of the *Mahāyānasūtrālaṃkāra*, where they are specified as inner science (*adhyātmavidyā*; *nang rig pa*), i.e., the *buddha-dharma*, epistemology and logic (*hetuvidyā*; *gtan tshigs rig pa*), linguistics (*śabdavidyā*; *sgra rig pa*), medicine (*cikitsāvidyā*; *gso ba'i rig pa*), and fine arts and crafts (*śilpakarmasthānavidyā*; *bzo rig pa*); see Seyfort Ruegg 1995: 101–32.

learnedness by including his name in a list of six Sakya luminaries known as the "six ornaments that adorn [Tibet,] the land of snows" (*gangs can mdzes pa'i rgyan drug*).[4] Such honors notwithstanding, Shākya Chogden's position in his own tradition was not uncontested, and some of his contemporaries even denied that he was a true Sakyapa.[5] This accusation, even if uttered only by a few, undoubtedly reflected the growing uneasiness that parts of the tradition felt about Shākya Chogden's scholarly exegesis from the 1470s onward when, for the first time, he brought his controversial questions concerning Sakya Paṇḍita's treatise on the three-vow theory—the *sDom gsum rab dbye*—before the learned public.[6] At around the same time he began to integrate a variety of the "emptiness-of-other" (*gzhan stong*) view into his own Madhyamaka approach, and this may have caused further annoyance on the part of his Sakya fellows.[7] After this, the study of Shākya Chogden's writings was more and more neglected by subsequent generations of Sakya scholars, who preferred the doctrinal exegesis of his contemporary Gorampa Sönam Sengge (1429–89). Later, during the mid-seventeenth century, Shākya Chogden's works suffered the same fate as the writings of Tāranātha (1575–1634) and other authors whose views were considered unsuitable by the newly established Ganden Podrang administration:

4. It is uncertain when this sixfold grouping was originally coined. For its appearance in contemporary Tibetan sources, see Amipa 1976: 53–54 and bCo brgyad Khri chen (n.d.): 47. It is interesting to note that along with Go rams pa bSod nams seng ge (1429–89), Shākya mchog ldan even holds an exceptional position among these "six ornaments," since those two are said to be masters of both sūtras and tantras, whereas the other four "ornaments"—g.Yag phrug Sangs rgyas dpal (1348–1414), Rong ston Shākya rgyal mtshan (1367–1449), Ngor chen Kun dga' bzang po (1382–1456), and Gong dkar rDo rje gdan pa Kun dga' rnam rgyal (1432–96)—were only regarded as masters of one of these fields, namely sūtras or tantras.

5. Kun dga' grol mchog, *Paṇḍi ta*, 142.2.

6. For a general survey of Shākya mchog ldan's writings that are relevant to the *sdom gsum* dispute and the reactions they provoked, see Jackson 1983: 16–18 and *passim*. See also the English translation of Sakya Paṇḍita's work by Jared D. Rhoton, the footnotes of which contain numerous references to Shākya mchog ldan's questions; Rhoton 2002, *passim*.

7. Shākya mchog ldan's mature approach to Madhyamaka philosophy is described in Tillemans and Tomabechi 1995, Mathes 2004, and Komarovski 2007. For reasons of reception history, mention should also be made of Seyfort Ruegg 1963, a study carried out more than a decade before Shākya mchog ldan's "Collected Works" were made available by Kunzang Tobgey in 1975, which contained the first rough survey of Shākya mchog ldan's view on *gzhan stong* Madhyamaka in a Western language. In recent years, Yaroslav Komarovski has translated several of Shākya mchog ldan's Madhyamaka writings; see Komarovski 2000 and 2006.

they were banned, as the contemporary Tibetan scholar Dongtog Rinpoche (b. 1933) puts it, "by some partisans of the [Central Tibetan] government who were intoxicated with the brewed liquor of sectarianism."[8] However, this ban may not have been solely due to the sharp polemics against Tsongkhapa (1357–1419) that are found in a number of Shākya Chogden's writings. Another factor that contributed to his becoming *persona non grata* in government circles may have been political animosities harbored by the new ruling power, for Shākya Chogden had entertained intimate relations with the Rinpung lords, who were certainly not remembered as great benefactors of the Gelug school by the Ganden Podrang administration.[9]

As a result of the banning of his works—which were therefore believed not to be extant in later times—Shākya Chogden remained a hazy figure for Western scholars until some decades ago. For instance, in 1958 Alfonsa Ferrari stated in a gloss to her translation of a Tibetan pilgrimage guidebook that nothing is known about "Shākya-mchog-ldan of Sa-skya" except for some dates.[10] The situation improved considerably in 1975 when the Bhutanese publisher Kunzang Tobgey made available a facsimile edition based on a twenty-four volume manuscript set of Shākya Chogden's "Complete Works" (*gsung 'bum*), which had been rediscovered in a monastery near Thimphu

8. Dongthog Rinpoche 1976: 22, *phyogs ris chang gis myos pa'i srid dbang 'dzin pa 'ga' zhig*. But cf. Davidson 1981: 97 n. 30, where one informant, namely Ngor mKhan po bSod nams rgya mtsho, denies that Shākya mchog ldan's writings were banned in Tibet. According to bSod nams rgya mtsho, copies of Shākya mchog ldan's works were kept in the libraries of Ngor Ewaṃ Chos ldan and rTa nag Thub bstan rnam rgyal monasteries, but scarcely anybody took an interest in these works.

9. For Shākya mchog ldan's ties to the Rin spungs pas, see for example Kun dga' grol mchog, *Paṇḍi ta*, 138.5; 160.4 and 162.4. There is also a telling "letter of benediction" preserved in *gSung 'bum* XVII, 177.5–178.4, that Shākya mchog ldan had written "on the occasion when the protector of the realm, [the Rin spungs pa] Don yod rdo rje (1463–1512), had arrived at the head of [his] troops and was moving towards"—that means "invaded"—"the sNe'u estate [in dKyid shod]" (*sa skyong don yod rdo rje dpung gi thog tu phebs nas gzhis ka sne'u phyogs su bskyod skabs shis brjod du gnang ba*); see also Jackson 1989a: 26 and 51n74.

10. Ferrari 1958: 70 and 162n626.

at that time.[11] Due to this edition—and the subsequent reprints[12]—we have now begun to understand Shākya Chogden's place in the religio-intellectual landscape of fifteenth-century Tibet more fully. His scholastic writings dealing with Madhyamaka, Pramāṇa, and—to a lesser extent—the three-vow theory have attracted most interest, while other fields of his enormous literary output are to this day virtually neglected.

The present paper aims at presenting the rich hagiographical material available on Shākya Chogden. I will particularly dwell on the two main hagiographies, namely Künga Drölchog's *The Life of Liberation of the Great Paṇḍita Shākya Chogden,* [*entitled*] *"A Detailed Analysis"* (hereafter *Detailed Analysis*), and Shākya Rinchen's *The Life of Liberation of the Glorious Shākya Chogden Drime Legpai Lodrö, the Great Charioteer of* [*Tibet,*] *the Land of Snows,* [*entitled*] *"Sun that Illuminates the Muni's Teachings"* (hereafter *Sun that Illuminates the Muni's Teachings*). Since our perceptions of Shākya Chogden are often limited to the more controversial aspects of his career, these sources may be helpful in drawing a more comprehensive picture of his long life. Moreover, they may shed some light on the precise historical conditions that rendered possible his remarkable scholarly activities.

To begin with, I would like to list, in approximately chronological order,

11. For the production of this set at the behest of the Bhutanese monk-scholar Shākya rin chen (1709/10–59), see paragraph 2.2 below. A short account of the modern publication of the *gsung 'bum* is given in Dhongthog 1976: 23–24. Prior to 1975 only very few of Shākya mchog ldan's writings were readily available and these were very difficult to obtain. Probably in 1969 one of his commentaries on the *Abhisamayālaṃkāra*, the *mNgon par rtogs pa'i rgyan 'grel pa don gsal ba dang bcas pa'i rnam par bshad pa*, was published in Bhutan (see the online catalogue of the Library of Congress, LC Control Number 77911690). His *Lugs gnyis rnam 'byed rtsa 'grel* coupled with a work by his teacher Rong ston was made available in New Delhi as *Two Controversial Māhyamika* [sic] *Treatises* by Trayang Samten and Jamyang Samten in 1974. Also worthy of mention is a bundle of twenty-eight folios consisting of the incomplete eighth chapter of his *Theg pa chen po dbu ma rnam par nges pa'i bang mdzod*. This fragmentary Madhyamaka treatise was among the Tibetan books that Rahula Sankrityayana gave to the Bihar Research Society, Patna, in 1936; see Jackson 1989b: 59, no. 1035. However, a catalogue of books preserved in the Tibetan 'Bras spungs Monastery, published only recently, shows that numerous works by Shākya mchog ldan have survived in the library of this monastery; see bsTan 'dzin phun tshogs 2004, *passim*.

12. There are two Indian reprints published by Nagwang Topgyal, Delhi: 1988 and 1995. In 2006 a new version based on inputs of Kunzang Tobgey's edition was prepared by Sachen International, Kathmandu. Furthermore, Gene Smith informed me in an e-mail of 23th January 2008 that there is also supposed to be a further input edition from Dzongsar in Kham.

the relevant textual sources. These are of two kinds: proper hagiographies belonging to the indigenous namtar (*rnam thar*) genre and short sketches found in traditional religious histories:[13]

(01) Dorje Gyalpo (b. fifteenth century): [title unknown]

(02) Gelong Lodrö Sangpo (b. fifteenth century): *The Life of Liberation of the Glorious Shākya Chogden,* [*entitled*] *"A Wondrous Mind-Vehicle"*[14]

(03) Shākya Gyaltsen Pal Sangpo (b. fifteenth century): *The Life of Liberation of Paṇchen Shākya Chogden,* [*entitled*] *"A Garland of White Lotus Flowers"*[15]

(04) Jonang Jetsün Künga Drölchog (1507–66): *The Life of Liberation of the Great Paṇḍita Shākya Chogden,* [*entitled*] *"A Detailed Analysis"*

(05) Pawo Tsuglag Trengwa (1504–66): short hagiographical account in *The History of the Buddhadharma,* [*entitled*] *"A Feast for the Scholars"*

(06) Mangtö Ludrub Gyatso (1523–96): short hagiographical account in *The Sun that Illuminates the Chronology of the Doctrine,* [*entitled*] *"Thoroughly Good* (lit. 'white') *Superior Aspiration"*

(07) Ngorpa Könchog Lhündrub (1497–1557) and Jadral Sangye Püntsog (1649–1705): short hagiographical account in *The Excellent Elucidation of How the Noble Buddhadharma Emerged,* [*entitled*] *"Great Ship that Sets Out on the Ocean of the Doctrine"*

(08) Drug Je Khenpo Shākya Rinchen (1709/10–59): *The Life of Liberation of the Glorious Shākya Chogden Drime Legpai*

13. Apart from the first three works, the respective Tibetan titles are given in the bibliography below.

14. Tibetan title: *dPal ldan shākya mchog ldan gyi rnam thar ngo mtshar yid kyi shing rta*. The Tibetan phrase *yid kyi shing rta* ("mind-vehicle") corresponds to Skt. *manoratha,* which is a poetical expression for "wish," "desire," etc.

15. Tibetan Title: *Paṇ chen shākya mchog ldan gyi rnam par thar pa padma dkar po'i phreng ba*.

Lodrö, the Great Charioteer of [Tibet,] the Land of Snows, [entitled] "Sun that Illuminates the Muni's Teachings"

(09) Situ Paṇchen Chökyi Jungne (1699/1700–1774): short hagiographical account in *The Countless "Lives of Liberation" Belonging to the Attainment-Lineage, the Precious Karma Kamtsang Kagyü Tradition, [entitled] "A Garland of Moonstones"*

Since this purely chronological order reveals nothing about how the sources relate to each other, I have arranged them in the following discussion into four groups:

(1) Hagiographies written by direct disciples
(2) Künga Drölchog's *Detailed Analysis* and further texts based on it
(3) Hagiographical accounts handed down in the Karma Kagyü tradition
(4) The short hagiographical account in Mangtö's *Chronology of the Doctrine* and further texts based on it

(1) Hagiographies written by direct disciples

From Künga Drölchog's *Detailed Analysis,* composed in the middle of the sixteenth century, we know of three earlier hagiographies to which he refers as *rNam thar rdor rgyal ma*, *rNam thar ma ti ma*, and *rNam thar rje dbon ma*. These are not the original titles but short titles derived from the names of their respective authors. Since these hagiographies were already known in Künga Drölchog's lifetime, it makes sense to look for their authors among the disciples of Shākya Chogden. Leonard van der Kuijp had already taken this approach and thus tentatively identified the following disciples of the Serdog Paṇchen as possible authors of these works: Dorje Gyalpo (*rNam thar rdor rgyal ma*), Shākya Gyaltsen (*rNam thar rje dbon ma*) and, erroneously, Lodrö Namgyal (*rNam thar ma ti ma*).[16] Due to a recently published catalogue of books preserved in the library of the Tibetan Drepung Monastery, it is now

16. Van der Kuijp 1983: 10.

possible to identify the authors and original titles of at least two of these three works beyond any question.

(1.1) Dorje Gyalpo: [title unknown]

This hagiography, which we know only by its short title *rNam thar rdor rgyal ma*, is not contained in the aforementioned Drepung catalogue, and nothing is known about its whereabouts. Künga Drölchog mentions this so-called *Life of Liberation [composed] by Dorgyal* several times in his *Detailed Analysis* as one of his sources. Its author's name, "Dorgyal," refers to Shākya Chogden's disciple Dorje Gyalpo, who was also known as the "man from Nyangtö Tsechen [in Tsang]" (*nyang stod rtse chen pa*). Just like his teacher, Dorje Gyalpo carried the title "great paṇḍita" (*paṇ chen*) and had some acquaintance with Sanskrit.[17]

(1.2) Gelong Lodrö Sangpo: The Life of Liberation of the Glorious Shākya Chogden, [entitled] "A Wondrous Mind-Vehicle"

Another hagiography of Shākya Chogden was written by Gelong Lodrö Sangpo. This work is preserved in the library of the Tibetan Drepung Monastery as a handwritten manuscript of sixty-two folios.[18] Lodrö Sangpo, also a disciple of Shākya Chogden, is said to be from Khartse Changra.[19] Künga Drölchog refers to this hagiography as *rNam thar ma ti ma*, in which the word *mati* is the Sanskrit equivalent of Lodrö in the author's name.

17. Kun dga' grol mchog, *Paṇḍi ta*, 229.4; Shākya rin chen, *Gangs can*, 462.4–5. Note that Shākya rin chen writes the abbreviation rDor rgyal in full as rDo rje rgyal mtshan and not as rDo rje rgyal po. Further historical data on rDo rje rgyal po is scarce. The register (*dkar chag*) of Sha ra Monastery states that he was the founder of sNa mkhar Monastery and that the stūpa (*mchod rten*) with his relics is located at Sha ra dGon pa in 'Phan po (north of lHa sa); see Roesler 2004: 63. Furthermore, we learn from a *rnam thar* collection by the great 'Jam mgon Kong sprul (1813–99) that rDo rje rgyal po conferred the *pravrajyā* vows on gTer ston Shes rab 'od zer (1518–?84). Later he taught Shes rab 'od zer various tantras of the Sa skya pas as well as the *Kālacakra Tantra*; see 'Jam mgon Kong sprul, *Zab mo'i gter*, 560.2–4.

18. bsTan 'dzin phun tshogs 2004, *smad cha*, 1525, no. 017193.

19. Kun dga' grol mchog, *Paṇḍi ta*, 229.4; Shākya rin chen, *Gangs can*, 462.3.

(1.3) Shākya Gyaltsen Pal Sangpo: The Life of Liberation of Paṇchen Shākya Chogden [entitled] "A Garland of White Lotus Flowers"

In his *Detailed Analysis*, Künga Drölchog mentions the *Life of Liberation [composed] by the nephew*, i.e., the *rNam thar rje dbon ma*. Shākya Chogden's disciple and nephew Shākya Gyaltsen Pal Sangpo composed this hagiography, and according to a gloss in Shākya Rinchen's *Sun that Illuminates the Muni's Teachings*, Shākya Gyaltsen was later installed on the teaching-throne of Serdogchen Monastery as Shākya Chogden's successor.[20] The hagiography written by him is listed in the Drepung catalogue as a handwritten manuscript of seventy-seven folios.[21]

(2) The extensive hagiography authored by Künga Drölchog and further texts based on it

(2.1) Künga Drölchog: The Life of Liberation of the Great Paṇḍita Shākya Chogden, [entitled] "A Detailed Analysis"

The most important source for the life of Serdog Paṇchen Shākya Chogden is this extensive hagiography stemming from the pen of Jonang Jetsün Künga Drölchog. Its twenty-seven chapters recount in chronological order the important events of Shākya Chogden's life, including an account of his previous existences. Although this work is in many respects a typical Tibetan namtar—that is, a "life of liberation" presenting the spiritual career of its protagonist in a given soteriological framework—it also contains some unusual elements, to be discussed in greater detail below. I have been able to locate at least four textual witnesses so far, and arranged these into two groups.

(A1) A Tibetan blockprint in Uchen script, probably from the sixteenth century (7 lines, 108 folios):

20. Ibid., 460.5.

21. bsTan 'dzin phun tshogs 2004, *smad cha*, 1573, no. 017762. Kun dga' grol mchog informs us in one of his autobiographical writings that a certain Sangs rgyas dBon Rin po che once related this *rnam thar* to him as a supplementary teaching (*zur chos*). I assume that this Sangs rgyas dBon Rin po che was none other than Shākya mchog ldan's nephew (*dbon*) Shākya rgyal mtshan; see Kun dga' grol mchog, *Rang rnam Ib*, 44.

One print taken from these blocks is kept in the library of the Tibetan Drepung Monastery and further copies are preserved in the "Nationalities Library" (*mi rigs dpe mdzod khang*), Beijing, and in the Tucci Fund, Rome. The Tibetan Buddhist Resource Center (TBRC), New York, holds digitally scanned files of another copy.[22] The marginal annotation of the prints, which reads *gi*, implies that this blockprint was originally part of a quite bulky collection, presumably of miscellaneous works by Jonang authors.

(A2) An eighteenth-century Uchen manuscript from Bhutan (7 lines, 117 folios):
This version is part of the twenty-four-volume set of Shākya Chogden's "Complete Works," which were prepared at the behest of Drug Je Khenpo Shākya Rinchen.[23] The hagiography is found in vol. 16 (*ma*), pp. 1–233. Since (A2) differs from (A1) only in minor scribal errors, I assume the manuscript to be a more or less direct copy from (A1).

(A3) A Ume manuscript from Dzamtang (7 lines, 193 folios):
Although I have not yet been able to check the manuscript thoroughly, it also appears to be a copy of (A1), with which it shares the same fascicle-marking on the margin, *gi*.

(B) A Ume manuscript from Nepal (5–6 lines, 247 leaves):
The Nepal-German Manuscript Preservation Project (NGMPP) microfilmed this manuscript in Tsagkhang Gönpa, Dolpo. It is abundant in variant spellings, most of which are scribal errors. The Tibetan punctuation mark (*shad*) is used in a different way than in the witnesses of group (A), in which the punctuation is basically the same. Moreover it contains, albeit to a very small extent, wordings not found in (A).

22. bsTan 'dzin phun tshogs 2004, *smad cha*, 1558, no. 017586; Sun wun zing 1989: 72, no. 002751(4); Rossi Filibeck 2003: 341, no. 708; TBRC W25586.

23. See paragraph 2.2 below. Although (A1) is the original from which (A2) is copied, I cite from the latter, since this edition is more easily accessible.

Genesis of the hagiography

Jetsün Künga Drölchog was well suited for writing the *Detailed Analysis*. Not only was it the case that generally he "was very much a product of the Sakya tradition, which he upheld through practice and teaching," as Cyrus Stearns puts it,[24] but that in going through his autobiographical writings[25] we see that he maintained close ties to Shākya Chogden's former seat Tubten Serdogchen and its teaching tradition throughout his whole life. We are told that already during his childhood in Lowo Möntang (i.e., present-day Mustang) he listened to eulogies and "lives of liberation" of Shākya Chogden as well as of the latter's teacher Dönyö Pal, and that these accounts impressed him to the extent that he developed a strong inclination toward both of them.[26] Moreover, his main religious master during that time was Drungpa Chöje Künga Chogdrub, who had been a former student of Serdog Paṇchen.[27] Later, when the thirteen-year-old boy traveled to Ü and Tsang for further studies, one of his first stops after visiting Sakya and Khau Dragdzong was Serdogchen.[28] There he continued his studies under the tutelage of another

24. Stearns 1999: 65. Here Kun dga' grol mchog and his doctrinal affiliations are further characterized in the following way: "[H]e was an excellent model of a completely unbiased upholder of nonsectarian (*ris med*) sentiments, and there is extremely little evidence that he felt any special allegiance to the Jonang tradition, which he led, over that of others that he also taught and practiced. The three main lineages of tantric practice which seem to have been the most important for Kunga Drolchok were the Sakya teachings of the Path and Result, the esoteric instructions of the Shangpa Kagyü school, and the Jonang tradition of the Six-branch Yoga."

25. Seven autobiographical accounts are found in the recently published volume of "rJe btsun Kun dga' grol mchog's outer, inner, and secret lives of liberation"; see *Rang rnam Ib–VII*. In this regard *Rang rnam Ib–V* constitutes one successive narrative, whereas *Rang rnam VI* and *VII* serve as a supplementary twin, the latter being the "uncommon" (*thun mong ma yin pa*), that is the "secret," counterpart to the former. Unfortunately Kun dga' grol mchog provides us only very sporadically with precisely specified dates, which holds true especially for the first group of five accounts.

26. Kun dga' grol mchog, *Rang rnam Ia*, 306.1–2; *Rang rnam Ib*, 33.

27. Kun dga' grol mchog, *Rang rnam Ib*, 26; *Rang rnam VI*, 330; *Rang rnam VII*, 380. For the mention of Kun dga' mchog grub's name in the list of Shākya mchog ldan's disciples, see Kun dga' grol mchog, *Paṇḍi ta*, 229.2.

28. This may be an indication that Shākya mchog ldan was not only still remembered in Glo bo, but that even after his death there was some kind of exchange between gSer mdog can monastery and Mustang.

disciple of Shākya Chogden, namely Paṇchen Dönyö Drubpa.[29] Although, for the time being, this stay was brought to a sad and untimely end by an outbreak of smallpox, as a consequence of which his elder brother passed away, Künga Drölchog returned again and again—both as a student and later as a teacher—to this monastic institution.[30] His good knowledge of Shākya Chogden's writings, which is attested by a number of quotations from these works found in the *Detailed Analysis*, thus comes as no surprise.[31] He tells us in a brief section, also found in the *Detailed Analysis*, that he took pains to obtain the reading-authorization (*lung*) for the Paṇchen's "Collected Works," which he received, according to one of his autobiographical accounts, from the so-called Khenchen Rinpoche (i.e., Künga Tashi Namgyal), again a former disciple of Shākya Chogden.[32] The puzzle becomes a little clearer when we realize that it was this Khen[chen] Rinpoche[33] who later requested Künga Drölchog to compose the *Detailed Analysis*.

The namtar itself and the autobiographical writings of Künga Drölchog provide us with some information about the circumstances under which the hagiography was written. Not many "hard" facts are given in the colophon of the work. There it is only stated that Künga Drölchog, commissioned by the aforementioned Khenchen Rinpoche, authored the text to "cleanse his idle

29. Kun dga' grol mchog, *Rang rnam Ib*, 40. At that occasion Kun dga' grol mchog studied, among other texts, two works by Shākya mchog ldan, namely the *gSer gyi thur ma* (*gSung 'bum* VI, 439–647; VII, 1–229), i.e., the latter's controversial treatise on the three-vow theory, and the *Bya pa dris lan* (*gSung 'bum* XVII, 178–82). See also Kun dga' grol mchog, *Rang rnam VI*, 342; *Rang rnam VII*, 381. Don yod grub pa, who was also a native of Glo bo, is mentioned as a disciple of Shākya mchog ldan in Kun dga' grol mchog, *Paṇḍi ta*, 229.4.

30. See, for instance, Kun dga' grol mchog, *Rang rnam Ib*, 99; *Rang rnam III*, 257, 259; *Rang rnam IV*, *passim*; *Rang rnam V*, 291, 307, 317; *Rang rnam VI*, 348.

31. See note 40 below.

32. Kun dga' grol mchog, *Paṇḍi ta*, 227.6–7, where it is also said that the old Tibetan *gsung 'bum* edition comprised eighteen volumes. But cf. Khenpo Appey 1987: 437, according to which there were once sets of twenty-one volumes preserved in gSer mdog can and other monasteries. For the list of some fifty works, the *lung* of which Kun dga' grol mchog received from mKhan chen Rin po che, see Kun dga' grol mchog, *Rang rnam II*, 182–83. Although it is here not explicitly stated that the *lung* encompassed the whole of Shākya mchog ldan's writings, the arrangement of works very much resembles other lists; see for example Khenpo Appey 1987: 103.

33. mKhan Rin po che is found as mKhan chen Rin po che bKra shis rnam rgyal in the list of Shākya mchog ldan's disciples; see Kun dga' grol mchog, *Paṇḍi ta*, 230.2–3. See also Shākya rin chen, *Gangs can*, 464.4–465.1.

acts" (*snyoms las kyi bgyi ba cung zhig bsal*).[34] A little bit more is said in one of the autobiographies of Künga Drölchog:

> While [I] was staying in strict seclusion in Geser Monastery at Tsechen Pu for two months, [I] wrote a very extensive "Life of Liberation" of Paṇchen [Shākya Chogden], after Khen Rinpoche had urged [me to do so]. Moreover, Khen Rinpoche granted [me] the kindness of this [composition] being completed in golden letters [by the scribe].[35]

This is complemented by an interesting account, found at the beginning of the last chapter of the *Detailed Analysis*, where Künga Drölchog describes how he actually composed the text:

> [I] have not repeated the three previous[ly written] "Lives of Liberation" [but I] have rested [on them] (*gdan bkod du byas*), and concerning what was missing, [I] have supplemented marginal [points]. Moreover, with intense endeavor, I have obtained mostly from sixteen *kalyāṇamitra*s—that is to say from the twelve supreme ones of the *ācārya*s who have touched the feet of Paṇchen [Shākya Chogden] himself and who have personally drunk the nectar of [his] speech, as well as from the four holders of the lineages [of Shākya Chogden's] disciples—the gates of empowerments, reading[-authorizations] and instructions that were transmitted [to me] by these [disciples, as well as] the pronouncements from the magnificent spiritual songs of [this] king of doctrine. Without forgetting [anything, I] have committed to memory all the bits and pieces of the different narrative strands of the life story [I] heard from each [of these masters] on these occasions. [I] arranged [these bits and pieces on which I] relied, and—like the [proper]

34. Kun dga' grol mchog, *Paṇḍi ta*, 233.6. The full name of mKhan chen Rin po che is only mentioned in the *dbu med* manuscript microfilmed by the NGMPP.

35. Kun dga' grol mchog, *Rang rnam IV*, 283: *rtse chen phu'i gad ser dgon par zla ba gnyis nang mtshams bsdams pa'i ring | mkhan rin po ches bkas bskul nas paṇ chen gyi rnam thar rgyas par spel ba'i rtsom pa bgyis shing | de nyid gser yig tu sgrub pa'i bka' drin yang mkhan rin po che nyid kyis gnang |*

> sequence of the [successively] rising constellations of stars—[this life story] is without any gaps in the course of the eighty years [of Shākya Chogden's life], and [its] whole body [of events] never became disordered.[36]

Here it is clearly stated that Künga Drölchog based his work not only on the "three earlier lives of liberation" (i.e., the hagiographies written by the direct disciples described above), but also relied on what some of his teachers—who had been students (or students of students) of Serdog Paṇchen—related about the latter. Also this account reveals, again, Künga Drölchog's intimate ties to some of the representatives of Shākya Chogden's teaching tradition. Most of the above-mentioned twelve direct disciples, "who have touched the feet of the paṇchen himself," can be identified by name through the scattered references found on them in the *Detailed Analysis*. Among them were his early teacher Drungpa Chöje Künga Chogdrub, the above-mentioned Khen Rinpoche Künga Tashi Namgyal, Gelong Tugje Palgön (who served as *gnas kyi slob dpon*—the "master of learning"—of the young Künga Drölchog),[37] Dönyö Drubpa (styled, too, as Serdog Paṇchen in other sources),[38] Doringpa Künsang Chökyi Nyima (1449–1524), Changlungpa Shönnu Chödrub, Karma Trinlepa Chogle Namgyal (1456–1539), Dorje Lopön Rabsal Dawa Gönpo, and Drungtsün Sherab Paljor.[39]

Moreover, Künga Drölchog made use of Shākya Chogden's writings to

36. Kun dga' grol mchog, *Paṇḍi ta*, 230.5–231.1: (...) *rnam thar snga ma gsum gdan bkod du byas ma zlos shing | gang ma tshang ba'i thad khol du kha skong bgyis | rang res 'bad rtsol drag pos paṇ chen nyid kyi zhabs la gtugs shing | gsung gi bdud rtsi dngos su bzhes pa'i slob ma'i mchog bcu gnyis | yang slob brgyud pa 'dzin pa bzhi ste | dge ba'i bshes gnyen bcu drug gi drung du gang las brgyud pa'i dbang lung gdams pa'i sgo | chos kyi rgyal po'i dpal gyi mgur las bka' stsal ba phal cher thob cing | de skabs re re nas kyang rnam thar gyi zur mi 'dra ba'i cha phra ba thos pa kun kyang ma brjed par blo la gzungs su bsten pa dag so sor bkod | dgung lo brgyad cu'i bar la hor kongs med cing dbu zhabs gtan ma log pa | rgyu skar 'char ba'i go rim ltar bris* (...).

37. Ibid., 32.7.

38. See, for example, Khenpo Appey 1987: 72, where gSer mdog Paṇ chen Don yod grub pa is mentioned as the author of a commentary on Sa skya Paṇḍita's *sDom gsum rab dbye*.

39. References to these scholars as sources for the *rnam thar* are found in Kun dga' grol mchog, op. cit., 52.5; 80.7 (Kun dga' mchog grub); 41.6 (mKhan Rin po che); 32.7 (Thugs rje dpal mgon); 175.6 (Don yod grub pa); 43.7; 79.4; 153.3; 196.7 (rDo ring pa); 21.7; 25.2; 29.6; 37.7; 43.4; 53.3; 64.2; 86.3; 103.1; 129.6; 164.4; 203.7; 204.2 (sPyang lung pa); 24.6; 41.7 (Karma phrin las pa); 19.4; 24.2 (Rab gsal zla ba mgon po); 11.6; 57.6; 103.4; 129.2; 132.4; 147.3 (Shes

obtain additional information. In this regard, his sole reference to the "magnificent spiritual songs (*mgur*) of [this] king of doctrine" is a little bit misleading: Although Künga Drölchog mentions the *Collection of Spiritual Songs* (*mgur 'bum*) several times, he also referred to numerous other texts such as the register (*dkar chag*) of the Maitreya statue in the main temple of Serdogchen, the colophon of a commentary to Guṇaprabha's *Vinayasūtra*, and a eulogy to Shākya Chogden's forty teachers, to name only a few.[40]

Eventually, he informs us in two of his autobiographical writings how he propagated the life story of Shākya Chogden. Shortly after completing the text, he bestowed its reading-authorization (*lung*) upon the monastic community of Serdogchen while seated on Shākya Chogden's former teaching throne. Some time later he gave the *lung* again in Tingkye.[41] Unfortunately, he doesn't provide us with dates for these events, including the precise date of composition. Thus we can only very tentatively infer from the course of events in the main narrative of the autobiographies that Künga Drölchog authored the *Detailed Analysis* around the middle of the sixteenth century, maybe in the late 1540s or early 1550s.[42]

---

rab dpal 'byor). Compare also the list of Shākya mchog ldan's disciples, ibid., 228.5–230.2, with the names of Kun dga' grol mchog's teachers given in Kun dga' grol mchog, *Padma*, 3–9.

40. See, for instance, Kun dga' grol mchog, *Paṇḍi ta*, 78.7, 155.6 (*dkar chag* of the great Maitreya statue in gSer mdog can: *gSung 'bum* XVII, 244–72); 26.3, 30.6, 31.7 (*'Dul ba'i dka' 'grel nyi ma'i shing rta*: *gSung 'bum* XXII, 1–265); 12.4, 14.4 (*bShes gnyen dam pa bcu phrag bzhi'i bstod pa*: *gSung 'bum* XVII, 2–8); 190.3 (*bca' yig* of gSer mdog can Monastery: *gSung 'bum* XVII, 307–9).

41. Kun dga' grol mchog, *Rang rnam IV*, 285; *Rang rnam V*, 314. It should be noted that it was the "three dharma kings of gTing skyes that were brothers" (*gting skyes chos rje sku mched rnam pa gsum*) who sponsored the printing of Shākya mchog ldan's *gsung 'bum* shortly after his passing; see Kun dga' grol mchog, *Paṇḍi ta*, 227.6. See also note 79 below.

42. On the one hand, Kun dga' grol mchog must have been an experienced and mature teacher when he put together the *rnam thar*, since he had already been giving initiations and teachings such as the Path with Its Result (*lam 'bras*) and the Six Dharmas of Niguma (*ni gu chos drug*) for many years at that time; see, for example, Kun dga' grol mchog, *Rang rnam Ib*, 138–39, 140; *Rang rnam II*, 198; *Rang rnam IV*, 282. On the other hand, mKhan Rin po che, who had been a disciple of Shākya mchog ldan, was still alive—though he seems to have died only shortly later; see *Rang rnam V*, 302.

Some remarks on the text

As already mentioned above, the *Detailed Analysis* contains some unusual elements. In this regard, its most striking feature is Künga Drölchog's critical appraisal of sources. Not only does he frequently refer to his written and oral sources by name, remarkable in itself since this approach is unusual in Tibetan hagiographical literature,[43] but he also cross-checks his source material, and when there is disagreement on a particular point, he discusses the differences.[44] In addition, we find a number of passages in which he lets Shākya Chogden (or other individuals involved) comment upon some events just narrated. This style, when applied by Künga Drölchog, brings about several narrative levels, and the particulars contained in these digressions often go beyond the scope of a single narration of Shākya Chogden's life story. This means, as Leonard van der Kuijp stated already in 1983, that "because of its wealth of information, [this namtar] should be destined to become one of the major sources for an as of yet unwritten intellectual history of fifteenth-century Tibet."[45]

But despite Künga Drölchog's noteworthy efforts to clarify the various inconsistencies found in the middle of the sixteenth century in written and oral accounts of Shākya Chogden's life story, his *Detailed Analysis* is not without shortcomings. Some of the data given by him is, to say the least, problematic. For instance, the brief account of Serdog Paṇchen's life in Mangtö Ludrub Gyatso's *Chronology of the Doctrine* gives alternative dates for some important events in Shākya Chogden's life.[46] Further discrepancies show up

43. See, for instance, notes 39 and 40 above. It will suffice to quote the following passage from *Paṇḍi ta*, 27.4–5, in order to give an impression of how Kun dga' grol mchog refers to his sources. After giving a philosophical excursus on some points of dGe lugs scholasticism, Kun dga' grol mchog says: "This was personally told by Paṇ chen [Shākya mchog ldan] to the sNar thang Ka bzhi pa Grags pa shes rab tshul khrims (i.e., the twentieth abbot of sNar thang, mKhan chen Grags pa shes rab), who later acted as *chos dpon* of rGyal byed tshal in Pu rangs [district] of mNga' ris. [I, Kun dga' grol mchog, heard] the oral report [of Shākya mchog ldan's account] from Drung btsun bZang po brtan pa (*zhes paṇ chen dngos kyis snar thang ka bzhi pa grags pa shes rab tshul khrims phyis mnga' ris kyi pu rangs rgyal byed tshal gyi chos dpon gnang ba de la gsungs pa'i ngag rgyun drung btsun bzang po brtan pa las so |*)."

44. See, for instance, ibid., 56.4–57.5, where several details of Shākya mchog ldan's taking of the *upasaṃpadā* vows are discussed.

45. Van der Kuijp 1983: 10.

46. See paragraph 4.1 below.

when one compares several passages of the *Detailed Analysis* with the information recorded in various colophons of Shākya Chogden's writings.[47] An obvious error on Künga Drölchog's part is the date he provides for the death of Shākya Chogden's teacher Rongtön, which conflicts with Shākya Chogden's own account in his namtar of Rongtön.[48]

Nevertheless, for all its shortcomings and difficulties, Künga Drölchog's *Detailed Analysis*—if carefully compared with other sources—remains an indispensable source for exploring the life of Shākya Chogden. The following chapter outline (with added years for easier reference) may therefore be helpful for the further study of the text.[49] Cross-references to Shākya Rinchen's *Sun that Illuminates the Muni's Teachings*[50] are given in brackets.

I. [Preliminaries], pp. 2.1–4.2
II. [Main Part], pp. 4.2–230.4
  (01) Introductory account of earlier incidents [from past lives], pp. 4.2–8.5 (pp. 181.5–202.5): pre 1428
  (02) [His] birth, pp. 8.5–13.4 (pp. 4.2–13.1): 1427–early 1430s
  (03) [His] early years, pp. 13.4–17.4 (pp. 14.1–19.5): ca. 1435–ca. 1436
  (04) [He] obtained the *pravrajyā* and [later on] the *śrāmaṇera* vows, pp. 17.4–26.1 (pp. 19.5–39.1): 1436–40
  (05) As [it] had happened before, [when] Dharmakīrti requested the method of logical reasoning from Kumārila[, in the same way it happened to Shākya Chogden], pp. 26.1–28.6 (pp. 40.4–44.1): ca. 1440–42

47. See also Komarovski 2007: 79.

48. This was already indicated by Jackson 1989a: 8. It should be noted that in addition several "minor" inconsistencies have found their way into the text. They, however, do not affect the main narrative. For example, in a short digression (*Paṇḍi ta*, 86.2) Kun dga' grol mchog gives the following account: "At that time (i.e., 1456), the *siddha* of our days, dBus smyon pa (1458–1532), dwelled as mDzo herder [in the retinue] of lHun sde pa (*de dus da lta'i grub thob dbus smyon pa 'di lhun sde pa'i mdzo rdzi la 'dug*)." If Kun dga' grol mchog had been right, dBus smyon's yogic accomplishments would have been indeed remarkable, since he was born only two years later in 1458.

49. The Tibetan "headings" are found at the end of the respective chapters.

50. See paragraph 2.2 below.

(06) The scholar [Shākya Chogden] is counted among the number of scholars, pp. 28.7–33.7 (pp. 44.1–50.4): 1442–45
(07) [He] demonstrated how [he] trained in the fields of knowledge, pp. 33.7–44.5 (pp. 50.4–72.3): 1445–48
(08) [He] trained in the field of the ocean[like] scriptural [tradition of the] Mantra[yāna], pp. 44.5–50.7 (pp. 73.3–82.3): 1449–50
(09) [He obtained] the *upasaṃpadā* vows, pp. 50.7–61.1 (pp. 82.3–101.5): 1450–52
(10) In Sangpu [he] increased extensively the accumulation of that which is wholesome, pp. 61.1–70.2 (pp. 102–119.3): 1452–53
(11) At the great monastic seat [of Sakya he] propounded the immense scriptural tradition, pp. 70.3–84.6 (pp. 119.3–147.3): 1454–55
(12) [He] received a vast [number of] empowerments, pp. 84.6–93.5 (pp. 147.3–159.4): 1456–59
(13) Some sections on wondrous [events], pp. 93.5–102.2 (pp. 159.4–172.3): 1460–68
(14) The natural outflow of [his] realization became manifest, pp. 102.2–107.6 (pp. 172.3–210.4): 1468–69
(15) [He] propounded the words of the doctrine in the province of Ngari (mNga' ris), pp. 107.6–117.5 (pp. 210.4–232.1): 1469/70–75
(16) [He] was accepted by the *yidam* [deities] and [he realized] the field of supernatural knowledge, pp. 117.5–130.7 (pp. 232.1–258.5): 1475–78/79
(17) The miraculous display of the deeds of [his] learnedness, pp. 130.7–141.3 (pp. 258.5–275.1): 1479–83
(18) Jamgön (Maitreyanātha) Dönyö Pal passed away to the [heavenly] sphere, the holy [realm of] Tuṣita, pp. 141.3–148.5 (pp. 275.1–286.3): 1483–84
(19) [At Shākya Chogden's command] the Maitreya statue was manufactured, pp. 148.5–163.7 (pp. 287.4–319.3): 1484–90
(20) Some sections [showing that he] was worthy of praise, pp. 163.7–172.6 (pp. 320.2–339.2): 1490–91

(21) [He was a man] endowed with the glory of a scholar as well as a spiritually accomplished master, pp. 172.6–180.2 (pp. 339.2–351.2): 1492–94
(22) [He] turned the marvelous wheel of the doctrine, pp. 180.2–187.7 (pp. 353.2–369.1): 1494–95
(23) [His] extraordinary qualities, pp. 187.7–200.3 (pp. 369.1–391.4): 1495–1500
(24) Rejoicing at impartial scholars, pp. 200.3–208.1 (pp. 393.3–407.2): 1501–3
(25) [His] *parinirvāṇa*, pp. 208.2–224.5 (pp. 407.2–446.5): 1504–7
(26) The continuous [turning of] the wheel of [his] enlightened activity, pp. 224.5–230.4 (pp. 448.1–468.1)
(27) The final chapter, pp. 230.4–233.4

III. [Colophon], pp. 233.4–7

(2.2) Drug Je Khenpo Shākya Rinchen: The Life of Liberation of the Glorious Shākya Chogden Drime Legpai Lodrö, the Great Charioteer of [Tibet,] the Land of Snows, [entitled] "Sun that Illuminates the Muni's Teachings"

By far the most extensive description of Shākya Chogden's life story is this hagiography authored by the Bhutanese monk-scholar Shākya Rinchen, who served as ninth head abbot of his native land (*'brug rje mkhan po*) during the years 1744–55. The work is preserved in the fourth volume of Shākya Rinchen's "Collected Works" (*gsung 'bum*), which were originally prepared as a manuscript edition in eight tomes after his death.[51] Kunzang Topgey, whose name was already mentioned above in connection with the publication of Shākya Chogden's "Collected Works," made available this *gsung 'bum* collection as a modern facsimile edition in 1976.

According to the colophon of the work, Shākya Rinchen had already cherished the wish to write a namtar of Shākya Chogden in the past, but only began with the composition after his disciple Yönten Taye (1724–84) urged him to do so. Furthermore we are told that for the most part Shākya Rinchen drew upon Künga Drölchog's *Detailed Analysis*, but also added minor points

51. See the bibliographical note to the individual volumes of the *gsung 'bum* edition.

from other namtars—although he remains silent on what his sources actually were. He eventually completed the text at Tubten Jagö Pungpo Monastery on the sixteenth day of the eighth month in an unspecified year.[52] Unfortunately, if taken as an additional source, Shākya Rinchen's autobiography, or rather its supplement that was written by two of his disciples,[53] has nothing to say about the namtar of Shākya Chogden, let alone its year of composition. However the possible timeframe in this regard is limited to the years 1749–59. The first date denotes the year of foundation of Jagö Pungpo Monastery[54]—that is, the place where the text was completed—while the latter is the *terminus ante quem* since Shākya Rinchen died on the thirteenth day of the ninth month of that year.[55]

The head abbot and the "mahāpaṇḍita" of Serdogchen

Already during his lifetime Shākya Rinchen was considered to be the re-embodiment of Shākya Chogden. For example, his contemporary, Tendzin Chögyal (1700–1766/67), mentions two incidents concerning this matter in a sketch of Shākya Rinchen's life that is found in his famous religious history of Bhutan (i.e., the *lHo'i chos 'byung*).[56] Here we learn that it was revealed to the young Shākya Rinchen in a dream that one of his former births had been Milarepa's disciple Rechungpa (1085–1161). Subsequently

52. Shākya rin chen, *Gangs can*, 470.4–471.4. Thub bstan Bya rgod phung po'i ri Monastery is situated in Pha jo sdings (i.e., "the plateau of Pha jo ['Brug sgom zhig po]," b. twelfth cent.) in the vicinity of Thimphu.

53. Only the first eight and a half chapters were authored by Shākya rin chen himself (i.e., *lHag pa'i bsam pa*: 1–294), whose disciples Yon tan mtha' yas and Kun dga' rgya mtsho (1722–72) finished the work. Like their teacher, they both served as head abbots of Bhutan (*'brug rje mkhan po*) in later years: Kun dga' rgya mtsho as twelfth 'Brug rJe mKhan po (r. 1769–71) and Yon tan mtha' yas as thirteenth rJe mKhan po (r. 1771–75). It should be noted that the latter is the same person who had asked Shākya rin chen to compose the *rnam thar* of Shākya mchog ldan.

54. For the foundation of Thub bstan Bya rgod phung po, see Shākya rin chen, *lHag pa'i bsam pa*, 335.4–337.2; 422.3.

55. Ibid., 508.4–5.

56. Tendzin Chögyal completed the *lHo'i chos 'byung* on the fifteenth day of the fourth month (*sa ga zla ba*) in the female earth-hare year (1759), that is, a few months before Shākya rin chen's passing. During the time of composition, Tendzin Chögyal served as tenth head abbot of Bhutan (r. 1755–62); see Tendzin Chögyal, *lHo'i chos 'byung*, 149r5–6. For further information on this work, see Martin 1997: 136.

Shākya Rinchen composed a supplication to his own line of pre-existences, which also included Shākya Chogden. The second incident, as mentioned by Tendzin Chögyal, occurred some time later, only a few years before Shākya Rinchen was appointed as ninth head abbot of Bhutan in 1744: During a retreat, we are told, the bodhisattva Maitreya appeared to him, as a consequence of which the line of Shākya Chogden's former births emerged lucidly in his mind.[57] It is interesting to compare Tendzin Chögyal's narrative with Shākya Rinchen's own description of these incidents as found in his autobiography, for Shākya Rinchen is much more discreet on this matter. Although he explains that his teacher recognized him to be Rechungpa's rebirth, nothing is said about Shākya Chogden in this regard.[58] However, whatever the meaning of this conspicuous lacuna, Shākya Rinchen apparently accepted the above-mentioned attributions concerning his former existences that were uttered by his contemporaries. In this connection some passages in the opening chapter of his *Sun that Illuminates the Muni's Teachings*, which are not contained in Künga Drölchog's *Detailed Analysis*, are telling. This chapter deals with the line of Shākya Chogden's former births, to which Shākya Rinchen has added a further name: that of his own pre-embodiment Rechungpa, thus closing the circle.[59]

But Shākya Rinchen's affinity for Shākya Chogden finds its expression also on a more worldly level. It is by now a well-known fact that it was mainly due to him that Shākya Chogden's "Collected Works" were preserved in Bhutan at a time when they were becoming rare in Tibet, thus saving most of them from destruction. As will be shown below, his contacts with Serdogchen in this regard are well documented, and according to the contemporary Tibetan scholar Dhongthog Rinpoche, he was even installed on the teaching throne of this monastery while in Tibet. Later, when Shākya Rinchen left for Bhutan, he took manuscripts of Shākya Chogden's complete works to his native land, where they were copied.[60] However, it should be noted

57. Tendzin Chögyal, *lHo'i chos 'byung*, 84v4–6; 85r6–85v1.

58. Shākya rin chen's own version of the above mentioned two incidents is found in Shākya rin chen, *lHag pa'i bsam pa*, 128.1–5; 284.2 et seq. For an additional account of the visions and dreams he experienced at these occasions, see Shākya rin chen, *Rang nyid*, 534.2–5; 552.1 et seq.

59. Shākya rin chen, *Gangs can*, 192.5 et seq.

60. Dhongthog Rinpoche 1976: 23.

that Dhongthog Rinpoche's description of this event is problematic.[61] The date he provides for Shākya Rinchen's enthronement in Serdogchen, namely the water-sheep year of the tenth sixty-year cycle (that is, 1583),[62] is an obvious mistake. Further, it seems that the event itself never took place. Apart from an earlier attempt that failed hopelessly, Shākya Rinchen traveled to Tibet only once, in 1740.[63] But he didn't succeed in reaching Serdogchen. Instead, Shākya Rinchen tells us:

> [I] arrived at a village called Gyangro Khangmar. From this place there was a route leading to Tsang province. Like a thirsty man longing for water, I wished to see [places] such as the great Serdogchen Monastery—[which is like] Śrāvastī—where Paṇchen Chökyi Gyalpo (i.e., Shākya Chogden) spread the teachings of the Buddha in previous times. [But I] was without resources, and because of that, [I] had to follow [the entourage] as the attendant of Tulku Rinpoche. It would therefore have been improper [to leave for Serdogchen]. Full of sadness [I] set off [in company of Tulku Rinpoche and the others] and arrived at Nelung.[64]

Shākya Rinchen may have decided not to go to Serdogchen because his journey was not a simple pilgrimage to the holy places of Tibet. As mentioned

61. This was already pointed out by Anne Burchardi in an unpublished paper on Shākya mchog ldan's literary heritage in Bhutan. See now Burchardi (forthcoming).

62. Even if we fix for this event a water-sheep year in the eighteenth century, the problem with the date cannot be solved, since the respective years, namely 1703 and 1763, won't fit with Shākya rin chen's dates (1709/10–59).

63. For an account of this travel, see Shākya rin chen, *lHag pa'i bsam pa*, 233–79. See also his travelogue: Shākya rin chen, *Shākya'i dge sbyong*, *passim*.

64. Shākya rin chen, *lHag pa'i bsam pa*, 240.6–241.3: *rgyang ro khang dmar zhes bya ba'i grong du slebs | sa phyogs de nas gtsang gi phyogs su 'gro ba'i lam 'dug cing | sngon gyi dus paṇ chen chos kyi rgyal pos sangs rgyas kyi bstan pa rgyas par mdzad pa'i chos sde chen po mnyam yod gser mdog can la sogs pa mjal 'dod kyi blo skom pa chu dran pa ltar byung yang | rang la rgyu chas kas dben pas sprul sku rin po che'i zhabs phyir bsnyegs dgos kyis stabs ma 'grig par sems 'phreng bzhin du song ste nas lung du 'byor |*. For a translation of this passage, see also Anne Burchardi (forthcoming). In this context, it is interesting to see that in Shākya rin chen's travelogue written sometime after the journey, and on which the account of the autobiography seems to be based, even the mention of the name of gSer mdog can Monastery as found in the autobiography is reduced to an enigmatic allusion; see Shākya rin chen, *Shākya'i dge sbyong*, 212.2–3.

above, Shākya Rinchen traveled as the attendant of the so-called Tulku Rinpoche, that is, Drubwang Künga Migyur Dorje, alias Yunggön Dorje (1721–69). This Tibetan master, who was considered to be a rebirth of Drug Nyön Künga Legpa (1455–1529), played an important role in the rapprochement between Bhutan and Tibet after hostilities between the two countries during the Bhutanese civil war (1729–35).[65] Since the "pilgrimage" was part of the reconciliation process and Shākya Rinchen participated as an officially selected "exchange student," one can speculate that it was considered politically unsuitable to visit Serdogchen Monastery. But though Dhongthog Rinpoche's account seems highly improbable when set against this background, there may be an element of truth in what he related. There is some evidence that Shākya Rinchen was considered as Shākya Chogden's rebirth by the monastic community of Serdogchen, too. When describing the ceremonies held for the deceased Shākya Rinchen, the authors of the supplement to his autobiography provide us with an interesting passing remark. At the end of the last chapter, it is said that one Tulku Khyenrab Tendzin Lhündrub Shab, who was the abbot of Serdogchen at that time, let the monks of his monastery recite for many days, invoking prayers for Shākya Rinchen's swift return from the heavenly abode of Tuṣita to Tibet (*gangs ri'i ljongs*).[66]

Be that as it may, we find in the same source a number of important facts which more clearly reveal Shākya Rinchen's affiliation to Shākya Chogden and his former monastery. In this regard we learn of at least one actual meeting with a scholar from Serdogchen.[67] And the eleventh chapter of this work incorporates a long register, which records in great detail Shākya Rinchen's numberless acquisitions for several monasteries and various other projects he fathered during the years 1744–59.[68] For instance, in 1751 he (or rather the Bhutanese state) spent more than three hundred *bal traṃ*[69] on donations for Serdogchen, consisting of various articles for adorning the interior of the temple such as brocade streamers,

65. Ardussi 1999: 68–73.

66. Shākya rin chen, *lHag pa'i bsam pa*, 514.5–515.2.

67. See ibid., 389.4–5, according to which sometime after 1756 Shākya rin chen welcomed Shangs pa Bla zur from gSer mdog can, who "came to pay homage" (*mjal phyag la 'byor*) and who asked for teachings.

68. Ibid., 397.5–476.2.

69. According to ibid., 427.5–6, sixty "Nepalese *traṃ*" (*bal traṃ*) amounts to nine silver *srang* (*dngul srang*).

silk ribbons and garments for the statues, supplies for tea gatherings, butter lamps, fine silk scarves for ceremonies held for the dedication of merit, and provisions for the lamas and common monks.[70] Similar donations are attested for the years 1753 and 1755.[71] Moreover, we can at least partly reconstruct Shākya Rinchen's undertakings to compile the writings of Shākya Chogden, which eventually formed the basis of the *gsung 'bum* collection Kunzang Topgey published as a facsimile edition in 1975. We learn from the above-mentioned register that Shākya Rinchen obtained more than six volumes of Shākya Chogden's collected works from Serdogchen in 1750, for which he paid approximately forty *ma traṃ*.[72] Three years later, in 1753, he spent seventy *ma traṃ* for the copying of eleven new volumes of the *gsung 'bum* edition, and in the same year he laid out five *ma traṃ* for another tome.[73] In 1754 he commissioned three more new volumes of Shākya Chogden's writings and, later on, spent eight *ma traṃ* for six hundred sheets of paper, which were needed for copying further volumes.[74]

Chapter outline of the text

As indicated above, Shākya Rinchen based his namtar heavily on Künga Drölchog's *Detailed Analysis*, from which he extracted the main narrative in paraphrase. However, he chose to ignore the more unusual elements that characterize the earlier work. Thus every mention of sources, and the majority of Künga Drölchog's digressions, failed to find a place in Shākya Rinchen's text, whereas the idealization and elevation of Shākya Chogden's character are further elaborated. Nonetheless, it is a useful work, since it rephrases several passages of the *Detailed Analysis* that are somewhat difficult to understand. Therefore I provide below a chapter outline of the text. In this context, one oddity of the modern facsimile edition should be noted. Shākya Rinchen's work originally consists of three parts with separate Tibetan foliation (but with ongoing Western pagination added in the

70. Ibid., 444.6–445.4.

71. Ibid., 458.1–459.1; 468.5–469.3. The donations of the year 1753 included various articles for adorning Shākya mchog ldan's reliquary shrine (*gdung rten*) as well as the life-size statues of Rong ston, Ngor chen, Don yod dpal, and Shākya mchog ldan himself.

72. Ibid., 428.5–6. For a translation of this passage, see Burchardi (forthcoming).

73. Shākya rin chen, *lHag pa'i bsam pa*, 457.3; 462.2.

74. Ibid., 464.3–4; 466.1.

reprint). The publisher erroneously placed the first part, which deals with the line of Shākya Chogden's previous existences, in the second position, thus now beginning at page 179. Moreover, page 102 is missing, having been replaced with page 202.

I. [no title], pp. 179–202
 (00) Preliminaries, pp. 180.1–181.5
 (01) An account of [how he] practiced the bodhisattva conduct in the vast ocean [of] buddha-fields, and to what an extent [this] lamplike emanation, who illuminates the teachings, appeared also in Jambudvīpa, pp. 181.5–202.5 (pp. 4.2–7.6)

II. Part One: Ü, pp. 1–177
 (02) An account of how [he] took rebirth as an emanation [body] in [Tibet,] the land of snows, pp. 2.1–13.4 (pp. 8.5–12.5): 1427–early 1430s
 (03) An account of the leisure activities of [his] early years, pp. 13.4–22.4 (pp. 13.4–18.3): early 1430s–ca. 1435
 (04) An account of [how he] entered into the ocean[like] gate of learning after [he] had been accepted by the noble *kalyāṇamitras*, and [how he] obtained the *śrāmaṇera* vows, pp. 22.4–39.4 (pp. 18.3–25.4): 1437–40
 (05) An account of [how he] reached the other shore of the ocean-like tenets of his own [tradition] and of others, and [how he] was installed as head [teacher] of the monk assembly of the Nego [college], pp. 39.4–56.4 (pp. 26.1–36.7): 1440–46
 (06) An account of [how he] turned the wheel of the noble doctrine, and [how he] displayed once more the way [he] trained in all fields of knowledge, pp. 56.4–73.2 (pp. 36.7–43.7): 1446–48
 (07) [chapter heading on missing page 102], pp. 73.2–102 (pp. 44.5–60.2): 1449–52
 (08) An account of [how he] celebrated among other things the religious festival in Sangpu, and in particular, [how he] performed a scholastic debate in the glorious Sakya [Monastery] [consisting of] a presentation of the doctrine, pp. 102–137.5 (pp. 61.1–78.2): 1452–55

(09) An account of [how he] extensively studied once more the sūtras and tantras, [how he] extensively acted for the benefit of the teachings and sentient beings in the region of Uru, [and how he] gained full confidence in [his] realization, pp. 137.5–177.3 (pp. 78.2–104.3): 1455–69

III. Part Two: Tsang, pp. 203–471

(10) An account of [how he] took over the great monastic seat of Serdogchen, [which is like] Śrāvastī, and how [he] acted for the benefit of others in the region of Lowo in Ngari, pp. 204.1–241.5 (pp. 104.3–122.1): 1468–75

(11) An account of all [his] scholarly deeds, and [how] Jamgön Dönyö Pal passed away to [the realm of] Tuṣita, pp. 241.5–287.1 (pp. 122.1–147.5): 1476–84

(12) An account of [how] the statue of Bhaṭṭāraka Ajita (i.e., Maitreya) was set up, and [how he] dwelled on the level of the highest siddhis, pp. 287.2–320.1 (pp. 148.5–162.7): 1484–90

(13) An account of [how he] commissioned the great appliqué thangka, and of the extent of [his] deeds of scholarship and spiritual accomplishment, pp. 320.2–352.5 (pp. 163.7–179.3): 1490–94

(14) An account of [how he] acted for the benefit of the teachings and sentient beings while extensively turning the wheel of the profound and vast dharma, pp. 352.5–392.3 (pp. 180.2–199.3): 1494–1500

(15) An account of [how he] performed many virtuous (lit. "completely white") activities [to which he] diligently applied himself at the end of [his] life, pp. 392.3–433.2 (pp. 200.3–218.6): 1501–7

(16) [without chapter heading], pp. 433.3–470.4 (pp. 218.6–230.4): 1507

IV. [Colophon], pp. 470.4–471.4

(2.3) Accounts by contemporary Tibetan authors

There are at least three short hagiographical narratives by contemporary Tibetan scholars that are based on Künga Drölchog's *Detailed Analysis*.

Dhongthog Rinpoche compiled two very reliable summaries of the namtar, the first one of which is found in his booklet on the history of Shākya Chogden's writings. The second account, which differs from the first, is included in his historiographical work on the Sakya school. Moreover, the Nyingma scholar Khetsun Sangpo composed a versified summary of the *Detailed Analysis*, which is contained in the eleventh volume of his *Biographical Dictionary of Tibet and Tibetan Buddhism*. These narratives do not contain any new information, and thus I mention them only in passing.[75]

(3) Hagiographical accounts handed down in the Karma Kagyü tradition

(3.1) Pawo Tsuglag Trengwa: Short hagiographical sketch in *A Feast for the Scholars*

Another hagiographical tradition, namely accounts handed down in the Karma Kagyü school, is represented by the historian Pawo Tsuglag Trengwa (1504–66). A short sketch of Shākya Chogden's life is included in the eighth chapter of the third part of Pawo's religious history *A Feast for the Scholars*.[76] This chapter deals with the Karma Kamtsang tradition, and Shākya Chogden's life story is contained therein because he is counted among the "root disciples" (*rtsa ba'i slob ma*) of the Seventh Karmapa hierarch Chödrag Gyatso (1454–1506). The hagiographical note was put down around the middle of the sixteenth century—that is, approximately at the same time when Künga Drölchog was writing his *Detailed Analysis*.[77] Although the narrative is very short, it contains some minor details not known from other sources. According to the Pawo, Shākya Chogden's father was "a certain Kongtön."

75. Dhongthog 1976: 3–21; Dhongthog 1977: 243.1–253.5; Khetsun Sangpo 1979: 426–65. Furthermore, Jörg Heimbel (Hamburg) informed me that the monks of gSer mdog can Monastery (which was rebuilt in recent years after its total destruction during the Cultural Revolution) are preparing a booklet on the history of their monastery, apparently based on the *Detailed Analysis* (oral communication, October 2007).

76. Pawo Tsuglag Trengwa, *Chos 'byung*, 1157–58.

77. According to Martin 1997: 88, Pawo Tsuglag Trengwa composed the *chos 'byung* during the years 1545–64. The eighth chapter dealing with the Karma Kaṃ tshang tradition was completed on the twenty-third day of the seventh month of a bird year, that is 1549 or 1561; see Pawo Tsuglag Trengwa, *Chos 'byung*, 1333.

Furthermore, we learn that at the age of thirteen or fourteen, Shākya Chogden had become a "qualified geshe (*dge bshes*) in regard to the entire [Buddhist] teachings, thus officiating as a *chen po* [in later times]."[78] Finally, there is a further passage of interest, which is found earlier in the same chapter. At the end of an extensive hagiography of the Seventh Karmapa hierarch, we are provided with a description of the meeting between Chödrag Gyatso and Shākya Chogden at the Rinpung court in 1502.[79]

(3.2) Situ Paṇchen Chökyi Jungne: Short hagiographical account in *A Garland of Moonstones*

A slightly expanded version of the above-mentioned hagiographical sketch by Pawo Tsuglag Trengwa and the account of Shākya Chogden's meeting with the Seventh Karmapa are found in Situ Paṇchen's renowned history of the Karma Kagyü tradition.[80] To the former portrayal Situ has added the comment that Shākya Chogden and Chödrag Gyatso shared the same doctrinal views when it came to epistemology (*pramāṇa*; *tshad ma*) and the "emptiness-of-other" (*gzhan stong*) interpretation of Madhyamaka philosophy. Moreover, we are told that both Serdog Paṇchen and the Seventh Karmapa were of an identical mind stream (*thugs rgyud*).[81]

78. Ibid., 1158: *dgung lo bcu gsum bcu bzhi nas bstan pa yongs rdzogs kyi dge bshes tshad ldan du gyur te chen po mdzad*. The term *chen po* denotes a high position in the administration of monasteries in those days.

79. Ibid., 1103, 1104. Mention should be made of two other hagiographical sketches found in the same chapter of dPa' bo's *chos 'byung*. Since these accounts deal with two of Shākya mchog ldan's disciples, namely Ngo khro Rab 'byams pa dBang phyug dpal and sDe bdun Rab 'byams pa dBang phyug rgyal mtshan, they may be of interest; see ibid., 1159–60, 1168. Here sDe bdun Rab 'byams pa is said to have been the proctor (*zhal ngo*) of rTing khebs Monastery in gTsang and later took charge of the printing of Shākya mchog ldan's writings. See in this regard also Kun dga' grol mchog, *Paṇḍi ta*, 227.6, where it is stated that it was the "three dharma kings of gTing skyes who were brothers" (*gting skyes chos rje sku mched rnam pa gsum*) who were responsible for the printing of Shākya mchog ldan's works; see Kun dga' grol mchog, *Paṇḍi ta*, 227.6. See also note 41 above.

80. Si tu Paṇ chen, *History*, 646.4; 582.5; 583.1. For further information on Si tu's *chos 'byung*, see Martin 1997: 139.

81. This claim is already found in Kun dga' grol mchog, *Paṇḍi ta*, 6.1.

(4) The short hagiographical account in Mangtö's *Chronology of the Doctrine* and further texts based on it

(4.1) Mangtö Ludrub Gyatso: Short hagiographical account in *The Sun that Illuminates the Chronology of the Doctrine,* [*entitled*] *"Thoroughly Good Superior Aspiration"*

The earliest witness of the fourth group of hagiographical writings concerning Shākya Chogden's life story can be found in Mangtö Ludrub Gyatso's famed "chronology of the doctrine" (*bstan rtsis*), which was compiled between the years 1566–87.[82] It is interesting to see that Mangtö's dating of several important events in Shākya Chogden's life differs from the respective specifications given by Künga Drölchog. For instance, Mangtö states that Shākya Chogden obtained his first monastic vows, the *bar ma rab byung,* in 1435, yet Künga Drölchog's *Detailed Analysis* gives the year as 1437.[83] The same applies to the dating of the taking of the *śrāmaṇera* vows. According to Mangtö, Shākya Chogden received these vows in 1437, whereas Künga Drölchog places this event in 1440.[84] Unfortunately, the sources Mangtö relied upon for this short namtar remain unidentifiable.[85] Since the dates for the above-mentioned two events are not discussed any further by Künga Drölchog, it seems that the three earlier hagiographies composed by Shākya Chogden's disciples concur with the *Detailed Analysis* in this regard. Therefore they can be ruled out as possible sources used by Mangtö.

82. Mang thos, *bsTan rtsis*, 228–30. See also Martin 1997: 94.

83. Mang thos, *bsTan rtsis*, 228; Kun dga' grol mchog, *Paṇḍi ta*, 18.5–19.1.

84. Mang thos, *bsTan rtsis*, 228; Kun dga' grol mchog, *Paṇḍi ta*, 25.2–4.

85. For a short discussion of the sources Mang thos drew upon for the composition of his *Thoroughly Good Superior Aspiration*, see Mang thos, *bsTan rtsis*, 3–4.

(4.2) Ngorpa Könchog Lhündrub and Jadral Sangye Püntsog: Short hagiographical account in *The Excellent Elucidation of How the Noble Buddhadharma Emerged,* [*entitled*] *"Great Ship that Sets Out on the Ocean of the Doctrine"*

An abridged version of the above-mentioned hagiographical account by Mangtö is contained in Jadral Sangye Püntsog's supplement (*kha skong*) to Ngorpa Könchog Lhündrub's *chos 'byung.*[86] Sangye Püntsog attached this supplement in 1692 to the work.[87] Since the short hagiographical narrative contains no new information, it is of no further interest.

(4.3) Accounts by contemporary Tibetan authors

Also of no further interest are several short hagiographical sketches based on Mangtö's account that were compiled by contemporary Tibetan authors. In this regard, it will suffice to mention two well-known reference works, namely Koshül Dragpa Jungne's compilation of short hagiographies of Tibetan masters and Dungkar Losang Trinle's encyclopedia of Tibetan culture. Both contain short descriptions of Shākya Chogden's life that are faithful renderings of Mangtö's narrative.[88]

Concluding Remarks

The examination of available Tibetan sources on Shākya Chogden's life has shown that there are different hagiographical strands, the most important being constituted by Künga Drölchog's *Detailed Analysis.* This extensive namtar was based on three earlier hagiographies written by direct disciples of Shākya Chogden. In addition, Künga Drölchog made use of further sources mostly consisting of oral accounts given to him by some of his teachers who had been students of Shākya Chogden. The only other full-fledged namtar, Shākya Rinchen's *Sun that Illuminates the Muni's Teachings*, is for

86. dKon mchog lhun grub, *A History*, 354.5.

87. Fur further information on this *chos 'byung*, see Martin 1997: 112.

88. Ko zhul Grags pa 'byung gnas and rGyal ba Blo bzang mkhas grub 1992: 984–85; Dung dkar Blo bzang 'phrin las 1997: 1268.

the most part an extended paraphrase of Künga Drölchog's *Detailed Analysis*. Moreover, there are two further traditions preserving descriptions of Shākya Chogden's life, but these do not seem to have been used as sources for any extensive namtars. The first one is represented by a brief hagiographical sketch found in Pawo Tsuglag Trengwa's religious history *A Feast for the Scholars*, which later served as a blueprint for the short portrayal of Shākya Chogden included in Situ Paṇchen Chökyi Jungne's *Garland of Moonstones*, a historiographical work mainly dealing with the Karma Kamtsang tradition. The earliest witness of the second minor tradition is a short hagiographical account in Mangtö Ludrub Gyatso's famed "chronology of the doctrine." An abridged version of this sketch can be found in Jadral Sangye Püntsog's supplement to Ngorpa Könchog Lhündrub's *Great Ship that Sets Out on the Ocean of the Doctrine*, which is, again, a traditional work on religious history.

In closing, it should be mentioned in passing that several passages complementing the hagiographical sources discussed in this paper are scattered throughout Shākya Chogden's *gsung 'bum*. Attached to quite a number of his works are colophons that not only give information on the exact place and time of composition but often also on sponsors, scribes, and the purpose for writing the respective work. In addition, many texts that are of historical interest are preserved particularly in the sixteenth and seventeenth volumes of his *gsung 'bum*. Here we find hagiographies, invocations, and praises of his teachers and other contemporaries, as well as two extensive collections of letters, and textual material on Serdogchen Monastery. While Künga Drölchog utilized some of the information found in these writings when composing his *Detailed Analysis*, a thorough investigation of this material remains a desideratum, as it might yield hitherto unknown details on the master's life.

Bibliography

Classical Tibetan Sources

bsTan 'dzin chos rgyal, rJe mKhan po X (1700–66/67). *lHo'i chos 'byung bstan pa rin po che'i 'phro mthud 'jam mgon smon mtha'i 'phreng ba*. (Computer file by courtesy of Lumbini International Research Institute.)

dKon mchog lhun grub, Ngor mKhan chen X (1497–1557), and Bya bral Sangs rgyas phun tshogs (1649–1705). *A History of Buddhism, Being the Text of: Dam pa'i chos kyi 'byung tshul legs par bshad pa bstan pa'i rgya mtshor 'jug pa'i gru chen zhes bya ba rtsom 'phro kha skong bcas*. New Delhi: Ngawang Tobgey, 1973.

dPa' bo gTsug lag phreng ba (1504–66). [*A Feast for the Scholars* =] *Chos 'byung mkhas pa'i dga' ston*. (Reprint of the Beijing ed., 1986.) Vol. 2 (*smad cha*). Varanasi: Vajra Vidya Library.

'Jam mgon Kongs sprul Blo gros mtha' yas (1813–99). *Zab mo'i gter dang gter ston grub thob ji ltar byon pa'i lo rgyus mdor bsdus bkod pa rin chen bai ḍūrya'i phreng ba* (short title: *gTer ston brgya rtsa'i rnam thar*). In *Rin chen gter mdzod chen mo* (sTod lung mTshur phu redaction), vol. 1 (ka), pp. 291–759. Paro: Ngodrup and Sherab Drimay, 1976.

Kun dga' grol mchog, Jo nang rJe btsun (1507–66). *Padma dkar po'i chun po*. In *rJe btsun kun dga' grol mchog gi phyi nang gsang gsum gyi rnam thar*, pp. 3–10. Beijing: Mi rigs dpe skrun khang, 2005.

———. *Paṇḍi ta chen po shākya mchog ldan gyi rnam par thar pa zhib mo rnam par 'byed pa*. In *The Complete Works (gSuṅ 'bum) of gSer-mdog Paṇ-chen Śākya-mchog-ldan*, vol. 16, pp. 1–233. Thimphu: Kunzang Tobgey, 1975.

———. [*Rang rnam Ia* =] *Zhen pa rang grol gyi lhug par brjod pa'i gtam skal bzang dad pa'i shing rta 'dren byed*. In *Kun dga' grol mchog blo gsal rgya mtsho'i gsung 'bum: The Autobiographies of Jo-naṅ Kun-dga'-grol-mchog and His Previous Embodiments*, vol. 2. New Delhi: Tibet House, 1982.

———. [*Rang rnam Ib* =] *rJe btsun kun dga' grol mchog gi rnam thar skal bzang dad pa'i shing rta 'dren byed*. In *rJe btsun kun dga' grol mchog gi phyi nang gsang gsum gyi rnam thar*, pp. 21–178. Beijing: Mi rigs dpe skrun khang, 2005.

———. [*Rang rnam II* =] *rNam thar skal bzang dad pa'i shing rta 'dren byed kyi 'phros zur 'debs mdzes rgyan*. In *rJe btsun kun dga' grol mchog gi phyi nang gsang gsum gyi rnam thar*, pp. 179–208. Beijing: Mi rigs dpe skrun khang, 2005.

———. [*Rang rnam III* =] *rNam thar yang rgyan nor bu'i phra bkod*. In *rJe btsun kun dga' grol mchog gi phyi nang gsang gsum gyi rnam thar*, pp. 209–66. Beijing: Mi rigs dpe skrun khang, 2005.

———. [*Rang rnam IV* =] *rNam thar spel rgyan nor bu'i do shal*. In *rJe btsun kun dga' grol mchog gi phyi nang gsang gsum gyi rnam thar*, pp. 267–87. Beijing: Mi rigs dpe skrun khang, 2005.

———. [*Rang rnam V* =] *rNam thar mtshar rgyan*. In *rJe btsun kun dga' grol mchog gi phyi nang gsang gsum gyi rnam thar*, pp. 288–319. Beijing: Mi rigs dpe skrun khang, 2005.

———. [*Rang rnam VI* =] *rMyong ba rgyan gyi me tog ces bya ba thun mong gi sgo'i rnam thar*. In *rJe btsun kun dga' grol mchog gi phyi nang gsang gsum gyi rnam thar*, pp. 320–76. Beijing: Mi rigs dpe skrun khang, 2005.

———. [*Rang rnam VII* –] *rMyong ba rgyan gyi me tog ces bya ba thun mong ma yin pa'i rnam thar*. In *rJe btsun kun dga' grol mchog gi phyi nang gsang gsum gyi rnam thar*, pp. 377–404. Beijing: Mi rigs dpe skrun khang, 2005.

Mang thos Klu sgrub rgya mtsho (1523–96). [*Thoroughly Good Superior Aspiration* =] *bsTan rtsis gsal ba'i nyin byed lhag bsam rab dkar*. In *bsTan rtsis gsal ba'i nyin byed [dang] lha snyad rig gnas lnga'i byung tshul*, pp. 3–251. Lhasa: Bod ljong mi dmangs dpe skrun khang, 1987 (= Gangs can rig mdzod 4).

Shākya rin chen, rJe mKhan po IX (1709/10–59). *Gangs can gyi shing rta chen po dpal shākya mchog ldan dri med legs pa'i blo gros kyi rnam thar thub bstan gsal ba'i nyin byed*. In *The Collected Works (gSuṅ 'bum) of rJe Śākya-rin-chen*, vol. 4, pp. 1–471. Thimphu: Kunzang Topgey, 1976.

———. *Rang nyid kyi gsang ba'i tshul cung zad bsnyad pa sgyu 'phrul dra ba'i rol rtsed*. In *rJe Śākya rin chen gyi rnam thar daṅ gsuṅ thor bu: The Autobiography and Selected Writings of Śakya-rin-chen, the Ninth rJe mKhan-po of Bhutan*, vol. 1, pp. 521–87. Delhi: Thamchoe Monlam, 1974.

———. *Shākya'i dge sbyong shākya'i ming gis mtshon pa bdag nyid lha ldan 'phrul gyi gtsug lag khang chen por phyin pa'i gtam lha mi kun tu dga' ba'i zlos gar*. In *The Collected Works (gSuṅ 'bum) of rJe Śākya-rin-chen*, vol. 6, pp. 201–54. Thimphu: Kunzang Topgey, 1976.

———. *lHag pa'i bsam pa bskul zhing byang chub kyi spyod pa la 'jug pa'i gtam dam pa'i chos kyi gaṇḍi'i sgra dbyangs snyan pa'i yan lag rgya mtsho*. In *rJe Śākya rin chen gyi rnam thar daṅ gsuṅ thor bu: The Autobiography and Selected Writings of Śakya-rin-chen, the Ninth rJe mKhan-po of Bhutan*, vol. 1, pp. 1–519. Delhi: Thamchoe Monlam, 1974. [The work was left unfinished by Shākya Rinchen and was completed by Künga Gyatso and Yönten Taye.]

Si tu Paṇ chen VIII Chos kyi 'byung gnas (1699/1700–1774). [*A Garland of Moonstones* =] *History of the Karma bKa'-brgyud-pa Sect Being the Text of "sGrub brgyud karma kaṃ tshang [bka'] brgyud pa rin po che'i rnam par thar pa rab 'byams nor bu zla ba chu s[h]el gyi phreng ba"* (dPal spungs ed.). New Delhi: D. Gyaltsan and Kesang Legshay, 1972. [The work was left unfinished by Situ Paṇchen and was completed by Belo Tsewang Künkhyab ('Be lo Tshe dbang kun khyab), b. 1718.]

Modern Tibetan Sources

bCo brgyad Khri chen Thub bstan legs bshad rgya mtsho (n.d.). *Gangs ljongs mdo sngags kyi bstan pa'i shing rta dpal ldan sa skya pa'i chos 'byung mdor bsdus skal bzang yid kyi dga' ston*. Dharamsala: Tibetan Educational Printing Press.

bsTan 'dzin phun tshogs, ed. 2004. *'Bras spungs dgon du bzhugs su gsol ba'i dpe rnying dkar chag*. 2 vols. Beijing: Mi rigs dpe skrun khang.

Dhongthog Rinpoche, T. G. [gDong thog Theg mchog bstan pa'i rgyal mtshan] 1976. *A History of the Complete Works of gSer mdog Paṇ chen Śākya mchog ldan: Paṇḍi ta chen po shākya mchog ldan dri med legs pa'i blo gros kyi gsung rab rin po che par du bskrun pa'i tshul las brtsams pa'i gleng ba bstan pa'i nyi gzhon yid srubs sprin las grol ba'i dga' ston tshangs pa'i bzhad sgra*. Thimphu: Kunzang Tobgey.

——— 1977. *Byang phyogs thub pa'i rgyal tshab dpal ldan sa skya pa'i bstan pa rin po che ji ltar byung ba'i lo rgyus rab 'byams zhing du snyan pa'i sgra dbyangs: A History of the Sa-skya-pa Sect of Tibetan Buddhism*. New Delhi.

Dung dkar Blo bzang 'phrin las mchog 2002. *Bod rig pa'i tshig mdzod chen mo shes bya rab gsal*. Beijing: Krung go'i bod rig pa dpe skrun khang.

Hor rgyal, ed. 2005. *Jo nang dkar chag shel dkar phreng mdzes*. Beijing: Mi rigs dpe skrun khang.

Khenpo Appey [mKhan po A pad] 1987. *dKar chag mthong bas yid 'phrog chos mdzod bye ba'i lde mig: A Bibliography of Sa-skya-pa Literature*. New Delhi: Ngawang Topgyal, 1987.

Khetsun Sangpo [mKhas btsun bzang po] 1979. *Biographical Dictionary of Tibet and Tibetan Buddhism. Vol. XI: The Sa-skya-pa Tradition (Part Two)*. Dharamsala: Library of Tibetan Works and Archives.

Ko zhul Grags pa 'byung gnas and rGyal ba Blo bzang mkhas grub 1992. *Gangs can mkhas grub rim byon ming mdzod*. Lan chou: Kan su'u mi rigs dpe skrun khang.

Sun wun zing, ed. 1989. *Bod gangs can gyi grub mtha' ris med kyi mkhas dbang brgya dang brgyad cu lhag gi gsung 'bum so so'i dkar chag phyogs gcig tu bsgrigs pa shes bya'i gter mdzod*. Vol. 2 (*bar cha*). Mi rigs dpe mdzod khang. Beijing: Mi rigs dpe skrun khang.

Sources in Western Languages

Amipa, Sherab Gyaltsen 1976. *A Waterdrop from the Glorious Sea: A Concise Account of the Advent of Buddhism in General and the Teachings of the Sakyapa Tradition in Particular*. Rikon: Tibetan Institute.

Ardussi, John 1999. "The Rapprochement between Bhutan and Tibet under the Enlightened Rule of sDe-srid XIII Shes-rab-dbang-phyug (r. 1744–63)." Reprint with minor corrections from *Proceedings of the 7th Seminar of the International Association for Tibetan Studies, Graz 1995*, ed. by Ernst Steinkellner, vol. I, pp. 17-27. Wien: Verlag der Österreichischen Akademie der Wissenschaften. *Journal of Bhutan Studies* 1.1: 64–83.

Burchardi, Anne (forthcoming). "Shākya mchog ldan's Literary Heritage in Bhutan." In *Proceedings of the International Conference on "Written Treasures of Bhutan."* Thimphu.

Davidson, Ronald M. 1981. "The Ṅor-pa Tradition." In *Wind Horse: Proceedings of the North American Tibetological Society*, ed. by Ronald M. Davidson, vol. 1, pp. 79–98.

Jackson, David Paul 1983. "Commentaries on the Writings of Sa-skya Pandita: A Bibliographical Sketch." *The Tibet Journal* 8.3: 3–23.

——— 1989a. *The Early Abbots of 'Phan-po Na-lendra: The Vicissitudes of a Great Tibetan Monastery in the 15th Century*. Wiener Studien zur Tibetologie und Buddhismuskunde 23. Wien: Arbeitskreis für tibetische und buddhistische Studien, Universität Wien.

——— 1989b. *The "Miscellaneous Series" of Tibetan Texts in the Bihar Research Society, Patna: A Handlist*. Tibetan and Indo-Tibetan Studies 2. Wiesbaden: Franz Steiner Verlag.

Komarovski, Yaroslav Lvovich 2000. *Three Texts on Madhyamaka by Shakya Chokden*. Dharamsala: Library of Tibetan Works and Archives.

——— 2006. "Reburying the Treasure—Maintaining the Continuity: Two Texts by Śākya Mchog Ldan on the Buddha-Essence." *Journal of Indian Philosophy* 34.6: 521–70.

——— 2007. "Echoes of Empty Luminosity: Reevaluation and Unique Interpretation of Yogācāra and Niḥsvabhāvavāda Madhyamaka by the Fifteenth Century Tibetan Thinker Śākya mchog ldan." PhD diss., University of Virginia.

Kuijp, Leonard W. J. van der 1983. *Contributions to the Development of Tibetan Buddhist Epistemology: From the Eleventh to the Thirteenth Century*. Alt- und Neu-Indische Studien 26. Wiesbaden: Franz Steiner Verlag.

Martin, Dan 1997. *Tibetan Histories: A Bibliography of Tibetan-Language Historical Works*. London: Serindia Publications.

Mathes, Klaus-Dieter 2004. "Tāranātha's 'Twenty-One Differences with Regard to the Profound Meaning': Comparing the Views of the Two *gŹan stoṅ* Masters Dol po pa and Śākya mchog ldan." *Journal of the International Association of Buddhist Studies* 27.2: 285–328.

Roesler, Ulrike and Hans-Ulrich 2004. *Kadampa Sites of Phempo: A Guide to Some Early Buddhist Monasteries in Central Tibet*. Bauddha Books 2. Kathmandu: Vajra Publications.

Rossi Filibeck, Elena de 2003. *Catalogue of the Tucci Tibetan Fund in the Library of IsIAO*, Vol. 2. Rome: Istituto Italiano per l'Africa e l'Oriente.

Rhoton, Jared Douglas 2002. *A Clear Distinction of the Three Codes: Essential Distinctions Among the Individual Liberation, Great Vehicle, and Tantric Systems*. SUNY Series in Buddhist Studies. Albany: State University of New York Press.

Seyfort Ruegg, David 1963. "The Jo naṅ pas: A School of Buddhist Ontologists According to the *Grub mtha' šel gyi me loṅ*." *Journal of the American Oriental Society* 83: 73–91.

——— 1995. *Ordre Spirituel et Ordre Temporel dans la Pensée Bouddhique de l'Inde et du Tibet*. Collège de France. Paris: Diffusion de Boccard.

Stearns, Cyrus 1999. *The Buddha from Dolpo: A Study of the Life and Thought of the Tibetan Master Dolpopa Sherab Gyaltsen*. SUNY Series in Buddhist Studies. Albany: State University of New York Press.

Tillemans, Tom J. F., and Tomabechi, Toru 1995. "Le *dBu ma'i byuṅ tshul* de Śākya mchog ldan." *Asiatische Studien* 44.4: 891–918.

Narratives of Reincarnation, Politics of Power, and the Emergence of a Scholar

The Very Early Years of Mikyö Dorje[1]

Jim Rheingans

Introduction

The boy who was to become the eighth in the line of the Karmapas, Mikyö Dorje (1507–54), did not have an easy childhood. His status as an incarnation was disputed, and while his school enjoyed special favors from the Rinpungpa rulers particularly dominant in the period of 1498–1517, unrest in Ü set in again after 1517. Despite this, he became one of the most important scholars of the primarily meditation-orientated Karma Kagyü tradition next to the Third Karmapa, Rangjung Dorje (1284–1339), and exerted political influence in places where his school held large estates. During a period of growing systematization, Mikyö Dorje was a prolific writer: he commented on four of the five main sutra subjects,[2] tantric doctrines, and other traditional fields of knowledge, his oeuvre filling more than thirty volumes.[3]

1. Part of this paper is related to my PhD research *The Eighth Karmapa's Life and His Interpretation of the Great Seal* 2008. I would like to acknowledge the generous support of the School of Historical and Cultural Studies, Bath Spa University, and the Tara Foundation. I am indebted to David Jackson, Burkhard Scherer, and Franz-Karl Ehrhard for useful suggestions regarding this publication. I would like to thank the editors of the present volume for including this paper.

2. Abhidharma, Madhyamaka, Prajñāpāramitā, Vinaya, and Pramāṇa (see Brunnhölzl [2004]: 19). For his scholastic contributions, see also Rheingans 2008: 135–47.

3. *mKhas pa'i dga' ston*, p. 1313: *bka' 'bum ni rje pakṣi la'ang da lta po ti bcu drug las mi bzhugs la rje 'di'i bka' 'bum po ti sum bcu lhag bzhugs.* According to *Kaṃ tshang*, p. 355 (completed

With regard to his studies, scholastic accomplishments, and the founding of institutes, the Eighth Karmapa continued the aims of his predecessor, the Seventh Karmapa, and tried to raise the educational standard of the Karma Kagyü.[4] His scholastic proficiency is illustrated in a spiritual memoir (*rang rnam*): he mainly taught the five topics, Abhidharma, Pramāṇa, Prajñāpāramitā, Vinaya, and Madhyamaka, augmented by Sakya Paṇḍita's *Treasury of Reasoning* (*Tshad ma rig gter*), the *Differentiation of the Three Vows* (*sDom gsum rab dbye*), and the trainings of the Vinaya.[5] Despite the scholastic challenge and use of strong language in some of his writings, the summary of the Eighth Karmapa's life reveals his keen interest in different traditions of learning, as well as humbler overtones.[6] The Karmapa's intellectual engagement culminated in the composition of large scholastic commentaries to

1715), about twenty volumes (*pusti*) made up the Eighth Karma pa's works. Such a difference in volume numbers does not necessarily indicate a different number of texts. The 1984 catalogue of the Beijing Nationalities Library claims (Mi rigs dpe mdzod khang [ed.], *Bod gangs can gyi grub mtha',* p. 17.): "it is clear in the spiritual biography that there are twenty-eight volumes, however..." (*pod nyi shu rtsa brgyad tsam yod tshul rnam thar du gsal yang*). However, this claim is not verified in any of the spiritual biographies. See Rheingans 2008: 57–71 for a more detailed analysis.

4. Both scholars of the Karma bKa' brgyud tradition and the number of his writings lend support to this claim (see also Rheingans 2008: 150–56). mKhan po Nges don, a scholar of the Karma bKa' brgyud tradition who had studied in Rumtek, considered it a particular feature of the Eighth Karma pa that he spread the doctrine mainly through *mchad nyan*, e.g., exposition and study of the Buddha's teaching (as practiced in Tibet) (oral communication, Malaga, March 2007). In sheer number, the Karma pa's writings may be compared to the likes of Shākya mchog ldan (twenty-four volumes) and, most importantly, 'Brug chen Padma dkar po (twenty-four volumes). For the monasteries and centers of learning founded, see *Mi bskyod rdo rje'i spyad pa'i rabs*, fol. 10b–11b (pp. 369–71). While the dGe lugs monastic education focused more on debate, the non–dGe lugs schools developed commentarial schools (*bshad grwa*) stressing exegesis. This development took place after the fifteenth century (Dreyfus 2005: 276–92). In general, one must distinguish between a lineage of spiritual instructions, passed down from teacher to student, and a religious school, which is an organized form of the studies and practices connected with a particular transmission lineage (Kapstein 1980: 139; 1996: 284n2).

5. *Mi bskyod rdo rje'i spyad pa'i rabs*, fol. 9b (p. 367).

6. The Eighth Karma pa's straightforward language is indicated at other occasions: around 1539, the Karma pa met Jo nang Kun dga' sgrol mchog (1507–65/66), a famed Jo nang pa master. This would have been his disciple prophesied as "sun-like," but the Karma pa used a few straightforward words in typical Khams pa fashion and the student ran away (*Kaṃ tshang*, p. 342).

treatises, such as the *Madhyamakāvatāra* and *Abhisamayālaṃkāra*.[7] Despite the Eighth Karmapa's significance, the only academic study of the Karmapa's life has been Gregor Verhufen's master's thesis from 1995,[8] in which he only briefly hints at the existence of a rival candidate for the title of Karmapa and the ensuing tensions.[9]

This paper wishes to analyze the Eighth Karmapa's early years, the dispute about his identification, and the intricate religio-political context. The study touches upon the politics of reincarnation and its documentation in the narratives about a Buddhist saint. The main sources are spiritual memoirs and biographies (*rnam thar*) of the Eighth Karmapa, recently made

7. In his famed Madhyamaka commentary he explored the language of his opponents and the tools of Buddhist logic to the fullest, yet he was clearly skeptical of overanalyzing (Williams [1983]: 129). Williams 1983 a and b and Ruegg 1988, 2000 have dealt with the *spyi don* of Mi bsykod rdo rje's *dBu ma la 'jug pa'i rnam bshad*. Brunnhölzl 2004 offers the most extensive study of the Eighth Karma pa's Madhyamaka. For further previous research on the Eighth Karma pa's doctrines, see also Rheingans 2008: 15–30.

8. Verhufen has focused mainly on the Karma pa's relationship to his most important teacher, Sangs rgyas mnyan pa (1445/57–1510/25). His main reference for the Eighth Karma pa's life was Si tu and 'Be lo's *Kaṃ tshang*: after briefly translating a passage surrounding the pre-birth of the Karma pa (Verhufen 1995: 75–80), he has summarized the remainder of his life (ibid., 80–89). The list of visions of the Eighth Karma pa along with indices of places and names in *Kaṃ tshang* (Verhufen 1995: 104–31) are a most welcome contribution. For the Eighth Karma pa's life, Verhufen has not drawn from the older *mKhas pa'i dga' ston*, composed by one of the Eighth Karma pa's students, and the spiritual biographies from the *Collected Works of the Eighth Karmapa* were not available to him. Richardson 1980: 347–50 has briefly discussed the Karma pa's invitation to China and its conflicting portrayal in Chinese, dGe lugs, and bKa' brgyud pa sources. Two traditional accounts of the Eighth Karma pa's life were published earlier: In *Black Hat Lama*, Nik Douglas and Meryl White 1976: 86–90 have offered a very brief summary, and in *The Sixteen Karmapas of Tibet,* Karma Thinley Rinpoche 1980: 89–96 has composed four pages about the Eighth Karma pa that contain no citation of sources. It is made clear from the appendix that he has used the *mKhas pa'i dga' ston*, *Kaṃ tshang*, Padma dkar po's *Tibetan Chronicle*, and Nges don bstan rgyas' *Karma pa sku 'phreng gyi rnam thar* for his summary. See Rheingans 2008: 95–164 for a more extensive summary and analysis of the Eighth Karma pa's life.

9. In a footnote, Verhufen 1995: 31n51 quotes the *Karmapa Papers* edited by Nesterenko 1992: 7, where the Tibetan scholar sTobs dga' Rin po che rightly mentions that there were two candidates for the title of Eighth Karma pa. Although Verhufen 1995 asserts he has not found this story confirmed in any available spiritual biography, he refers to it later himself (80). He does not mention it in detail, and his argument is based on the highly abbreviated version in *Kaṃ tshang*, pp. 304–5. Verhufen 1995: 96n59 has included, however, two brief sentences indicating this conflict in Stein 1972: 147, who had employed the *mKhas pa'i dga' ston* as source. Van der Kuijp 2001: 59 has very briefly noted the situation, referring to *mKhas pa'i dga' ston*, pp. 1207–25.

available through the publication of his collected works.[10] Since previous research has rarely taken this textual corpus into account, I will briefly evaluate the sources, their intertextuality, and genres. One of the main sources employed is the spiritual biography authored by Jangchub Sangpo, alias Akhu Atra.[11]

Religio-Political Tension in Ü and Tsang

The religio-political climate that likely contributed to the tensions built up in the early years of the Eighth Karmapa needs to be considered first. In the era extending from 1354 to 1642, three families successively controlled most areas of Tibetan Ü and Tsang: the Pagmo Drupa (1354–ca. 1478), the Rinpungpa (1478–1565), and the Tsangpa (1565–1642). In the decades preceding the Eighth Karmapa's birth, the religio-political situation was characterized by tension and clashes between the Pagmo Drupa of Ü and the Tsang-based Rinpungpa.[12]

Despite this, from the 1480s the Karma Kagyüpa under the religio-political influence of the Fourth Shamarpa, Chödrag Yeshe (1453–1524), and the Seventh Karmapa, Chödrag Gyatso (1454–1507), enjoyed a time of unprecedented honor and support from the Rinpungpa, reaching its peak in the period between 1498 and 1517. During the first ten years of the Eighth

10. The twenty-six volume *Collected Works of the Eighth Karmapa* consists of newly discovered texts digitally inputted in Tibetan *dbu can* script. Its compilation, editing, and printing were funded by the Tsadra Foundation. For an analysis of the history and transmission of his writings and the rubrics and sources for the *Collected Works of the Eighth Karmapa* published 2000–2004, see Rheingans 2008: 57–71. In a forthcoming publication, a descriptive and comparative catalogue of the Eighth Karma pa's writings will be made available.

11. The full title is: *rGyal ba kun gyi dbang po dpal ldan karma pa mi bskyod rdo rje'i zhabs kyi dgung lo bdun phan gyi rnam par thar pa nor bu'i phreng ba* (*The Spiritual Biography up to the Seventh Year of the Glorious Karmapa Mi bskyod rdo rje, the Mighty One of All Jinas: A Garland of Jewels*). See below for a detailed description of the sources.

12. A comprehensive study of this period's history based on a wide range of Tibetan sources is not yet accomplished (Kapstein 2006: 116, 130). Accounts can be found in overviews on Tibetan history such as Tucci 1949, Snellgrove and Richardson 1968, Tucci 1980, Stein 1972, Samuel 1993, and, recently, Kapstein 2006. Alternatively, information on related persons or topics is found in various monographs and articles, such as for example Jackson 1989, Petech 1990, Sperling 1980, Vitali 1996, Schwieger 1996, Wylie 2003, van der Kuijp 1991, 1994, and 2001, and Ehrhard 2002a, 2002b, 2004, and forthcoming, or in unpublished master's theses such as Krupa 1999, Rheingans 2004, and Caumanns 2006.

Karmapa's life, the Rinpungpa and the most powerful man of the day, General Dönyö Dorje (1463–1512), were at the height of their power and wealth, directly ruling major areas of Tibet (Ü, Tsang, and even parts of Ngari).[13] The Eighth Karmapa witnessed the transition from relative peace and strong central rule to increasing instability, especially in Ü, culminating in the period of great unrest in the late 1540s.[14]

In 1354, after the decline of the Eastern Mongol empire, Tai Situ Jangchub Gyaltsen (1302–64), from the Kagyüpa seat Pagmo Dru, ended the primacy of the Sakyapas under Mongolian patronage and ruled from his residence in Neudong.[15] While the Pagmo Drupa lords were initially affiliated with the Kagyüpa, they were also to become strong supporters of Gelug founder Tsongkhapa (1357–1419) and his disciples,[16] as Tsongkhapa represented an appealing example of learning and monasticism.[17]

Gradually, the Pagmo Drupa's rule was superseded by their own ministers, the lords of Rinpung in eastern Tsang: after the civil war of 1434 and the death of the ruling head, Dragpa Gyaltsen (1385–1432), the Pagmo Drupa leaders (*gong ma*) Dragpa Jungne (1414–45) and Künga Legpa (1433–82) became increasingly weakened.[18] The year 1478 saw the gradual seizure of power by the Rinpungpa, under the leadership of Tsokye Dorje (1462–1510)

13. See below and Jackson 1989: 29ff.

14. During the preceding Mongol overlordship and Sa skya rule (1244–1354), monasteries had become more powerful than the nobility. Some consider this period crucial for the evolution of a more formal patron-priest relationship (*mchod yon*) and the interplay of religion and politics in Tibet (Ruegg 1991: 448). While the patron often sought to gain control over a certain area or population through presenting offerings to a revered teacher, lamas were in need of funding for and protection of their expanding monastic complexes (Schuh 1976: 219). For the Mongol period as a whole, see Petech 1990; see also Schuh 1986, Wylie 1978, and the later analysis of Everding 2002.

15. Snellgrove and Richardson 1968: 153ff. Petech 1990: 85–119 briefly documents the rise of Phag mo gru after the Mongol overlordship. For the life of Byang chub rgyal mtshan, see van der Kuijp 1991 and 1994. Byang chub rgyal mtshan had founded the monastery of rTse thang close to his residence (see van der Kuijp [200]1: 64–65, for an outline of the abbots of rTse thang).

16. Kapstein 2006: 128.

17. Kapstein 2006: 121, Snellgrove and Richardson 1968: 180–82. Ruegg 2004: 326–43 examines Tsong kha pa's impact and exegetical method. For Tsong kha pa's life, see Kaschewsky 1971; for his relation to Red mda' ba, see Roloff 2003.

18. Jackson 1989: 52.

and his nephew Garpa Dönyö Dorje (1463–1512), general of the Rinpungpa army encampment. Taking advantage of Pagmo Drupa's weakness, he assumed rule of the crucial Dzong Shigatse in western Tibet.[19]

The Fourth Shamarpa played an important role in these events and was one of the most interesting figures of this period; he had close ties to Dönyö Dorje and to the Pagmo Drupa. Like Gö Lotsāwa (1392–1481), he acted as teacher of Chenga Ngagi Wangpo (1439–90), who was installed by the Rinpungpa as Pagmo Drupa leader (*gong ma*) in 1481.[20] In 1493, after Ngagi Wangpo's passing, the Fourth Shamarpa was officially installed as Chenga of Densatel Monastery, the highest religious authority of the Pagmo Drupa. Since Ngagi Wangpo's successor, Ngagwang Tashi Dragpa, was still a minor, the Shamarpa *de facto* shared political responsibilities with some ministers beginning in 1491.[21]

Meanwhile, the Rinpungpa generals marshalled campaigns to gain control of the Lhasa region. In 1480, Dönyö Dorje closed in on Central Yarlung, together with armies from Yargyab and Gongkar.[22] The Gelugpa felt threatened by the growing political power of the Rinpungpa and their chief gurus;

19. Shakabpa 1967: 86; Jackson 1989: 16–20.

20. Richardson 1980: 346f. For the Fourth Zhwa dmar pa, see also Ehrhard 2002a: 9–33, Ehrhard 2004: 249–50, and Tucci 1949: 29–31. Extensive Tibetan sources are *mKhas pa'i dga' ston*, pp. 1115–50, and *Kaṃ tshang*, pp. 194–224. On the occasion of Ngag gi dbang po's installment the Fourth Zhwa dmar pa was present, as was bKra shis dar rgyas, ruler of Bya yul and supporter of Karma 'phrin las pa and the Seventh Karma pa (Ehrhard 2002a: 23n19, who used *mKhas pa'i dga' ston*, pp. 1123–24). See also *mKhas pa'i dga' ston*, pp. 1140–43, for frequent meetings of the Fourth Zhwa dmar pa and Don yod rdo rje between 1501–4, where they exchanged teachings and offerings. For the relation of Bya bKra shis dar rgyas, the Seventh Karma pa, and Karma 'phrin las pa, see Rheingans 2004: 64–66 and *Kaṃ tshang*, p. 246. A monograph study of the Fourth Zhwa dmar pa's life and works is highly needed for the history of medieval Tibet.

21. Paṇ chen bSod nams grags pa, *Deb ther dmar po gsar ma*, p. 88 (translation by Tucci 1971: 226). It is uncertain to what extent the Fourth Zhwa dmar pa was actually involved in the different campaigns. dGe lugs historians such as Sum pa mkhan po Ye she dpal 'byor believe that he was the instigator of the 1481 invasion—the biography of the Zhwa dmar pa credits him with a diplomatic role (Jackson 1989: 47n61). Richardson 1980: 347 generally depicts the Zhwa dmar pa as more politically involved than the Karma pa lamas, but his pioneering research was a first attempt to come to terms with the complicated political issues of that time and may be slightly outdated (see note 20 above).

22. Jackson 1989: 38. The Rin spungs pa also appointed Glang ri thang pa Blo gros rgyal mtshan as abbot of the important Sa skya pa monastery Nalendra, which was very close to Lhasa.

already mounting tensions magnified when, in 1489 and 1490, Dönyö Dorje accompanied the Seventh Karmapa twice to Lhasa, where he laid the foundation for the Tubchen Chökor Monastery east of the city.[23]

After the Rinpungpa were temporarily halted by the revolt of the Ganden abbot Mönlam Pal (1414–91) and distracted by a defeat in Gyaltse, Ü again became their main focus.[24] This time, they were more difficult to stop. In 1492, an army of Tsang led by Dönyö Dorje and Nangso Künga Tashi came through Yardrog and took some districts from Yargyab, Gongkar, and Nel. A further incident increased tensions significantly: around 1497, the Seventh Karmapa was attacked by Gelugpa monks in the vicinity of Lhasa and only survived by launching an escape to the Jokhang temple.[25]

The Rinpungpa and the Fourth Shamarpa were sorely provoked by the incident, though the Seventh Karmapa tried to calm the situation. Rinpungpa lords pressed on to control the Lhasa region, and 1498 saw their victory: a great army of Ü and Tsang marched to Kyishö. This time the Chapa lord, angered by the attack on the Seventh Karmapa, joined in.[26]

23. According to the spiritual biography of the Seventh Karma pa, he founded the monastery (*Kaṃ tshang*, edition Si tu Paṇ chen Chos kyi 'byung gnas, *sGrub brgyud karma kaṃ tshang*, vol. I, p. 586: *lha sa'i shar du thub chen chos 'khor gyi sde'i rmang bting / 'di la rten 'brel ha cang 'grig che ba ma byung bar rje phrin las pa gsung bzhin bstan pa'i rgyun 'bring tsam zhig byung / der chos rje mi nyag pa gshegs nas karma phrin las pa bskos /*). An earlier passage, describing the spiritual biography of Karma 'phrin las pa, suggests (ibid., p. 652) that Karma 'phrin las pa may also have been involved in laying its foundation stone. In any case, it was situated to the east of Lhasa, and Karma 'phrin las pa acted as a teacher there (Rheingans 2004: 72–73, 102–9). Sangs rgyas dpal grub, fol. 37b (p. 223), attributes the founding of Thub chen to the Fourth Zhwa dmar pa; his testimony is the earliest one (see below, "Spiritual Memoirs and Biographies of the Eighth Karmapa").

24. Jackson 1989: 65. The monks of 'Bras spungs and dGa' ldan gathered behind the powerful dGa' ldan and 'Bras spungs abbot, sMon lam dpal. He tried to shake off Rin spungs pa dominance through sorcery and the strengthening of their Central Tibetan patrons. Indeed, they revolted from 1485 to ca. 1488, when the Rin spungs pa were partly distracted from their hold on Central Tibet, mainly due to a defeat to the forces of rGyal rtse in 1485 (Jackson 1989: 54–58).

25. An exact date has not yet been proven, though 1481 or 1497 are likely (Shakabpa 1967: 87; Jackson [1989]: 49n64). Jackson (ibid.) claims the Karma pa was a peaceful figure, refraining from using violence here. This incident led, however, to the Bya pa Khrid dpon (a student of the Seventh Karma pa) breaking away from the Central Tibetan alliance and joining the gTsang pa forces. To what extent these events motivated the campaigns has not been discovered and should be examined with the aid of proper and extensive source work.

26. Jackson 1989: 39.

In 1499, urged by the Taglungpa and the Seventh Karmapa, the Fourth Shamarpa negotiated a relatively mild settlement for the Nelpa and Gelug monasteries.[27] The Gelug attack, however, did not go unpunished. Between 1498 and 1517, the Rinpungpa enjoyed unlimited rule of Ü and Tsang. During this time they did not allow Gelug monks of Sera and Drepung to take part in the Great Prayer Festivals (*smon lam chen mo*), which were instead conducted by Kagyü and Sakya monks.[28]

From 1498 until his death in 1512, General Dönyö Dorje held quite a powerful position. Dönyö Dorje commanded the construction of the Fourth Shamarpa's Yangpachen Monastery (situated north of Lhasa) in 1503/5.[29] This, along with the newly founded Tubchen Monastery (1498) east of Lhasa may have reinforced the clashes between the Gelugpa and the Karma Kagyüpa.[30] Given this context, it is likely that strategic, rather than religious, motivations were at heart of the issue, since it would have been futile for the Rinpungpa to gain supremacy over the Pagmo Drupa in Central Tibet without first controlling the Gelug monasteries of Sera and Drepung.[31]

During the Rinpungpa control (1498–1517) the Pagmo Drupa, under Ngagwang Tashi Dragpa (enthroned in 1499 by the Rinpungpa), continued to exist as mere figureheads. It was only in 1518, after the Rinpungpa lords lost direct rule of Ü, that the ban of the Gelug monks from the Great Prayer Festivals was removed at the petition of Gendün Gyatso (1475–1542), the person later referred to as the Second Dalai Lama. He was able to do so in conjunction with the re-emerging power of the Pagmo Drupa ruler, who on that occasion (in 1518) donated to him an estate close to Drepung called "Ganden

27. Ibid. has used *Kaṃ tsang* for the respective paragraph.

28. In his work on the Second Dalai Lama, Mullin (1994: 94–98) accuses the Fourth Zhwa dmar pa of banning the prayer festivals; according to this author, he was attempting to strengthen his political position. However, he admits (ibid., 98): "I have not looked into the actual history of the conflict over this festival in detail."

29. For the founding of the Yangs pa chen Monastery and the Fourth Zhwa dmar pa, see Wylie 2003: 485. Richardson 1980: 339 has the founding date of Yangs pa can as 1489.

30. This was the opinion of the Eighth Karma pa's biographer and attendant Sangs rgyas dpal grub. Sangs rgyas dpal grub, fol. 37b (p. 223), explains that the dGe lugs pa and the Karma bKa' brgyud pa were not in accord. The main reasons were the founding of the monasteries of Yangs pa can and Thub chen.

31. Kapstein 2006: 130.

Palace" (dGa' ldan pho brang).[32] While the successor of the Second Dalai Lama, the Third Dalai Lama Sönam Gyatso (1543–88), sought to intensify relations with the Mongols, the Seventh and Eighth Karmapas continued to maintain links from afar with the Chinese Ming court, a practice begun by the Fourth Karmapa, Rölpai Dorje.[33]

As far as religious practice was concerned, the fifteen and sixteenth centuries were characterized by scholastic systematization and a progressive solidification of teaching lineages and scholastic and monastic establishments into religious sects.[34] A model of succession for powerful hierarchs of these sects was the reincarnate lama. The Karma Kagyü tradition credits its founder, the First Karmapa Düsum Khyenpa (1110–93), with being the first reincarnate lama of Tibet.[35] And although there have been antecedents in the early period

32. Kapstein 2006: 131. It became the seat of him and his successors, and after 1642, under the Fifth Dalai Lama, the name of the estate became a label for the Central Tibetan government in general.

33. For the Fourth Karma pa's relation to the Mongols, see Sperling 2004; for the Fifth Karma pa bDe bzhin gshegs pa's relation to Ming China, see Sperling (1980) and Schuh (1976). The Second and the Third Karma pas also had occasional ties with the Mongol court during its overlordship (*Kaṃ tshang*, pp. 386; Richardson 1980: 341–44, Kapstein 2006: 131ff.). The dGe lugs pa ties with the Mongols later ripened when the Fifth Dalai Lama called for help and thereby consolidated his power. But during the late sixteenth and early seventeenth centuries, the rivalry between dBus and gTsang continued, deepening the rivalry of the dGe lugs and bKa' brgyud schools. During this period the Karma bKa' brgyud tradition still enjoyed influence, a situation that continued until the Tenth Karma pa, Chos dbyings rdo rje (1605–74) (Smith 2001: 42).

34. Smith 2001: 241. For scholastic traditions, the fourteenth-century systematization was the work of successive masters of the gSang phu and Sa skya (for gSang phu, see Van der Kuijp 1987). Scholars such as Klong chen Rab 'byams pa (1308–63) (see Kapstein 2000: 97–105), Dol po pa Shes rab rgyal mtshan (1292–1361), and the Third Karma pa, Rang byung rdo rje (1284–1339), were influenced by these traditions in developing their peculiar interpretations (for the Third Karma pa, see Schaeffer 1995: 6–25 and 72–110). The Sixth Karma pa, mThong ba don ldan (1416–53), received most of his scholastic teaching from the famed Sa skya pa master Rong ston Shes bya kun rig (1367–1449), who, along with the gSang phu traditions, constituted a major source of the Karma bKa' brgyud sūtra exegesis (Brunnhölzl 2004: 19; for Śākya mchog ldan's education with Rong ston, see Caumanns 2006: 65–68). There were also masters more skeptical of scholastic ideas, such as the Second Karma pa, Karma Pakṣi (1206–83), or the 'Bri gung 'Jig rten mgon po (this is the thesis of Kapstein 2000: 101–6).

35. The First Karma pa founded the monastery of Karma dgon in Eastern Tibet in 1147, and in 1193 founded mTshur phu, the main monastic seat of the Karma bKa' brgyud in Central Tibet (Richardson 1980: 337; Wylie 1978: 38). While Richardson (ibid.) assumes that the name "Karma pa" stems from the founding of the Karma monastery, tradition asserts that it is a slightly Tibetanized Sanskrit *karma* ("action") combined with the Tibetan nominalizer *pa*,

of Tibetan history, Wylie has argued that the system in fact emerged with the Third Karmapa at the time of Mongol supremacy in order to replace the powerful Khön family of the dominant Sakyapa.[36] In either case, in the fifteenth and sixteenth centuries the system of reincarnation had become formalized, freeing monastic orders from the institution of family inheritance. The system was an innovation with advantages and problems, the latter clearly visible in the case of the Eighth Karmapa's selection. Families and monasteries were keen on having one of "their" members obtain the title of a great reincarnate, a denomination cherished for its socio-political advantages.[37] On the

---

making: "the person [doing] the [Buddha] activity" (Karma 'phrin las pa, *Dris lan*, p. 162: *rgya skad karma zhes pa bod skad du las shes bya bar bsgyur dgos pas / sangs rgyas thams cad kyi phrin las pa yin pa'i don gyis na karma pa zhes grags pa'o*). For an elaborate presentation of the history of the bKa' brgyud tradition and the Karma pas, the most significant Tibetan sources are *mKhas pa'i dga' ston*, *Kaṃ tshang*, and, as far as the Karma pas are concerned, Nges don bstan rgyas' *Karma pa sku 'phreng gyi rnam thar*. In English, see Roerich 1996: 473ff., Smith 2001: 39–87, Thinley 1980, and Thaye 1990.

36. Wylie 1978: 581–82. He argues that it had the advantage of being free from patrimonial connections and a "charisma of office." Samuel 1993: 495–97 explains the concept of reincarnation emerging with the bKa' brgyud pa during the Mongol period as a political device that would bring political and economical advantages to monasteries (see also Goldstein 1973: 446–48). Van der Kuijp 2005: 29f. argues that the system emerged even at an earlier stage, the early kings of Tibet being considered emanations of bodhisattvas. In the spiritual biography of the First Karma pa, the lines "I will care for protecting the doctrine" were considered a prophecy for his future rebirth (*mKhas pa'i dga' ston*, p. 870: *ngas kyang chos skyong ba la bcol ba yin zhes sprul pa'i sku dngos su byon par don gyis lung bstan te*). The Karma bKa' brgyud assertion that Karma pa and Zhwa dmar pa are inseparable (and called "Black Hat Karmapa" and "Red Hat Karmapa") is sometimes referred to as a prophecy of the Second Karma pa Karma Pakṣi (1204–83). Karma 'phrin las pa states: "It was obvious that these two, [Zhwa dmar II] rJe mKha' spyod dbang po (1350–1405) and [Karma pa V] bDe bzhin gshegs pa (1384–1415), were the ones [who were mentioned in the prophecy]. And it is said that body, speech, and mind of the two are not different from body, speech, and mind of [the Second Karma pa] Karma Pakṣi. Therefore, it is acknowledged that the two—Red Hat and Black Hat—are of one mind stream (*thugs rgyud*). Even the (manner of speaking) of the Red Hat and Black Hat Karmapa is based on this circumstance" (Karma 'phrin las pa, *Dris lan*, fol. 43b/p. 172: *rje mkha' spyod dbang po dang rje bde bzhin gshegs pa gnyis yin par grags / de gnyis kyi sku gsung thugs dang / karma pakṣi'i sku gsung thugs tha mi dad par gsungs pas / zhwa dmar nag gnyis thugs rgyud gcig par grags pa yin / karma pa zhwa dmar nag / ces zer ba'ang don 'di la brten pa yin no*). For the First Zhwa dmar pa's life see also Roerich 1996: 523–32.

37. Kapstein 2006: 105, 109. The dispute about the succession of the Eighth Karma pa's contemporary, 'Brug chen Pad ma dkar po (1527–92), for example, led to two different lines. dPag bsam dbang po (1593–1641) from the house of 'Phyongs rgyas was supported by the gTsang pa lord. The candidate from the house of Rwa lung, Zhabs drung Nga dbang rnam rgyal (1594–1651), fled to Bhutan in 1616 and succeeded in establishing a monastic state (Aris

other hand, the incarnation system provided security for the growth of scholasticism and was favored by the secular rulers.[38]

What, almost inevitably, followed was a more or less active involvement of important religious hierarchs in political affairs, including the seeking of funding from wealthy and powerful patrons, who in turn aimed for dominance over a particular area of Tibet. The Gelugpa quickly adopted the incarnation model and their two reincarnate lamas, the Dalai Lama (or his regents) and Paṇchen Lama, dominated Tibetan politics from the seventeenth century onward.[39]

Spiritual Memoirs and Biographies of the Eighth Karmapa

The primary sources for an investigation of the Eighth Karmapa's life belong to the *rnam thar* and *rang rnam* genres. In general, these provide the greatest detail of events in the life of a Tibetan saint, being a type of hagiography, a biography of a saint or an idealized biography, as studied in other religious contexts.[40] The label *rnam thar* signifies that they were intended to be read

1979: 205–28; Smith [2001]: 84). Ensuing conflicts were sometimes resolved by resorting to the concept of manifold emanations. For the Zhabs drung's successors, see Aris 1979: 258f.

38. According to Samuel 1993: 497, it was a method for synthesizing what he calls the monk and shaman ideals. Over the course of history, the various bKa' brgyud schools have oscillated between scholastic institutionalization and mystic reform. In the bKa' brgyud lineages of the fifteenth and sixteenth centuries, this particularly refers to the movement of the "crazy yogins" (*smyon pa*), which is briefly described by Smith 2001: 59–61 and Stein 1993: 170–72. See Ehrhard (forthcoming), for the "madman of dBus," Kun dga' bzang po, and his relation to rulers. See also Kögler 2004: 25–55, who suggests that this movement emerged due to social factors such as the absence of central political authority and the important role of the clergy.

39. Samuel 1993: chapter 26. As is well known, the Dalai Lamas also obtained their Mongolian title in retrospect. The gap in the succession of the Third Dalai Lama (1543–88) was used by the Mongol court to recognize the Fourth Dalai Lama as Altan Khan's great-grandson (Elverskrog 2007: 8). Yumiko 2003 has argued that the political power of the Fifth Dalai Lama increased through a series of actions taken (especially empowerments of Avalokiteśvara) between 1642 and 1653, presenting himself as a manifestation of the bodhisattva Avalokiteśvara (ibid., 550). Apart from the Fifth, the Seventh, and the Thirteenth Dalai Lamas, they mostly did not exercise much real authority and died early (Petech 2003).

40. Other genres that can assist the acquiring of information regarding the life of a Tibetan master are abbatial chronicles (*gdan rabs*), records of teachings received (*gsan yig, thob yig*; see Sobisch 2003), and tables of contents (*dkar chag*). As with other aspects of Tibetan Studies, the *rnam thar* genre as such has not been extensively examined. Vostrikov 1994 has been a pioneer in the field, surveying historical literature, as has been Ruegg 1966 with his study of

as an account of a saint's life.[41] Spiritual biographies vary immensely in both type and scope, ranging from informative life accounts, rich in historical and ethnographic detail, to tantric instructions, eulogies, and even works containing empowerment rituals. However, their predominant characteristic is that they form a narrative genre in which certain topoi of the life of a Buddhist saint are included, with features that are easily discernible to readers and that form the key constituents of the plot.

The term *rnam thar* translates the Sanskrit *vimokṣa*, meaning "liberation, the experience of a meditating saint."[42] A Tibetan definition of the term *rnam thar* claims: "(1) an historical work of the deeds of a holy (*dam pa*) person or a treatise which tells his [religious] achievement (*rtogs pa brjod pa*); (2) liberation."[43] To emphasize the fact that these works portray the liberation or

---

Bu ston's *rnam thar*. In his study of Tibetan historiographical literature, van der Kuijp 1996: 46–47 examined the "history of religion" *chos 'byung* genre to some extent. Analysis of Indian spiritual biographies is found in Robinson 1996 and of Tibetan spiritual memoirs (*rang rnam*) and Tibetan life-writing in general in Gyatso 1998: 101–23. Remarks can also be located in the further studies mentioned below. Southeastern Buddhist hagiography has been studied by, for example, Kieschnik 1997 and Tambiah 1984. Compared to Buddhist hagiography, Christian hagiography has been studied extensively; see Dubois and Lemaitre 1993 for research about Christian hagiography; and Head 2000 for an anthology of medieval Christian hagiography. I would like to thank Burkhard Scherer for helpful remarks and suggestions for this publication.

41. One may thus consider the *rnam thar* sources "tradition" as opposed to "remains," "remains" being used for artifacts not intended as sources for the subject investigated. However, the classification seems to be controversial (Faber and Geiss 1992: 82ff.). Marwick 2001: 172–79 discusses what he terms "witting and unwitting testimony." The extent to which, in Tibetan culture, the *rnam thar* genres provide what one may term "historical information" depends on individual texts and the chosen research methodology.

42. Smith 2001: 273n2. A noun form of *vi-mokṣ, A.* "to set free, let loose, liberate," related to *vi-muc*, "to unloose, to unharness" (Monier-Williams 1996). Tibetans mechanically rendered the prefix *vi* with the prefix *rnam pa* and *mokṣa* with *thar pa/ba*, hence: *rnam par thar ba*, transformed into *rnam par thar pa* and then abbreviated to *rnam thar*. Roberts 2007: 3–5 has indicated that the term *rnam thar* in a Tibetan title probably first occurred within the early bKa' gdams tradition and was also used by sGam po pa. Early bKa' gdams pa scholars likely adapted the term as found in a verse of the translated *Bodhicaryāvatāra*. Roberts points out that in *Bodhicaryāvatāra* V.103 the term is used to indicate a part of the *Gaṇḍavyūha-Sūtra*, see also P. A. Roberts' article in the present volume. Some actual *rnam thar* texts were probably patterned after Indian examples of spiritual biography, for instance *avadāna* and *jātaka*.

43. Zhang Yisun: *rnam thar- 1. skyes bu dam pa'i mdzad spyod lo rgyus kyi gzhung ngam / rtogs pa brjod pa'i bstan bcos / 2. rnam grol.* A related genre, *rtogs brjod* (Skt. *avadāna*), literally means "presentation of accomplishment."

accomplishment of a person, one could render the term as "liberation story." To give more nuance to their historical content, the term "spiritual biography" is also appropriate, and is the translation chosen for this paper. The related *rang rnam* genre (literally "one's own liberation [story]") may be translated as "spiritual memoir." The use of "biography" or "autobiography" without any prior explanation overlooks the primary function of the genre.[44]

Previous scholars have interpreted and used texts of this genre in various ways.[45] It is certainly helpful to be aware of the genre's functions in its culture, when employing it for research. Willis has argued that a major function is not only to inspire the reader but also to impart exoteric and esoteric instruction. She has interpreted the sometimes used outer, inner, and secret (*phyi*, *nang*, and *gsang*) levels of *rnam thar* as: (1) the "historical," (2) the "inspirational," and (3) the "instructional" dimensions.[46] Those sources used in this paper mainly belong to the outer level; the spiritual memoirs can also be regarded as inner. Smith had already succinctly summarized the genre's main characteristics in 1969:

> The rnam thar genre [is] a type of literature that the non-Tibetan will equate with biography or hagiography. Yet while there is often much in a rnam thar that is of biographical nature, a rnam thar has for the Buddhist a considerably greater significance. (...) The rnam

44. Although the subject of the work is the life of a Buddhist master and contains some historical information, the function of the title and its primary content is mostly to tell the story of a person's spiritual development and not to give historical detail about his career or motives. Kongtrul in his autobiography stresses the function of engendering faith (Kongtrul 2003: 3); see also the spiritual biography of the Eighth Karma pa by Sangs rgyas dpal grub, fol. 3b (p. 155) and below. That rather implies "liberation," not "biography." Dargyay 1994: 99 uses "features of liberation." For a study of English biographies, see for example Pritchard 2005.

45. Gyatso 1998: 107–9 tends to see *rang rnam* as related to the Western genre of autobiography in that postmodern theories of the self can be usefully applied to its study. Schuh and Schwieger 1985: xxix–xxx have focused on the writers' hidden motives: for example favoritism toward their own tradition and particularly their own monastery. Aris 1988 has also drawn conclusions as to the possible motivations of the protagonists Padma gling pa and the Sixth Dalai Lama. Robinson 1996: 64, regarding the *rnam thar* of great Indian adepts, has argued they should be read as hagiography, not as biography. Unless vast comparative studies of many instances of this genre are achieved, conclusions as to its nature must remain preliminary.

46. Willis 1995: 5. This interpretation is useful, though it may have to be adapted to various types of *rnam thar*. Templeman 2003: 141 argues that understanding the genre as inspirational has become commonplace and favors viewing the genre as an actual instruction.

> thar is ultimately a practical instruction, a guide to the experience, insights, and vision of one developed being.[47]

Spiritual biographies have thus more functions than the narrating of the life of a saint: they act as role model and instruction for Buddhist practitioners.[48] But who are the role models a Tibetan medieval saint is meant to emulate? Tiso elaborates on three types of Buddhist roles intended to inspire: (1) the arhat in the Theravāda tradition, (2) the bodhisattva in the Mahāyāna, and (3) the *mahāsiddha* in the Vajrayāna. In Tibet, which produced an exceptional number of these texts, the ideal projected on some early Kagyüpa masters such as Marpa was the third: the tantric saint, the "great accomplished one" or mahāsiddha.[49] Following the introduction of incarnation as a model of spiritual succession and the monasticization of lay tantric lineages, the dimension of the reincarnate monk is often added to narratives of incarnate lamas like the Karmapa, depicting the "abstract role of an incarnate lamaist priest."[50] The Karmapas are supposed to mirror all three levels, as mentioned above, of the Buddha's teaching.[51] The spiritual biographies and memoirs consequently portray the Eighth Karmapa after the ideal of a "learned and accomplished one" (*mkhas sgrub*), an accomplished scholar and realized meditator, an ideal characteristic for important religious hierarchs in late medieval Tibet.[52]

47. Smith 2001: 13–14. It is a reprint of a foreword from 1969.

48. Karma Thinley Rinpoche, a contemporary master of the bKa' brgyud and Sa skya traditions, explains his motives for composing such a work: "I wish to demonstrate the marvellous example set forth by former masters such as the First Karma Thinleypa, in their spiritual training and work for sentient beings" (Thinley 1997: 1).

49. According to the bKa' brgyud tradition's "golden rosary" narratives (*gser phreng*), spiritual biographies reflect the enlightened principle of the tantric Buddha Vajradhara (Tiso 1989: 113ff.). See Roberts 2007, for a study of the evolution of the spiritual biography of Ras chung pa. For sources on the life of Mar pa, see Martin 1984; for a detailed—albeit controversial—discussion of Mar pa's life vis-à-vis the roles projected upon him by the tradition, see Davidson 2004: 141–48.

50. Schuh and Schwieger 1985: xxix.

51. Jampa Thaye in his preface to *History of the Sixteen Karmapas of Tibet* (Thinley 1980: 21–38). The function of visions and miracles is also described. The three levels of Buddhist teaching are reflected in the three vow theories which developed to a considerable level in Tibet (see Sobisch 2002).

52. Kapstein 2006: 231; Kapstein 2000: 19.

When using spiritual biographies as sources, it is thus important to analyze their content with regard to narrative function. Though it is fruitful to use the "filter method," to "filter" historical events or conclude historical realities from the text, whether information can be taken at face value depends on each source and the function of particular events within the story.[53] Too many "breaks" in the narrative may be a particular indicator that there are events to be read "in between the lines." Otherwise, the narratives may at times tell us more about the ideas and ideals prevalent at the author's time than the historical facts about the protagonist.[54] Although this method is not formally applied in this paper, an avenue of further research may be to investigate systematically the function of events within the narrative, rather than drawing conclusions about the author's or protagonist's character. If carefully applied, tools from narratology can add to a better comprehension.[55]

In the following the main sources from this genre are examined with attention paid to the earliest textual witnesses. Most stem from volume 1 of the *Collected Works of the Eighth Karmapa* and have not been published before the year 2000.[56] As well as preparing the way for the ensuing section, this will facilitate work for future researchers.

53. A term used by Mills in an address to the Tibetologists present at the International Association for Tibetan Studies Conference, Bonn, August 2006.

54. Roberts 2007 has undertaken an extensive comparative study of various versions of Ras chung pa's spiritual biography. It has been shown that elements of Ras chung pa's and Mi la ras pa's spiritual biographies emerge from inventive storytelling, but also that *rnam thar* usually develop from earlier realism to later idealization. One example is the story of the yak horn (ibid., 183–210).

55. Ohnuma 1998: 324, 335–46 has examined what she calls "gift of body stories" (*dehadāna*) and the literalization of metaphors through analysis of narratives. In his *Moderne Literaturtheorie und Antike Texte*, Schmitz 2002: 55–75 describes how narratology was applied to classical texts. For further applications of narratology see also Scherer 2006: 2–7; for narratology in general, see Bal 1997.

56. A supplement at least partly authored by Karma bde legs outlines the sources vaguely. Using the editorial supplement (Karma bde legs, *dPe sgrigs gsal bshad*, p. 4) and a survey of the individual colophons, one can determine as main origins and new contributions two versions of manuscripts stored in 'Bras spungs (i), manuscripts from the Potala (ii), and manuscripts from the Nationalities Palace in Bejing (iii). For a brief evaluation, see Rheingans 2008: 65–71.

(a) Spiritual Memoirs by the Eighth Karmapa

i. *Karma pa mi bskyod rdo rje'i rnam thar legs spyad mar grags pa rje nyid kyis mdzad pa* (4 fols.) is a short text composed in verse.[57] In the beginning, the Karmapa states he has written on his experiences at some students' request, who are specifically named in the interlinear commentary (*mchan*) as Drigung Rinpoche and Paṇchen Dorgyalba.[58] The work is an instruction with philosophical and motivational content; dates and information regarding events in his life are completely absent. A text designed as a commentary (*'grel pa*) to this work is one of the significant spiritual biographies by his early students (examined below).

ii. *Karma pa mi bskyod rdo rje'i rnam thar la bslab pa'i khrid*[59] (18 fols.) is a spiritual memoir designed as an instruction to the Eighth Karmapa's disciples. Though few dates are mentioned, the influence of his teachers is illustrated well. Composed in 1536 (his thirtieth year), the Karmapa revised it later, in 1548 (his forty-second year). The work is an outline of the Karmapa's practices, experiences, and reliance on his four great teachers (*rje btsun chen po bzhi*).[60]

iii. *Pha mi bskyod rdo rje'i rnam thar rje nyid kyis rnam thos kyi ri bor mdzad pa*[61] (7 fols.) is a short account in verse composed in his twenty-eighth year (1534) in Namtökyi Riwo. It details the main phases of the Karmapa's life from his perspective,

57. *Collected Works of the Eighth Karmapa*, vol. 1, pp. 107–14. Though full references are to be found in the bibliography, they are given here for easier access.

58. Mi bskyod rdo rje, *Karma pa mi bskyod rdo rje'i rnam thar legs spyad mar grags pa*, fol. 1a (p. 108). In 1536 the Karma pa visited 'Bri gung monastery, exchanged questions with Paṇ chen rDor rgyal ba, met the fifteenth abbot of 'Bri gung, sKyu ra Rin po che Rin chen rnam rgyal (1527–70) (both are characterized as students of Śākya mchog ldan in *mKhas pa'i dga' ston*, p. 1239), and the local lord Bya bKra shis dar rgyas (*Kaṃ tshang*, pp. 338–39; see also Rheingans 2008: 137–39).

59. *Collected Works of the Eighth Karmapa*, vol. 1, pp .115–49.

60. Mi bskyod rdo rje, *Karma pa mi bskyod rdo rje'i rnam thar la bslab pa'i khrid*, fol. 3a (p. 119).

61. *Collected Works of the Eighth Karmapa*, vol. 1, pp. 331–43.

occasionally providing dates. It is crucial in that it exposes some of the motivations and feelings of the Karmapa himself.

iv. *rJe mi bskyod rdo rje'i 'phral gyi rnam thar tshigs su bcad pa nyer bdun pa rje nyid kyis mdzad pa*[62] (3 fols.) comprises twenty-seven verses of motivational teachings, and could be considered a "song of experience" (*mnyam mgur*). It was composed in the Karmapa's thirty-third year (1539) at Tsurpu.

v. *Mi bskyod rdo rje'i spyad pa'i rabs*[63] (19 fols.) begins with an autobiographical summary of the Karmapa's life up to his fortieth year (1546). Therein he briefly describes how he attended his teachers and lists his compositions. This list is a valuable resource (next to the Fifth Shamarpa's *dKar chag*) for determining the content and authenticity of the Eighth Karmapa's writings.

vi. *gDul bya phyi ma la gdams pa'i rnam par thar pa*[64] (16 fols.) is a part of the Karmapa's spiritual biography taught to his "later students" (*gdul bya phyi ma*). It contains autobiographical elements and mainly describes his spiritual development. The word "instruction" (*gdams pa*) in the title indicates the work was designed as such; consequently it found entry in the "advice" (*bslab bya*) section of the *Collected Works of the Eighth Karmapa*.

vii. *Nyid bstod kyi rang 'grel*[65] (5 fols.) is a peculiar work: a commentary by the Eighth Karmapa on a "self-praise" (*nyid bstod*) also attributed to the Eighth Karmapa.[66] It focuses on Buddhist tantra and philosophy.

62. *Collected Works of the Eighth Karmapa*, vol. 1, pp. 344–49.

63. This is an abbreviation. The full title reads: *Byang phyogs 'di na karma pa / / rim par byon las bdun pa rang byung ni / / kun mkhyen chos rje'i slob mar gyur 'ga' yi / / bka' 'bangs mi bskyod rdo rje'i spyad pa'i rabs [The Succession of Deeds of Mi bskyod rdo rje: He Obeys the Command of Some Students of the Omniscient Master, the Self-Arisen Seventh among the Karmapas, Who Have Appeared One after the Other* (rim par) *in this Northern Land]*, *Collected Works of the Eighth Karmapa*, vol. 1, pp. 350–87.

64. *Collected Works of the Eighth Karmapa*, vol. 3, pp. 519–49.

65. *Collected Works of the Eighth Karmapa*, vol. 1, pp. 430–38.

66. This is clearly stated in the beginning of the text. The more elaborate title of the "self-

viii. *rGyal ba karma pa mi bskyod rdo rje'i rnam thar bdag tshul bcu gnyis*[67] (10 fols.) is a spiritual memoir written in 1527 in Kongpo. The Karmapa's story is therein fashioned after the ideal of the twelve deeds of the Buddha. The Karmapa's sojourn in the pure land of Maitreya is depicted, a mystic placc where he is supposed to have dwelt before his birth. It contains descriptions of various Buddhist practices undertaken by the Karmapa, and laments the degenerate nature of disciples and teachers in Central Asia during this period.

ix. *Chos kyi rje 'jigs rten dbang po dpal karma pa brgyad pa'i zhabs kyi mtshan rab tu brjod pa rje nyid kyis mdzad pa*[68] (3 fols.) explains the meaning of the Eighth Karmapa's full name. The mentioning of the names is also a benefit of this text: "Glorious Fame Accomplishing the Teaching, Victorious in All Directions at All Times in Manifold [Ways], Unmovable Good One, [and] Melodious Sound of Adamantine (*vajra*) Joy."[69] The text is an example of the creative and poetic methods by which the author relates each element of the names to various doctrinal concepts and qualities of Buddhism. The text has a commentary by Pawo Tsuglag Trengwa (1504–66) which is described below.

(b) Spiritual Biographies by Direct Students of the Eighth Karmapa

The first three texts are the earliest, most extensive, and historically significant primary sources for the study of the Karmapa's life. Additionally, the

---

praise" is *Tshigs su bcad pa bzla med mar 'bod pa* (ibid., fol 1b: *bdag nyid la gdag nyid kyis bstod pa byas pa'i tshigs su bcad pa bzla med mar 'bod pa de nyid kyi tshig don dgrol bar bya /*).

67. *Collected Works of the Eighth Karmapa*, vol. 1, pp. 488–507.

68. *Collected Works of the Eighth Karmapa*, vol. 1, pp. 388–92.

69. Mi bskyod rdo rje, *Chos kyi rje 'jig rten dbang po dpal karma pa brgyad pa'i zhabs kyi mtshan rab tu brjod pa*, fol. 1b (p. 389): *dpal ldan chos grub grags pa phyogs thams cad la dus kun tu sna tshogs par rnam par rgyal ba mi bskyod bzang po rdo rje dga' ba'i dbyang*. In the English translation of the main text above, the beginning of a discernible sub-name or epithet is capitalized for easier comprehension, though the sub-names can be determined in various ways (ibid., fol. 2b/p. 391).

spiritual biography composed by Sangye Paldrub (ii) contains a hint about two important sources unfortunately still missing. Research has to be based on these three accounts, combined with the spiritual memoirs presented earlier. The Eighth Karmapa's two main students and authors of spiritual biographies were also crucial to the first compilation of the Eighth Karmapa's writings: Shamarpa Könchog Yenlag (1525–83) had authored a title list (*dkar chag*), and Pawo Tsuglag Trengwa had served as scribe for some of the Karmapa's works.[70]

i. *rGyal ba kun gyi dbang po dpal ldan karma pa mi bskyod rdo rje'i zhabs kyi dgung lo bdun phan gyi rnam par thar pa nor bu'i phreng ba*, (37 fols., abbreviated A khu A khra in the notes) by Akhu Atra Gelong Jangchub Sangpo, contains the most detailed account of the Karmapa's early years. Its author was an attendant of the Eighth Karmapa who met the then seven-month-old Karmapa in 1507, attending him until shortly before completion of his eighth year (1514).[71] He indicates in

70. The Fifth Zhwa dmar pa had received the blessing by the Eighth Karma pa to complete a table of contents in rTsa ri (*Kaṃ tshang*, p. 391) and began compiling it in 1547. *dKar chag*, fol. 14b (p. 27), states that the Zhwa dmar pa started when the Eighth Karma pa was forty years old and completed it one year after his death, i.e., 1555 (in the ninth month of the wood-hare year) in Yangs pa can. dPa' bo gTsug lag phreng ba was the second main student of the Karma pa (see *Kaṃ tshang*, pp. 357–65, and his spiritual memoir *Rang gi rtogs pa brjod pa 'khrul pa'i bzhin ras 'char ba'i me long zhes bya ba bzhugs so* in *mKhas pa'i dga' ston*, pp. 1530–74). He met the Karma pa for the first time in 1531 (*Kaṃ tshang*, p. 337) and later acted as note-taker and scribe for Karma pa VIII, *Slob dpon dbyangs can bzang pos nye bar stsal ba'i dril bu rim pa lnga pa'i khrid*, fol. 103a (p. 981) and *dPal rdzogs pa'i sangs rgyas karma pa mi bskyod rdo rje*, fol. 128a (p. 1139) (see also: NGMPP, Reel no. E 2944/2, 101 fols., manuscript, dBu med; the colophons are identical). The latter, a commentary to the first section (*tshoms dang po*) of the 'Bri gung pa "same intention" doctrine (*dgongs gcig*), was composed from notes (*zin bris*) dPa' bo Rin po che had made of the Karma pa's teaching on the fifteen points (*gnad rim bco lnga*) of the *dgongs gcig* in the presence of the Fifth Zhwa dmar pa, dKon mchog yan lag, when he taught in 'Bri gung in 1536 (*Kaṃ tshang*, p. 339). The Karma pa's *dGongs gcig gi gsung bzhi bcu'i 'grel pa* was composed in the same year (1536) (see also Rheingans 2008: 136–39). For a list of the Eighth Karma pa's students, see also *Kaṃ tshang*, p. 356; *mKhas pa'i dga' ston*, pp. 1332–33.

71. A khu A kra, fol. 36b (p. 104): *zhes pa 'di ni dge slong byang chub gzang po bya ba ming gzhan a khu a khrar grags pa / yang dag pa'i rdzogs pa'i sangs rgyas karma pa chos grags rgya mtsho las bka' drin cung zad mnos pa'i rten 'brel gyis / sprul pa'i sku 'di yang dgung zla bdun bzhes nas mjal / dgung lo bgryad du ma longs kyi bar zhabs pad bsten nas ngo mtshar gyi mdzad pa kha shas mthong ba kun zin bris byas par 'dug /*. The title does not talk of the seventh month but the seventh year (*dgung lo bdun pa*) of the Karma pa (being 1513/14). However, this seems to be wrong.

the colophon that he was a student of the Seventh Karmapa, Chödrag Gyatso. He was likely an administrator under the Seventh Karmapa, and also compiled a collection of meditation instructions of the *Ras chung snyan rgyud*.[72] The colophon further mentions that he noted several miraculous events that he witnessed and affirms the authenticity of the events depicted.

Since this spiritual biography was composed by an attendant of the Karmapa, one can assume its author was close to him. Furthermore, it is clear that the Karmapa himself was familiar with, or at least aware of, this source: in the title list of the spiritual memoir the Eighth Karmapa composed in his fortieth year (1546), he writes: "The spiritual biography up to [my] seventh year, arranged by the monk (*dge slong*) Byang chub bzang po."[73]

This work became the primary source on the Karmapa's early years for later biographers. Pawo Rinpoche, too young to witness the events, remarks that he had summarized Akhu Atra's work for depicting the Karmapa's early years in his own work (see below). Sangye Paldrub, author of the next source, also mentions that he used Akhu Atra's account. At times they added different perspectives, interpretations, and some additional information.[74]

ii. *rGyal ba spyan ras gzigs dbang brgyad pa'i legs spyad ma'i don 'grel gsal ba'i sgron me*[75] (90 fols., abbreviated Sangs rgyas dpal grub), by Sangye Paldrub, is an extensive spiritual biography

72. *mKhas pa'i dga' ston*, p. 1225, calls him *dpon chen* of the Seventh Karma pa, literally meaning "great lord" but here probably indicating "great administrator." The work he compiled is A khu A kra Byang chub bzang po, *bDe mchog mkha' 'gro snyan rgyud*.

73. *Mi bskyod rdo rje'i spyad pa'i rabs*, fol. 5a (p. 358): *dge slong byang chub bzang pos dgung lo bdun yan gyi rnam thar bsgrigs pa /*.

74. *mKhas pa'i dga' ston*, p. 1225: *de ltar gzhon nu rol rtsed kyi rnam thar cung zad tsam dge slong byang chub gzang po zhes bya ba drung gong ma'i dpon chen a khu a khra zhes grags pa des bsrgigs pa'i rnam thar las bsdus pa yin la 'di phyin gyi mdzad pa sa bon tsam nyid la nyid kyis bstod pa dang sbyar te brjod par bya'o /*.

75. *Collected Works of the Eighth Karmapa*, vol. 1, pp. 150–329.

by a student of the Eighth Karmapa, containing lengthy doctrinal discussions. The text is designed as a "commentary" on the Karmapa's spiritual memoir (i), listed above.[76] According to the colophon, the author attended the Karmapa from his thirty-third year on (1539).[77] Thus, the text was composed some time after that year. Sangye Paldrub was appointed by the Eighth Karmapa as a lama somewhere in Tsang and is also found requesting a brief Mahāmudrā commentary.[78]

The outline shows that this spiritual biography is designed as a pedagogical tool. In the statement of purpose, Sangye Paldrub explains that the work seeks to inspire faith in students and in those who "have the eye of wisdom," so that when seeing or hearing this spiritual biography they would want to learn and emulate it.[79] To that end, events in the Karmapa's life are subsumed under topics such as the deeds of the bodhisattva (e.g., the six *pāramitās*), and are consequently not ordered chronologically. Often the narrator inserts reflective remarks about the bad times and boastful teachers around "these days" (*deng sang*).[80] However, on the closing pages where the author details his sources, some interesting information is offered. Again, mention is found of Akhu Atra's account of the Eighth Karmapa's early years, but the author then mentions two more texts, presently unavailable: a spiritual biography composed by Drubpai Wangchug Gampo Khenpo Shākya Gelong Sangpo, and one authored by Lama Pönyig.[81]

76. Mi bskyod rdo rje, *Karma pa mi bskyod rdo rje'i rnam thar legs spyad mar grags pa rje nyid kyis mdzad pa*. This is also corroborated by Sangs rgyas dpal grub, fol. 90b (p. 329): *karma pa brgyad pa legs spyad ma'i grel pa.*

77. This date is confirmed by *Kaṃ tshang*, p. 341.

78. *Kaṃ tshang*, p. 346. He requested the notes (*zin bris*) of the Eighth Karma pa's *rGya gar gyi phyag chen sngon byung dwags brgyud kyi sgros kyis rgyan pa* (ibid., fol. 7a/p. 1071).

79. Sangs rgyas dpal grub, fol. 3b (p. 155).

80. For example Sangs rgyas dpal grub, fol. 22a (p. 192).

81. Sangs rgyas dpal grub, fol. 83b (p. 315): *zhes a khu a khra pas bsgrigs pa'i rnam thar dang grub pa'i dbang phyug sgam po mkhan po śākya dge slong bzang pos mdzad pa'i rnam thar dang*

Some passages[82] are more extensive than in Pawo's *mKhas pa'i dga' ston*, though they use similar wording. The intertextuality might suggest that Sangye Paldrub's work is older, or alternatively that here we find remnants of the two missing sources that may have partly served as templates for other early texts. This quality makes this source very valuable. Yet the full extent of the relationship will remain unclear until the two missing accounts are located and the spiritual biographies can be analyzed together in greater detail.

iii. *mKhas pa'i dga' ston* (vol. 2, pp. 1206–1334) by Pawo Tsuglag Trengwa (1504–66) contains the longest account of Karmapa Mikyö Dorje. The passage on the Karmapa is contained in the blockprint volume *pa* of this "history of Buddhism" (*chos 'byung*), and it follows a narration strategy similar to that of a spiritual biography as is evident from its structure and content. Across various published editions there are no differences in content, with dissimilarities being limited merely to orthography.

The whole of the *mKhas pa'i dga' ston* was composed between 1545 and 1565. The spiritual biography of the Eighth Karmapa is found in chapter 3, section 8: the religious history of the Karma Kagyü school. In his colophon, Pawo Rinpoche explains that he was urged by Khedrub Paldingpa Kirtishvara (Skt. Kīrtīśvara) to compose such a spiritual biography and had promised to do so twelve years before. He then completed the spiritual biography of the Eighth Karmapa in a bird year (probably 1561) at the Ganden Mamo temple in Kong-

---

bla ma dpon yig gis mdzad pa'i rnam thar dang drung nyid gsungs pa'i rnam thar yin pa rnams nang nas khungs dag re re.

82. See, for example, the passage describing how the Eighth Karma pa studied with Karma 'phrin las pa in Sangs rgyas dpal grub, fol. 23b–24a (pp. 195–96) (*thog mar mngon rtogs rgyan rtsa 'grel la nyi ma bzhi lngar chos thun gsum mdzad pa la tshig don gnyis kar mkhyen pa la tshegs ma byung bas / chos thun drug bdun du spar dgos zhus pas*) as compared to *mKhas pa'i dga' ston*, p. 1237 (*rje phrin las zhabs las thog mar mngon rtogs rgyan gyi 'grel pa don gsal la nyin re mthun gsum gyis gsan par mdzad pa na thun mang du spar par zhus pas*). For a translation of the whole passage, see Rheingans 2008: 131–33.

po.[83] Tsuglag Trengwa was one of the Karmapa's two principal disciples, and as such his testimony can be regarded as trustworthy within the framework of the genre.

Looking at the intertextuality of this work, along with the other major spiritual biographies composed by the Eighth Karmapa's students, it seems that Pawo Rinpoche took these other accounts into consideration in creating his own work, though the other texts can, at times, be more extensive. Nevertheless, of single works treating the whole of the Karmapa's life, Pawo's account may be considered the most extensive to date. While sometimes following a chronological order of events, it is divided into different topics such as his youth, his receiving the various levels of vows of Buddhism, his ascetic practices, and his benefiting of others—a structure which again elevates the religious function of the text over the historical.

iv. *Chos kyi rje 'jigs rten dbang po dpal karma pa brgyad pa'i zhabs kyi mtshan rab tu brjod pa'i 'grel pa*[84] (19 fols.) is a commentary by Pawo Tsuglag Trengwa on the spiritual memoir about the different names of the Eighth Karmapa (ix).

v. *Mi bskyod rdo rje rnam thar tshigs bcad ma* (5 fols.) and

vi. *rGyal ba mi bskyod rdo rje'i rnam thar la bstod pa zol med mes pa 'dren byed* (26 fols.) are found in the *Selected Writings* (vol. II) of the Fifth Shamarpa, another prominent student of the Eighth Karmapa. These are two accounts, in verse, of the deeds of his teacher, Mikyö Dorje. They are not extensive yet constitute early sources on the Eighth Karmapa's life. However, they do not contain extensive new historical information.

(c) Spiritual Biographies by Later Tibetan Scholars

i. *Kaṃ tshang brgyud pa rnam thar* contains the most extensive spiritual biography among the numerous later compilations. It is part of the great history of the Kagyü tradition by Situ

83. *mKhas pa'i dga' ston*, p. 1333.

84. *Collected Works of the Eighth Karmapa*, vol. 1, pp. 393–430.

Paṇchen and Belo Tsewang Kunkhyab. The account of the Eighth Karmapa is twenty-five folios long[85] and mainly consists of a summary of Pawo Tsuglag Trengwa and other earlier works.[86] *Kaṃ tshang* was completed in 1715, 161 years after the Eighth Karmapa's death. Nevertheless, at times passages elucidate the cryptic parts of the older sources as events are ordered in a more intelligible and predominantly chronological way. Further, some passages suggest that Situ Paṇchen might have had access to the two now unavailable sources. The other, later compilations listed are often based on the *Kaṃ tshang* of Situ Paṇchen, which has apparently become the standard source for scholars in the Karma Kagyü lineage.[87]

ii. *Chos rje karma pa sku 'phreng rim byon gyi rnam thar mdor bsdus dpag bsam khri shing* by Karma Ngedön Tengye (nineteenth century) is a compilation of Karmapa biographies from the First to the Fifteenth, written in 1891. It provides a section on the Eighth Karmapa of over forty-one pages, consisting of a summary of Situ Paṇchen's *Kaṃ tshang*.

iii. The short account regarding the Eighth Karmapa in the *Biographical Dictionary of Tibet and Tibetan Buddhism* (vol. 7, pp. 163–84) compiled by Khetsun Sangpo in 1973, amounts to a review of *Kaṃ tshang* and, as such, adds nothing new. Brief accounts and summaries based on the aforementioned texts can be found in various modern bibliographies of Tibetan scholars. Though they are of no independent value, these later sources can help to determine the reception and transformation of the narrative.[88]

85. This refers to the edition in the collected works of Si tu Paṇ chen; in this paper I will use a reprint from 2004. The editions differ only in minuscule orthographical variations.

86. *mKhas pa'i dga' ston* is sometimes referred to in the text. Concerning the other sources, we can only speculate whether Si tu Paṇ chen had access to them or not. I assume that he had.

87. One main reason may be that this is because *Kaṃ tshang* poses less of a challenge to the reader and is organized more chronologically (oral communication mKhan po Nges don, February 2005).

88. Listed after date of publication: 1984: Mi rigs dpe mdzod khang (ed.), *Bod gangs can gyi grub mtha'*, pp. 15-17. 1992: Grags pa 'byung gnas and Blo bzang mkhas grub, *Gangs can mkhas*

In summary, the most useful primary sources for depicting the life of the Karmapa are the three spiritual biographies by his students (i–iii) and some spiritual memoirs (mainly ii, iii, and v). Two of the five early sources by his students are still missing.[89] Of the later compilations, the extensive and well-structured *Kaṃ tshang* by Situ Paṇchen can be useful, as it seems to contain remnants of the two lost sources. The single most important source for the very early years of the Eighth Karmapa is Akhu Atra.

The Very Early Years of the Eighth Karmapa (1507–16)

The boy who would become the Eighth Karmapa was born on the fourth day of the eleventh *hor* month of the fire-hare year (1507) in Eastern Tibet in today's Chamdo prefecture, close to the Ngomchu River.[90] The area was called Kartipug in a village called Satam. To the north lay the main Karma

---

grub rim byon ming mdzod, pp. 27–29. 1997: rGyal mtshan, *Kam tshang yab sras dang spal spungs dgon pa*, pp. 52–57. 1997: lDan ma 'Jam dbyangs tshul khrims, *dPal karma pa sku phreng rim byon gyi mdzad rnam*, pp. 158–68. 1999: Mi nyag mgon po, *Gangs can mkhas dbang rim byon gyi rnam thar mdor bsdus*, pp. 248–51.

89. *'Bras spungs dkar chag*, p. 1506, lists an alleged autobiography entitled *rNam thar rin chen 'od phreng*. This could not, however, be verified in any of the title lists. As the text is also unavailable, its nature remains doubtful.

90. A khu A khra, fol. 9b (p. 50). It is likely the seventh of December 1507, assuming these dates are given according to the mTshur phu astrological tradition used by scholars of the Karma bKa' brgyud tradition (see Schuh 1973 and Vogel 1964: 225–26 for the Tibetan calendar and the sexagenary cycle; see Henning 2007: 337–39 for the mTshur phu tradition). *Kaṃ tshang*, p. 302, has the fourth day of the eleventh *hor* month as the Karma pa's birthday. Verhufen 1995: 78, 92n33, who used this source, states that some astrological traditions add a month in this ninth *rab 'byung* cycle (which would account for the difference) and assumes (using Schuh 1973: 123) that according to both the mTshur phu and other traditions this would be the second of February 1507. A khu A khra, fol. 1bff. (pp. 2ff.), starts out by outlining the Karma pa's former incarnations as great masters of Indian and Tibetan Buddhism (ibid., fols. 16a–21a/pp. 32–42). Before the narration of the actual birth, most narratives expound on the qualities of the Karma pa's parents. For the prebirth stories and the nature of the parents see A khu A khra, fols. 2a–5b (pp. 4–10); Sangs rgyas dpal grub, fols. 1a–7a (pp. 2–14); *mKhas pa'i dga' ston*, pp. 1206–9; and *Kaṃ tshang*, pp. 299–302. The latter *Kaṃ tshang* has been translated in an excellent manner into German in Verhufen 1995: 75–79. Most narratives initially establish the Eighth Karma pa's continuity with his predecessor, the Seventh Karma pa Chos grags rgya mtsho: "I am unborn and yet show birth, I do not abide and [yet] show abiding, there is no death and yet I show dying; and again, though there is no birth, I will show [re]birth" (A khu A khra, fol. 5a/p. 41: *bdag ni skye ba med la skye tshul ston / / gnas pa med la gnas tshul ston / / 'chi ba med la 'chi ba'i tshul ston / / slar yang skye ba med la skye tshul bstan /*).

Kagyü seat in Eastern Tibet, Karma Gön; to the southwest, the Taglung Kagyü seat Riwoche.[91] The future Karmapa's father was Ser Jadrel Jampa Shenyen, occasionally abbreviated A Jampa; his mother was Lama Drön, a wife from the Dong clan, also called Önmo Lama Drön.[92]

Following the style of spiritual biographies, the element of self-recognition is introduced: immediately after his birth the Karmapa is said to have rolled his eyes back and to have uttered "I am the Karmapa."[93] When news spread of the birth of a special boy, the Karma Situpa, whose main seat was Karma Gön, decided to examine the case after just seven days.[94] The Seventh Karmapa had apparently left letters regarding his rebirth for the Gyaltsab Rinpoche and Situ Rinpoche respectively.[95] In Situpa's prediction letter, the future Karmapa's parents were named Jampa and Lama Tso. However, these did not accord precisely with those of the boy's parents (A Jampa / Jampa Shenyen, Lama Drön). Therefore, Situpa decided to test the matter.[96]

The story goes that at first Situpa told the parents to keep the special nature of the boy secret for three months and gave them various presents

91. *Kaṃ tshang*, p. 300; *Mi bskyod rdo rje'i spyad pa'i rabs*, fol. 1b (p. 351). For the area, see also Dorje 1999: 395–97.

92. A khu A khra, fol. 5b (p. 42). According to his spiritual memoir (*Mi bskyod rdo rje'i spyad pa'i rabs*, fol. 1b/p. 251) the father was gSer bya bral Byams pa bShes gnyen. And the mother is called Bla ma sgron, identified with an attendant of Birwapa, when he was invited by the Chinese king. The father had apparently received Mahāmudrā teachings from the Seventh Karma pa and descended from the patrilineage (*gdungs*) of the nine generals of the time of the Sa skya hierarch 'Gro mgon 'Phags pa (1235–80) (ibid., fol. 1b/p. 251). As the boy is sometimes (ibid., fol. 13a /p. 57) called "Son of lDag li" (*ldag li'i bu*) or "Father and Son Lho rong Nang so pa" (*lho rong nang so yab sras*), these two names of the Karma pa's father may be added.

93. A khu A khra, fol. 9b (p. 50), mentions that he uttered this phrase three times, whereas *mKhas pa'i dga' ston*, p. 1212, writes that he said it twice. According to his spiritual memoir the Karma pa said: "Om ma ṇi pad me hung," "Karmapa, Karmapa," and "a, ā, i, ī" (*Mi bskyod rdo rje'i spyad pa'i rabs,* fol. 1b).

94. There seems to be some confusion about the dates of the Si tu pa: Richardson 1980: 377 gives the dates of Si tu II bKra shis rnam rgyal (1450–97) and Si tu III bKra shis dpal 'byor (1498–1541). But A khu A khra, fol. 18b (p. 68), and Zhang Yisun assert that the Karma Si tu pa passed away in 1512. Furthermore, circa 1516, the Eighth Karma pa recognized the incarnation of Si tu bKra shis dpal 'byor and gave him the name Chos kyi 'od zer (*mKhas pa'i dga' ston*, p. 1234). It would follow that the Si tu at hand here is the third Si tu bKra shis dpal 'byor. That means he would have had to die in 1512 and been reborn before 1516.

95. *mKhas pa'i dga' ston*, p. 1207.

96. A khu A khra, fol. 10a (p. 51).

for the boy, including a silk scarf and ritual pills (*rten 'dus ril bu*). He said to the infant Karmapa: "I will bring you clothes and invite you for tea [later]."[97] He then instructed the parents to serve the pills and burn incense. If the boy were the incarnation, nothing would happen. If not, he would show signs the next day. If he were to say verses in the evening, it would be maximum four phrases (*tshig*) and minimum three; then the parents should come to Situpa. The father acted accordingly and said: "If you are the rebirth of the Karmapa, Karma Situpa will bring you clothes and invite you for tea; therefore clothes and tea invitation are marginal and can be left for later!" The boy replied: "E ma ho! Do not harbor doubts about me; I am [the one] called the Karmapa." He said more verses but these were subsequently forgotten.[98]

Following this, the spiritual biographies relate events in support of the boy being the re-embodiment of the Seventh Karmapa.[99] During the first months, he traveled through eastern Tibet, mainly to Riwoche, Lhorong, and Gyatön, probably accompanied by his parents and some attendants. Among them was the author of the spiritual biography, Jangchub Sangpo, and various other "part-time" attendants, among them an Önpo Gawa and Sangye Gyaltsen.[100]

At the age of three months, the boy was invited by the Riwoche Chöje Sönam Rinchen Pal Sangpo (1454–1532) and the Lhorong Depa (the ruler of Lhorong, sometimes called Lhorong Gochri) to Lhorong.[101] At the age of

97. Ibid., fol. 10a (p. 51): *karma si tu bas khyod la na bza 'ja 'dren dang bcas pa bskur yod zhus la /*.

98. Ibid., fol. 10a–b (pp. 51–52): *khyed karma pa'i sku skye yin na / karma si tu bas khyed la na bza' ja 'dren dang bcas pa bskur byas pas / na* [fol. 10b] *bza' ja 'dren yang zur 'phyis gsung nas / e ma ho / nga la the tshom ma byed dang / / nga ni karma pa zhes bya / zhes gsungs.* The translation for *zur 'phyis* is "free," as a spelling error is suspected. The meaning used was supported by mKhan po Nges don (oral communication, March 2007). Sangs rgyas dpal grub, fol. 8a (p. 164), adds that the event took place nine days after the birth on the thirteenth day of the month. Later tradition considered the whole event important; Thinley 1980: 89 reports comparatively extensively on it (one assumes he used the *mKhas pa'i dga' ston* for this passage).

99. He recognized students and ritual implements from his past life and showed signs of remarkable spiritual abilities; he caused rains of flowers and rainbows (A khu A khra, fol. 17b/p. 66).

100. A khu A khra, fol. 17b (p. 66).

101. It is not entirely clear from the sources whether he actually went to the places of Ri bo che and Lho rong respectively, or whether these two persons invited him while being in another place. Ri bo che, however, is quite close to the area of his birth: the temple of Ri bo che was

seven months, it is recounted that he gave blessings to a large assembly near Riwoche.[102] The abbot of Riwoche and Lhorong Goshri would become supporters of the future Karmapa; the Riwoche Chöje being characterized as decided from the outset. During that period, Riwoche was the largest monastery in Kham and commanded increasing secular power in Eastern Tibet.[103]

Around 1508, the Tsurpu Gyaltsab Tashi Namgyal (1490–1518) received news about the signs of the rebirth of the Karmapa, in the area of the Ngom River from a Lama Sönam Gyaltsen, in conjunction with the rising sun shining on his tent and his first tea. This was considered auspicious by the Gyaltsab Rinpoche.[104] However, he also received news about another possible candidate: a boy staying in Kongpo.

The story that unfolds from the proclamation of the rival candidate until

---

founded in 1246 by Sangs rgyas dbon, third lineage holder and abbot of the sTag lung branch of the bKa' brgyud school (Schwieger 1996: 122, Dorje 1999: 391). The area, and the town of Lho rong, is southeast of the Karma pa's birthplace in Ngom, and further south than Ri bo che (ibid., 403). The Ri bo che Chos rje is almost certainly the eighth abbot of Ri bo che 'Jig rten dbang phyug bSod nams rin chen (1454–1531) (his life is depicted in Ngag dbang rnam rgyal, *sTag lung chos 'byung*, pp. 657–61; see also Schwieger 1996: 126 and van der Kuijp 2001: 59).

102. A khu A khra, fol. 12b (p. 56).

103. Ngag dbang rnam rgyal, *sTag lung chos 'byung*, pp. 659–60, at first cites *mKhas pa'i dga' ston* (p. 1207: *kho bo la phyi nang gsang ba'i pha ma yod de* ... [p. 1208] ... *shes pa mi gsal ba yin*; then paraphrases until: *de gnyis sngags kyi sbyor lam pa yin*) employing the concept of outer, inner, and secret parents of the Eighth Karma pa (mostly referring to the "real" physical parents as well as to "parents" on a more spiritual plane such as enlightened masters and various buddhas). The phrase *chos rje 'jig rten dbang phyug* in the passage referring to the secret father *chos rje 'jig rten dbang phyug 'khor lo sdom par bzhengs pa'i zhal nas zhugs te* may refer to the Ri bo che Chos rje appearing as the Heruka Cakrasaṃvara. Ngag dbang rnam rgyal, *sTag lung chos 'byung*, p. 660, then explains that when most of the inmates of the encampment (*sgar pa*) decided that the son of Bla ma A mdo ba was the Karma pa, Chos rje 'Jig rten dbang phyug distinguished well and identified the one who would become the Karma pa (namely the other one) correctly and made vast offerings to him. This refers probably to the later visit to Ri bo che in 1510 (see below). According to *sTag lung chos 'byung*, p. 660, the Eighth Karma pa has interpreted the backing by Chos rje 'Jig rten dbang phyug's as an auspicious coincidence for the growth of the latter's teaching. Sangs rgyas dpal grub, fol. 9b (p. 167), too, reports Chos rje 'Jig rten dbang phyug as having made up his mind early on. For the prosperity and influence of Ri bo che during the late fifteenth and sixteenth century, see Schwieger 1996: 125–27; he also refers to the *Blue Annals* (Roerich 1996: 652), which consider Ri bo che the largest monastery in Kham in 1478.

104. A khu A khra, fol. 13a (p. 57); *mKhas pa'i dga' ston*, p. 1215. In Tibetan culture, the interpretation of events as auspicious or inauspicious (*rten 'brel*) is a widely accepted practice rooted in pre-Buddhist beliefs (Samuel 1993: 176; Tucci 1980: 202; for the role of dreams, see Wayman [1967]). In the spiritual biographies, the interpretation of dreams and various kinds

1513 illustrates some of the religio-political concerns in determining an incarnation, and was likely a decisive factor in the Eighth Karmapa's development. The other boy proclaimed a Karmapa candidate was the son of Lama Amdowa, residing in Kongpo Dragsum (southwest of Lhasa). The son of Lama Amdowa is also called "western candidate" while the later Karmapa, due to his provenance from Kham, is called "eastern candidate." At this time, the Karma encampment (*sgar*), the movable tent village of the previous Karmapa, was probably pitched in the area of Kongpo.[105] Pawo Rinpoche recounts in retrospect that as the Lama Amdowa had offered those residing in the encampment food and beer (*chang*), they became partial toward the view that his son was the Karmapa.[106]

The Gyaltsab Rinpoche quickly went to Kongpo Dragsum to meet the other candidate. According to Pawo Rinpoche, although reportedly clear about the eastern boy being the Karmapa through various dreams, he went in order to accord with the worldly view of the residents in his encampment. When the western candidate returned all three gifts to him, the Gyaltsab Rinpoche considered this a bad omen. In a dream afterward, he saw the west as black and the east (the Karmapa's birth place) as bright.[107] Previously, while in a retreat in Nyewo Sapug, the Gyaltsab Rinpoche dreamt of a similar scenario: at the right side of a tiger there was a lion who could not roar and the tiger was also unable to roar. While he was contemplating: if the lord of all wild animals, the lion, has no voice, how can there be a voice to the tiger, from the left a dragon's roar pervaded all directions. After the roar sounded, the lion became a white dog and vanished. When later that day Gyaltsab Rinpoche examined the dream, he concluded that the tiger was him, the lion

---

of divination play key roles in identifying the Karma pa. Verhufen 1995: 50 points out the importance of visions as transmission in the Eighth Karma pa's spiritual biography.

105. From the time of the Seventh Karma pa, Chos grags rgya mtsho, the encampment became more permanent and was occasionally called mTshur phu sgar. The camp moved periodically in a nomadic way (oral communication mKhan po Nges don; Thinley 1980: 90; D. Jackson 1996: 167). The Tibetan *sgar pa* can also refer to the inmates of the encampment, consisting of monks and lamas, as well as laypeople acting as guards for the religious hierarchs (Snellgrove and Richardson 1968: 137).

106. *mKhas pa'i dga' ston*, p. 1216. dPa' bo's account of the two incarnations is, in general, more bitter in this matter. He says, for example, that Bla ma A mdo ba was wild.

107. A khu A khra, fol. 13bf. (p. 58f.); *mKhas pa'i dga' ston*, p. 1216.

the western incarnation, and the dragon the eastern. He related this to Lama Chöpa from Rongpo.[108]

The matter did not seem so obvious to the Gyaltsab Rinpoche, according to other sources, and the path to the resolution of this issue and the enthronement of the Eighth Karmapa would be a long one. Sangye Paldrub indicates that the rival candidate's party had the political support of the Pagmo Drupa regents and their priests (*yon mchod*), the Gyaltsab Rinpoche, and Tsurpu monks, and what is more, the powerful Rinpungpa general, Dönyö Dorje.[109] Thus, the most powerful and wealthy patrons along with the encampment lamas and monks had become partial to the western candidate.

It is worth noting the role the Fourth Shamarpa played in this process. A passage in the *mKhas pa'i dga' ston* indicates that the Fourth Shamarpa, when asked whether he would invite the western candidate from Kongpo Dragsum for tea, declined and mentioned to those in the encampment that the incarnation from the east would be undisputed.[110] Still, it appears he assumed a relatively low-key role: he had not met the young Karmapa and consequently did not act as his principal tutor. This is surprising, as the Shamarpa had been the main lineage holder after the passing of the Seventh Karmapa and was a respected spiritual teacher.

Pawo Rinpoche and Sangye Paldrub, too, explain that the Fourth Shamarpa would have indeed been a most suitable teacher for the Karmapa, but first he could not go to Dokham, and later the conditions (*rten 'brel*)

108. *mKhas pa'i dga' ston*, p. 1216; A khu A khra, fol. 14a (p. 59).

109. Sangs rgyas dpal grub, fol. 10a (p. 168): *de'i dus kong po brag gsum du karma pa'i sprul sku 'khrungs pa la dbus gtsang nas sde srid phag mo gru pa yon mchod / sde pa sgar pa don yod rdo rje / chos rje sgar gyi rgyal tshab sprul sku mtshur dkar gyi rin po che rnam pas gtso mdzad / karma pa'i grwa slob yon bdag thams cad kyis sku skyer mod pa*. Sangs rgyas dpal grub is the only source explicitly mentioning this political support. Interestingly, here the rGyal tshab Rin po che (including the monks from mTshur phu) is also depicted as supporting the western candidate. This is likely to mean that, as the main lords of Tibet and all the monks in his camp supported the rival candidate, he had to give in to the pressure at least outwardly. The phrase *phag mo gru pa yon mchod* is not precise; could it possibly indicate Ngag dbang bKra shis grags pa (1488–1564) and the Fourth Zhwa dmar pa (1453-1524)? Ngag dbang rnam rgyal further mentions sKya se rTogs ldan pa as supporter of the boy from A mdo (*sTag lung chos 'byung*, p. 660: *skya se rtogs ldan pa dang sgar dmangs thams cad*). sKya se rTogs ldan -pa had studied under the Seventh Karma pa and was venerated by all important people (*mi chen po rnams*) of dBus and gTsang and most importantly Don yod rdo rje (*mKhas pa'i dga' ston*, pp. 1152–53).

110. *mKhas pa'i dga' ston*, p. 1219.

of his meeting the Karmapa did not materialize.[111] Sangye Paldrub adds that Dokham and Ütsang were separated by a great distance.[112] However, large distances did not usually matter to Tibetans, particularly great hierarchs such as the Fourth Shamarpa, who commonly spent their entire lives traveling in Tibet, China, and Mongolia.[113]

But as the Shamarpa's (and the Karma Kagyü's) main patron, and most powerful figure in Tibet at the time, Dönyö Dorje, apparently supported the western candidate, it would not have been wise to publicly oppose him, a strategy also apparently applied by the Gyaltsab Rinpoche. Was it mere coincidence that the Eighth Karmapa was only enthroned in 1512, after Dönyö Dorje passed away?[114]

This may account for Shamarpa and Karmapa not meeting before 1512. But the reason behind their inability to meet between 1512 and 1524 seems to have been the two lamas' entourages and Tibetan etiquette: both had very powerful positions which would not allow them to look weak in the eyes of their administration.

In 1523 (*chu lug*), while traveling in Kongpo, the young Karmapa received a letter from the Fourth Shamarpa via the latter's student Önpo Chökyongwa. In this letter, the Shamarpa expressed his deep wish to meet the Karmapa

111. Sangs rgyas dpal grub, fol. 20b (p. 189); *mKhas pa'i dga' ston*, p. 1232. The Fourth Zhwa dmar pa approved of Sangs rgyas mnyan pa. A letter left by the Seventh Karma pa stated that, while there would be many suitable teachers among his direct students, Sangs rgyas mnyan pa was praised as the most suitable. Zhwa dmar told the bla mas and lord in the encampments of dBus and mDo that as the rGyal tshab Rin po che and most of the Seventh Karma pa's students were already dead, the most suitable teacher among the living would be Sangs rgyas mnyan pa.

112. Sangs rgyas dpal grub, fol. 13a (p. 194). The *Collected Works of the Eighth Karmapa* contain a song praising the Fourth Zhwa dmar pa (Mi bskyod rdo rje, *Mon sha 'ug stag sgo dom tshang ngur mo rong du gsungs pa'i mgur*).

113. Furthermore, the Fourth Zhwa dmar pa died in 1524 and thus had seventeen years to travel to mDo khams and meet the young Karma pa. Previously, he had traveled widely and visited his seat in dGa' ldan Ma mo in Kong po (Ehrhard 2002a: 15).

114. For the passing of Don yod rdo rje, see Paṇ chen bSod nams grags pa, *Deb ther dmar po*, p. 89; see also the translation in Tucci 1971: 229. As has been pointed out, the Zhwa dmar pa frequently met and traveled with Don yod rdo rje in the last part of the latter's life (*mKhas pa'i dga' ston*, pp. 1141–48). In 1504 (last mentioned date before the passage on ibid., p. 1146), for example, he gave dharma lessons in the dGe lugs monastery of 'Bras spungs and later visited the Potala together with Don yod rdo rje (ibid., p. 1147). It may be suspected that as the Zhwa dmar was greatly involved in the power struggles in dBus and gTsang at that time, his absence could have led to difficulties for the Karma bKa' brgyud pa in those areas.

despite his previous inability to come, and suggested a rather low-key meeting in Kongpo Dragsum. The Shamarpa would come as an old monk (most likely in order not to harm etiquette as perceived by the Karmapa's camp), and the Karmapa should avoid the main route via Yarlung (probably in order not to disturb the Shamarpa's entourage as he was head of Densatel). But the Karmapa's encampment-leaders considered this inappropriate, as such a step would amount to the Karmapa requesting a teaching from the Shamarpa (*chos gsan*).[115]

As a consequence, Shamarpa received a response in which the Karmapa said that despite his wish to meet, "those [from my] encampment are not under control, thus I cannot come."[116] The Shamarpa in turn is depicted as desperate: "He held his head with his hands and said: 'There is no need for me to remain [in this world] now,'" later adding: "this [position as] head of Densatel came to really harm me."[117] Shortly afterward, in 1524, the Shamarpa passed away, having entrusted a secret letter to Önpo Chökyongwa, expressing his wish to meet the Karmapa in his next life.[118] These passages indicate

115. *mKhas pa'i dga' ston*, pp. 1259–60 (and *Kaṃ tshang*, pp. 322–24, in slightly abbreviated manner), quote the letter from the Fourth Zhwa dmar pa to the Eighth Karma pa in the account about the Eighth Karma pa's life. According to *mKhas pa'i dga' ston*, p. 1258, in the second month of the water-sheep year (1523) Mi bskyod rdo rje was invited by various people such as Śākya bzang po from upper and lower Kong po (*Kaṃ tshang*, p. 322, adds the places rNam thos kyi ri bo and Gyi ling). The spiritual biographies then explain that Zhwa dmar Rin po che had previously sent tea invitations through Bla ma gDan sa pa and dBon po Chos skyong ba. As he knew the seeming difficulties of a harmonious teacher-student relationship from before (*sngar*; does this also relate to some problems of not having been able to meet the Seventh Karma pa at some point earlier as indicated in *mKhas pa'i dga' ston*, p. 1144?) he sent dBon po Chos skyong ba to deliver the letter. A passage in the Fourth Zhwa dmar pa's spiritual biography in *mKhas pa'i dga' ston*, pp. 1149–50, indicates that while the Karma pa went to Kong po he was invited again and again, especially by dBon po Chos skyong ba (who was a student of the Fourth Zhwa dmar pa).

116. *mKhas pa'i dga' ston*, p. 1150: *sgar pa rnams kyis dbang ma 'dus pas ma slebs*. The Karma pa related the same to the messenger of these letters, dBon po Chos skyong ba (ibid., p. 1149: *rje karma pa nyid phebs par spro na'ang sgar pa rnams kyis mi phebs par zhus* / "The Karma pa himself said that he would like to come but those from his encampment had asked him not to").

117. Ibid., p. 1149: *dbu phyag gis 'phur zhing da ni kho bo bsdad pa la dgos pa mi 'dug* [p. 1150] *gungs nas ... gdan sa thel gyi go sa 'di nga la shin tu gnod par byung gsungs*.

118. Ibid., p. 1150: *rje karma pa'i drung du kong stod du sngags kong gi mtshams tsam du mjal gi grub smon zhes dang / dbon po chos skyong ba la'ang log shog gi bka' lung phebs te / dgung lo don gnyis pa sprel lo zla ba bcu gcig pa'i nyer nga la dgongs pa chos kyi dbyings chen po'i klong du thim*. Sources for this account are the passages in the Fourth Zhwa dmar pa's spiritual biography

how religious hierarchs were dependent not only on their patrons but also on the will of their religio-political administration.[119]

Be that as it may, at some point before 1512, the western candidate was invited into the encampment from Kongpo Dragsum. The future Karmapa, however, continued traveling to various places in eastern Tibet, such as Lhorong and Riwoche, where he inspired the local people and monks and gained their loyal support.[120] Sangye Paldrub evokes an intense image which may be considered a crucial moment in the Eighth Karmapa's life, in spite of the eulogical undertones peculiar to spiritual biographies.[121] The supporters (e.g., the people from Riwoche and Lhorong) of the future Karmapa were poor, and when he fell sick could not even provide medicine. The boy contemplated sadly that in such times having the name of an "incarnation" (*sprul sku*) would be of no benefit for the next life, and it would also seem that, in this life, there was no control over food or clothing.

Finding the name of an incarnation unnecessary, he was delighted about not having it. The boy thus resolved that the only thing that mattered was to seek out a qualified teacher and to determine what the true dharma was and was not, feeling joy in contemplating the great fortune it would be to know the Buddhist teachings.[122] The event is rounded off with the narrative

---

(*mKhas pa'i dga' ston*, pp. 1149–50, almost quoted verbatim in *Kaṃ tshang*, pp. 223–24) and the related passage from the account about the Eighth Karma pa (*mKhas pa'i dga' ston*, pp. 1258–60, and *Kaṃ tshang*, pp. 322–24). The respective passages and their manifold contexts demand further studies.

119. It is noteworthy that a lama's entourage as somewhat responsible for the lama's deeds may as well be a topos.

120. Mi bskyod rdo rje, *Karma pa mi bskyod rdo rje'i rnam thar*, fol. 2b (p. 333), explains that he stayed (due to the issue of the other candidate) in the area around Lho rong until he was six years old. From the sources it is evident that the Karma pa traveled around and that the other candidate stayed in the camp in Kong po Brag gsum until the Karma pa finally arrived in 1513 (see below).

121. Sangs rgyas dpal grub, fol. 10a (p. 168), follows the passage that indicated the missing support from the powerful rulers and lamas. Although the narratives aim to portray the Karma pa as a buddha, the difficulties surrounding the incarnation were certainly a historical reality and must have had a considerable impact on the child.

122. According to mKhan po Nges don, this resolve to seek out the teaching was, among other factors, a decisive one for the Karma pa to become one of the most learned among the Karma pas. mKhan po Nges don further commented that he had seen a text putting forth this position. Unfortunately, the title was not remembered (oral communication, March 2007).

of an ascetic, a student of the previous, Seventh Karmapa, who performed a divination (*pra phab*) with the aid of Mahākāla. He received a prophecy that all beings would honor and have confidence in this young boy as the Karmapa.[123]

Later, a similar skepticism about his title is expressed in a spiritual memoir that offers insight into some of the young Karmapa's motives for his refusal to journey to the Chinese court, around 1520.[124] The passage at first recounts the belief that the Seventh Karmapa had prophesied that he had—in order to protect the doctrine—manifested in his own form and that of the king of China. When the king urgently wished to receive teachings from the rebirth of the Karmapa, the spiritual memoir states:

> At that time [I] was still a child, [and] even if I had not been one, I did not have in my mind even partially the qualities needed for going to serve as a spiritual teacher of a magically emanated [Chinese] emperor. Therefore, feeling intimidated, I was fed up with my own past deeds. [And I wondered] about my being called "Karmapa," asking, for what [action] is it the punishment (*nyes pa*)?[125]

This passage is imbued with a pleasant humility and exhibits some rather personal traits. Back in his early years, the spiritual biographies portray the future Karmapa's abilities during his travels in eastern Tibet with the often employed topoi of recognizing ritual implements such as hats, rosaries, and statues from his predecessors. At the age of nine months (1508) he was invited to the Namkha Dzö temple in Lhorong Dzongsar.[126] In his third year (1509) he met Önpo Gawa, and when he was four (1510), on his way to Riwoche,

123. Sangs rgyas dpal grub, fol. 10b (p. 169).

124. Mi bskyod rdo rje, *Pha mi bskyod rdo rje'i rnam thar*, fol. 3b–4b (pp. 335–38). See also Rheingans (2008): 124–28.

125. Mi bskyod rdo rje, *Pha mi bskyod rdo rje'i rnam thar*, fol. 4a (p. 336): *de tshe bdag ni lang tsho ma rdzogs shing / / lang tsho rdzogs kyang sprul pa'i rgyal po yi / dge ba'i bshes su 'gro ba'i yon tan ni / / cha shas tsam yang rgyud la ma 'tshal bas / sems zhum rang gi las la yi chad de / / bdag la karma pa zhes grags pa yi / bla dwags 'di 'dra ci yi nyes pa yin /*

126. A khu A khra, fol. 14a (p. 59). There he was presented with the hat of the Sixth Karma pa and another one, and two statues of the Sixth Karma pa, and in both cases chose the right one.

he encountered Kinog Lama Sönam Rinchen. Kinog Lama offered the Karmapa a turquoise and asked him to reveal himself as Karmapa. The boy is said to have answered with a famous utterance, and regular topos: equation with other important Buddhist masters: "Sometimes I am Padmasambhava, sometimes I am Saraha, and at other times I am Maitreya."[127]

Upon his arrival in Riwoche in 1510, the Karmapa met the local sangha and again successfully performed various tests. In Tashö he related that he would like to go to Kongpo, and a letter was prepared for him to go to the encampment. In his fifth year (1511), he proceeded to the area of Omolung, where he visited the house of Önpo Gawa. Sources subsequently depict a dialogue asserting the Karmapa's superiority over his rival, suggesting clairvoyant abilities. Önpo Gawa asked:

> "Is the son of Amdowa the Karmapa?"
>
> "I am Karmapa. The son of Amdowa is a rebirth of the Surmang incarnation," [Karmapa] answered.
>
> [Önpo Gawa] asked again: "Is he the one who passed away in Tselakang or the one who passed away in Tsarshi?"
>
> "He is the one who passed away in Tsarshi; he is my monk."[128]

In 1512 the Situpa passed away at Karma Gön, and some of the monks from the encampment came for the funeral rites, thus establishing some contact. After the passing of the Situpa, the Gyaltsab Rinpoche became active in establishing the Karmapa's recognition.[129] In the tenth lunar month of the ape year

127. A khu A khra, fol. 15b (p. 62): *lan re padma 'byung gnas yin / lan re sa ra ha pa yin / lan re byams pa mgon po yin*; *mKhas pa'i dga' ston*, p. 1217. This saying is considered "famous" in that it was reproduced by *Kaṃ tshang* and found entry in all accounts of the Eighth Karma pa's life (Verhufen 1995: 30; Thinley [1980]: 90 attributes the date wrongly to 1512; Douglas and White 1976: 86). Visionary meetings with Saraha or connection to him are a mark of all Tibetan Mahāmudrā traditions, including the Second and Third Karma pas (Schaeffer 2000: 95–98; Braitstein 2004: 64–66) and the dGe lugs pa (Willis 1995: 117).

128. A khu A khra, fol. 17a (p. 65): *karma pa nga yin a mdo bu zur mang sku skye'i skye ba yin / rtse lha khang la 'das pa de yin nam / rtsar shis na 'das pa de yin zhus pas rtsar shis na 'das pa yin / khong nga'i gra pa yin gsungs /*

129. A khu A khra, fol. 18b (p. 68). This is Lho rong rDzong gsar in Lho rong and probably not the monastery rDzong gsar, which is further in the east (Dorje 1999: 465). A khu A khra first mentions only the word rDzong, later it is said he would be in rDzong gsar; the area however is the one of Lho rong.

(1512), the Karmapa was invited to the Karma encampment for the first time. Two messengers (Lama Ripa and Deshin Shegpa Önpo) were sent by Gyaltsab Rinpoche from the encampment to Dzongsar, where the young Karmapa abided.[130] In the twelfth lunar month of the same year the Karmapa traveled, via Olung Monastery, Drangra Monastery, Rushö, and Tsangrag Sumdo, in the direction of the encampment in Kongpo.[131]

As the rival candidate was in the encampment at that time, the conflict over the two reincarnations reached its climax. Again, Lama Yangripa (who had acted as a messenger earlier) came with many offerings to invite the Karmapa for tea.[132]

The inmates of the encampment then decided to greet and invite the Lhorong Goshri, who—among others—was traveling with the Karmapa as attendant. However, a rule had been laid down that no one should offer silk scarves, tea invitations, or prostrations to the arriving boy, as it was not yet settled whether he was truly the Karmapa and because the rival candidate from the west was still present. Nevertheless, the spiritual biographies report that most people, on seeing the boy from the east arriving, were overwhelmed by his charismatic presence and started to prostrate and venerate him, some with tears in their eyes.[133] Finally, the Karmapa was received in the encampment on the New Year day of the bird year (1513). Before the sun set, he met the Gyaltsab Rinpoche, Tashi Döndrub Namgyal, for the first time.[134]

While the future Karmapa had arrived, it would still be more than a month before his enthronement. In the first days, both boys were brought in front of a large assembly where they were asked to answer questions and give blessings. On this occasion, two sources depict the Karmapa as fearless and

130. A khu A khra, fol. 18b (p. 68). The rGyal tshab had given his messengers two envelopes (or covers) with similar appearance. One contained words of truth (*bden thob*) and the other one was empty. As the young Karma pa, upon arrival of the messengers, chose the one with the words of truth, the messengers developed strong trust.

131. A khu A khra, fol. 18b (p. 68).

132. Ibid., fol. 19a (p. 69).

133. Ibid., fol. 19b (p. 70).

134. A khu A khra, fol. 19b (p. 70), *mKhas pa'i dga' ston*, p. 1221f.; Sangs rgyas dpal grub, fol. 10b (p. 169).

compassionate in all circumstances, whereas the second candidate, Amdowa's son, is portrayed as crying and confused.[135]

The source tells that by that time the inmates of the encampment had been split into two parties, each supporting one candidate: the Gyaltsab Rinpoche tried to reconcile the parties and urged them not to become partial but to be upright and to trust in the analysis (*dpyod pa*) and careful examination of the candidates. Upon analysis it was revealed that the second candidate—though already seven years old—did not know more words than "father, mother, and food and drink."[136]

The Gyaltsab's efforts did not bear results at first. On one occasion the future Karmapa (the eastern boy) was even stopped from stepping on the throne.[137] While public identifications continued, the boys were brought again into a row to identify statues and scroll paintings of former Karmapas. At the first occasion, on the twenty-ninth day of the first lunar month, the rival candidate is reported to have failed. The second time, on the first day of the second lunar month, he managed to recognize a painting with the seal of a previous Karmapa. His supporters immediately proclaimed he had been recognized, which the other party doubted; an interlinear remark in Akhu Atra expresses scepticism about the "public recognitions" "these days."[138]

So heated was the atmosphere that the Gyaltsab Rinpoche seems to have pondered a possible outbreak of violence. Though he is portrayed as having had no doubts inwardly as to the identity of the Karmapa, the party supporting the other candidate was politically strong and had powerful allies. On the other hand, the people from Lhorong and Gyatön were fervent adherents of the boy the Gyaltsab had chosen. As no concurrence could be reached, the Gyaltsab suggested to the religious and political heads of the

135. Sangs rgyas dpal grub, fol. 11b (p. 171); *mKhas pa'i dga' ston*, p. 1223. One should note that these two sources are written in retrospect. A khu A khra, whose author should have witnessed these events, fails to go into detail regarding the other candidate's abilities.

136. Sangs rgyas dpal grub, fol. 11b (p. 171); *mKhas pa'i dga' ston*, p. 1223.

137. A khu A khra, fol. 20a (p. 71); *mKhas pa'i dga' ston*, p. 122.

138. A khu A khra, fol. 21a (p. 73). The interlinear remark (*mchan*) is found in A khu A khra, fol. 21a–b (pp. 73–74) (it is not clear from which time this interlinear remark stems): to examine an incarnation in such a manner and then carry out the recognition would not be suitable for high incarnations such as the Karma pa, since, in fact, one would go to ask the common mob. Therefore, a master would not make an effort in such a recognition other than to catch the minds of ordinary people.

powerful provinces of Lhorong and Gyatön that they might remove the Karmapa from the camp.[139]

The inhabitants of these areas and their leaders considered this unacceptable, as the Karmapa had been decided as far as they were concerned, and they threatened to drive out the other candidate and his party if they would not agree on the rightful Karmapa. Tensions mounted and the Gyaltsab worried that if he did not enthrone the eastern boy and future Karmapa, some of his supporters might be tempted to start a war.[140] Finally, adherents of the second candidate made concessions and informed the Gyaltsab they would concur.[141] Specific reasons are not given, and it must be noted that as stated previously Dönyö Dorje had just passed away in 1512.

As is typical, spiritual biographies describe a dream of the Gyaltsab Rinpoche as providing guidance.[142] On the thirtieth day of the first lunar month, he had a dream where the Karmapa himself (the eastern candidate) urged the Gyaltsab Rinpoche to end the dispute which was underlined by the symbolic appearance of a white and a red ḍākinī. They incited him to let the truth be known and staunch the spread of lies. The Gyaltsab Rinpoche, probably under enormous political and spiritual pressure to take a public decision, resolved to enthrone the eastern candidate and confer upon him the title of Karmapa.[143]

Narratives subsequently establish the Karmapa's authority and his conti-

139. Sangs rgyas dpal grub, fol. 11b (p. 171).

140. *mKhas pa'i dga' ston*, p. 1223; Sangs rgyas dpal grub, fol. 12a (p. 172).

141. Ibid.

142. Wayman 1967: 2 explains dreams as literary themes in India and Tibet; he also discusses the dream (ibid., 11) as a means developed in the Buddhist tantras. For dreams in the Tibetan traditions and their interpretations, see Sumegi 2008: 71–94, 107–9; for dreams in spiritual biographies, see also Young 1999: 8–15.

143. A khu A khra, fol. 21b (p. 74). The whole incident was pictured in a slightly mistaken manner in previous accounts. Thinley 1980: 90: "but when he [the rGyal tshab] met Mikyo Dorje, he spontaneously felt compelled to bow down to him." Douglas and White 1976: 73–74: "Gyaltsap Tulku Tashi Namgyal and Lama Yang Ripa travelled to Ri Wo Che in order to settle the matter, and vowed not to show any distinction between the two little boys until it was determined beyond doubt which of them was the true incarnation. However when they were presented before Mikyo Dorje they found themselves automatically doing full prostrations to him and thus realized that he must be undoubtedly the real Karma pa." Verhufen (1995: 96n59) has at least noted that Stein (1972: 147, employing *mKhas pa'i dga' ston*) indicates in two brief sentences the potential conflict of the situation.

nuity with his predecessor, Seventh Karmapa Chödrag Gyatso, through the ritual of enthronement. In the morning light of the eleventh day of the second lunar month of the bird year (1513), the boy from the east ascended the throne. He received the black hat, symbol of the Karmapas, and the title "Victorious Great Karmapa" (*rgyal ba karma pa chen po*).[144] The Gyaltsab saw the face of the late Seventh Karmapa in the sun, and all the inhabitants of the encampment are reported to have woken up as if from a bad dream to a great trust in the Karmapa, asking themselves: "What happened to us, that we were deluded before in such a way?"[145] The whole ceremony was a festivity, probably directly witnessed by a sangha of over three thousand and celebrated by an even larger number of devotees in the local markets. The omniscient Chenga, the Shamarpa, sent offerings,[146] and it is also said that offerings were sent by the Chinese king after the Karmapa was recognized.[147]

After the enthronement, on the fifteenth day of the second month of the bird year (1513), the Karmapa uttered praise to dharmapāla Mahākāla Bernagchen and said that it would do away with all harm from non-human beings for the *garpa*s.[148] This suggests that they had been under such an influence in the first place. The last doubters in the camp were persuaded by the genuine Karmapa, when he exhibited clairvoyance in knowing that "official" adherents of the western boy's party secretly already venerated him.[149]

The story of the rival candidate is taken up later in the sources, illustrating the negative result of wrong views (*log lta*). It seems that with the unfavorable turn of events, Lama Amdowa, the candidate's father, became unhappy and

144. A khu A khra, fol. 22a (p.75); Sangs rgyas dpal grub, fol. 12a (p. 172).

145. *mKhas pa'i dga' ston*, p. 1224: *sngar nged rang tsho de 'drar 'khrul pa ci byung ngam zhes.*

146. Ibid.

147. A khu A khra, fol. 22a (p. 75). In the days thereafter, a series of visions of masters are described (ibid., fol. 22b/p. 76). Verhufen 1995: 49–51 explains the function of such visions as a sign of development of tantric practice and purity of the mental continuum. With special emphasis on the Eighth Karma pa, he has noted that visions take a special place in spiritual biographies. Stott (in Thinley 1980: 3) even deems them the crucial factor of the Karma pa biographies, while Chögyam Trungpa (Nālandā Translation Commitee 1980: 313) underlines them as indicators of spiritual transmision.

148. Ibid., fol. 22b (p. 76). The text was entitled *mGon po ma hung mgu ma*, and may refer to a fragment with a slighlty different title in the Eighth Karma pa's *Rang la nges pa'i tshad ma*, fols. 9b4-10a (pp. 1056–58).

149. A khu A khra, fol. 22b (p.76); *mKhas pa'i dga' ston*, p. 1225.

wanted to leave the camp with his son. Though the Gyaltsab Rinpoche urged him to stay, he grudgingly departed, which in turn led to a deterioration of his merit due to his wrong views.[150] This is related to a topos well known in spiritual biographies: the bad times and the hesitation to take rebirth. Its positioning close to the events surrounding the reincarnation dispute may suggest at least a connection. The Karmapa is said to have related to the Gyaltsab Rinpoche:

> From when I died in the tiger year (*stag lo*, 1506) [as the Seventh Karmapa] until my rebirth in the hare year (*yos lo*, 1507), I stayed in [the pure realm of] Tuṣita with Maitreya and in [the pure realm] Sukhāvatī and was happy. Then, because I was tired of people,[151] I thought it would be pointless to come here for the time being. When [thinking so] the protector Maitreya and the wisdom-ḍākinīs said, "you have to take rebirth in the world (*jambudvīpa*)." Having taken rebirth I have until this year stayed in Lhorong.[152]

Following this, the Karmapa takes the first steps toward monkhood, and while the issue with the two candidates is not mentioned in the sources from then on, the narrative progresses to depict the deeds expected from a reincarnate Buddhist master and scholar: exposition (*bshad*), debate (*rtsod*), and composition (*rtsom*). Upon his enthronement in the third month of the bird year (1513), news of the Karmapa spread to all Karma Kagyü monasteries in Ü and Tsang.[153] It seems that at this time people became aware that his name, Mikyö Dorje ("Unshakable Vajra"), was given to him by Padmasambhava.[154]

150. A khu A khra, fol. 23a (p. 77).

151. The phrase *Mi rnams la yid chad pas* may also be read as *yid chad yod pas* = "the people have broken faith."

152. A khu A khra, fol. 25b, (p. 82). In the same year the Karma pa himself remarked to his biographer A khu A khra that his followers should not look down upon a Zur mang Bya bral as he would remember many previous lives (ibid., fol. 32b/p. 96). It may possibly refer to the rival candidate.

153. dPa' bo Rin po che himself was witness to it at ten years old (*mKhas pa'i dga' ston*, p. 1224).

154. *Kaṃ tshang*, p. 306. The earlier sources such as A khu A khra, Sangs rgyas dpal grub, and *mKhas pa'i dga' ston* do not mention the granting of the name at this stage.

On the third day of the fourth lunar month the Karmapa received from the Gyaltsab Rinpoche the *upavāsatha* vows of the Mahāyāna-prātimokṣa, and the name Chökyab Dragpa Palsang ("Dharma Refuge, Good Radiant Glory").[155] Then the Gyaltsab Rinpoche, his first Buddhist teacher, taught him step by step to read and write (*yi ge*) and gave the empowerments of Hayagrīva and Vajravārāhī,[156] as well as meditation instructions (*khrid*) for the practice of Buddha aspects such as Jinasāgara, Vajrayoginī, and Mahākāla.[157]

After his enthronement, the Karmapa began traveling more extensively, journeying to various places in Kham such as Sagyukhang, Redraglung, Sholhade, and Ganden. Then a few months later, on the third day of the eighth lunar month (*khrums kyi zla ba*), it was again the Gyaltsab Rinpoche who inducted him into the *śrāmaṇera*-vows of a novice monk (*pravrajyā*) in conjunction with an official hair-cutting ceremony. This ritual took place in Olung Yanggön.[158] In the same bird year (1513), dialogues occur in Akhu Atra that portray the Eighth Karmapa as a capable and realized teacher through teaching Mahāmudrā: two occur between the first and second teachings of the Gyaltsab, and two follow them.[159] In the ninth month, the Karmapa delivered his first sermon to a large assembly. On the twentieth day he left Dzongsar[160] for Dokham and, ultimately, Riwoche.[161]

155. *mKhas pa'i dga' ston*, p. 1226. *Kaṃ tshang*, p. 307, reads the name variation "Chos kyi grags pa dpal bzang po" and gives the thirteenth day. The *upavāsatha* vows are the observance of eight precepts for twenty-four hours (Tsomo 2004: 673).

156. A khu A khra, fol. 24a (p. 78).

157. *Mi bskyod rdo rje'i spyad pa'i rabs*, fol. 3b (p. 355).

158. A khu A khra, fol. 31b (p. 94). The phrase used is: *gtso bor sems rab tu byung ba'i zhar la khyim pa'i rtags spong ba'i ched du dbu skra bcad cing*. The hair-cutting is often associated with the Buddhist refuge (*śaraṇa*). The Eighth Karma pa had most probably received the Buddhist refuge before in conjuction with the *upavāsatha* vows. *mKhas pa'i dga' ston*, p. 1226, summarizes the taking of vows in the context of depicting the Karma pa's renunciation. He explains that he received the *upāsaka* vows together with observing the eight precepts of the *poṣadha* (which is probably his account of the *upavāsatha* vows), the *pravrajyā*, and the hair-cutting, plus the name.

159. Showing these abilities as teacher is a likely function of the embedded dialogues in the overall structure of this narrative. The dialogues are partly translated and their contexts and functions analyzed in my forthcoming paper "Great Seal Dialogues in a Spiritual Biography about Mi bskyod rdo rje (1507–54)."

160. Probably Lho rong rDzong gsar.

161. *mKhas pa'i dga' ston*, p. 1330f.

Local monks and lamas invited him to the temple (*mchod khang*) and presented him with tea and other large gifts (in a welcome ceremony). After uttering auspicious prayers, he taught the meditation instruction (*zab khrid*) on the guruyoga and others to a pleased assembly. Later, he is said to have given the reading transmission to the meditation (*sgom lung*) of Avalokiteśvara to more than ten thousand people assembled in a marketplace.[162] The earliest mentioned text was composed at the age of eight (1514): a commentary to a song (*mgur*) of Milarepa, dealing with Mahāmudrā.[163]

The Karmapa then returned to Ngom, where he visited the birthplace of the Sixth Karmapa in Ngomshel. In the Rene Gön seat he appointed Palden Tashi as abbot.[164] He finally went to the famed Karma Monastery, where he was received with great pomp.[165] After briefly meeting two of his most important teachers, he was invited by Sangye Nyenpa of Denma to his monastery, Jangchub Ling, where he was greeted by a large gathering.[166] He then journeyed slowly to Litang and Nyagrong, which at that time was a stronghold of the Karma Kagyüpa, and finally returned northeastward to Surmang Dechentse.[167]

During these early years a patron-priest connection is forged, related by

162. A khu A khra, fol. 34b (p. 100). At that point the source talks about a Zhwa dmar ba. This does not refer, however, to the Fourth Zhwa dmar pa but to some unidentified lama with a red hat.

163. Mi bskyod rdo rje, *rJe btsun mi las rje sgam po pa gdams pa mgur 'grel, Collected Works of the Eighth Karmapa*, vol. 15, pp. 1105–1110, 3 fols. Subsequently, further visions are introduced linking the Karma pa to both the epistemological tradition of Dignāga and Dharmakīrti and the epitome of the tantric yogin, Padmasambhava. He replied to a prayer: "I am Padmasambhava; you (Karma pa) are rGyal [ba] mchog dbyangs. Inseparable, [we] are the great Vajradhara; [we] rest in the unborn *dharmakāya*."

164. Ibid., fol. 35b (p. 102). Visions of Maitreya and Karma Pakṣi are reported.

165. Ibid., fol. 36b (p. 103).

166. *Kaṃ tshang*, p. 311. The monastery was founded by Sangs rgyas mnyan pa and is located in the area of lDan ma, in the region of sDe dge in eastern Tibet. It is an area located at the 'Bri chu river and synonymous with 'Dan ma and 'Dan khog (Dorje 1999: 474; Kessler 1983: 56, 65). The following events, in particular the travel to 'Jang sa tham, are mentioned at a later stage in *mKhas pa'i dga' ston* than in *Kaṃ tshang*.

167. *mKhas pa'i dga' ston*, p. 1231. For notes on the area of Li thang, where the First Karma pa had founded the monastery of Kham po gnas nang, see Dorje 1999: 433. *Kaṃ tshang*, p. 312, mentions that the Karma pa also visited this monastery on his travel. For the various Zur mang monasteries, see Dorje 1999: 484, 486.

the sources in typical fashion. The Karmapa accepted an invitation sent by the king of Jang Satam, an area very much south of Kham in today's southwest China.[168] On the third day of the third month of the mouse year (1516) the Eighth Karmapa arrived in Jang Satam, staying for seven days. The event is described as a pompous exchange of gifts, and the young Karmapa passed on teachings to the king, his wives, and the local population. As a result, the king promised not to engage in war with Tibet for thirteen years; he sent five hundred boys for a monastic education to Tibet each year, and founded a hundred monasteries. The king also provided extensive funding for religious buildings.[169] It shows that his position as Karmapa was widely accepted, and that he (likely urged by his retinue) became involved in the politics of the day, indicating the attraction he may have been for local lords.

The period after Mikyö Dorje's early years is characterized by extensive study with his four most important teachers, leading to the composition of the Karmapa's first major scholastic works:[170] from 1516 to 1529 he studied extensively with Sangye Nyenpa Tashi Paljor (1445/57–1510/25), who was his main lama of Mahāmudrā. Dümoma Tashi Öser (b. fifteenth century, d. ca. 1545),[171] Khenchen Chödrub Sengge (b. fifteenth century), and in particular Karma Trinlepa Chogle Namgyal (1456–1539) were important for his intellectual development. It is likely that he avoided the traditional main centers of Ü and Tsang for thirty years until coming to his Central Tibetan main seat Tsurpu in 1537.[172] During the later part of his life, he was confronted by,

168. This area had been a Karma bKa' brgyud and rNying ma (Kaḥ tog branch) stronghold already during the Yuan period. In the Yuan dynasty, Lijang became the capital, and in the Ming period the authority of its kings was recognized (Dorje 1999: 423).

169. *Kaṃ tshang*, pp. 312–13. It is important to note that such numbers are not to be taken literally.

170. The Karma pa himself named them the *rje btsun chen po rnam pa bzhi* (Mi bskyod rdo rje, *Karma pa mi bskyod rdo rje'i rnam thar la bslab pa'i khrid*, fol. 3a).

171. Si tu and 'Be lo, *Kaṃ tshang*, p. 345: *rje bkra shis 'od zer 'das pa'i dgongs rdzogs bsrubs shing.* This was in 1545 (*sprul lo*).

172. *Kaṃ tshang*, p. 344. See also Rheingans 2008: 135–47. One passage in *Kaṃ tshang* indicates that he had approached dBus before 1537. According to *Kaṃ tshang*, p. 321, he went to Phu lung, where he spent the New Year of the *lug lo* (probably *chu lug*, 1523) and then to De mo. According to Ferrari 1958: 53 and 131n307, Phu lung is in a side valley of 'Phyong rgyas (see also Dorje 1999: 210–11). But according to Ferrari 1958: 131n307, Phu lung is only accounted for in Tucci 1949 and otherwise unknown; the other spiritual biographies about the Karma pa refer to places in Kong po for the given time.

and had to balance, an unstable situation in Ü and Tsang, involving numerous local lords and ruling families, in particular the Rinpungpa and Pagmo Drupa. He had the support of the Ja, Yarlung, and especially the Dagpo Kurab lords and connections with the non-Tibetan kings of Jang Satam and Mön. Karmapa Mikyö Dorje passed away in 1554 after a pilgrimage to Tsari.[173]

Conclusions: Lives Lived—Lives Imagined

It will be a long time before we can appreciate fully the Eighth Karmapa's life, his contributions to Tibetan scholasticism and practice, and the intricate religio-political contexts. A thorough comprehension of the *rnam thar* genre as such will surely need intensive future research, too. Some preliminary conclusions, however, may be allowed from this brief study. The first half of the sixteenth century emerged as a crucial period. The Ü and Tsang wars and the Gelug and Kagyü political clashes have been related to the founding of two key monasteries near Lhasa. It is most likely that geo-strategic underpinnings propelled spiritual transmissions even more into becoming sects, entangled in political affairs. Despite, or one might say because of, involvement in Tibetan politics from a young age, the Eighth Karmapa's attitude toward his position was not overtly enthusiastic. It is probable that the dispute over the incarnation and its underpinnings had a considerable impact on the young Karmapa. According to Akhu Atra he reacted by resolving to seek out a genuine teacher and to study diligently.

Some of the intricate religio-political situation in which the hierarchs were engulfed was also uncovered: probably due to the dependence on the powerful Rinpungpa, the Gyaltsab Rinpoche had apparently not publicly opposed the rival candidate for some time, and the Fourth Shamarpa, despite sending letters and offerings, did not meet the boy. The enthronement was conducted only after Dönyö Dorje's passing, although the significance of this fact remains speculative. The decisions to be reached about the authenticity of the candidate are depicted by the narrative as derived from a mixture of self-recognition, letters, exhibition of extraordinary spiritual abilities, public tests, dream-visions, and omens. The conflict is not resolved by resorting to

173. See Rheingans 2008: 116–50, for a summary of the remainder of the Eighth Karma pa's life.

the concept of different emanations of one person, but the rival candidate is recognized as a spiritually able but different reincarnate lama.

With regard to the development of the narrative, the slightly later sources by Pawo Tsuglag Trengwa and Sangye Paldrub come to a more stark judgment of the situation. A whole range of actions from bribery through Tibetan beer to the threatening of violence is depicted. Additionally, Sangye Paldrub's judgment of the political situation seems what may be termed more realistic with regard to the Gyaltsab Rinpoche's involvement and the role of Dönyö Dorje. Sources are, on the whole, negative about the political state of affairs of the day, which may go beyond the commonplace lament about degenerate times. Sangye Paldrub explains that people in Kongpo, as in Ü and Tsang, behaved like animals, killing each other.[174] In the future, we are in need not only of a thorough study of the Fourth Shamarpa's life and works, but also of some precise distinguishing of narrative functions in the story of a saint, with specific examples.

The case of the Eighth Karmapa supports the view that reincarnation disputes are strongly linked to Tibet's peculiar intersection of religion and politics and were not unusual in pre-modern Tibet. Indeed, along with their stories and justifications, such disputes continue to haunt Tibetan Buddhists in the West, shaking the faith of some "prisoners of Shangri-la."[175] The dispute over the Eighth Karmapa has a striking resonance in the disputes over the identities of the current Paṇchen Lama and the Seventeeth Karmapa.[176]

174. Sangs rgyas dpal grub, fol. 37b (p. 223).

175. Lopez 1998 has coined this term for the Western imaginations of and about Tibet. On Lopez's work and a critique of the again imagined boundaries between a fantasized and real Tibet, see also Germano 2005.

176. The Chinese Communist Party tried to influence the choice of the succession of the Tenth Paṇ chen Chos kyi rgyal mtshan of the dGe lugs school, who passed away 1989. A boy recognized in 1995 by the Fourteenth Dalai Lama as Eleventh Paṇ chen Bla ma called Ge 'dun Chos kyi nyi ma disappeared and instead the Chinese government installed a boy named rGyal mtshan nor bu. The topic remains a human rights issue; see Hinton 2001. After the Sixteenth Karma pa, Rang byung rig pa'i rdo rje (1924–81) passed away, a dispute about his successor emerged in the late 1990s. Two candidates currently carry the title of the Seventeenth Karma pa: mTha' yas rdo rje, approved of by the Fourteenth Zhwa dmar pa (see Curren 2005) and 'O rgyan 'phrin las having the support of the Tibetan Government-in-Exile in the person of the Fourteenth Dalai Lama and the current Si tu Rin po che (see Terhune [2004]). For the reception of these issues in two encyclopedias of Buddhism, see the entries of Quintman 2004 and Powers 2007.

As Tibetan Buddhism is received and transformed in the West, the cross-cultural encounter adds further dimensions to the issue: Tibetan society in exile has considerably changed the balances of power and the spheres of influence of various *bla brang*. And although the concept of reincarnation and transmigration of souls has existed in the West, the cultural role of the reincarnate lama is not a familiar model in Europe and the Americas.[177] Will the long intertwinement of religion and politics (*chos srid zung 'brel*) come to an end in Tibetan Buddhism?

177. See Zander 1999 for the history of reincarnation ideas in Europe. See Samuel 2005: 288–817 and 317–45 on thoughts about Tibetan Buddhism in the West and the role of lamas in this process; see also Germano 2005.

General Abbreviations

HR	*History of Religion*
IATS	International Association of Tibetan Studies
JAOS	*Journal of the American Oriental Society*
JIABS	*Journal of the International Association of Buddhist Studies*
JIATS	*Journal of the International Association of Tibetan Studies*
JIP	*Journal of Indian Philosophy*
JTS	*Journal of the Tibet Society*
LTWA	Library of Tibetan Works and Archives
NGMPP	Nepal German Manuscript Preservation Project
PIATS	*Proceedings of the Seminar of the International Association of Tibetan Studies*

Bibliography

Primary Sources in Tibetan Language

A khu A khra dGe slong Byang chub bzang po (b. sixteenth century). *bDe mchog mkha' 'gro snyan rgyud (Ras chung snyan rgyud): A Manuscript Collection of Orally Transmitted Precepts Focusing upon the Tutelaries Cakrasamvara and Vajravārāhī, Representing the Yig cha compiled by Byang chub bzang po*. 2 vols. New Delhi, 1973. (Reproduced from a rare manuscript in the library of Apho Rinpoche.)

———. [A khu A khra =] *rGyal ba kun gyi dbang po dpal ldan karma pa mi bskyod rdo rje'i zhabs kyi dgung lo bdun phan gyi rnam par thar pa nor bu'i phreng ba*. In *Collected Works of the Eighth Karmapa*, vol. 1, pp. 33–106, 37 fols.

[*'Bras spungs dkar chag*.] 'Bras spungs dPal brtsegs Bod yig dpe rnying zhib 'jug khang (eds). *'Bras spungs dgon du bzhugs su gsol ba'i dpe rnying dkar chag / dpal brtsegs bod yig dpe rnying zhib 'jug khang nas bsgrigs*. 2 vols. Beijing: Mi rigs dpe skrung khang, 2005.

Collected Works of the Eighth Karmapa. Mi bskyod rdo rje, Karma pa VIII (1507–54). *dPal rgyal ba karma pa sku 'phreng brgyad pa mi bskyod rdo rje'i gsung 'bum*. 26 vols. Lhasa: Dpal brtsegs Bod yig Dpe rnying zhib 'jug khang, 2000–2004. Phyogs bsgrigs theng dang po [First ed.]. (Printed from blocks kept at 'Bras spungs dGa' ldan Pho brang and Khams dPal spungs dgon, later reset electronically in Tibet. Distributed by the Tsadra Foundation, New York.)

dKon mchog 'bangs, Zhwa dmar V (1525–83). [*dKar chag* =] *rGyal ba thams cad kyi ye shes kyi sku rnam pa thams cad pa'i thugs can karma pa mi bskyod rdo rje bzhad pa'i gsung 'bum gyi dkar chag*. In *Collected Works of the Eighth Karmapa*, vol. 1, pp. 1–28, 14 fols.

———. *Mi bsykod rdo rje rnam thar tshig btsad ma*. In dKon mchog 'bangs, *Selected*

Writings on Vajrayāna Buddhist Practice: Volume II, pp. 119–28. Gangtok, Sikkim: Dzongsar Chhentse Labrang, Palace Monastery, 1979.

———. *rGyal ba mi bskyod rdo rje'i rnam thar la bstod pa zol med mes pa 'dren byed ldeb*. In dKon mchog 'bangs, *Selected Writings on Vajrayana Buddhist Practice: Volume II*, pp. 89–110. Gangtok, Sikkim: Dzongar Chhentse Labrang, Palace Monastery, 1979.

dPa' bo gTsug lag phreng ba (1504–66). *Chos kyi rje 'jig rten dbang po dpal karma pa brgyad pa'i zhabs kyi mtshan rab tu brjod pa rje nyid kyis mdzad pa*. In *Collected Works of the Eighth Karmapa*, vol. 1, pp. 388–92, 3 fols.

———. [*mKhas pa'i dga' ston.*] *Chos 'byung mkhas pa'i dga' ston*. 2 vols. Beijing: Mi rigs dpe skrun khang, 1986.

Grags pa 'byung gnas and Blo bzang mkhas grub. *Gangs can mkhas grub rim byon ming mdzod*. [Lan chou:] Kang su'u mi rigs dpe skrun khang, 1992.

[*Kaṃ tshang*]. See Si tu Paṇ chen Chos kyi 'byung gnas and'Be lo Tshe dbang kun khyab.

Karma Nges don bstan rgyas (nineteenth century). *Chos rje karma pa sku 'phreng rim byon gyi rnam thar mdor bsdus dpag bsam khri shing*. P. O. Ochghat, Tibetan Bonpo Monastic Center: New Thobgyal, 1973.

Karma 'phrin las pa I, Phyogs las rnam rgyal (1456–1539). *Dri lan gyi phreng ba rnams*. In *The Songs of Esoteric Practice (Mgur) and Replies to Doctrinal Questions (Dris-lan) of Karma-'phrin-las-pa*, pp. 87–223. New Delhi: Ngawang Topgay, 1975. (Reproduced from Prints of the 1539 Rin chen ri bo Blocks.)

———. *mGur kyi 'phreng ba rnams*. In *The Songs of Esoteric Practice (Mgur) and Replies to Doctrinal Questions (Dris-lan) of Karma-'phrin-las-pa*, pp. 1–86. New Delhi: Ngawang Topgay, 1975. (Reproduced from Prints of the 1539 Rin chen ri bo Blocks.)

Khetsun Sangpo [mKhas btsun bzang po] (ed.). *Biographical Dictionary of Tibet and Tibetan Buddhism*. 12 vols. Dharamsala: Library of Tibetan Works and Archives, 1979.

lDan ma 'Jam dbyangs tshul khrims. *dPal karma pa sku phreng rim byon gyi mdzad rnam*. [Lan chou:] Kan su'u mi rigs dpe skrun khang, 1997.

Mi bskyod rdo rje, Karma pa VIII (1507–54). *dBu ma la 'jug pa'i rnam bshad dpal ldan dus gsum mkhyen pa'i zhal lung dwags brgyud grub pa'i shing rta*. In *Collected Works of the Eighth Karmapa*, vol. 14, pp. 1–975, 487 fols.

———. *dPal rdzogs pa'i sangs rgyas karma pa mi bskyod rdo rje'i zhabs kyis skyob pa 'jig rten gsum gyi mgon po'i dbon mkhyen rab kyi dbang phyug rin chen rnam rgyal chos kyi grags pa la dam pa'i chos dgongs gcig pa'i bshad pa dgyes par gnang ba'i gsung rgyun dang por slob ma dag gis reg zig tu byas shing phyis rgyal ba thams cad mkhyen pa nyid kyi zhal lung dri ma dang bral ba bdud rtsi'i 'dod ster grub pa'i dpyid thig gzhon nu bde ba'i lang tshor gar dgu'i sgeg pa kun mkhyen rab tu 'bar ba'i phung po bskal me[d?] 'jigs byed ces bya ba tshoms dang po gzhan 'grel du mdzad pa rnams*. In *Collected Works of the Eighth Karmapa*, vol. 4, pp. 885–1139, 128 fols. (see also: NGMPP, Reel No. E 2944/2, 101 fols, manuscript, dBu med.)

———. *gDul bya phyi ma la gdams pa'i rnam par thar pa'o*. In *Collected Works of the Eighth Karmapa*, vol. 3, pp. 519–49, 16 fols.

———. *Karma pa mi bskyod rdo rje'i rnam thar legs spyad mar grags pa rje nyid kyis mdzad pa*. In *Collected Works of the Eighth Karmapa*, vol. 1, pp. 107–14, 4 fols.

———. *Karma pa mi bskyod rdo rje'i rnam thar la bslab pa'i khrid*. In *Collected Works of the Eighth Karmapa*, vol. 1, pp. 115–49, 18 fols.

———. [*Mi bskyod rdo rje'i spyad pa'i rabs.*] *Byang phyogs 'di na karma pa / / rim par byon las bdun pa rang byung ni / / kun mkhyen chos rje'i slob mar gyur 'ga' yi / / bka' 'bangs mi bskyod rdo rje'i spyad pa'i rabs*. In *Collected Works of the Eighth Karmapa*, vol. 1, pp. 350–87, 19 fols.

———. *Mon sha 'ug stag sgo dom tshang ngur mo rong du gsungs pa'i mgur*. In *Collected Works of the Eighth Karmapa*, vol. 2, pp. 592–97.

———. *Nyid bstod kyi rang 'grel*. In *Collected Works of the Eighth Karmapa*, vol. 1, pp. 430–38, 5 fols.

———. *Pha mi bskyod rdo rje'i rnam thar rje nyid kyis rnam thos kyi ri bor mdzad pa*. In *Collected Works of the Eighth Karmapa*, vol. 1, pp. 331–43, 7 fols.

———. *Rang la nges pa'i tshad ma zhes bya ba'i 'grel pa gnas lugs bdud rtsi'i nyin khu*. In *Collected Works of the Eighth Karmapa*, vol. 15, pp. 1039–58, 10 fols.

———. *rGya gar gyi phyag chen sngon byung dwags brgyud kyi sgros kyis rgyan pa*. In *Collected Works of the Eighth Karmapa*, vol. 15, pp. 1059–71, 7 fols.

———. *rGyal ba karma pa mi bskyod rdo rje'i rnam thar bdag tshul bcu gnyis*. In *Collected Works of the Eighth Karmapa*, vol. 1, pp. 488–507, 10 fols.

———. *rJe mi bskyod rdo rje'i 'phral gyi rnam thar tshigs su bcad pa nyer bdun pa rje nyid kyis mdzad pa*. In *Collected Works of the Eighth Karmapa*, vol. 1, pp. 344–49, 3 fols.

———. *Slob dpon dbyangs can bzang pos nye bar stsal ba'i dril bu rim pa lnga pa'i khrid*. In *Collected Works of the Eighth Karmapa*, vol. 20, pp. 776–982, 103 fols.

Mi nyag mgon po. *Gangs can mkhas dbang rim byon gyi rnam thar mdor bsdus*. [Beijing:] Khrung go'i bod kyi shes rig dpe skrun khang, 1999.

Mi rigs dpe mdzod khang (ed.). *Bod gangs can gyi grub mtha' ris med kyi mkhas dbang brgya dang brgyad cu lhag gi gsung 'bum so so'i dkar chag phyogs gcig tu sgrigs pa shes bya'i gter mdzod*. Sichuan: Si khron mi rigs dpe skrun khang, 1984.

Ngag dbang rnam rgyal (1571–1626). *sTag lung chos 'byung*. Gangs can rig mdzod 22. Lhasa: Bod ljongs bod yig dpe rnying dpe skrun khang, 1992.

Paṇ chen bSod nams grags pa. *Deb ther dmar po gsar ma*. Chengdu: Si khron mi rigs dpe skrun khang, 1989.

rGyal mtshan. *Kam tshang yab sras dang spal spungs dgon pa*. Sichuan: Si khron mi rigs dpe skrun khang, 1997.

rTa tshag Tshe dbang rgyal (fifteenth century). *Dam pa'i chos kyi byung ba'i legs bshad lho rong chos 'byung ngam rta tshag chos 'byung zhes rtsom pa'i yul ming du chags pa'i ngo mtshar zhing dkon pa'i dpe khyad par can*. Gangs can rig mdzod 26. Lhasa: Bod ljongs bod yig dpe rnying dpe skrun khang, 1994.

Sangs rgyas dpal grub (sixteenth century). *rGyal ba spyan ras gzigs dbang brgyad pa'i rnam thar legs spyad ma'i don 'grel gsal ba'i sgron me*. In *Collected Works of the Eighth Karmapa*, vol. 1, pp. 150–329, 90 fols.

Si tu Paṇ chen Chos kyi 'byung gnas (1699/1700–1774) and 'Be lo Tshe dbang kun khyab. *bKa' brgyud gser phreng rnam thar zla ba chu sel gyi phreng ba smad cha* (*The Golden Garland of Kagyü Biographies, vol. 2*). Sarnath: Vajra Vidya Institute Library, 2004. (Reprint of *sGrub brgyud karma kaṃ tshang brgyud pa rnam thar rin po che'i rnam par thar pa rab 'byams nor bu zla ba chu shel gyi phreng ba*.)

———. *sGrub brgyud karma kaṃ tshang brgyud pa rin po che'i rnam par thar pa rab 'byams nor bu zla ba chu sel gyi phreng ba*. New Delhi: D. Gyaltsan und Kesang Legshay, 1972. (Reproduced from a print of dPal spungs edition belonging to Nam mkha' rdo rje of Nang chen.)

Zhang Yisun et al. (eds). [Zhang Yisun =] *Bod rgya tshig mdzod chen mo*. 2 vols. Beijing: Mi rigs dpe skrun khang, 1985.

Secondary Literature

Aris, Michael 1979. *Bhutan: The Early History of an Himalayan Kingdom*. Warminster: Aris and Phillips.

——— 1988. *Hidden Treasures and Secret Lives: A Study of Pemalingpa (1450–1521) and the Sixth Dalai Lama (1683–1706)*. New Delhi: Motilal.

Bal, Mieke 1997. *Narratology: Introduction to the Theory of Narrative*. Toronto, Buffalo, London: University of Toronto Press.

Braitstein, Lara 2004. *Saraha's Adamantine Songs: Texts, Contexts, Translations and Traditions of the Great Seal*. PhD Thesis, McGill University Montreal

Brunnhölzl, Karl 2004. *The Center of the Sunlit Sky: Madhyamaka in the Kagyü Tradition*. Ithaca, NY: Snow Lion Publications.

Caumanns, Volker 2006. "gSer-mdog Paṇ-chen Shākya-mchog-ldan (1428–1507): Erschließung einiger wichtiger Quellen zu seinem Leben und Gesamtwerk unter besonderer Berücksichtigung seiner scholastischen Ausbildung." Master's thesis, University of Hamburg.

Curren, Erik D. 2005. *Buddha's Not Smiling: Uncovering Corruption at the Heart of Tibetan Buddhism Today*. Lexington: Alaya Press.

Dargyay, Eva K. 1994. "Srong bstan sgam po of Tibet: Bodhisattva and King." In *Monks and Magicians: Religious Biographies in Asia*, ed. by P. Granoff and K. Shinhohara, pp. 99–119. Delhi: Motilal.

Davidson, Ronald M. 2004. *Tibetan Renaissance: Tantric Buddhism in the Rebirth of Tibetan Culture*. New York: Columbia University Press.

Dorje, Gyurme 1999. *Tibet Handbook: With Bhutan*. Bath: Footprint Handbooks.

Douglas, Nik and Meryl White 1976. *Karmapa: The Black Hat Lama of Tibet*. London: Luzac & Company.

Dreyfus, Georges 2005. "Where do Commentarial Schools come from? Reflections on the History of Tibetan Scholasticism." *JIABS* 28.2: 273–99.

Dubois, Jacques and Jean-Loup Lemaitre 1993. *Sources et méthodes de l'hagiographie médiévale*. Paris: Editions du Cerf.

Ehrhard, Franz-Karl 2002a. *The Life and Travels of Lo-chen Bsod-nams rgya-mtsho*. Lumbini: Lumbini International Research Institute.

——— 2002b. *A Buddhist Correspondence: The Letters of Lo-chen Bsod-nams rgya-mtsho*. Lumbini: Lumbini International Research Institute.

——— 2004. "Spiritual Relationships between Rulers and Preceptors: The Three Journeys of Vanaratna (1384–1468) to Tibet." In *The Relationship Between Religion and State (chos srid zung 'brel) in Traditional Tibet: Proceedings of a Seminar held in Lumbini, Nepal, March 2000*, ed. by Christoph Cüppers, pp. 245–65. Lumbini: Lumbini International Research Institute.

——— 2006. "gNas Rab-'byams-pa Byams-pa phun-tshogs (1503–1581) and His Contribution to Buddhist Block Printing in Tibet." Unpublished manuscript of the IATS Conference, Bonn, 2006.

——— (forthcoming). "The Madman of dBus and His Relationships with Tibetan Rulers of the 15th and 16th Centuries."

Elverskog, Johan 2007. "An Early Seventeenth Century Tibeto-Mongolian Ceremonial Staff." *JIATS* 3: 1–24. www.thdl.org?id=T3127.

Everding, Karl-Heinz 2002. "The Mongol States and their Struggle for Dominance over Tibet in the 13th Century." In *Tibet, Past and Present, PIATS 2000*, ed. by Henk Blezer et al., pp. 109–29. Leiden: Brill's Tibetan Studies Library.

Faber, Erwin and Immanuel Geiss 1992. *Arbeitsbuch zum Geschichtsstudium*. Heidelberg, Wiesbaden: Quelle and Meyer.

Ferrari, Alfonsa 1958. *mKhyen rtse's Guide to the Holy Places of Central Tibet*. Serie Orientale Roma 16. Rome: Istituto Italiano per il Medeo ed Estremo Oriente.

Germano, David 2005. "Encountering Tibet: The Ethics, Soteriology, and Creativity of Cross-Cultural Interpretation." *Journal of the Amercian Academy of Religion* 69: 165–82.

Goldstein, Melvyn C. 1973. "The Circulation of Estates in Tibet: Reincarnation, Land and Politics." *The Journal of Asian Studies* 32.3: 445–55.

Gyatso, Janet 1998. *Apparitions of the Self: The Secret Autobiography of a Tibetan Visionary; A Translation and Study of Jigme Lingpa's Dancing Moon in the Water and the Ḍākki's Grand Secret-Talk*. Princeton: Princeton University Press.

Head, Thomas, ed. 2000. *Medieval Hagiography: An Anthology*. New York: Garland Publications.

Henning, Edward 2007. *Kālacakra and the Tibetan Calendar*. New York: American Institute of Buddhist Studies/Columbia University Press.

Hinton, Isabel 2001. *The Search for the Panchen Lama*. New York: W. W. Norton & Company.

Jackson, David P. 1989. *The Early Abbots of 'Phan-po Na-lendra: The Vicissitudes of a Great Tibetan Monastery in the 15th Century*. Wiener Studien zur Tibetologie und Buddhismuskunde 23. Wien: Universität Wien.

——— 1996. *A History of Tibetan Painting: The Great Tibetan Painters and Their*

Traditions. Philosophisch-historische Klasse Denkschriften 242, Beiträge zur Kultur- und Geistesgeschichte Asiens 15. Wien: Österreichische Akademie der Wissenschaften.

Kapstein, Matthew T. 1980. "The Shangs-pa bKa'-brgyud: An Unknown Tradition of Tibetan Buddhism." In *Tibetan Studies in Honour of Hugh Richardson*, ed. by Michael Aris and Aung San Suu Kyi, pp. 138–44. Warminster: Aris and Philips.

——— 1996. "*gDams ngag*: Tibetan Technologies of the Self." In *Tibetan Literature: Studies in Genre*, ed. by José Ignacio Cabézon and Roger R. Jackson, pp. 275–90. Ithaca, NY: Snow Lion Publications.

——— 2000. *The Tibetan Assimilation of Buddhism: Conversion, Contestation and Memory*. Oxford, New York: Oxford University Press.

——— 2006. *The Tibetans*. Malden, Oxford, Carlton: Blackwell.

Kaschewsky, Rudolf 1971. *Das Leben des lamaistischen Heiligen Tsongkhapa Blo-bzaṅ grags-pa (1357–1419)*. Asiatische Forschungen 32, parts 1 and 2. Wiesbaden: Otto Harrossowitz.

Kessler, Peter 1983. *Die historischen Königreiche Ling (Gling) und Derge (sDe dge)*. Laufende Arbeiten zu einem Ethnohistorischen Atlas Tibets; Lieferung 40,1. Rikon: Tibet Institut.

Kieschnick, John 1997. *The Eminent Monk: Buddhist Ideals in Medieval Chinese Hagiography*. Studies in East Asian Buddhism 10. Honolulu: University of Hawaii Press, Kuroda Institute.

Kögler, Annette 2004. "sMyon-pa: Verrückte Heilige in Tibet. Theoretische Diskussion und Fallstudien am Beispiel von 'Bri-gung A-mgon Rin-po-che und weiterer monastischer Exzentriker." Master's thesis, University of Bonn.

Krupa, Jowita 1999. "The Life and Works of Glo-bo mKhan-chen (1456–1532)." Master's thesis, University of Hamburg.

van der Kuijp, Leonard W. J. 1987. "The Monastery of Gsang-phu ne'u thog and Its Abbatial Succession from ca. 1073 to 1250." *Berliner Indologische Studien* 3: 103–29.

——— 1991. "On the Life and Political Career of Ta'i-si-tu Byang-chub rgyal-mtshan (1302–?1364)." In *Tibetan History and Language: Studies Dedicated to Uray Géza on his Seventieth Birthday*, ed. by Ernst Steinkellner, pp. 277–328. Wien: Arbeitskreis für Tibetische und Buddhistishe Studien Universität Wien.

——— 1994. "Fourteenth Century Tibetan Cultural History I: Ta'i-si-tu Byang-chub rgyal-mtshan as a Man of Religion." *Indo-Iranian Journal* 37: 139–49.

——— 1996. "Tibetan Historiography." In *Tibetan Literature: Studies in Genre*, ed. by José Ignacio Cabézon and Roger R. Jackson, pp. 39–57. Ithaca, NY: Snow Lion Publications.

——— 2001. "On the Fifteenth Century Lho rong chos 'byung by Rta tshag Tshe dbang rgyal and Its Importance for Tibetan Political and Religious History." *Lungta* 14: 57–76.

——— 2005. "Die Dalai Lamas von Tibet und die Ursprünge der Lama-Wiedergeburten." In *Die Dalai Lamas: Tibets Reinkarnationen des Bodhi-*

sattva Avalokiteśvara, ed. by Martin Brauen, pp. 14–31. Stuttgart: Arnoldsche Verlagsbuchhandlung.

Lopez Jr., Donald S. 1998. *Prisoners of Shangri-La.* Chicago: University of Chicago Press.

Martin, Dan 1984. Review of Tsang Nyön Heruka (= gTsang smyon He ru ka, 1452–1507); Nālandā Translation Comittee (trans.) 1982, *The Life of Marpa the Translator* (Boulder: Prajña Press). *The Journal of the Tibet Society* 4: 83–91.

Marwick, Arthur 2001. *The New Nature of History: Knowledge, Evidence, Language.* Hampshire: Palgrave.

Monier-Williams, Monier 1996. *Sanskrit-English Dictionary: Etymologically and Philologically Arranged.* Delhi: Motilal Banarsidass. (First ed. Oxford, 1872.)

Mullin, Glenn 1994. *Mystical Verses of a Mad Dalai Lama.* Wheaton: The Theosophical Publishing House.

Nālandā Translation Commitee, trans.; Mi-bskyod rdo rje, Karmapa VIII et al., ed. 1980. *The Rain of Wisdom: The Essence of the Ocean of the True Meaning.* Boulder: Shambhala.

Nesterenko, Michel, ed. 1992. *The Karmapa Papers.* Paris.

Ohnuma, Reiko 1998. "The Gift of the Body and the Gift of Dharma." *HR* 37.4: 333–59.

Petech, Luciano 1990. *Central Tibet and the Mongols: The Yüan-Sa-skya Period of Tibetan History.* Rome: Istituto Italiano per il Medeo ed Estremo Oriente.

——— "The Dalai-Lamas and Regents of Tibet." In *The History of Tibet: Volume II*, ed. by Alex McKay, pp. 567–83. London, New York: RoutledgeCurzon. (First published: *T'oung Pao* XLVII [1959]: 368–94.)

Powers, John 2007. "Karmapas, the Gyelwas." In *Encyclopedia of Buddhism,* ed. by Damien Keown and Charles Prebisch, pp. 439–440. London, New York: Routledge.

Pritchard, Allan 2005. *English Biography in the Seventeenth Century: A Critical Survey.* Toronto: University of Toronto Press.

Quintman, Andrew 2004. "Karma pa." In *Encyclopedia of Buddhism*, ed. by Robert E. Buswell, pp. 417–19. New York: Macmillan Reference USA.

Rheingans, Jim 2004. "Das Leben und Werk des ersten Karma 'phrin las pa: Ein bedeutender Vertreter der bKa' brgyud und Sa syka Traditionen Tibets." Master's thesis, University of Hamburg.

——— 2008. "The Eighth Karmapa's Life and His Interpretation of the Great Seal." PhD diss., University of the West of England, Bristol.

——— (forthcoming). "Great Seal Dialogues in a Spiritual Biography about Mi bskyod rdo rje (1507–1554)." In *Yogācāra Models of Truth or Reality in Indo-Tibetan Buddhism*, ed. by Klaus-Dieter Mathes. *Journal of the International Association for Buddhist Studies* special volume. Boston: Wisdom Publications.

Richardson, Hugh 1980. "The Karma-pa Sect: A Historical Note." In *Tibetan Studies in Honour of Hugh Richardson*, ed. by Michael Aris and Aung San Suu Kyi, pp. 337–78. Warminster: Aris and Philips. (Reprint of *Journal of the Royal Asiatic Society* 1959, parts 1 and 2.)

——— 2003. "The Political Role of the Four Sects in Tibetan History." In *The History of Tibet: Volume II*, ed. by Alex McKay, pp. 165–74. London, New York: RoutledgeCurzon. (Reprint of *Tibetan Review* 11.9 1976: 18–23.)

Roberts, Peter Alan 2007. *The Biographies of Rechungpa: The Evolution of a Tibetan Hagiography*. London, New York: Routledge.

Robinson, James Burnell 1996. "The Lives of Indian Buddhist Saints: Biography, Hagiography and Myth." In *Tibetan Literature: Studies in Genre*, ed. by José Ignacio Cabézon and Roger R. Jackson, pp. 57–70. Ithaca, NY: Snow Lion Publications.

Roerich, George N. 1996. *The Blue Annals*. Delhi: Motilal Barnasidass. (First published in 2 vols., Calcutta: Royal Asiatic Society of Bengal, 1949–53.)

Roloff, Carola 2003. "Red mda' pa (1349–1412) und Tsong kha pa (1357–1419): Zwei zentrale Figuren des tibetischen Buddhismus und ihr wechselseitiges Lehrer-Schüler-Verhältnis." Master's thesis, University of Hamburg.

Ruegg, David Seyfort 1966. *The Life of Bu ston Rin po che: With the Tibetan Text of the Bu ston rNam thar.* Serie Orientale Roma 28. Rome: Istituto Italiano per il Medeo ed Estremo Oriente.

——— 1988. "A Karma bKa' brgyud Work on the Lineages and Traditions of the Indo-Tibetan dBu ma (Madhyamaka)." In *Orientalia Iosephi Tucci Memoriae Dicata*, ed. by G. Gnoli and L. Lanciotti, pp. 1249–80. Serie Orientale Roma LVI, 3. Rome: Istituto Italiano per il Medeo ed Estremo Oriente.

——— 1991. "*Mchod yon, yon mchod* and *mchod gnas/yon gnas*: On the Historiography and Semantics of a Tibetan Religio-Social and Religio-Political Concept." In *Tibetan History and Language: Studies Dedicated to Uray Géza on his Seventieth Birthday*, ed. by Ernst Steinkellner, pp. 441–53. Wien: Arbeitskreis für Tibetische und Buddhistische Studien Universität Wien.

——— 2004. "The Indian and the Indic in Tibetan Cultural History, and Tsong kha pa's Achievement as a Scholar and Thinker: An Essay on the Concept of Buddhism in Tibet and Tibetan Buddhism." *JIP* 32.4: 321–43.

Samuel, Geoffrey 1993. *Civilized Shamans: Buddhism in Tibetan Societies*. Washington, London: Smithsonian Institute Press.

——— 2005. *Tantric Revisionings: New Understandings of Tibetan Buddhism and Indian Religion*. Hants, UK: Ashgate.

Schaeffer, Kurtis Rice 1995. "The Enlightened Heart of Buddhahood: A Study and Translation of the Third Karma pa Rang byung rdo rje's Work on Tathāgatagarbha, the *bDe bzhin gshegs pa'i rnying po gtan la dbab pa*." Master's thesis, University of Washington.

Scherer, Burkhard 2006. *Mythos, Katalog und Prophezeiung*. Palingenesia 87. Wiesbaden: Franz Steiner Verlag.

Schmitz, Thomas A. 2002. *Literaturtheorie und antike Texte*. Darmstadt: Wissenschaftliche Buchgesellschaft.

Schuh, Dieter 1973. *Untersuchungen zur Geschichte der tibetischen Kalenderrechnung*. Verzeichnis der Orientalischen Handschriften in Deutschland, Supplement Band 16. Wiesbaden: Franz Steiner Verlag.

——— 1976. "Wie ist die Einladung des fünften Karma-pa an den chinesischen Kaiserhof als Fortführung der Tibetpolitik der Mongolen-Khane zu verstehen." In *Altaica Collecta*, ed. by Walther Heissig, pp. 209–44. Wiesbaden: Otto Harrassowitz.

——— 1977. *Erlasse und Sendschreiben mongolischer Herrscher für tibetische Geistliche*. St. Augustin: VGH-Wissenschaftsverlag.

——— 1986. "Tibet unter der Mongolenherrschaft." In *Die Mongolen*, ed. by Michael Weiers. Darmstadt: Wissenschaftliche Buchgesellschaft.

Schwieger, Peter, ed. 1985. *Die Werksammlungen Kun-tu bzaṅ-po'i dgoṅs-pa zaṅ-thal, Ka-dag raṅ-byu raṅ-śar and mKha'-'gro gsaṅ-ba ye-śes-kyi-rgyud*. Tibetische Handschriften und Blockdrucke 9. Wiesbaden: Franz Steiner Verlag.

——— 1996. "The Lineage of the Noblehouse of Ga-zi in East Tibet." *Kailash—A Journal of Himalayan Studies* 18.3–4: 115–32.

——— (forthcoming). "The Long Arm of the 5th Dalai Lama: Influence and Power of the 5th Dalai Lama in Southeast Tibet." *Buddhist Himalaya: Studies in Religion, History and Culture*, The Golden Jubilee Conference of the Namgyal Institute of Tibetology, Gangtok, Sikkim, India (1–5 October 2008), organized by Anna Balikci-Denjongpa and Alex McKay.

Shakabpa, Tsepon 1967. *Tibet: A Political History*. New Haven: Yale University Press.

Smith, E. Gene 2001. *Among Tibetan Texts: History and Literature of the Himalayan Plateau*. Studies in Indian and Tibetan Buddhism. Boston: Wisdom Publications.

Snellgrove, David and Hugh Richardson 1968. *A Cultural History of Tibet*. London: Weidenfeld and Nicolson.

Sobisch, Jan-Ulrich 2002. *Three-Vow Theories in Tibetan Buddhism: A Comparative Study of Major Traditions from the Twelfth through the Nineteenth Centuries*. Contributions to Tibetan Studies 1. Wiesbaden: Dr. Ludwig Reichert Verlag.

——— 2003. "The 'Records of Teachings Received' in the Collected Works of A mes Zhabs: An Untapped Source for the Study of Sa skya pa Biographies." In *Religion and Secular Culture in Tibet: Vol. 2*, ed. by Henk Blezer, pp. 59–77. Leiden: Brill's Tibetan Studies Library.

Sperling, Elliot 1980. "The 5th Karmapa and Some Aspects of the Sino-Tibetan Relationship between Tibet and the Early Ming." In *Tibetan Studies in Honour of Hugh Richardson*, ed. by Michael Aris and Aung San Suu Kyi, pp. 280–89. Warminster: Aris and Philips.

——— 2004. "Karmapa Rol-pa'i rdo-rje and the Re-Establishment of Karma-pa Political Influence in the 14th Century." In *The Relationship Between Religion and State (chos srid zung 'brel) in Traditional Tibet: Proceedings of a Seminar*

Held in Lumbini, Nepal, March 2000, ed. by Christoph Cüppers, pp. 229–43. ·Lumbini: Lumbini International Research Institute.

Stein, Rolf A. 1972. *Tibetan Civilization.* London: Faber and Faber.

Sumegi, Angela 2008. *Dreamworlds of Shamanism and Tibetan Buddhism: The Third Place*. Albany: SUNY.

Tambiah, Stanley J. 1984. *The Buddhist Saints of the Forest and the Cult of Amulets: A Study in Charisma, Hagiography, Sectarianism, and Millennial Buddhism.* Cambridge: Cambridge University Press.

Templeman, David 2003. "The Mirror of Life: The Structure of a 16th Century Tibetan Hagiography." In *Religion and Biography in China and Tibet*, ed. by Benjamin Penny, pp. 132–47. London: Curzon.

Terhune, Lea 2004. *Karmapa: The Politics of Reincarnation.* Boston: Wisdom Publications.

Thaye, Jampa 1990. *A Garland of Gold: The Early Kagyü Masters in India and Tibet.* Bristol: Ganesha Press.

Thinley, Rinpoche Karma 1980. *The History of the Sixteen Karmapas of Tibet*. Boulder: Prajña Press.

——— 1997. *The History of the First Karma Thinleypa*. Bristol: Ganesha Press.

Tiso, Francis Vincent 1989. "A Study of the Buddhist Saint in Relation to the Biographical Tradition of Milarepa." PhD diss., Columbia University.

Tsomo, Karma Lekshe 2004. "Prātimokṣa." In *Encyclopedia of Buddhism*, ed. by Robert E. Buswell, pp. 667–69. New York: Macmillan Reference USA.

Tucci, Giuseppe 1949. *Tibetan Painted Scrolls.* Rome: Libreria dello Stato.

——— 1971. *Deb ther dmar po gsar ma: Tibetan Chronicles.* Serie Orientale Roma 24. Rome: Istituto Italiano per il Medeo ed Estremo Oriente.

——— 1980. *The Religions of Tibet.* Berkeley: University of California Press.

Verhufen, Gregor 1995. "Die Biographien des Achten Karmapa Mi bskyod rdo rje und seines Lehrers Sangs rgyas mnyan pa: Ein Beitrag zur Geschichte der Karma bKa'-brgyud-pa-Schulrichtung des tibetischen Buddhismus." Master's thesis, University of Bonn.

Vitali, Roberto 1996. *The Kingdoms Gu-ge Pu-hrang: According to mNga'-ris-rgyal-rabs by Gu-ge-mkhan-chen Ngag-dbang-grags-pa.* London: Serindia.

Vogel, Claus 1964. "On Tibetan Chronology." *Central Asiatic Journal* 9.3: 224–38.

Vostrikov, A. L. 1994. *Tibetan Historical Literature.* Surrey: Curzon Press. (Reprint of the first English ed. Calcutta, 1970.)

Wayman, Alex 1967. "Significance of Dreams in India and Tibet." *HR* 7.1: 1–12.

——— 1978. *Calming the Mind and Discerning the Real: Buddhist Meditation and the Middle View; From the Lam rim chen mo of Tsong-kha-pa.* New York: Columbia University Press.

Williams, Paul 1983. "A Note on Some Aspects of Mi bskyod rdo rje's Critique of dGe lugs pa Madhyamaka." *JIP* 11: 125–45.

Willis, Janice 1995. *Enlightened Beings: Life Stories from the Ganden Oral Tradition.* Boston: Wisdom Publications.

Wylie, Turell V. 1978. "Reincarnation: A Political Innovation in Tibetan Buddhism." In *Proceedings of the Csoma de Körös Memorial Symposium*, ed. by Lajos Ligeti, pp. 579–586. Bibliotheca Orientalis Hungaricae 23. Budapest: Akademiai Kaido.

——— 2003. "Monastic Patronage in 15th Century Tibet." In *The History of Tibet: Volume II*, ed. by Alex McKay, pp. 483–91. London, New York: RoutledgeCurzon. (First published *Acta Orientalia Academiae Scientiarum Hungaricae* 34.3 1980: 319–28.)

Young, Serenity 1999. *Dreaming in the Lotus: Buddhist Dream Narrative, Imagery, and Practice*. Boston: Wisdom Publications.

Yumiko, Ishihama 2003. "On the Dissemination of the Belief in the Dalai Lama as a Manifestation of the Bodhisattva Avalokitseśvara." In *The History of Tibet: Volume II*, ed. by Alex McKay, pp. 538–53. London, New York: Routledge Curzon. (First published *Acta Asia* 64 [Tokyo 1993]: 38–56.)

Zander, Helmut 1999. *Geschichte der Seelenwanderung in Europa: alternative religiöse Traditionen von der Antike bis heute*. Darmstadt: Wissenschaftliche Buchgesellschaft.

The Good, the Bad, and the Ugly

The Circumscription of Saintly Evil in Tibetan Biography

Charles Ramble

Biography and Evil

The word "biography" in English means two different things. On the one hand, it refers to the series of events that take place in, or in relation to, the life of an individual; and on the other, it denotes the category of literature, or an example of that category, that relates such events. In Tibet, the nearest equivalent to the latter is the literary genre known as *rnam thar* ("namtar"). Corresponding to the Sanskrit term *vimokṣa*, the name derives from the ostensible purpose of such works: to recount an exemplary life that passes through various trials to achieve "complete liberation" (*rnam* [*par*] *thar* [*pa*]). An indication of how widely the generic application of the term has come to prevail over its literal meaning is to be seen in its current use to designate the libretti of the so-called "Tibetan opera" (A lce lha mo).

Namtar vary greatly in the degree to which they are truly biographical in the conventional Western sense. At one end of this spectrum they are regarded by scholars (Tibetan and non-Tibetan alike) as being among the most reliable sources of historical information, especially with respect to the local perspective and the minutiae of daily life that are typically passed over in "official" historical literature. At the other extreme, namtar may be wholly occupied with the inner, visionary world of an individual's spiritual endeavor, or else they may be formulaic to such a degree that they transcend and efface the particularities of their subjects' lives. A hypothetical instance of such a narrative could typically be reduced to the following sequence of literary formulae:

- Miraculous signs before the birth of the subject, such as unseasonable good weather, as well as portentous dreams on the part of the mother.
- Extraordinary neonatal gestures, precocious learning abilities, and a strong attraction to religious figures and institutions.
- A highly charged meeting with the "root lama," who may well have had a prophetic dream about the disciple's advent.
- Stock tribulations through which cumbersome karmic traces are patiently sloughed off.
- Missionary activities in the course of which the hero converts savages in inhospitable regions, causing them to give up hunting and animal sacrifice; he receives honor and reverence from local potentates.
- The hero's passing away, attended by various miraculous phenomena; these include unusual transformations of the body as well as instances of pathetic fallacy, such as clouds of rainbow light and rain of flowers.

In view of the overwhelming preoccupation of such literature with the lives of saints and other spiritual giants, the term namtar is therefore generally glossed as "hagiography." Biographies—especially autobiographies—of secular figures in Tibet are to be found, but these are rather rare, and cannot be said to constitute a well-developed biographical genre. There were no professional writers in Tibetan and it would not have happened, for example, that someone might set out to write the life story of a reprobate or fiend on the grounds of public or literary interest.

This does not mean that Tibetans have never written unkind things about one another, only that sustained critical appraisals are never applied to the protagonists of namtar. This uniformly affirmative feature of the Tibetan case is therefore quite unlike, say, the dual character of biographical writing in Classical Greek, where the laudatory genre of encomium is opposed to the invective's elegant demolition of its chosen subject (Pelling 1990).

A few words of explanation are in order here about the eye-catching term "evil" that features in the title. Above all, this article is *not* an exploration of the nature of evil in Buddhism or in Tibetan society, nor is "evil" meant to correspond to any Tibetan term. I have chosen the word simply because it is the most versatile available in the English language to cover the wide range of behaviors, acts, and characters that I wish to explore in this study. The implications of the term and its referents over an extended historical period and across a wide range of cultures are admirably explored in David Parkin's *The Anthropology of Evil* (Parkin 1985). For comparative perspectives on the subject of evil, the present article will draw principally on articles contained in that collection. Paradoxically, the milder terms "wrongdoing" or "badness," while less immediately dramatic than "evil," trap us, by their narrower semantic range, into implicit value-judgments that the context may not warrant. "Evil" had both a weak and a strong sense. The current predominance of the strong sense—Macfarlane (1985) suggests that it may have originated as late as the Industrial Revolution—has largely overshadowed the more casual tones of the older usage, which does, nevertheless, survive in stock expressions such as "evil necessity" and "lesser of two evils." (This weak sense has been resurrected in some modern sociolects, where it even acquires a complimentary character as a quasi-synomym for "magnificent.")

Following a discussion of the way in which evil is understood in certain African contexts, David Parkin observes that:

> ...we can see at a glance why the English word "evil" has been so useful to social anthropologists. It can refer to extreme fear, death and destruction, but also to lesser misfortunes. It may denote an agent's firm intention to harm, or instead may be seen as originating in an unintended human or non-human condition. Evil agents may be abhorrent, but they may also be admired for their cleverness. While people may be terrified of the deadly effects of the worst kinds of evil, they can at other times joke about it and make humorous parallels. Talk about evil thus ranges over the terrible and serious as well as the playful and creative. (Parkin 1985: 1)

Etymologically, "evil" is related to the word "over" (an association that is more obvious in the corresponding German words *Übel* and *über*), and may originally have had the sense of "excessive" (Pocock 1985). Another band in the spectrum of connotations the word may have is provided by the Hebrew word *ra* that it translates in the King James version of the Bible: "*Ra* meant primarily worthlessness or uselessness, and by extension it came to mean bad, ugly or even sad. Thus *ra* originally meant evil in a weak sense..." (Taylor 1985: 27).

Examples of Invective: Karu Drubwang and Pema Lingpa

Attacks on the character or scholarship of a rival are not confined to any one genre of writing in Tibetan. I shall give just two examples here. The first is an assault by a nineteenth-century Bönpo on the figure of the well-known—perhaps even the best-known—Buddhist saint and poet, Milarepa (1040–1123). The passage appears in the *Gangs ti se dkar chag*, a Bönpo pilgrimage guide to Mt. Kailash that was written in 1844 by Karu Drubwang Tendzin Rinchen (1801–62). To judge from his autobiography, the author was keenly sensitive to what he perceived as the Buddhist appropriation of sites that had originally been associated with Bön. The most widely read biography of Milarepa, compiled by Tsangnyön Heruka (1452–1507) contains a section in which the hero of the work engages a Bönpo named Naro Bönchung in a series of magical contests. The issue at stake is the ownership of Mt. Kailash itself, hitherto the territory of the Bön religion. The series of engagements—each of which is won by Milarepa—culminates in the fall and humiliation of Naro and his relegation to a nearby minor mountain. Karu's dismissal of these stories is not limited to a scornful rejection of the historicity of the conflicts—which he catalogues and dismisses as "a small part of a fabricated, revisionist account" (*Gangs ti se dkar chag*: 92)—but extends to the person of Milarepa himself:

> Ordinary Buddhists say that this is a place that was won by that man called Milarepa, and this is what they preach to credulous people. For a start, [Tise] appeared at the origin of this world age—Milarepa certainly did not create it; and later in the good days, at the time when the Victorious Shen[rab] was promulgating his teachings and bestowing his blessings, even the name "Milarepa" was not around; and in a still later age, when the senior disciples were visiting the holy place and knowledge-holding yogis were meditating there, at the time when the lands of the eighteen

> royal lines of Shangshung were being founded, there was no one called Milarepa... (ibid.: 99)[1]

This passage is followed by a contemptuous summary of his life story and a stinging critique of the insipidity of his celebrated songs:

> He was born in Tsalung, in Gungthang, to a father named Milay Shegyal and a mother named Nyangtsa Kargyenma, and he was called Milarepa. Early in his life he had a falling out with his neighbors, and killed around thirty people and horses by means of a magic spell. In remorse, he wandered about Tibet until he met someone called Uncle Marpa the Translator in Lhodrag. He worked for him as a servant for several years, and received some so-called Indian religious teachings from him. He then returned to his village, but the masters of the people and the owners of the horses he had killed said, "Here comes that destructive demon!" and assaulted him with blows and with firebrands. Saddened by this, he spent a long time in the place known as Dragkar Taso. Then, after wandering around for a lengthy period in the area of Nyanam, Dingri, Labchi, and Kyirong he managed to secure a couple of patrons and even made something of a name for himself, and, like the proverbial beggar talking idly in the sunshine in his cave, he prattled his views and sang about his understanding, and to ordinary people he passed off his arrogant babble and his moronic words from the lesser vehicle as his "achievement"... (ibid.: 99–100)[2]

1. *chos pa phal gyis kho mi la ras pa zer ba'i mi des [grub pa] thob pa'i gnas yin zer zhing khas len pa rnams la bshad bkrol / de ci ltar na'ang gangs rin po che 'di ni dang po srid pa 'di srid / bskal pa 'di chags pa'i dus der byung ba ma gtogs / kho bo mi la ras pas kyang gangs ri 'di ma bzos / bar du skal bzang rgyal ba gshen gyis lung bstan cing byin gyis brlabs pa'i dus der / kho mi la ras pa zer ba'i ming yang med / de 'og dus kyi bskal pa la 'phags pa'i gnas brtan rnams kyis gnas brten cing rig 'dzin grub thob rnams kyis sgrub pa mdzad / zhang zhung rgyal rabs bco brgyad kyi yul chags pa'i dus su yang / kho mi la ras pa zer ba zhig med /*

2. *gung thang tsa lung gi yul du pha mi las shes rgyal dang / ma mnyang tsha dkar rgyan ma bya ba gnyis la / bu mi la ras pa bya ba skyes te / der kho tshe stod du yang khyim mtshes dang ma 'cham nas / mi rta sum cu tsam mthu btang ste bsad / de la 'gyod pa skyes nas bod yul du 'khyams tshe / lho brag a khu mar lo zer ba zhig dang 'phrad nas / der lo mang tsam du bran g.yog tu rgyugs*

A defensive procedure that is commonly used by targets of criticism (if, unlike Milarepa, they happen still to be alive) is to cite the accusation, dismiss it as nonsense, and attribute it to the malice or stupidity of the accuser. One figure who has generated more controversy than most is the treasure-discoverer Pema Lingpa (1450–1521). In recent times, Michael Aris's study of his biography has acted as a lightning rod for reciprocal attacks on Pema Lingpa's detractors by his modern-day devotees, but the biography leaves us in no doubt that he was fully capable of dealing sharply with his contemporary critics. Among the prophecies he revealed there is an allusion to one of his greatest critics, a certain Lama Namkha:

> A holder of a tantric lineage,
> The rebirth of the Bönpo minister Takna,
> Will appear from the direction of Shang
> With the name of Namkha.
> This vow-breaker will reverberate in all directions
> The dharma-sound of the Five Poisons.
> White without and black within,
> The seed of hell will issue forth.
> Whoever has contact with him
> Will be led to the lower conditions of life. (Aris 1988: 64)

The karmic retribution Lama Namkha and his supporters suffer is sure and terrible: the lama himelf dies of leprosy, while the crops of the communities that supported this malefactor are devastated by hail (ibid.: 66). Pema Lingpa even parodies his critics by means of the bold device of a polemic against Padmasambhava: the implication is that if he, Pema Lingpa, is to be the object of people's doubt, then Padmasambhava himself should also be.

Does this mean that the subjects of biographies are never portrayed as

---

/ rgya gar gyi chos zer ba zhig zhus / de nas rang yul du log pa la mi rta bsad pa'i bdag po rnams kyis yul gyi phung 'dre bsleb 'dug zer nas rdung rdeg 'bar gsum byas pas kho de la skyo ba skyes te / brag dkar rta so zer ba la mang du bsdad / de mthar snya nam ding ri la phyi skyid grong sogs la yar 'gro mar 'gro mang du byas pa'i mthar / yon bdag re gnyis shig kyang 'byor / ming yang chen po tsam byung ba la / brag phug gi nyi ma dang sprang po'i kha dal gyi dpe bzhin / lta ba kha ru khyer rtogs pa glu ru blang zhing / theg pa dman pa'i glen tshig dang / nga rgyal che ba'i 'chal tshig dang / tha mal pa la grub tshul du bstan... /

being in any way less than perfect? Not at all. But in the same way as there are official ways of being good, there are conventionally sanctioned ways of being evil. As far as the namtar as a literary genre is concerned, the necessary excellence of the subjects raises the problem of the devices whereby a degree of narrative tension can be salvaged from the sterile environment of perfection.

Forms of acceptable evil seem to fall into three broad categories:

1. Trifling misdemeanors,
2. Youthful errors for which the hero later atones (sometimes with dreadful penances),
3. Acts of destruction that are justified by reference to a higher moral order.

These are all conventionally acceptable forms of evil. The last part of this article will deal with the matter of unacceptable conduct, but for now I wish to examine examples of necessary—that is to say, doctrinally or theatrically necessary—evil.

Youthful Error and Expiation

A good example of a minor misdemeanor in an otherwise saintly life is found in the biographies of Yangtön Sherab Gyaltsen, an eleventh-century Bönpo master of the spiritual system known as the Dzogchen Shangshung Nyengyü. The transmission of this system belongs to the category known as "single line" (*chig rgyud*), according to which a master may pass on the teaching to only one disciple. Sherab Gyaltsen was asked by a widow (in one version, a widower) to transmit the teachings to her (or him), but could not do so because he had already given the instructions to one of his followers. Apparently unwilling to disappoint his petitioner, he adhered to the single-line restriction by not bestowing the teaching orally, but instead transmitted it in writing. The ruse did not work: he quickly fell ill, and died shortly afterward (Ramble 1985: 65). Within the arena of the Bönpo and Buddhist esoteric traditions, the consequences are unsurprising, but to the ordinary reader (or listener) the fate of Sherab Gyaltsen might seem a little harsh: after all, his only crime was an overzealous commitment to the edification of his disciples.

This was hardly a heinous sin: generosity killed the cat. The message to the lay reader is: such are the uncompromising standards of integrity expected of the great teachers.

More commonly, the badness of saints is confined to the early part of their lives. Indeed, the worse they are, the better. It is as if the degree of badness they manifest in the early part of their lives is commensurate with the magnitude of the goodness they will display following their conversion. Here is the case of Togden Önpo, another adept of the Dzogchen Shangshung Nyengyü.

> While he was a youth he followed in the footsteps of his father, who was a brigand. He engaged in fighting and banditry over a number of years. ...As he and his companions were returning [from a raid] they were ambushed by a party who hurled spears at them, killing his father and many of the bandits. He himself was stabbed with a sword and his intestines spilled out onto the ground. One of [the attackers] said, "Judging from the prominence of the veins in this one's eyes, he could be the son of Ogye Rogpo. Stab him again!" "There's no need to stab him," said another, "he is sufficiently wounded." And they went away. He had lain there for a while protecting his innards from the crows with his hands, when two servants who had escaped arrived. They pushed his intestines into his body and sewed him up with silken thread so that he did not die. Later he cremated his father's body and took revenge for his death. (*Bon-po Niṣpanna-Yoga:* 88–89)[3]

In particular, we should note the reference to Togden Önpo's piety, which implicitly entails the killing of his father's assassins. He then sought to atone for his wrongs by turning to the religious life. However, his chosen teacher

3. *gzhon dus yab ar ba yin pa'i rjes su 'breng nas / dmag chus dang jag rkun kyang lo 'ga' byas res shig na mo mas ra re / da res rta sngon po snying dom dmar po yod pa khugs par 'dug gis / de khug na nga la blang zer tsam na / khong rang la tshur la mal mdung rgyab ste / yab dang ar ba mang du bsad khong pa rang la yang ral gri brgyabs rgyu ma thad la blug / cig gi na re 'di'i mig rtsa mtho lugs kyis / 'o brgyad rog po'i bu ma yin nam / da rung gcig rgyobs zer bas / gcig na re brgyab mi dgos non nas 'dug zer nas song ngo / der rgyu ma la bya rog phyag gis bsrungs shing yod tsam na / g.yog po gnyis rta dang rkya bros byas pas thar nas 'ong ste / rgyu ma nang du bcug dar skud kyis btsem pas ma grongs so / phyis pha'i ro bsregs sha yang lon par byas so /*

angrily dismissed him because of his inability to learn to read. He then turned to his celebrated maternal uncle, Tashi Gyaltsen:

> "O Lama, I have studied letters but I cannot learn them. Even though I do not know my letters, if you have a teaching for attainment of enlightenment, fix it in my mind, otherwise I shall become a bandit again." The lama replied, "I have certain precepts known as the Dzogchen Shangshung Nyengyü, which make manifest the mind of Samantabhadra without depending on a piece of paper so much as a dog's tongue in size." (ibid.: 89–90)[4]

Togden Önpo's salvation was assured, and he himself went on to become an adept.

The *locus classicus* in Tibetan literature for the malefactor who renounces his evil ways and turns to the religious life is the biography of Milarepa, a sixteenth-century work that has already been mentioned above. Following the death of Milarepa's father, the family estate was given to the boy's uncle and aunt to be held in trust until he was old enough to take charge. However, the uncle and aunt simply appropriated the inheritance and reduced Milarepa and his mother to penury. The despairing widow turned to her son for help:

> "I wish you were dressed in the mantle of a man and mounted on a horse, so that your stirrups would rip the necks of our detested enemies. That is not possible. But you could do them harm by guileful means. I would that, having thoroughly learned magic together with the destructive spell, you first destroy your uncle and aunt, then the villagers and the neighbors who have treated us so cruelly. I want you to curse them and their descendants down to the ninth generation. ...If you return without having shown signs of your magic in our village, I, your old mother, will kill myself before your eyes." (Lhalungpa 1977: 23)

4. *bla ma lags / ngas yi ge bslab pas ni mi shes par 'dug / yi ge mi shes kyang sangs rgyas pa'i gdams pa zhig yod na ni thugs la thog / de min na da rung nga ar ba la 'gro zhus pas / bla ma'i zhal nas / 'o bu nga la shog gu khyi lce tsam la rag ma lus par / kun tu bzang po'i dgongs pa mngon du 'char ba'i gdams pa / rdzogs pa chen po zhang zhung snyan rgyud bya ba yod...*

Milarepa duly took up the study of dark arts and, in time, returned to his native village with his arsenal of spells. While his uncle and aunt were hosting a large gathering he performed a ritual that induced the horses to kick down the pillars supporting the house. The ritual resulted in the deaths of thirty-five people. He then went on to raise a hailstorm that wiped out the entire harvest of the community that had offended him. His mother was delighted by the outcome; indeed, the reader feels that she is just a little too gleeful about the obliteration of her oppressors. Tormented by remorse for his actions, Milarepa then set off to find a spiritual master who would enable him to expiate his sins. The penances endured under the brutal tutelage of his chosen master, Marpa the Translator, eventually rid him of the burden of his wickedness, and paved the way for a life of mystic devotion.

How wicked was Milarepa? To be sure, he killed a large number of people and destroyed the crops of the survivors; and where karma is concerned, the law is the law and the author is intractable in his didactic insistence that the debt had to be paid. But it is equally clear that Milarepa acted out of devotion to his wronged mother (who, moreover, put him in a decidedly awkward position by threatening suicide in the event that he should fail her). We, the ordinary reader, dutifully accept the tenets of the Buddhist doctrine but secretly admire Milarepa's championing of the human over the dogmatic. He is like Albert Camus, who earned the opprobrium of the right-thinking intellectuals in 1956 by disengaging from active support of Algerian independence, on the grounds of the difficulties this might create for his mother, a cleaning woman in Algiers: "Entre ma mère et la justice, je préfère ma mère." In truth, no reader in the world is going to think the worse of Milarepa for despatching thirty-five wealthy and arrogant oppressors of a cheated widow.

Justifiable Homicide: The Case of Ra Lotsāwa

The same ordinary reader's sympathy with the disproportionate exaction of justice is tested by the biography of one of Milarepa's earlier contemporaries, Ra Lotsāwa Dorje Drag (b. 1016). For the purposes of the present article, there are three episodes in this work that I would like to examine: one because it presents us with a caricatural image of an enemy of the Buddhist doctrine, and the two others because they push the limits of what we might see as the acceptability of saintly violence. Ra Lo made several visits to the

Kathmandu Valley, where he was the disciple of a tantric master named Baro. It was from this teacher that he received the cycle of Vajrabhairava (Dorje Jigche), which he subsequently introduced to Tibet. The setting for the first encounter is the sacred site of Swayambhunath, where we find Ra Lo (who is referred to here as Rwa chen, the "Great Ra [Lo])," circumambulating the famous stupa:

> On one road he met a certain [Hindu] heretic named Pūrṇa the Black, who said, "You should be my disciple."
>
> "Who are you?" asked Rachen. "What do you know by way of dharma?"
>
> "I am the [Hindu] heretic Pūrṇa the Black, and I know such things as the Four Vedas."
>
> Rachen took an aversion to him. "I'm not going to dismount from a horse just to mount a donkey," he replied. "After entering the Buddhist path it wouldn't be right for me to adopt an alien faith."
>
> "You're a willful idiot. If we were to debate the merits of Buddhism and Hinduism the issue would be resolved," he said. They duly had a debate and the lama won.
>
> "You may be a smooth talker," he said, "but just see what happens in seven days," and he went on his way. Then Rachen stayed at Swayambhunath, performing circumambulations and prostrations.
>
> The heretic performed a ritual of sending darts and arrows. For five days Rachen experienced strange apparitions. He repelled them by means of Vajravārāhī, but then they returned. Rachen became uneasy and consulted his lama. He decided that, since these disturbing things had been happening, he should go and ask his teacher for a ritual repulsion technique that he possessed. When he arrived, the lama said, "Boy, have you by any chance provoked some fierce god or demon? Or been cursed by some heretic? Or violated your vows to your lama and the doctrine? Last night I dreamed that a golden stupa had been turned upside-down, and that the sun and moon had fallen to earth. Your turning up here

this morning is a very bad omen!" When Ra Lo subsequently told him about his brush with the heretic, he said,

"Not good! This is not good! Pūrṇa the Black is the most powerful of three hundred heretics. He has killed several Indian and Nepalese Buddhists. Profound techniques are required to reverse this spell; nothing will work except for an Ushni repulsion technique that I shall give you." Rachen gave him a *srang* of gold, and the lama bestowed on him the Ushni precepts and the technique for using them.

Rachen attached a tangka of Vajravārāhī to the side of his bed. He climbed into an earthenware jar, and after drawing the "circle of repulsion" on the rim he closed it and sat there reciting the mantras. At dusk he heard a rushing sound and, on looking, saw a cutch-wood dart with a red cloth attached flying through the air and hitting the door, splitting it open. In the middle of the night he heard another whoosh, and saw a dart strike the tangka, reducing it to dust. At dawn a third dart struck the capital of the pillar, transforming it to sawdust. But when day broke, the lama was unharmed.

The story spread until it reached the ears of the heretic Pūrṇa the Black, who fell into deep despair and killed himself. (*Rwa lo rnam thar*: 15–17)[5]

5. *lam kha gcig na mu stegs purṇa nag po bya ba gcig dang 'phrad / kho na re / khyod nga'i slob ma byas na 'ong zer ba la rwa chen gyis khyod su yin / chos ci shes gsungs pas / kho na re / nga mu stegs purṇa nag po yin / chos rig byed bzhi la sogs pa shes zer bas / rwa chen thugs log nas / nga rta las babs nas bong bu zhon pa mi 'ong / sangs rgyas kyi bstan pa la zhugs nas phyi rol pa'i chos sgor 'jug pa mi 'ong gsungs pas / kho khros te khyod glen pa u tshugs can zhig 'dug / phyi nang gi chos gang bzang rtsod pa byas na mngon zer nas / der rtsod pa byas pas bla ma rgyal / kho na re / khyod tshig la mkhas par 'dug ste / zhag bdun na ltos shig zer nas log ste song / der rwa chen ni 'phags pa shing kun la phyag dang bskor ba mdzad cing bzhugs / mu stegs de ni phur bu mda' 'phen gyi sgrub pa byed cing gnas pa las / zhag lnga na rwa chen la cho 'phrul sna tshogs pa byung nas / bla mas phag mo'i sgo nas phyir bzlog mdzad pas / re zhig zlog kyang slar sngar ltar byung ngo / der rwa chen thugs ma bde ste / nga la 'di lta bu 'ongs ma thad pa la byung bas / da bla ma chen po la bzlog pa'i thabs yod de 'ong bas zhu dgos snyam ste yar byon pa dang / bla ma'i zhal nas / bu khyod kyis lha 'dre drag po la ma bdos sam / mu stegs pa'i ngan sngags ma byung nam / bla ma dang chos kyi dam tshig ma nyams sam / mdang rmi lam na gser gyi mchod rten zhig mgo mjug ldog pa rmis / nyi zla gnyis pa thang la lhung ba rmis / da nangs khyod byon pas rtags ngan gsungs / der mu stegs pa dang 'gras tshul zhus pas / bla ma'i zhal nas / ma bzang / ma bzang / purṇa nag po de mu stegs sum brgya'i nang nas mthu che ba yin / rgya bal gyi chos pa mang po'ang*

There is nothing in this episode of the saintly evil with which we are concerned here: Ra Lo is guilty, at worst, of an injudicious slight. It is the figure of Pūrṇa the Black that is interesting, and we shall come back to this fiendish character presently.

When he returned to Tibet, Ra Lo was greeted with the news that his consort had been abducted by a neighboring community:

> She had been sought as a bride by the Drikhyimpa of Nyenam, but [the family] would not give her. Drikhyim raised a force of three hundred people and captured the nun, looted property, and beat the lama's parents nearly to death and imprisoned his siblings. His parents said:
>
> "Son, if you have magical powers you should show them to Drikhyim,
> otherwise what difference does it make whether you have received teachings or not?
> Even though we have practiced the dharma for the sake of karma,
> and have harmed no one,
> we have been made to suffer this without justification."
>
> So they said, and wept. Rachen said, "Don't worry, my parents; resolving the matter presents no difficulties." He meditated on Vajrabhairava and adopted the gesture of "Striking with the buffalo's horn," and the village was immediately reduced to dust. The

---

des bkrong / da mthu bzlog la zab dgos / de yang gzhan gyis mi phan te / nga la ushni'i bzlog pa zab mo zhig yod pas de sbyin no gsungs / der gser srang gang phul nas ushni'i gdams pa phyag len dang bcas pa rdzogs par zhus / de nas rwa chen gyis mal sa'i logs la phag mo'i thang ka bkram / rang nyid rdza ma'i nang du zhugs phyir bzlog gi 'khor lo g.yam pa la bris pas kha bcad / sngags bzlas shing bzhugs pas / srod la 'ur sgra chen po zhig byung ba bltas pas seng ldeng gi phur bu dar dmar gyi cod paṇ btags pa zhig 'ur gyis byung nas sgo la phog pas sgo tshal par gshags / nam phyed na yang sgra sngar ltar byung zhing bltas pas / phur bu gcig mal sa'i thang sku la phog nas thang ka thal bar btang / tho rangs kyi tshe sgra dang phur bu sogs sngar ltar byung nas khang pa'i ka gzhu la phog nas ka gzhu phyed mar gas / de nas nam yang langs te bla ma la ni gnod pa ma byung ngo / gtam de gcig nas gcig tu brgyud de mu stegs kyi rna bar thos pas mu stegs purṇa nag po yi mug nas lcebs te shi'o /

> bodies of those wicked people were ground to powder; they were "liberated," such that nothing was left of them, and they were led to the heavenly realm of Mañjuśrī. Everyone else, young and old alike, begged him, bowing to his feet in terror, to forgive the injuries they had committed. His siblings were released from their prison, while his consort and all the property—and more besides—were returned. They all became his patrons and subjects, irrespective of whether they had been his enemies or supporters. (ibid.: 41–42)[6]

As in the case of Milarepa, Ra Lo visited a terrible punishment on the persecutors of his family. The principal difference here is that the massacre was not the occasion for a salutary period of expiation: justice had been done, and that was that. The third episode recounts an act of magical violence that is even more startling, not just because it entails a higher body count but because the principal victim is a very prominent Buddhist hierarch: Khön Shākya Lodrö, the father of Khön Könchog Gyalpo, who founded Sakya Monastery.

> Khön Shākya Lodrö, who was very skilled in the rituals of Vajraheruka and Vajrakīla, became jealous. He invoked the twenty-eight forms of Durgā and produced many magical manifestations. Lama Ra Lo arose in the form of Pal Dorje Jigche, and through his mantras and mudrās the manifestations of Durgā became stiff and senseless. "If you do not submit to an oath I shall incinerate you," he said. The manifestations ceased, and they swore an oath to do whatever he said. When Khön heard this he became

6. *snye nam 'bri khyim pa'i chung mar dgos zer ba la ma gtad pas / 'bri khyim grong khyer sum brgyas dmag drangs nas / jo mo 'phrog nor rdzas rnams khyer / bla ma'i yab yum gnyis ma shi tsam du brdungs / sku mched rnams btson du bzung 'dug pa dang 'grigs / de'i tshe yab yum gnyis na re / bu gcig khyod la mthu yod na / 'bri khyim 'di la ston dgos te / gzhan du grub pa thob gyur kyang / ma thob pa dang khyad par ci / bdag cag las su chos byas shing / su la'ang gnod 'tshe ma byas kyang / don med sdug la 'di ltar sbyar / sdig can 'di rnams sgrol re ran / zhes mchi ma 'don bzhin smra bar byed / bla ma rwa chen gyi zhal nas / yab yum thugs khral mi 'tshal / 'di tsam sgrol ba la dka' tshegs ma mchis gsungs te / dpal rdo rje 'jigs byed kyi ting 'dzin du bzhugs nas / ma he'i rwas brdung ba'i stangs ka mdzad pas / grong khyer de thal ba bun gyis song / mi ngan de dag gi lus kyang phye mar 'thag ste gcig kyang ma lus par sgral nas 'jam dpal gyi zhing du drangs / mi rgan gzhon med pa thams cad skrag nas nyes pa bzod par gsol zhing zhabs la btud / sku mched btson du bzung ba rnams kyang btang / jo mo yang sngar gyi 'byor pa lhag dang bcas pa phyir gtad de / thams cad yon bdag dang 'bangs su gyur nas dgra gnyen med par byas so /*

exceedingly displeased. "This Ra Lo started out as the son of a [mere] tantrist; he received from a heretical lama called Bharo [the cult of] a divinity of the heretics with the head of a beast, and by practicing it, he deceives all the people. Whoever meets him will go to hell," he said in denigration.

Rachen's disciples said to him, "He has harmed us for no reason; please destroy him!"

"Whatever happens," he replied, "I shall never be an enemy to someone who is a holder of the doctrine. I would rather go and visit Lama Bharo in Nepal." At this, Ārya Avalokiteśvara, surrounded by a vast entourage, appeared in the sky in shining light, saying,

> "In this degenerate age,
> since it is difficult to convert savage sentient beings,
> I, too, tend to manifest the great treasure of my compassion
> in wrathful forms such as Hayagrīva;
> But especially, the benighted land of Tibet
> is accumulating bad karma because of misconceptions
> concerning the dharma, eminent [Buddhist] figures, and the
>   great philosophical positions,
> and should be the object of wrathful action;
> ...in the case of the truly savage and ferocious,
> a peaceful approach is of no use." (ibid.: 47–49)[7]

7. *'khon bal po'i sras 'khon shakya blo gros bya ba yang phur la mkhas shing nus pa thon pa zhig yod pas phrag dog byas te / dbang phyug nyer brgyad rbad nas cho 'phrul cher bstan byung ba la / bla ma rwa los dpal rdo rje 'jigs byed kyi skur bzhengs nas sngags dang phyag rgyas gzir bas dbang phyug ma rnams rengs shing brgyal / da dam 'og tu mi 'jug na bsreg go gsungs pas / der cho 'phrul zhi zhing ci gsung gi bka' sgrub pa dam bcas / de 'khon gyis gsan pas lhag par ma dgyes te / rwa lo bya ba 'di dang por sngags pa gcig gi bu yin pa la / khos bha ro bya ba'i mu stegs pa gcig la mu stegs lha dud 'gro'i mgo can zhig zhus nas sgrub pas mi thams cad mgo 'khor nas 'dug ste / kho dang 'phrad tshad dmyal bar 'gro gsungs nas skur ba btab / der rwa chen la bu slob rnams na re / khong gis nged rnams la don med du 'tshe bar byas pas bla mas tshar gcad pa zhu zer ba la / bla ma'i zhal nas / nged ci la thug kyang bstan 'dzin gyi skyes bu la dgra mi byed / de bas lho bal du bla ma bha ro'i spyan sngar 'gro ba dga' gsungs pas 'phags pa spyan ras gzigs 'od zer dpag med 'phro ba zhig 'khor mang pos bskor ba nam mkha' la byon nas 'di skad ces gsungs so / spyir na bskal pa snyigs ma'i dus / dmu rgod sems can 'dul dka' bas / thugs rje'i gter chen bdag gis kyang / rta mgrin la sogs khro bor sprul / khyad par bod yul mun pa'i gling / chos dang gang zag grub mtha' che /*

Khön Shākya Lodrö launches the first attack—a rain of rocks and earth—but Ra Lo repels this and responds with a fire ritual. Khön is killed—the first of about a dozen eminent Buddhist figures (among them the son of Marpa the Translator) to fall victim to Ra Lo's lethal powers. The retaliatory force that is launched against Ra Lo is scattered, two hundred villages are destroyed, and their inhabitants killed or dispersed (ibid.: 50). The late Khön's surviving followers then accept Ra Lo as their master.

Heroes and Villains

Pūrṇa the Black is a stage villain, the epitome of evil. He is the most powerful of the heretics, responsible for the deaths of numerous Buddhist masters: in word, deed, and appearance he resonates with similar figures in our own, Western popular and classical imagery: dark lords such as Darth Vader, Sauron, and their seventeenth-century propotype, the Satan of Milton's *Paradise Lost*.

Here is an eminent contemporary lama in defense of Ra Lo's actions:

> The great translator Ra Lotsāwa, one of the main Yamantaka lineage holders, is supposed to have killed many people through his tantric power, but *nobody regards Ra Lotsāwa as bad.* Tantric powers are attained on the basis of bodhicitta, the realization of emptiness, and the generation and completion stages of Highest Yoga Tantra, and when you gain the powers that come with the clear light and the illusory body and do wrathful actions—for example, separating evil beings' consciousness from their body—the main point is to transfer their consciousness to the pure land. That's the end result of wrathful tantric actions. Wrathful actions like that are done to benefit other sentient beings. When dealing with evil beings through peaceful actions doesn't benefit them the only way left to benefit them is through wrathful actions. If you possess the necessary powers and qualities you can benefit others in that way with no danger to yourself. Not only can you but you are supposed

sgro skur mang pos las ngan bsog / 'di dag mngon spyod bya ba'i yul / ...shin tu gdug cing gtum pa la / zhi bas phan par mi 'gyur... /

to. It's part of your samaya. (Kyabje Lama Zopa Rinpoche 2000; my emphasis)

Why would no one think that Ra Lo was bad? For the Buddhist (that is to say, Vajrayāna Buddhist) savant, the reason is given in the apologia cited above: as a realized master, Ra Lo was exercising his powers for the greater good of sentient beings. For the ordinary reader, the reason he is not bad is that his violence is magnificent and unapologetic.

Ra Lo and his principal adversaries belong to the same order of character: dangerous magi who command respect. Pūrṇa and Khön happen to be on the wrong side, but we could easily wish them on ours. (For many Tibetan Buddhists Khön *is* of course on the right side.)[8] It is likewise impossible not to feel sympathy with the Satan of *Paradise Lost*—the fault of Milton himself, who was, as Blake famously remarked, "a true Poet, and of the Devil's party without knowing it" (Blake 1975: xvii). But this tragic hero is the culmination of two thousand years of literary evolution. The earliest Satan, featured in the Torah, was something of a legal opponent (the name derives from a Hebrew verb meaning "to accuse"), and the character bifurcates in later Judaism and early Christianity. In the latter he becomes the antithesis to all God's creation, whereas in the former his significance dwindles to the point where he becomes otiose. He originates as the Adversary, often called upon by God to do his work by testing the devotion of his servants, and reaches his apotheosis with Milton. But he was at times a most inglorious figure, the object of demeaning titles—often the distortion of the names of pagan gods—intended to match his base character: the Father of Lies; Belial, the Worthless One; Beelzebub, Lord of the Flies. This is not the fallen Lucifer, the worthy opponent of the archangel Michael, but some vile creature, given to mean and base acts (Taylor 1985).

There are certain types of evil that are not only acceptable in Tibetan literature, but actually to the credit of the perpetrator, especially if they entail spectacular demonstrations of power. The same goes for the figures of teachers. No lama ever lost credibility for his predilection toward irrational behavior and even psychotic violence: the savage treatment meted out by their respective teachers to Nāropa, Milarepa, and Ani Lochen, and even Shardzawa

8. Darth Vader and the Terminator incidentally did switch their allegiances in the sequels.

Tashi Gyaltsen, whose master at one point shot him with a portable cannon, do not cast the perpetrators in an unfavorable light.[9]

There are some manifestations of evil that are *not* acceptable. Buddhism has sets of the greatest possible wrongs, notably the "five heinous sins." If there are examples of such acts being perpetrated by the subjects of biographies, I am not familiar with them, but in his assassination of numerous religious figures Ra Lo is certainly sailing very close to the wind, and although he may be excessive, he is still in the right. The manifestation of unacceptable evil to which I am referring has nothing to do with scale. On the contrary; as said earlier, these give an indication of power, and the potential of this power when it is turned to good. We do not hold it against Aśoka that the proximate cause for his conversion to Buddhism was the annihilation of Kalinga. We would look at him much more circumspectly if his greatest crime had been, say, the mutilation of small animals.[10]

The gravity of transgressions is culturally contingent. In Europe, pride of place for centuries was the Blood Libel, the accusation (first by Romans against Christians, later by Christians against Jews) of killing people, especially children, and consuming their flesh or blood. But as a source of visceral public horror this crime is largely a spent force in the Western public imagination, and can even be comfortably parodied in certain countries.[11]

In the film *The Silence of the Lambs*, the arch-villain is Hannibal Lecter, a serial murderer who eats his victims. And yet we, the audience, are on his side. The real object of our loathing is the pusillanimous psychiatrist Frederick Chilton, a minnow tormenting his captive whale with petty acts of deprivation. In the sequel, *Hannibal*, the true villain is Mason Verger, a vengeful patient of Lecter whom the latter has earlier induced to grotesque self-mutilation. He is eventually eaten alive by pigs. But we feel comfortable with the fate that the arbiter of moral justice, Hannibal Lecter, inflicts on him, because Verger has a record of sexual child abuse: he is guilty of the crime

9. For the life of Ani Lochen, see Havnevik 1999.

10. The torture of fishes and insects does, however, feature among the early activities of Zhang Rinpoche (1123–93). These juvenile transgressions, as well as the childhood peccadilloes of other lamas, are cited in Janet Gyatso's celebrated study of Tibetan autobiography (Gyatso 2001: 112).

11. Notably in the British television series *Blackadder*, which featured the character of the Baby-eating Bishop of Bath and Wells.

that has replaced cannibalism as the one inexpiable transgression in Western consciousness.

Murder on a massive scale, and even the murder of eminent Buddhist teachers, is justifiable, as long as the perpetrator is acting in the interests of the doctrine or out of filial piety. It does not matter if the punishment meted out by the lama in question is disproportionate to the crimes of which his opponents have been found guilty. But the acts of destruction should be conspicuous and magnificent: there should be no shabbiness or ugliness about them. Karu Drubwang's damning indictment of Milarepa was not primarily that he was a murderer, but that he was worthless as both a poet and a magus.

This manifestation of evil, behavior that is marked by worthlessness and ugliness, seems never to be associated with the protagonists of Tibetan biographies. Dereliction of filial duty, oppression of the weak and guiltless, and general spiritual impotence rarely, if ever, feature even as youthful peccadilloes for which the subject might then seek absolution. They are, by implication, inexpiable.

In Search of the Ugly

To return to a point that was made at the beginning of this article: "biography" might refer either to the content of a person's life or else to the literary genre that purports to present a life. So far, we have explored the phenomenon of saintly evil only as it appears in the Tibetan biographical genre. But if the conventions of this genre deprive us of the full spectrum of evil that lamas' lives might boast, we would do well to extend our search further into other literary domains.

The life I propose to examine briefly as an example is that of a certain Ösal Dorje, a nineteenth-century Nyingmapa lama from Mustang, in Nepal. All the information we have on this individual's life comes from the family's archives, which I was able to photograph in 1993. The background in brief: Ösal Dorje was the natural son of a woman named Purpa Wangmo. Because he was illegitimate, he inherited nothing from his errant father or two maternal uncles, who were also lineage lamas. The mother and son lived in a small house that one of the uncles had grudgingly allotted them.

There is no biography of Ösal Dorje, but we do find a short eulogy of his and his forebears' priestly qualities in a document drawn up to resolve a dispute he had had with his patrons in a neighboring village.

> Now you lamas and patrons have had a slight disagreement. But from the time of [the lamas' ancestor] Chönyi Rangdröl down to the present day, the lamas have served to the best of their ability and their patrons have revered them as the Buddha himself, accepting their words and marveling at their deeds, and were in a state of beatitude. The harvest was good, and there was more than enough to eat.[12]

Ösal Dorje was born into relative poverty, but thanks to astute money lending he was able to acquire a good deal of land from the forfeited securities of his debtors. He showed himself to be capable of acquiring land. Even if he did generally manage to stay on the right side of the law, his acquisitiveness was sometimes on the very edge of decency. A document from 1909 records his dealings with an impoverished blacksmith to whom he had once lent ten rupees. To summarize the content of the document: the blacksmith Künga Sitar of Tserog asked Lama Ösal Dorje of Tsognam Gönpa to lend him ten rupees. He gave the date of repayment as fifteen days thence, and the blacksmith's mother, Singha Ram, gave the lama seventeen coral beads and a rosary of black crystal as security. When the time came for the blacksmith to repay the debt, the lama denied that he had ever been given the coral beads or the rosary. The blacksmith brought a case (*bha sti*, Nep. *bhati*) against him, and the lama made a formal response (*spar sti*, Nep. *prati*) to the effect that he had not been given the missing items, and his son Tenpa Gyaltsen confirmed that there were no such corals in the house. The matter was sorted out by an intermediary. The lama paid the blacksmith eighteen rupees, and the blacksmith agreed to the arrangement. This document was written "so that, if the jewelry is found in the future, nothing so much as the buzzing of a fly (*rang*

12. Ramble (forthcoming): HMA/LTshognam/Tib/10. The references to the documents cited in this section correspond to those used in Ramble (forthcoming), where photographic reproductions are provided and "improved" readings suggested.

kad = sbrang skad) should be said about it in dispute." (HMA/UTshognam/Tib/22)[13]

If the lama had not been in possession of the blacksmith's mother's jewelry as a security for the loan, why did he consequently pay him eighteen rupees? Is it possible that Ösal Dorje took advantage of an indigent outcaste's fragile legal status to lie in court, appropriate the valuable deposit that his debtor's mother had made, and to silence the pair with a meagre out-of-court settlement?

Two years earlier, in 1907, the lama had been involved in a more serious disagreement. A certain Trogyal accused Ösal Dorje, his son Namkha, and two nuns of giving him a severe beating in the village of Tsognam. This is the accusation that Trogyal submitted:

> The lama's son Namkha grabbed me by the hair. Some of them seized me by the head and others by my legs and forced me to the ground. They pulled my hair and kicked me repeatedly and for a short time I lost consciousness. In the folds of my garment I had twenty-two corals of varying size and five rupees. These they stole from me, and left. I thought that, since they were many people against one, I should bring a case against them, and went to my sister's house. But in the evening lama Ösal Dorje and his son came, as before, and accused me of poisoning someone. I have witnesses who heard him say that. And on the matter [mentioned earlier in this petition] of them saying to me that, between seven days and seven months from that moment my family, my property, and my cattle would be wiped out: they'd pulled out some of my hair and taken it, and the four of them said that they would kill us all with

13. The unedited text of this document reads as follows: *tshog sgon bla ming bten bha rgyal tshen la tshe rog zo bha sku ka srid dar nas phyi su ur blang med pa'i yi ge bris nas phul snying don tsha tshog snam bla ming 'od gsal rdo rje nas dngul 10 dkar kyi zhu nas zhag 15 bha ka byi nas byu ru krug ma 17 dang stag bha shel nag 1 a ma shing ka dbram nas bha rtar zhag bdug zer zhin ngos bu mo sna ma sku ka srid dar bhi khu 100 mdzin nas bla ma'i ming su bha sti rgyabs nas bla ming ten bha rgyal tshen nas byu ru ngos nang med dgrang bha kyang med zer nas spar sti phul dkor ka zhin zhibs dar zhin mdzad ngang bha bla ha rti mi nang grig zhus nas bar dum nas zos bha sku ka srid dar la dngul 18 cod nas nang bha la ha sgos nas phyi su byu ru dang phrang bha byor zer nas ur blang rang skad tsam yang med bi yi ge bris nas phul.../*

> the magical spell called "The Evil Warrior-Support of the Fierce Silken Cloth." (HMA/UTshognam/Tib/18)[14]

Ösal Dorje and the other four responded to the accusation with a strong denial. Trogyal had accosted a woman from the De-Tangya area, they said, and she had taken refuge with the lama in Tsognam. They had not, contrary to the accusation, beaten and kicked Trogyal until he was unconscious. They had been unable to get the better of him—*he* was the one who had done the hitting and hair-pulling. They had not taken his jewelry, and furthermore:

> We never accused him of poisoning anyone. It is not true that we took some of his hair or said that his family, his property, and his livestock would be wiped out after seven days; and as for the magical spell called the All-Killing Evil Warrior, I've never done it and I don't even know how to do it, and I haven't had the instructions with which to perform it.[15]

The witnesses produced by Trogyal, the response continued, were personal enemies of the lama, liars who had perjured themselves in supporting the accusation (HMA/UTshognam/Tib/20).

This is a far cry from the epic mayhem wrought by the magical spells of Pema Lingpa, Milarepa, and Ra Lo. Ösal Dorje cannot be held guilty of using destructive magic (something for which, if we follow Zopa Rinpoche, nobody would have thought him bad anyway); but he is guilty of the far greater transgression of impotence; of thaumaturgic worthlessness.

14. *kho bo nam kha'i ngos kyi kyis skra nas bzung ste spi res kas mgo nas [...] res ka skang pa nas bzung rte gang kyel du g.yug nas skra spi u kri zhur dog ste zhur grang mang byas ste ngos dran med la yud rtsam song ba dang ngos kyis a bhag bug na byi ru dog che chung sdom nyi shu rtsa gnyis dang dngul lnga yod pa bcas khyer nas song gdug pas ngos kyang mi mang mi gcig yong bstabs bka' khrim zhu gro bsam nas / a ci nang na log nas dad pas yang kho bo 'od gsal rdo rje pha bu rnams sgong star yong nas khyod kyi mi la gdug gter nas bsad yod zer mi 'od gsal rdo rje yin 'di dus kyis phya dpang yang yod lags... / zhag bdun nas zla bdun kyi bar la mi rgyu phyug gsum med bar zos brgyu skor ngos kyi skra bcas spi nas khyer pas bzhi pas mthu gtad dar dug po'i dmag brten ngan pas rkun gsod ji bgyi yod pa...*

15. *dug gter mi bsad zer pa yang med zla dun zhag dun nang mi nor phyug gsum med pa zos rgyu zer...thu gtad dmag ngan skun gsod nga nas byas nus pa dang byas pa med byas rgyu bka' lung shes pa yang med... /*

And what of his filial piety, the quality of bedrock decency that is exhibited by the most ruthless of the avengers we have encountered above? In 1890 Purpa Wangmo gave the house and property she had inherited to her son, Ösal Dorje. However, she did not take it for granted that he would take care of her in her waning years, and drew up a deed in which she bequeathed to her son "the lower house, from its foundations to the prayer flag standing on top of it, together with the interior and exterior property attached to it, its land, and whatever credit and debts are accruing to it." She gave him the house on the condition that he provide her with a maintenance until her death. Along with the house he received two cattle pens, one big and one small field, one female donkey, one teapot, one frying pan, one small copper vessel, one bronze beer-cup, two boxes, one iron tripod, four earthenware jars, and one small rake.

The fields that the heirs to the estate, the Lamas Rigden and Rangdröl, had given their sister were intended for her use until her death. Even after her death, however, Ösal Dorje continued surreptitiously to harvest the crops, even though the fields should properly have reverted to the main house. In 1908, Tsewang Wangyal, the legitimate son of Lama Rigden, made a complaint to the district court that Ösal Dorje and his son had been harvesting—stealing, as he put it—the crop on land that was not theirs. According to a Nepali document from the case, the plaintiff, Tsewang Wangyal, had deeds to show that this field had been given to Purpa Wangmo by her brother Rigden as lifelong maintenance (*jivanbirta*) "*because her son had not looked after her properly*" (emphasis added: Karmacharya n.d. 3.49).

Conclusion

Tibetan biographies do sometimes present their subjects as being unequivocally good. Unfortunately, perfection and dullness are not incompatible qualities, and the characters of most saints and lamas are rounded out by a leaven of minor wrongdoing, token acts of evil that are tortuously expunged later in their lives. In addition to making the characters more interesting, this kind of evil, as well as its karmic consequences, serves the didactic function of showing us the terrifyingly high standards expected of aspirant saints. In extreme cases—and there are probably few biographies as extreme as that of Ra Lotsāwa—evil deeds provide a justification for the infallibility of their saintly perpetrators: however extravagant, the acts of violence are justifiable because of the intention of the agents, who see the bigger picture where we do not. Reinforcing our belief in saintly infallibility entails a test of our commitment to the principle that the end justifies the means, *upāya*: It tests this commitment to the limit, but not to destruction. In all probability, our faith would not be shaken however massive and ruthless the murderous devastation wrought by a trusted lama, because the difference in the evil exhibited is merely one of degree, not of kind. Since numbers of casualties become meaningless after a point, the evil remains cosmetic, and our acceptance of its rightness is in any case preferable to the specter of loss of faith. Heroes of such namtar may not be as two-dimensional as those who are irredeemably good, but—to take up an image used by Sarah Shaw in this volume—their characters are not fully rounded, just slightly curved. This is the outstanding deficiency of namtar as biography. To find truly three-dimensional characters we must look outside the genre, beyond mere badness, into other literary repositories of lives. The protagonists may not survive the test of sainthood, but they are likely to emerge as fully-rounded human beings: something that is arguably far more interesting than saintliness—even if the revelation is an ugly business.

Bibliography

Works in Tibetan

Autobiography of dKar ru

The Autobiography of dKar-ru Grub-dbang bsTan-'dzin rin-chen (*dPal snya chen rig 'dzin mchog gi rnam sprul bāi'u ldong btsun grub pa'i dbang phyug bstan 'dzin rin chen rgyal mtshan bde chen snying po can gyi rnam par thar pa rmad 'byung yon tan yid bzhin nor bu'i gter*). Dolanji: Tibetan Bönpo Monastic Centre, 1974.

Bon-po Niṣpanna-Yoga

Lokesh Chandra and Tenzin Namdak, eds. *History and Doctrine of Bon-po Niṣpanna-Yoga.* Śata-piṭaka series 73. New Delhi: International Academy of Indian Culture, 1968.

Gangs ti se dkar chag

Gans-ti-se'i dkar-chag: A Bon-po Story of the Sacred Mountain Ti-se and the Blue Lake Ma-paṅ. Ed. by N. Norbu and R. Prats. Roma: Istituto Italiano per il Medeo ed Estremo Oriente, 1989.

Rwa lo rnam thar

mThu stobs dbang phyug rje btsun rwa lo tsā ba'i rnam par thar pa kun khyab snyan pa'i rnga sgra zhes bya ba bzhugs so. Xining: mTsho sngon mi rigs dpe skrun khang, 1989.

Ya ngal

Yang sgom Mi 'gyur rgyal mtshan (sixteenth century). *Kun kyis nang nas dbang po'i dangs ma mig lar sngon du byung ya ngal bka' rgyud kyis gdung rabs un chen tshangs pa'i sgra dbyangs zhes bya ba bzhugs so.* Manuscript of 54 folios kept in the village of Lubra, Mustang District, Nepal.

Works in English

Aris, Michael V. 1988. *Hidden Treasures and Secret Lives: A Study of Pemalingpa, 1450–1521, and the Sixth Dalai Lama, 1683–1706.* Shimla: Indian Institute of Advanced Study; Delhi: Motilal Banarsidass.

Blake, William 1975 [1790–95]. *The Marriage of Heaven and Hell.* London: Oxford University Press in association with the Trianon Press.

Gyatso, Janet 2001 [1998]. *Apparitions of the Self: The Secret Autobiographies of a Tibetan Visionary.* Delhi: Motilal Banarsidass.

Havnevik, Hanna 1999. "The Life of Jetsun Lochen Rinpoche (1865–1951) as Told in Her Autobiography." DPhil diss., Acta Humaniora, Faculty of Arts, University of Oslo.

Karmacharya, M. K. (n.d.) *Mustang Documents in the Nepali Language (1667–1975 AD).*

Kyabje Lama Zopa Rinpoche 2000. "Practice Advice: Dorje Shugden." (Talk given

at Pomaia, Italy, October 2000.) Lama Zopa Rinpoche's Online Advice Book. http://www.lamayeshe.com/index.php?sect=article&id=455
Lhalungpa, Lobsang P. 1977. *The Life of Milarepa*. London: Granada.
Macfarlane, Alan 1985. "The Seeds of Evil Within." In *The Anthropology of Evil*, ed. by David Parkin, pp. 57–76. Oxford: Basil Blackwell.
Parkin, David 1985. "Introduction." In *The Anthropology of Evil*, ed. by David Parkin, pp. 1–25. Oxford: Basil Blackwell.
Pelling, Christopher 1990. "Childhood and Personality in Greek Biography." In *Characterization and Individuality in Greek Literature*, ed. by Christopher Pelling, pp. 213–44. Oxford: Clarendon Press.
Pocock, David 1985. "Unruly Evil." In *The Anthropology of Evil*, ed. by David Parkin, pp. 42–56. Oxford: Basil Blackwell.
Ramble, Charles 1984. "The Lamas of Lubra: Tibetan Bönpo Householder Priests in Western Nepal." DPhil diss., University of Oxford.
Ramble, Charles, in collaboration with Nyima Drandul (forthcoming). *Tibetan Sources for a Social History of Mustang (Nepal)*, volume 2: *The Archives of Tshognam*. Sankt Augustin: VGH Wissenschaftsverlag.
Taylor, Donald 1985. "Theological Thoughts about Evil." In *The Anthropology of Evil*, ed. by David Parkin, pp. 26–41. Oxford: Basil Blackwell.

Spellings of Tibetan Names

Ajampa	A Byams pa
Akhu Atra	A khu A kra
Ani Lochen	A ne Lo chen; full name: rJe btsun Lo chen rin chen
Belo Tsewang Kunkhyab	'Be lo Tshe dbang kun khyab
Bernagchen	Ber nag chen
Bharo	Bha ro
Chamdo	Chab mdo
Changlungpa Shönnu Chödrub	sPyang lung pa gZhon nu chos grub
Chapa	Bya pa
Chenga Ngagi Wangpo	sPyan lnga Ngag gi dbang po
Chödrag Gyatso	Chos grags rgya mtsho
Chödrag Yeshe	Chos grags ye shes
Chöje	Chos rje
Chökyab Dragpa Palsang	Chos skyabs Grags pa dpal bzang
Chönyi Rangdröl	Chos nyid rang grol
Dagmema	bDag med ma
Dagpo Kagyüpa	Dwags po bKa' brgyud pa
Dagpo Kurab	Dwags po sku rab
Denma	lDan ma
Densatel	gDan sa thel
Deshin Shegpai Önpo	De bzhin gshegs pa'i dbon po
Dingri	Ding ri
Dokham	mDo khams
Dong	lDong
Dongtog Rinpoche	gDong thog Rin po che
Dönmo Ripa	Don mo ri pa
Dönyö Dorje	Don yod rdo rje

Dönyö Drubpa	Don yod grub pa
Dönyö Pal	Don yod dpal
Doringpa Künsang Chökyi Nyima	rDo ring pa Kun bzang chos kyi nyi ma
Dorje Gyalpo	rDo rje rgyal po
Dorje Jigche	rDo rje 'jigs byed
Dorje Lopön Rabsal Dawa Gönpo	rDo rje Slob dpon Rab gsal zla ba mgon po
Dragpa Gyaltsen	Grags pa rgyal mtshan
Dragpa Jungne	Grags pa 'byung gnas
Dragkar Taso	Brag dkar rta so
Drangra	'Brang ra
Drigung Rinpoche	'Bri gung Rin po che
Drigung Kagyü	'Bri gung bKa' brgyud
Drigungpa	'Bri gung pa
Drikhyimpa	'Bri khyim pa
Dromtön	'Brom ston
Drubpai Wangchug Gampo Khenpo Shākya Gelong Sangpo	Grub pa'i dbang phyug sGam po mKhan po Shākya dge slong bzang po
Drubwang Künga Migyur Dorje	Grub dbang Kun dga' mi 'gyur rdo rje
Drug Je Khenpo Shākya Rinchen	'Brug rJe mKhan po Shākya rin chen
Drug Nyön Künga Legpa	'Brug smyon Kun dga' legs pa
Drungpa Chöje Künga Chogdrub	Drung pa Chos rje Kun dga' mchog grub
Drungtsün Sherab Paljor	Drung btsun Shes rab dpal 'byor
Dümoma Tashi Öser	bDud mo ma Bkra shis 'od zer
Dungkar Losang Trinle	Dung dkar Blo bzang 'phrin las
Düsum Khyenpa	Dus gsum mkhyen pa
Dzamtang	'Dzam thang
dzogchen	rdzogs chen
Dzogchen Shangshung Nyengyü	rDzogs chen Zhang zhung snyan rgyud
Dzongsar	rDzong gsar
Dzong Shigatse	rDzong gZhis ka rtse
Ganden	dGa' ldan
Ganden Mamo	dGa' ldan Ma mo
Ganden Podrang	dGa' ldan pho brang
Garpa Dönyö Dorje	sGar pa Don yod rdo rje
Garwang Dorje	Gar dbang rdo rje
Gelong Lodrö Sangpo	dGe slong Blo gros bzang po
Gelong Tugje Palgön	dGe slong Thugs rje dpal mgon
Gelug	dGe lugs
Gendün Gyatso	dGe 'dun rgya mtsho
Geser	Gad ser
Gö Lotsāwa	'Gos lo tsā ba

Gomtsül .... sGom Tshul; full name: sGom pa Tshul khrims snying po
Gongkar .... Gong dkar
Gorampa Sönam Sengge .... Go rams pa bSod nams seng ge
Götsang Repa .... rGod tshang ras pa
Gyadangpa Dechen Dorje .... rGya ldang pa bDe chen rdo rje
Gyaltsab Rinpoche .... rGyal tshab Rin po che
Gyaltse .... rGyal rtse
Gyangro Khangmar .... rGyang ro khang dmar
Gyatön .... rGya ston

Jadral Sangye Püntsog .... Bya bral Sangs rgyas phun tshogs
Jamgön .... Byams mgon
Jamgön Kongtrül .... 'Jam mgon Kong sprul
Jampa .... Byams pa
Jangchub Ling .... Byang chub gling
Jangchub Sangpo .... Byang chub bzang po
Jang Satam .... 'Jang Sa tham
Jonang Jetsün Künga Drölchog .... Jo nang rJe btsun Kun dga' grol mchog

Kadampa .... bKa' gdams pa
Karma Gön .... Karma dgon
Karma Kamtsang .... Karma Kaṃ tshang
Karma Ngedön Tengye .... Karma Nges don bstan rgyas
Karma Trinlepa Chogle Namgyal .... Karma 'Phrin las pa Phyogs las rnam rgyal
Kartipug .... Kar ti phug
Karu Drubwang Tendzin Rinchen .... dKar ru Grub dbang bsTan 'dzin rin chen
Khartse Changra .... mKhar rtse lcang ra
Khau Dragdzong .... Kha'u Brag rdzong
Khedrub Paldingpa Kirtishvara .... mKhas grub dPal sding pa Kir ti shwa ra
Khenchen Chödrub Sengge .... mKhan chen Chos grub seng ge
Khenchen Rinpoche Künga Tashi Namgyal .... mKhan chen Rin po che Kun dga' bkra shis rnam rgyal
Khetsun Sangpo .... mKhas btsun bzang po
Khön .... 'Khon
Khön Könchog Gyalpo .... 'Khon dKon mchog rgyal po
Khön Shākya Lodrö .... 'Khon Shākya blo gros
Khyungtsangpa .... Khyung tshang pa
Kinog Lama Sönam Rinchen .... Ki nog Bla ma bSod nams rin chen
Könchog Yenlag .... dKon mchog yan lag
Kongpo .... Kong po
Kongpo Dragsum .... Kong po Brag gsum
Kongtön .... Kong ston

Koshül Dragpa Jungne	Ko zhul Grags pa 'byung gnas
Künga Drölchog	Kun dga' grol mchog
Künga Legpa	Kun dga' legs pa
Künga Sitar	Kun dga' srid thar
Kyirong	sKyid grong
Kyishö	sKyid shod
Labchi	La phyi
Lama Amdowa	Bla ma A mdo ba
Lama Chöpa	Bla ma gCod pa
Lama Drön	Bla ma sGron
Lama Namkha	Bla ma Nam mkha'
Lama Pönyig	Bla ma dPon yig
Lama Shang	Bla ma Zhang
Lama Tso	Bla ma mtsho
Lama Yangripa	Bla ma Yang ri pa
Lhatsün Rinchen Namgyal	lHa btsun Rin chen rnam rgyal
Lhorong Depa	lHo rong sDe pa
Lingrepa	Gling ras pa
Lowo	Glo bo
Lowo Möntang	Glo bo sMon thang
Mangtö Ludrub Gyatso	Mang thos Klu sgrub rgya mtsho
Milay Shegyal	Mi las shes rgyal
Milarepa	Mi la ras pa
Mikyö Dorje	Mi bskyod rdo rje
Mönlam Pal	sMon lam dpal
Namkha Dzö	Nam mkha' mdzod
Namtökyi Riwo	rNam thos kyi ri bo
Nangso Künga Tashi	Nang so Kun dga' bkra shis
Naro Bönchung	Na ro Bon chung
Nāropa	Nā ro pa
Nego	gNas sgo
Nel	sNel
Nelung	Nas lung
Neudong	sNe'u gdong
Ngari	mNga' ris
Ngagwang Dragpa	Ngag dbang grags pa
Ngagwang Tashi Dragpa	Ngag dbang bkra shis grags pa
Ngendzong Tönpa	Ngan rdzong ston pa
Ngogtön	rNgog ston
Ngomshel	Ngom shel

Ngorpa Könchog Lhündrub .... Ngor pa dKon mchog lhun grub
Nyagrong .... Nyag rong
Nyanam .... sNya nam
Nyangtsa Kargyenma .... mNyang tsha dkar rgyan ma
Nyenam .... sNye nam
Nyewo Sapug .... sNye bo sa phug

Ogye Rogpo .... 'O brgyad rog po
Olung .... 'O lung
Omolung .... 'O mo lung
Önpo Chökyongwa .... dBon po Chos skyong ba
Önmo Lama Drön .... dBon mo Bla ma sgron
Önpo Gawa .... dBon po dGa' ba
Ösal Dorje .... 'Od gsal rdo rje

Pagmo Dru .... Phag mo gru
Pagmo Drupa .... Phag mo gru pa
paṇchen .... paṇ chen
Paṇchen Dönyö Drubpa .... Paṇ chen Don yod grub pa
Paṇchen Dorgyalba .... Paṇ chen rDor rgyal ba
Pawo Tsuglag Trengwa .... dPa' bo gTsug lag phreng ba
Pema Lingpa .... Padma gling pa
Purpa Wangmo .... Phur pa dbang mo

Ra Lotsāwa Dorje Drag .... Rwa Lo tsā ba rDo rje grags
Rangjung Dorje .... Rang byung rdo rje
Rechungpa .... Ras chung pa
Redraglung .... Ras brag lung
Rene Gön .... Re ne dgon
Rigden .... Rig ldan
Rigdzin Jatsön Nyingpo .... Rig 'dzin 'Ja' tshon snying po
Rinchen Sangpo .... Rin chen bzang po
Rinpung .... Rin spungs
Rinpungpa .... Rin spungs pa
Riwoche .... Ri bo che
Rölpai Dorje .... Rol pa'i rdo rje
Rushö .... Ru shod

Sagyukhang .... gZa' gyu khang
Sakya Paṇḍita .... Sa skya Paṇḍita
Sangpu .... gSang phu
Sangye Gyaltsen .... Sangs rgyas rgyal mtshan
Sangye Nyenpa Tashi Paljor .... Sangs rgyas mnyan pa bKra shis dpal 'byor

Sangye Paldrub........ Sangs rgyas dpal grub
Seben Repa........ Se ban ras pa
Serdog Paṇchen Shākya Chogden........ gSer mdog Paṇ chen Shākya mchog ldan
Serdogchen........ gSer mdog can
Ser Jadrel Jampa Shenyen........ gSer bya bral Byams pa bshes gnyen
Shākya Gyaltsen Pal Sangpo........ Shākya rgyal mtshan dpal bzang po
Shamarpa........ Zhwa dmar pa
Shamarpa Khachö Wangpo........ Shwa dmar pa mKha' spyod dbang po
Shardzawa Tashi Gyaltsen........ Shar rdza ba bKra shis rgyal mtshan
Shiwa Ö........ Zhi ba 'od
Sholhade........ Sho lha sde
Situ Paṇchen Chökyi Jungne........ Si tu Paṇ chen Chos kyi 'byung gnas
Sönam Gyatso........ bSod nams rgya mtsho
Sönam Rinchen Pal Sangpo........ bSod nams rin chen dpal bzang po
Sumtön........ Sum ston
Surmang........ Zur mang
Surmang Dechentse........ Zur mang bDe chen rtse

Taglung Kagyü........ sTag lung bKa' brgyud
Tai Situ Jangchub Gyaltsen........ Ta'i Si tu Byang chub rgyal mtshan
Tashi Döndrub Namgyal........ bKra shis don grub rnam rgyal
Tashö........ sTa shod
Tendzin Chögyal........ bsTan 'dzin chos rgyal
Tenpa Gyaltsen........ bsTan pa rgyal mtshan
Tilopa........ Ti lo pa
Tingkye........ gTing skyes
Togden Önpo........ rTogs ldan dbon po
Töpa Gawa........ Thos pa dga' ba
Trinle Gyatso........ Phrin las rgya mtsho
Trogyal........ Khro rgyal
Tsagkhang Gönpa........ bTsag khang dGon pa
Tsalpa Kagyü........ Tshal pa bKa' brgyud
Tsang........ gTsang
Tsangnyön Heruka........ gTsang smyon He ru ka
Tsangrag Sumdo........ Tshang rag gsum mdo
Tsarshi........ rTsar shis
Tsechen Pu........ rTse chen phu
Tserog........ Tshe rog
Tsewang Wangyal........ Tshe dbang dnang rgyal
Tsognam Gönpa........ Tshogs rnams dgon pa
Tsokye Dorje........ mTsho skyes rdo rje
Tsongkhapa........ Tsong kha pa
Tsurpu Gyaltsab Tashi Namgyal........ mTshur phu rGyal tshab bKra shis rnam rgyal

Tubchen Chökor .... Thub chen chos 'khor
Tubten Jagö Pungpo .... Thub bstan Bya rgod phung po
Tubten Serdogchen .... Thub bstan gSer mdog can
Tulku Khyenrab Tendzin Lhündrub Shab .... sPrul sku mKhyen rab bstan 'dzin lhun grub zhabs
Tulku Rinpoche .... sPrul sku Rin po che

Ü .... dBus
Uchen .... dbu can
Ume .... dbu med
Uru .... dBu ru

Yangpachen .... Yangs pa can
Yangtön Sherab Gyaltsen .... Yang ston Shes rab rgyal mtshan
Yardrog .... Yar 'brog
Yargyab .... Yar rgyab
Yarlung .... Yar (k)lung(s)
Yönten Taye .... Yon tan mtha' yas
Yunggön Dorje .... g.Yung mgon rdo rje

Contributors

VOLKER CAUMANNS is research associate (Wissenschaftlicher Mitarbeiter) at the Institute for Indology and Tibetology at Munich University. His research focuses on the Tibetan *rnam thar* literature and the history of the Sa skya tradition during the fifteenth and sixteenth centuries. He is currently working on a doctoral thesis on the life and works of the Tibetan scholar-saint gSer mdog Paṇ chen Shākya mchog ldan (1428–1507).

LINDA COVILL received her DPhil from the University of Oxford, where she conducted research on Buddhist literature in Sanskrit under the guidance of Richard Gombrich. She is the author of *Handsome Nanda* (2007)—a translation of the *Saundarananda*—and *A Metaphorical Study of Saundarananda* (2009).

MAX DEEG is the Head of School of the School of Religious and Theological Studies at Cardiff University, where he teaches Buddhism. He is interested in the history of Buddhism, especially the spread to East Asia, in Buddhist narratives and the history of Buddhist texts and their translation.

KHAMMAI DHAMMASAMI, a Theravada Buddhist monk of over thirty years standing, holds a DPhil from Oxford University. His interests include Pali, the Theravada Sangha, and the development of Buddhist universities. He is a Trustee and Fellow at the Oxford Centre for Buddhist Studies and Executive Secretary of the International Association of Buddhist Universities.

SARAH LEVINE was educated at Oxford, at the University of Chicago, and at Harvard, where she received her PhD. She retired in 2004 from the Harvard

Graduate School of Education and is currently an Associate of the Department of Sanskrit and Indian Studies. Her most recent books are *Rebuilding Buddhism* with David Gellner (Harvard University Press, 2005) and *The Saint of Kathmandu and Other Tales of the Sacred in Distant Lands* (Beacon Press, 2008).

Charles Ramble has a doctorate in Social Anthropology from the University of Oxford, where he is now Lecturer in Tibetan and Himalayan Studies at the Oriental Institute. His research interests include the Bön religion, pilgrimage, and archival literature. Among his most recent publications are *The Navel of the Demoness: Tibetan Buddhism and Civil Religion in Highland Nepal* (Oxford University Press, 2008) and *Tibetan Sources for a Social History of Mustang, Nepal* (VGH Wissenschaftsverlag, 2008).

Jim Rheingans is currently conducting research about history, doctrine, and literary genres of medieval bKa' brgyud pa Mahāmudrā traditions (monographs forthcoming about Karma 'phrin las pa and Mi bskyod rdo rje). After his MA in Tibetan Studies from Hamburg University (with Classical Indology and Ethnology) he did his doctoral dissertation about "The Eighth Karmapa's Life and his Interpretation of the Great Seal" (UWE Bristol). His further research interests include narrative and cultural dimensions of religious literature, Buddhist practice, and philosophy, along with Tibetan history and literature. Focus is laid on meditation guidebooks and hagiographies of the Indo-Tibetan Mahāmudrā traditions.

Peter Alan Roberts was born in Wales and lives in Hollywood, California. He obtained a BA in Sanskrit and Pali and a DPhil in Tibetan Studies (on the biographies of Rechungpa) from Oxford University (Harris-Manchester College). For more than twenty years he has been working as an interpreter for lamas and as a translator of Tibetan texts. He specializes in the literature of the Kagyü and Nyingma traditions with a focus on tantric practices.

Ulrike Roesler received her PhD in Indian Studies from the University of Münster (Germany) with a thesis on the concept of light in the *Ṛgveda* (published in 1997 as *Licht und Leuchten im Ṛgveda*). She held research and teaching positions at the Universities of Marburg (Germany) and Oxford

(UK) and is currently teaching Indian Studies at the University of Freiburg (Germany). Her research interests are in Indian and Tibetan Buddhism, narrative and biographical literature, and the history of the Tibetan Kadampa tradition.

SARAH SHAW read Greek and English at Manchester University, where she did her doctorate on the fiction of time travel in the nineteenth century. She studied Pali and early Buddhism at Oxford University. She has written three books on various aspects of Buddhism, meditation, and narrative. She teaches for the Oxford University Department for Continuing Education, Randolph College (US), and Taylor University (US) and is a member of Wolfson College, Oxford.

ROLAND STEINER studied Indology, Philosophy, Law, and Tibetology at the Universities of Bonn (MA) and Marburg (PhD). After holding positions as academic assistant and postdoctoral research fellow at the Department of Indology and Tibetology (Marburg University), he is currently a member of the Mokṣopāya Research Group of the Indological Institute, University of Halle-Wittenberg. His main research areas are classical Sanskrit and Prakrit literature, Indian philosophy, and Tibetan translations of Indian texts.

OCBS Monograph Series

THE OXFORD CENTRE FOR BUDDHIST STUDIES is a "Recognised Independent Centre" of Oxford University U.K.. It is a registered educational charity and a project of the Society for the Wider Understanding of the Buddhist Tradition. Its aims are to teach and conduct research into all branches of the Buddhist tradition while rigorously maintaining academic excellence.

Ronkin, Noa
Early Buddhist Metaphysics: The Making of a Philosophical Tradition
2005

Phuntsho, Karma
Mipham's Dialectics and the Debates on Emptiness: To Be, Not to Be, Or Neither
2005

Gombrich, Richard F.
How Buddhism Began: The Conditioned Genesis of the Early Teachings
2nd ed. 2005

Shaw, Sarah
Buddhist Meditation: An Anthology of Texts from the Pali Canon
2006

Hwang, Soon-Il
Metaphor and Literalism in Buddhism: The Doctrinal History of Nirvana
2006

Tuladhar-Douglas, Will
Remaking Buddhism from Medieval Nepal: The Fifteenth-Century Reformation of Newar Buddhism
2007

Roberts, Peter Alan
The Biographies of Rechungpa: The Evolution of a Tibetan Hagiography
2007

Wynne, Alexander
The Origin of Buddhist Meditation
2007

Kuan, Tse-fu
Mindfulness in Early Buddhism: New Approaches through Psychology and Textual Analysis, of Pali, Chinese and Sanskrit sources
2007

Gombrich, Richard F.
What the Buddha Thought
2009

Seongcheol, Ven.
(Trans. Hwang Soon-Il; ed. Linda Covill)
The Sermon of a Hundred Days
2010

About Wisdom

Wisdom Publications, a nonprofit publisher, is dedicated to making available authentic works relating to Buddhism for the benefit of all. We publish books by ancient and modern masters in all traditions of Buddhism, translations of important texts, and original scholarship. Additionally, we offer books that explore East-West themes unfolding as traditional Buddhism encounters our modern culture in all its aspects. Our titles are published with the appreciation of Buddhism as a living philosophy, and with the special commitment to preserve and transmit important works from Buddhism's many traditions.

To learn more about Wisdom, or to browse books online, visit our website at www. wisdompubs.org. You may request a copy of our catalog online or by writing to this address:

Wisdom Publications
199 Elm Street
Somerville, Massachusetts 02144 USA
Telephone: 617-776-7416
Fax: 617-776-7841
Email: info@wisdompubs.org
www.wisdompubs.org

The Wisdom Trust

As a nonprofit publisher, Wisdom is dedicated to the publication of Dharma books for the benefit of all sentient beings and dependent upon the kindness and generosity of sponsors in order to do so. If you would like to make a donation to Wisdom, you may do so through our website or our Somerville office. If you would like to help sponsor the publication of a book, please write or email us at the address above.

Thank you.

Wisdom is a nonprofit, charitable 501(c)(3) organization affiliated with the Foundation for the Preservation of the Mahayana Tradition (FPMT).